*GERMAINE GREER:*
*Untamed Shrew*

Also by Christine Wallace
*Hewson: A Portrait* (1993)

# GERMAINE GREER:
## Untamed Shrew

Christine Wallace

Faber and Faber, Inc.
A division of Farrar, Straus and Giroux
New York

Faber and Faber, Inc.
A division of Farrar, Straus and Grioux
19 Union Square West, New York 10003

Distributed in Canada by Douglas & McIntyre
Printed in the United States of America
First published in 1997 by Macmillan, Australia, as *Greer, Untamed Shrew*
First American edition published in 1999 by Faber / FSG

Library of Congress Cataloging-in-Publication Data
Wallace, Christine, 1960–
    [Greer, untamed shrew]
    Germaine Greer, untamed shrew / Christine Wallace.
        p.     cm.
    Originally published: Greer, untamed shrew. Sydney : Macmillan,
Pan Macmillan Australia, 1997.
    Includes bibliographical references and index.
    ISBN 0-571-19934-8 (hardcover)
    1. Greer, Germaine, 1939–   .  2. Feminists—Biography.
3. Feminism.   4. Feminist criticism.   5. Women's rights.   I. Title.
HQ1413.G74W35      1998
305.42'092—dc21
                                                                    98-20228

FOR
*the mavericks*

# Contents

# *Foreword*

This book is about Germaine Greer's life. Equally, it tells the story of *The Female Eunuch*, without which Greer might well have been just another talented expatriate antipodean making a splash on one side of the Atlantic.

With *The Female Eunuch* Germaine Greer secured an enduring place in the history of feminism. Nearly thirty years after the publication of that book, her principal works are overdue for review and evaluation. Given the unusual degree to which her life and work are entwined, neither a biography nor a work of review and criticism alone could succeed in doing justice to the subject as well as the two approaches do together.

One fascinating, and generally unnoticed, point about Greer and *The Female Eunuch* is the profound disjuncture in the way they have been received.

Ask baby boomers and their elders in the English-speaking world to name a feminist, and more often than not they will name Germaine Greer and mention *The Female Eunuch*. This response is far less common from the feminists among them, particularly those who read Greer's *Sex and Destiny*, widely considered to be second-wave feminism's first big backlash book. As well as telling the story of Greer's life and evaluating her main works, *Germaine Greer: Untamed Shrew* seeks to describe and explain this disjuncture.

Greer was initially highly effective as a polemicist: *The Female*

*Eunuch* really did change lives. Later characterizations of her as a 'bad feminist' or 'anti-feminist' somewhat miss the point. *Germaine Greer: Untamed Shrew* portrays an exceptionally talented, spirited, gutsy woman at odds in many ways with the family and era into which she was born, who went on to have a major, if not unambiguous, impact for the good on women in her time.

This book is not a conventional biography; it does not pretend to be an exhaustive account of Germaine Greer's life. Rather it focuses on why she was different from other second-wave feminists, why she could be so contradictory and why, despite this, the net impact of her influence has been generally positive. It concentrates on the formative experiences and intellectual influences which made the woman, and her contribution, so distinctive.

Feminism is one of the major political movements of the twentieth century, and it was Germaine Greer's unique role in it, as well as our shared Australian nationality, which drew me to her as a subject. From my vantage point as a political correspondent in our national capital when the book was conceived, it was intriguing to contemplate what her impact might have been had she engaged in parliamentary politics at home rather than in libertarian and sexual politics on the world stage.

I was still a child when the second wave began its great roll forward, and just eleven years old when *The Female Eunuch* was published in Australia. Germaine was a familiar figure early on in my psychic landscape – one shared with most others from my generation and the one before it. For the newest generation of feminists, the early groundwork covered by the major figures of the second wave is fading in memory or obscured by later work. Rediscovering the value, as well as dismissing the dross, in their pioneering contribution is a valuable endeavor for a movement prone to historical amnesia.

Greer opposed this book from the outset, and went to some lengths to sabotage what was always an honest and well-intentioned project. Her attack included personal threats and vilification, and the warning off of sources by letter, in print and through speeches.

This was part of her long-expressed hostility toward literary biography, in particular that concerned with living writers. The cooperation I received from Greer's family and friends tended to be in inverse relationship to their physical distance from her. Biographies which follow – especially those written, as she would prefer, after her death – will obviously provide more detail on her years in Britain.

The issue of authorized versus unauthorized biography was canvassed widely in the media during the writing and publication of this book. In the wake of Diana Spencer's death, one Australian commentator likened the authors of unauthorized biographies to paparazzi – an absurd and offensive comparison.

Where authorized biography is concerned, there is a serious risk that 'authorized' will mean 'compromised,' that some trimming of the sails will be required by the subject. This can jeopardise the ethical obligations incumbent on all writers dealing with the real world: obligations to readers as well as to subjects and sources. Interestingly, Greer commented to one reporter on a recent visit to Melbourne that authorized biographies tend to be boring anyway.

Not that it is all necessarily plain sailing with readers either. Biographer Norman White has commented that sometimes the audience can be the culprit in what he describes as the basic biographical dilemma. 'What often gets in the way of telling truths about someone's life,' White observed, 'is not the biographer's distortions or myopia, but the reader's preconceptions about what should be there, the way it should be told, and the conclusions which should be drawn.'[1]

When in October 1997 this book was published in Australia, the readers' preconceptions about Greer which emerged fell broadly into two camps: the one held that she is akin to a feminist saint and should be beyond critical evaluation, the other, conversely, that she is hell on wheels and the book is to blame for heightening public interest in her.

There was a small but interesting subtext from women who were broadly contemporaries of Germaine, pursuing a similar convention-smashing life. Some, sharing Greer's aversion to external examination, apparently took my analysis of Germaine's life and mores personally – as a commentary on their own life, too. We can expect, I think, a rash of 'life as it really was, not as you young impertinents think it was' memoirs from such figures.

This will be welcome. More direct accounts of this crucial period of social and political history will enrich our knowledge, and help sort out the blowhards and bulldust from the enduringly important. It will be timely, too, since that generation is approaching a perilous period, actuarially speaking.

Just as the idea of aristocratic legitimacy is rejected by the republicans among us, so we should dismiss the notion of a natural aristocracy in biographical writing, with authorized versions at its peak. In.the democracy of letters, may biography broadly thrive.

For help great and small I would like to thank Michael Alchin, Don Anderson, Christena Appleyard, Trish Barraclough, Peter Bartlett, Ruth Biegler, Anne Boston, John Bowan, Michael Bowers, Linda Brainwood, Pamela Bray, Elizabeth Brenchley, Karin Brennan, John Buchli, Gordon Burn, Peter Butler, Beatrix Campbell, Pat Chetwyn, Nikki Christer, Richard Cohen, Julia Costello, Michael Costello, Moira Curtain, Terry Cutler, Jennifer Dabbs, Arthur Dignam, Keiran Dwyer, Margot Edwards, Beatrice Faust, Liz Fell, Paul du Feu, Leon Fink, Margaret Fink, Andrew Fisher, Kate Fitzpatrick, Betty Friedan, Elise Simon Goodman, Lorrie Graham, Peggy Greer, Robin Grove, Stefan Gryff, Richard Hall, Barbara Grizzuti Harrison, Diane Hawke, Sophie Hennessy, Colette Hickey, Tom Hogg, Peter Hohnen, Robert Hughes, Barry Humphries, Bruce Hunter, Jill Johnston, Rosalie Jones, Jenny Lee, Kate Legge, Emanuel Lieberfreund, Vivienne Lincoln, Geoffrey Little, Virginia Lloyd, David McCulloch, Padraic McGuinness, Inez McLoughlin, Hilary McPhee, Karen Middleton, Kate Millett, Pat Milne, Rhyll Nance, Martha Nelson, the late Jill Neville, Richard Neville, Greg Newington, Jane Nicholls, John Passioura, Andrew Riemer, Jill Rowbotham, Ken Ruthven, Susan Ryan, Elaine Saunders, Nathan Silver, Sister Attracta, Sister Phillip, Roelof Smilde, Howard Smith, Judy Smith, Sasha Soldatow, Gloria Steinem, Catharine Stimpson, Albie Thoms, Robert Tickner, Glen Tomasetti, Dimity Torbett, Gabrielle Trainor, Lyn Tranter, Jo Upham, Bobbie Wallace, Chris Wallace-Crabbe, David Warwick, Dan Weaver, Gerry Wilkes, Sue Wills, Bruce Wilson, Elisabeth Wynhausen, the staff of the Baillieu Library at the University of Melbourne, Cambridge University Library, the Fisher Library at the University of Sydney, the National Library of Australia, the State Library of New South Wales and the Star of the Sea Archives.

Quotes without endnotes, unless otherwise indicated, come from interviews conducted by the author.

*Christine Wallace, 1998*

The author and publisher are grateful to the following people for permission to quote from their work: Jessica Anderson, Christena Appleyard, the Estate of M. C. Bradbrook, Eleanor Bron, Gordon Burn, Frances Cairncross, Beatrix Campbell, Anthony Clare, Anne Coombs, Anna Coote, Jennifer Dabbs, Geoffrey Dutton, Hester Eisenstein, Beatrice Faust, Liz Fell, Paul du Feu, Valerie Grove, Barry Humphries, Ramona Koval, Adrian McGregor, Juliet Mitchell, Richard Neville, Norman Page, Sheila Rowbotham, Jeffrey Sher, Catharine R. Stimpson, Richard Walsh and Bruce Wilson. The author would particularly like to thank Clyde Packer for permission to quote from his book *No Return Ticket* (Angus and Robertson: Sydney, 1984), and also Chris Hegedus and D. A. Pennebaker of Hegedus Pennebaker Films Inc. for permission to quote from their documentary *Town Bloody Hall* (1979).

The author and publisher wish to thank the following for permission to reproduce illustrations:

Associated Press 18; Derek Brook 4; Camera Press 21; Jennifer Dabbs 3; Hulton Getty Collection 15; News Limited 12, 13; *News of the World* 16; *Newspaper News*/Image Library, State Library of NSW 2; *Oz* 8; *Oz*/Keith Morris 9; Pennebaker Hegedus Films 11; The Photo Library-Sydney/Vernon Merritt/*Time Life* 10; Solo Syndication 19; *Table Talk*/Image Library, State Library of NSW 1; Albie Thoms 6; *Time* Inc. 5; Topham Picturepoint 14, 20; United Nations/T. Chen 17; Wesley/Hulton Getty Collection 7.

Our whole lives are lived in a tangle of telling, not telling, misleading, allowing to know, concealing, eavesdropping and collusion. When Washington said he could not tell a lie, his father must have answered, 'You had better learn.'

*Germaine Greer*[1]

MOTHER COURAGE: You don't think war might end, then?

THE CHAPLAIN: What, because the commander in chief's gone? Don't be childish. They're two a penny, no shortage of heroes.

*Bertolt Brecht*[2]

# 1

## Collateral Damage

It all began with Peggy and Reg.

It was the mid-1930s, when the pall of the Depression still lingered. Peggy Lafrank was making her way down the tree-lined boulevard of Collins Street, Melbourne, when a tall, well-dressed man standing with a group caught her eye. She was an apprentice milliner, just eighteen years old, long-legged, lively and smart; he was an urbane thirty-year-old who sold newspaper advertising space for a living in the city. Trying his luck, he tipped his hat and invited her for a coffee. Boldly, she accepted. They made an attractive couple as they strolled off down Collins Street to get better acquainted.

Australia's newspaper advertising men, smooth of patter and media patois, led mobile lives. Reg Greer had sold advertising space in Perth and Adelaide before moving to Melbourne, where he eventually became the local representative for the Adelaide *Advertiser*, a job he would hold for most of his working life. When Reg visited Peggy at home, he seemed a plausible suitor, despite the age gap. With his well-cut clothes and winning, worldly ways, he was apparently a man on the way up, and most solicitous of the Lafrank family's affairs. Reg charmed Peggy's mother, Alida 'Liddy' Lafrank, née Jensen. Reg Greer could be just the man to rein in her tall, attractive, headstrong daughter. Peggy was full of life, determined to be herself, her own person, and Reg appeared to be a moderating influence.

Reg escaped the spanners and screwdrivers that Peggy's father Albert had thrown at her previous boyfriends. Albert Lafrank, a salesman of Swiss-Italian heritage, had been cast off by Liddy and the children, who had packed up and left him a few months earlier. His son Bernard left first, sick of his father's strict ways; Liddy and the two younger siblings followed weeks later. But Peggy had not forgotten her father's lectures in the wake of the flying hand-tools. 'You think I'm hard, but if you knew how men talked about women and girls, *boasting . . .*' he would begin.

Years later after the marriage had gone awry, Liddy would tell Peggy to stop complaining about Reg. 'He just sits in front of telly, or talks about sport,' Peggy protested.

'He takes good care of you, settled you down,' Liddy would reply. 'I don't know what would have become of you if it hadn't been for Reg!'

Peggy resented the implication: 'Fancy saying to your daughter your husband sort of settled you down!' Liddy did not even object to the fact that Reg was not Catholic; she insisted only that the children of the marriage be educated in Catholic schools.

While Liddy saw Reg as a restraining influence on her young daughter, Peggy saw him as a suave and knowing guide to the bigger, more adventurous life to which she aspired. In the conservative, Anglophile, stultifyingly predictable Melbourne of the 1930s, this tall, worldly beau from the faintly glossy fringe of the fourth estate seemed to offer Peggy an escape from suburban mediocrity to excitement and sophistication.

Margaret Mary Lafrank and Eric Reginald Greer married in March 1937 at St. Columba's, a small Catholic church in the bayside suburb of Elwood. Peggy gave up her millinery job. Reg rented a modest flat in an improving middle-class area not far from St. Columba's, in Docker Street, near the beach. Peggy swam, sun-baked and did calisthenics on the sand; Reg came home from the office, poured himself cold beers and settled back to enjoy married life. The new Mrs. Greer's style would increasingly tend to the idiosyncratic, but at the outset she wore lashings of make-up, very much to her husband's taste. Before her marriage she modelled commercially once in a biscuit advertisement organized by Reg. The image – a winsome Peggy offering a biscuit to an appreciative older man – lived on as an icon in the Greer household, reminding the children of their mother's momentary public glamor.[1]

In the autumn of 1938 came the first conception. Peggy's pregnancy was easy, with little more than queasiness. But the labor was long and difficult. The baby, a girl, was bruised around the head from the traumatic delivery and arrived in floods of blood as Peggy hemorrhaged from a retained placenta. The baby was named Germaine, with no middle initial to interrupt the elegant alliteration with Greer. According to Peggy, it was the name of a minor British actress she found in an English magazine Reg had brought home from work. In Germaine's version, her mother was reading George Sand's *The Countess of Rudolstadt* when she fell pregnant, and drew the name from one of its characters, the Comte de Saint-Germain – 'because she liked the sound of it, I reckon.'[2] It was the height of the last Australian summer before the war: 29 January 1939.

Peggy, exhausted by the experience, decided one confinement was enough. Germaine compensated for the horror of the birth by being a good baby, sleeping soundly and breastfeeding peacefully. When other tenants objected to Germaine's nappies occupying the clothesline, the landlady offered an alternative flat, upstairs in a block around the corner on the Esplanade, directly overlooking the beach. Peggy, Reg and Germaine moved, taking the wet nappies with them.

After a year of contented breastfeeding, Germaine was reluctant to be weaned. 'It took ages to get her off the breast,' according to her mother. Nor was she quick to speak. 'I remember saying to our doctor when she was thirteen or fourteen months old, "When is she going to talk to me?" He said: "Just wait till she starts!"' If the words were slow to come, the drawings were not. While Peggy tidied the flat, Germaine would sit strapped in the high chair, with butcher's paper and crayons set in reach, or sometimes a plate of food would be set out to occupy her. One day a suspicious silence tweaked Peggy's concern. Germaine had fallen fast asleep, face flat in her plate of mush.

Germaine would remember nothing of this, nothing before Reg,

3

'Daddy,' went away to war. Her earliest memory of her father was that he was not there. Reg joined the Australian Imperial Forces (AIF) in January 1942, just before his daughter's third birthday, and moved away from home to train in the city with other volunteers for the Royal Australian Air Force. Three months later he was on a ship to Cairo, attached to Britain's Royal Air Force for classified cipher work. In the Esplanade flat, Peggy Greer got on with her young Elwood mother's life, consisting mainly of baby, beach and the bountiful attention of visiting American soldiers. 'I had a good time with the Yanks,' says Peggy. 'They were nice to Germaine too. They'd go into her nursery with their cigars and tell her bedtime stories.' Liddy, who lived not far away and doted on her grandchild, minded the baby while Peggy socialized with the young Americans. 'Perhaps I shouldn't have done that,' Peggy Greer ponders now.

Reg was still away when Germaine started at St. Columba's, the little school attached to the church where he and Peggy had married. In neat cursive script the St. Columba's ledger notes the arrival in February 1943 of student number 1664: 'Greer, Germaine. 57 Ormond Rd. Born 29.1.39. Religion: Catholic. Parent's name in full: Reginald. Parent's Occupation: A. I. F.' The entry was sandwiched between Marion Titheradge, also of Ormond Road, whose father Noel was a clerk, and Noel Olarenshaw of Byron Street, whose father John was in the Royal Australian Air Force. Of the thirty-six names listed under 'Parent's Name in Full' on that page in the register, only three were women: two engaged in 'Home Duties' and the other listing 'Library.' Many fathers were at the war; a few were manual workers – 'Railway Employee,' 'Factory,' 'Postal' and 'Engine Fitter.' Most were typical of the rising middle class that made up the bulk of the area's residents: draughtsmen, wool-classers, a builder, a doctor, a couple of journalists, a hotel-keeper, clerks. Only one Christian name stands out from the sea of Johns, Williams, Malcolms and Geralds: Verruccio, shopkeeper, of Glenhuntly Road. The town planners had added a little literary tone to the area, playing up to the residents' middle-class pretensions. Greer's classmates lived not only in Byron Street, but in Poets Grove, Dickens Street and Scott Street as well.

Germaine was bright, and people remarked on it to Peggy: 'The nuns told me I ought to be proud. I wasn't unproud. My response was that I ought to give her into the nuns' care because the Japanese were going to come down and get us.' The suggestion was half-serious, reflecting the Australians' real fear of Japanese invasion during the Pacific War. Like Reg, thousands of Australian troops were fighting on behalf of the British in Europe and the Middle East; reciprocal support in Asia and the Pacific from the over-stretched British was barely forthcoming. Australia struggled to redirect war resources and personnel to the Asia-Pacific theater as the Japanese assault moved south through Indo-China, Malaya, Singapore, the Dutch East Indies, Papua and New Guinea to the northern fringes of Australia. Darwin in the Northern Territory was bombed in February 1942; in May, three Japanese midget sub-marines sneaked into Sydney Harbour and sank a ferry. The Greers' home in Victoria was far from the danger, but Melburnians like Peggy were anxious nevertheless. Illness added to Peggy's con-cern about her daughter. 'Germaine was kind of sickly,' her mother recalls. 'She was injected against diphtheria, which was rife then, and you had to be careful of infantile paralysis – I was always wor-ried about that.' Germaine had attacks of croup: 'She'd sit up there, pale. Mum and I would make a fuss.'

Reg was invalided out of the forces long before the war ended, less than two years after he joined the AIF. Peggy and Germaine met him at Melbourne's main railway station. He returned a haggard, anorexic shell of the man he had been when he departed.

The Greers had to struggle to re-establish married life as Reg bat-tled with the debilitating effects of war-induced neurosis and Peggy came to terms with the damaged man who had returned in place of her pre-war husband. Reg was no carefree, cigar-wielding American serviceman enjoying rest and recreation leave; he was not even the smooth newspaper advertising sales rep with whom she had linked arms in Collins Street.[3] Peggy found the situation difficult to deal with, but as a Catholic she was committed to the marriage for the long haul.

There was an accommodation between the Greers, but not an easy one. Like many wives of the era, Peggy never knew the size of Reg's pay-packet, though she says he provided for the family adequately. There was no emotional, spiritual or material balm to melt Peggy's diffidence toward Reg. 'Reg and I weren't really good

5

friends,' she recalls. 'He was always polite.' Germaine's desperate desire for love from her hitherto missing father provided a peculiar symmetry to Peggy's distance from him. Reg's return intensified rather than assuaged Germaine's paternal longing. 'He was in a bad state when he got home from the war,' Peggy says. 'He ignored her.' Germaine was resentful. 'Daddy' never hugged her. When she put her skinny arms around him he would grimace, shudder and push her away – ostensibly as a joke, but it was one he played each time she sought fatherly comfort and affection. Germaine tried to rationalize his hurtful ploy as an anxiety-relieving ritual: 'I clung to the faith that he was not genuinely indifferent to me and did not really find me repulsive, although I never quite succeeded in banishing the fear of such a thing.'[4]

An added complication was Germaine's memory of Peggy's association with a particular American soldier when Germaine was a toddler. The Americans on rest and recreation leave produced a deep, competitive anger among Australian men fighting overseas who had left wives and girlfriends behind at home. According to Germaine, Peggy felt threatened because she thought her daughter might have witnessed an infidelity. 'And she's right,' Germaine reflected more than forty years later, in an interview with the psychiatrist Dr. Anthony Clare. 'I was a witness, and I could remember that relationship if I wanted to. I can remember one episode from it which was nearly fatal . . . I was given a knockout drop.' On that occasion she was fed some lobster thermidor, the smell of which makes her sick even now. 'People don't forget, you know,' Germaine continued. 'Mum thought she'd got away with it, and she still thinks she got away with it, I guess.'

Nobody wanted to know what she knew, this dynamite secret with the potential to blow the whole family apart. 'I'm sure that I was connected in his mind with the peak of his anxiety condition,' she said of her distant, sometimes tortured father, 'when he found that his marriage was extremely shaky and that things had gone on that he'd rather not think about – and in the middle of all of this is this brat. This knowing brat! God knows what I said to him! I'm sure I made the situation worse. And that's when the holding me off business began. No confrontations with this child, because this child will make the catastrophe happen.'[5]

Not only did Reg deny Germaine attention and affection, but he was also absorbing her mother's energy, on which she had previously had first claim. In Peggy's view, 'She thought of me as her personal property. She was rather a clinging child, to both of us. She liked to know what was going on, including between us.' Her possessiveness spilled over into reluctance to go to school. 'She liked to stay home. . . . She'd hang back rather than go to school. One morning she was dressed, and had on a straw hat. I said: "Go on, you've got to go." She banged the hat down on her head and put her neck out, and was in bed for a week.'

The rejection was sometimes reciprocated. In the local Elwood milk bar, the young Germaine picked out her mixed bag of lollies then looked to her mother for money. 'You'd better ask your father,' Peggy said. '*He's* not my father,' retorted Germaine. 'God in heaven's my father.' To which a grim-faced Reg responded: 'Well, you'd better get him to pay, then, hadn't you.'

Germaine's distress about the cold, nervous man who returned instead of the distinguished stranger whose photograph stood on the sideboard was complicated by the baby sister his arrival set in train. Reg's physical and mental deterioration had not extinguished his sexual being. Jane Greer was born on 5 February 1945, just after her father-hungry sister had turned six. 'I did it for him really, and Germaine and me,' Peggy says. '[We] needed something to settle us down.' Again the labor was long and complicated by another retained placenta which caused a major hemorrhage. After a further five-year interval, Barry Greer was born.

Peggy's reproductive travails did not deter Germaine from traditional girlish pursuits. 'Germaine liked dolls. She wasn't a tomboy,' Peggy remembers, although there was plenty of time outdoors too. 'I used to live at the beach with the kids. They had the best of everything. We'd clear up and then go to the beach all day. Meet your friends, play with canoes.'

At school, however, Germaine showed little interest in sport but displayed great aptitude for her lessons. She was powerfully influenced by Liddy Lafrank, who strongly favored a good education. 'A respect for school, learning, would've come from my mother,' according to Peggy. 'She used to say, "It's no load to carry."' Discord at home did not stop Germaine from taking

Liddy's cue and excelling at school, even if it made her less likely to develop a placid temperament. 'She was nearly always top of the class,' says Peggy, 'very good at spelling and writing. She would listen.' At the same time she would regularly misbehave. 'She was disrespectful of the nuns at primary school,' Peggy recalls. 'I wasn't the sort of mother to go down to the school. They have to fight their own battles – if they got the cane, tough.' Liddy was softer with her clever grandchild. She bought Germaine expensive toys, including a prized tricycle which Germaine, in a moment of childish generosity, redistributed to a needy friend. 'I said one day: "I haven't seen your trike,"' Peggy says. 'She said: "I gave it to Pammy, she doesn't have a good one."' Germaine remembered being smacked for her early altruism.

Corporal punishment and emotional conflict stud Germaine Greer's accounts of her childhood. She feared her mother and has said that she suffered intensely because of Peggy's personality: 'I'm supposed to be grown up and have forgotten about it but it's very difficult to forget being terrorized when you were only two feet high! It's not even that you remember it a lot: it's just unforgettable.'[6] She compared the situation to the plot of Mary Shelley's *Frankenstein*: 'A monstrous birth is the most terrifying thing a woman can confront and I was it.'[7] The relationship was not made any easier by her mother's readiness to use corporal punishment, according to Germaine, 'because my mother did physically abuse me as a child. She didn't do it very badly – I haven't got a cracked skull, I'm not burnt, I haven't got scars. But she did use weapons. She used a stick. And she used to hurt me pretty badly . . . I don't think she did it all that often, but it was always totally unexpected.'[8]

As late as 1992 Greer said she was unable to speak to her mother without anxiety setting in, her palms sweating and heart pounding;[9] she claimed in print that her mother later even attempted to undermine Germaine's confidence in Reg Greer's paternity itself.[10] By contrast, Germaine portrayed herself as placid and agreeable. 'Was I a bad girl?' she queried. 'Huh! Do you know, the first time I heard a child say "no" to its mother I felt as if the world had come to an end. I never said no to my mother; perhaps I should have. I mean, my theory used to be that when my mother belted me, I should have turned around and dropped her, and the fact that I didn't has been something that has affected my whole development. I've got one punch that I pulled that I should have let fly.'[11]

Peggy does not dispute that she used to smack Germaine when she believed she was being naughty. She considered the smack an indispensable part of any mother's child-rearing kit, particularly with headstrong children like Germaine: 'I can't see how you can get along without giving kids a whack. If they defy you, you'd have to be a saint not to give them a whack sometimes.'

A singular episode illustrates why Greer remembered her punishments as arbitrary. Germaine was late home one day from primary school, Peggy recalls:

> She'd walked home round the beach. Reg was sitting at the kitchen window. Germaine was hand-in-hand with this man ... He was carrying her books. I said: 'My God, what'll I do?' Reg said: 'I'm going to call the cops.'
>
> The cop came on a bike. They'd disappeared [into the bushes]. Reg went down and found the cop. The cop said to Reg: 'He's just a simple chap, always around.' I was angry with Germaine. She knew she shouldn't have come round that way! She would've been about ten. I can't help it – I belted her. Reg said to the cop: 'You should've let him get on with it. You shouldn't have stopped him. Then he could've been charged.' I wondered about what Reg had turned into that he took that attitude.
>
> For her to have walked the wrong way home! She didn't say much. I pulled the cord out of the toaster and hit her across the legs. I was far more upset than her. I had to make her understand there were other people in the world apart from her. There's a streak in her of incomprehension about other people's feelings. I don't think you should betray your family.

Peggy 'couldn't help it,' she said, of hitting her daughter with the toaster cord. But to Germaine, unlikely at that age to have learnt any concept of vulnerability to sexual assault, her mother's furious anxiety would have seemed mystifying.

Germaine loved her father for not hitting her but his failure to protect her from Peggy lost him her respect. He sat in the next room, 'where the thud of blows was clearly audible,' without intervening. To his daughter he was revealed as weak, craven, feeble: ' "It takes two to quarrel," he would say, apparently

9

unaware that I could not go off to my club until the mad dog in the kitchen had stopped foaming at the mouth. . . . Nevertheless I could not forgive my mother for calling him "a senile old goat," as she often did.'[12] Germaine remained unconvinced that her father loved her. Where were the demonstrations of pride and affection from him, let alone love?

Germaine's early passivity toward her parents extended to her quest for knowledge about her father's family, a mysterious entity lacking the usual cousins, grandparents, aunts, uncles – or, indeed, anybody at all. Reg had 'forbidden' Germaine to ask questions.[13] That there was some dark secret about him was, in retrospect, an unavoidable conclusion. 'You had to know there was,' she says, 'because you'd say to him: "Why don't I have any grandparents on your side of the family? Where are they?" And sometimes he'd say they were in England and sometimes he'd say they were dead.'[14] Fantasy fathers lived on in her mind until Germaine was nearly fifty years old. There was the idealized Daddy who lovingly dandled her on his knee before departing for the war; there was the war hero who had been away on top-secret cipher work, returning shattered by the harshness of his military debriefing; and there was the elegant, conservative, rather snobbish newspaper advertising executive who was dismissive of her intellectual achievements – by implication, because of his own superior education.

According to family myth, Reg was born to an English colonial family in Durban, South Africa, and raised in Launceston, Tasmania. His gloves, tailored suits, affability and well-modulated voice seemed to corroborate the story. Greer accepted her father's veto on inquiry into the wider family relations, and put off the search until after his death. As a result, it was not until middle age that she discovered her father had withheld the truth about his personal history. Meanwhile her perceptions of Reg continued to be based more on wish-fulfilment than on fact.

Writing later about her childhood home, Greer painted a picture of relative cultural deprivation. There were only twenty books in the bird's-eye maple bookcase of her parents' sitting room, she wrote, all of them aids to her father's alleged seduction of other women. 'Because of my infant reading of my father's books, literature and voluptuousness are inextricably entangled in my mind.' Reg's selection included Theophile Gautier's erotic classic *Mademoiselle de Maupin*, which provided Greer with 'my first, and will probably provide me with my last, masturbation fantasy'; Negley Farson's *The Way of a Transgressor*, where she read that 'whores make the best wives'; and Liam O'Flaherty's *Famine*, where she read how 'the parish priest used to nuzzle his housekeeper's ebullient breasts.' At eleven years of age she asked her father what a whore was, one of the other twenty books – a Shakespeare collection – propped in her lap in self-defence against the inevitable barked inquiry about what she had been reading.[15]

The passivity that characterized Germaine's relationship with her parents was reversed at school. She came up through the scholarship ranks, moving on from St. Columba's to Sacred Heart in Sandringham and Holy Redeemer in Ripponlea, a hot-house where talented young Catholics were prepared for scholarship exams. Germaine was successful, and in 1952 she enrolled as a scholarship student at Star of the Sea College, Gardenvale – motto *Facta Non Verba*, 'deeds not words' – a college of the Sisters of the Presentation of the Blessed Virgin Mary.

The Presentation Sisters, an Irish order, date from the eighteenth century. The founder, Honora 'Nano' Nagle, was educated at a French convent during a time of intense Catholic persecution in Ireland. In 1754 she opened a school for thirty girls, reputedly in a mud cabin in a back street of Cork, at a time when opening a Catholic school of any sort was an invitation to official persecution. Drawing on a small inheritance, she expanded her program of good works, opening more schools, arranging for Irish women to be trained as nuns by the Ursulines in France, and eventually establishing her own order in the 1770s. After the death of Nagle, who was by then known as Sister John of God, the Presentation Sisters were formally recognized by the Holy See.

The order was established in Australia a century later, in 1883, and the Australian wing immediately distinguished itself as one of strong women prepared to confront male authority. The two founding sisters, Mother Paul Fay and Mother John Byrne, were initially invited to establish a school in the New South Wales country town of Wagga Wagga, but they decamped to Melbourne after the local bishop appropriated the deeds to the school. They established their new college in Gardenvale, a leafy affluent suburb close to Melbourne's Brighton Beach. In Melbourne they enjoyed better relations with the clergy; as a welcoming gesture, the local parish priest gave the school a bell which still rang the Angelus three times a day during Germaine's student years.

The school bore no resemblance to any mud cabin in an Irish back street. It rose confidently in stone, two storeys high, surrounded by small, decorative gardens and later fronted by an asphalt playground. A tinge of the social conscience that drove Nano Nagle survived. Independent thought was encouraged among the girls to an extent unusual in a convent school, with a thread of compassion and sense of social justice woven through the teaching; 'strong Star women' became a catch phrase.[16] The nuns were well educated and full of the love of their job, teaching and even administering discipline quietly. Greer recalled: 'The worse trouble you were in, the softer the voice. They'd deliver this rabbit-killer punch in a soft, soft voice.'[17]

The principal, Mother Eymard Temby, was a Star girl herself, and exerted a major influence on the philosophical tone of the school. A significant figure in Australian Catholic education, she was forty-one when Germaine arrived. Mother Eymard believed that 'all people are precious in their very existence, and that everything possible should be done by individuals, churches and governments to draw out their potential as human beings – and to resist all manner of oppression.'[18] She was explicitly interested in the status of women and advocated an active role for women in the Catholic laity. At the time of Vatican II in the 1960s, a pivotal, liberalizing period of Catholic philosophical development, she urged women to examine the new concepts and embrace change. She would instruct Catholic women's groups that change could be a force for growth; it was something to be desired, something exciting, dynamic and challenging. 'Now the Holy Spirit is revealing some very significant truths here,' she told one group of women in the conservative rural Victorian region of Gippsland in 1967, during a discussion of Vatican II. 'Most importantly, that we are Christians every minute of the day, that for the laity their way to God lies in their family life, social life and work life. These measure the extent of our Christianity – not the number of novenas we make or the fervour with which we sing the Benediction.'[19]

The teaching at Star in the 1950s was built on the same intense moral conservatism that imbued Catholicism in the rest of Australia at the time, but Mother Eymard's activist influence subtly pervaded the school culture. While she was no raging feminist in the modern, secular sense, Mother Eymard ardently hoped that Star would produce girls who would become strong women, able to make an impact for good. Shortly after Greer's first book, *The Female Eunuch*,[20] was published, for example, Mother Eymard publicly defended Star's controversial graduate against the criticisms of a male doctor who had attacked the book's sexual orientation. Mother Eymard thanked the doctor for his comment, but continued that, while she didn't at all agree with everything Germaine had written, she acknowledged her intelligence, courage, ability and her strength to change the world.

Star of the Sea would be the tall, precocious thirteen-year-old's savior from unhappiness and sparse cultural stimulus at home. School archive records describe an adventurous, articulate, creative girl of keen intelligence and a great love of fine music and art. Germaine was well liked, according to one nun's report, but she was 'a bit of a mad-cap and somewhat erratic in her studies and in her personal responses.'[21]

Star's great, gray Gothic building and asphalt exercise yard at first seemed forbidding to Germaine, but the vigorous life of Star's community of women, the singing and drama, the motivated teachers ready to forgive the talented student her foibles quickly cemented its place in her affections, in contrast to home. She was always hanging around school, and rode her bicycle home by indirect routes to stave off going back to Peggy and Reg for as long as possible. Over her years at Star she spent longer and longer hours at the school, making up various extra-curricular activities to fill the period between four o'clock when school finished and meal time at home. School offered a wealth of culture and thought that put Germaine and her faith in a wider context, and she absorbed it eagerly.

At home the only relief from tedium was mischief-making. None of the elements of the good life that she later came to appreciate – wine, good food, good music, a decent library, beautiful furniture, flowers, parties, paintings – was evident at the Greer house; but

13

then such things were not to be found in most modest suburban middle-class homes in 1950s Melbourne. Reg used home chiefly as a place for basic maintenance and ablutions – food, laundry, bed and bathing.[22] He would bring home the foreign language editions of *Reader's Digest* for his daughter but rarely if ever attended school speech nights. Reg did not applaud Germaine's prizes in public and barely registered them in private.[23]

While Germaine's own recollections have emphasized the passive stance she remembered adopting toward her parents, there are conflicting memories of her verbal jousts with Reg. Germaine and her father could not have a discussion; it had to be a debate, with Germaine challenging Reg's definitive pronouncements, questioning, pushing, probing. Particularly in the years immediately after his return from the war, he lacked the psychological strength to deal with Germaine's power-charged onslaught. His strategy was to avoid engagement. Held at arm's length emotionally, Germaine carried through her teenage years the added burden of believing she was the only reason her mother had stayed with Reg – a revelation Peggy had made to her daughter when Germaine was twelve, on the threshold of adolescence. For Germaine: 'That was a really tough one to take, because their relationship to me seemed to be appalling.'[24]

Peggy Greer's own memories of the children's school years, by contrast, are happy ones: 'We'd sing over the washing up at home – hymns, Latin mass, cantatas. We'd dance to the radio. We enjoyed ourselves.' Germaine and her mother both liked reading Georgette Heyer's period romances, with their dashing heroes and swooning lace-clad heroines. Germaine took up fencing, a sport in which she could deploy her height and reach to advantage. Only menstruation seemed to flatten her energies. 'She was a complete wreck at period time,' Peggy recalls, 'great pain, lying about.' But the older Germaine grew, the more she felt the family happiness centered on Jane and baby Barry.

The younger children benefited from having a father whose psychological wounds were better healed, or at least better held together, than they had been immediately after his return from the war. As Peggy admits, 'Reg was more affectionate with Barry than the other two.' Reg's support for his son was unequivocal. 'He helped me identify that I was worthwhile,' Barry recalls, 'which is pretty good stuff for parents to do.'[25]

Germaine thought Barry adorable too, and Barry worshipped her in return, but she felt a burning sense of unfairness at the contrast with Reg's attitude toward her. She did not have a dog as a child. Barry did, 'but then my brother had everything. My brother got into Daddy's bed every morning of his life until he was at least twelve years old. Daddy mightn't have been able to hug me, but he had no difficulty doting on my brother.'[26]

To Germaine her sister and particularly her brother were clearly loved, while she was criticized, attacked and literally spurned by her father. The more Germaine strove to win her parents' praise through her efforts at school, the less her academic achievements seemed to impress them: 'When my brother was expected my father tried out names, "Dr. Gideon Greer," "Dr. John Greer." He never tried out "Dr. Germaine Greer." '[27]

Peggy's relationship with the younger children was totally different from her attitude to her first-born, according to Germaine, 'because I was a disaster.' She came to believe that Peggy had not wanted a baby so early in her marriage. Combined with a terrible labor and the subsequent vicissitudes of an unexpected war – not least its impact on Peggy's marriage – this profoundly impaired their bonding. 'What she wanted to do was dance on the deck of an ocean liner under the stars to the strains of Nelson Riddle,' Greer commented drily in her interview with Anthony Clare. 'She really did not want to be on her back, in pain, in a dreary rented apartment.'[28] Germaine simply could not shake off the feeling that she was unwanted. The affection of the most important woman in her life was apparently unwinnable.

While the most important man in her life, her father, also continued to wound and mystify her, Germaine was engaging ever more deeply with his spiritual rival. The passion and mystery of the nuns' love affair with Christ, 'the archetypal lover,' touched her too. She had been confirmed 'Germaine Frances' in the church before arriving at Star, and had a new simple, white dress with a veil for her first communion. 'She was jealous of the kids with orange-blossom embroidery on their veils,' Peggy recalls. In adolescence the intensity of her religious belief rose to a new plane.

At fourteen she fasted and was gathered up, unconscious, from the floor of the church 'because I'd go there and kneel with my arms stretched out for hours on end, making love to this image . . . this person really.'[29]

> The one thing the nuns don't do is take sex for granted, or trivialise it or turn it into a sport. For all convent girls sex is hugely attractive, dark, mysterious and very powerful. . . . It's been an ongoing disappointment in my life to discover that other people don't give it that much importance. I really expected the stars to shoot from their spheres when I finally undid more than one button. We were all sex-struck and that's the nuns' fault entirely.[30]

By the time Germaine was fifteen her religious belief was weakening, though she did not completely abandon her faith until the year after she left school. She blamed the nuns. 'The wanting to be a saint has to do with adolescent passion,' she said later. 'You're thinking you're going to love God, you're going to love him hard. I mean to death! He has to have your whole life, because anything else in your whole life is not worth giving.' For Germaine, however, the central premise collapsed after one of the nuns tried to teach the philosophical proofs of the existence of God. She found the case unconvincing, intellectually deficient: 'If my Church had any brains, children like me would be taught by Jesuits – not by nuns at all. We require much higher educational levels. The nuns were not smart enough. If I'd been taught by Jesuits I would still be Catholic.'[31]

Lanky and clever, Germaine stood out in class from the beginning. One of her first teachers, Sister Phillip, who taught her German in Year 9, recalls an obviously able though not outstanding student who could deliver pat answers even when not apparently paying attention: 'She didn't really shine, but at the same time you knew she was doing well.' Thirty years later Sister Phillip recalls the acclaim Germaine earned by passing intermediate Italian without any formal instruction in the subject.

Germaine was taught art by the large, loud and popular Sister Raymonde – nicknamed 'Bomb' by some of the girls because she always arrived in a rush, and 'Metho' by others for her custom of awarding better marks for spirit. Sister Attracta took Special Choir, an activity for which one had to audition and give up recreational time for practice and performance. The repertoire ranged from High Mass to Latin motets. 'Germaine had a nice voice – not outstanding, but nice,' says Sister Attracta. 'She was a very lovable girl and used to get on with the others well. She never gave me any trouble at all.' Others found her more difficult: Greer recalled being sent to stand in the corridor outside class for disagreeing with the proposition that communism was the work of the devil. Inevitably, Reverend Mother walked by: 'And she'd say, "Oh, Germaine, you could be a great saint or a great sinner. The choice is entirely up to you." I'd be thinking: "great sinner, great sinner!"'[32]

Germaine's attempts to be friendly and caring were sometimes bizarre according to Moira Curtain, a younger student who met her through school drama productions. The school library was housed in a classroom with locked glass-fronted cupboards which Germaine used to raid: 'I don't know whether she forced the lock or whether perhaps some things like the Bible were left open. She'd say: "If you want to come up to the library, I'll show you the dirty bits in the Bible." I used to go staggering up, absolutely intrigued by this. I'd never heard of Onan and his seed, but Germaine showed it to me, and onanism – every time I hear it, I think of Germaine.'

It was in art and drama that Germaine made her reputation at school. Although she was accident-prone, her cultural passions led teachers to place special trust in her. Sister Raymonde, for example, allowed her to take the school's prized art book home overnight – the only copy, worth a mighty £70 in the currency of the day. In pelting rain Germaine drifted out of the school ground with her hair sticking out, her hat perched on top and her gloves full of holes, the precious book sitting just inside the top of her school bag. It fell out of her bag into the gutter, and down through the gutter grate. Germaine lay flat on her stomach in the middle of the running drain trying to fish out the sodden book. It was months before the Greers could afford to replace it.

Germaine was a gangly and awkward teenager, six feet tall by her matriculation year. As one fellow student put it, in her later years at school 'she looked all wrong, like a woman dressed up as a twelve-year-old.' Greer describes herself at fourteen as 'so grey and drawn with adolescent misery' that she could easily have been taken for someone nearing thirty.[33]

In theatrical productions, however, she transcended her physical awkwardness. She was a brilliant Duke of Plaza-Toro in the school's production of *The Gondoliers*. In her final year at Star she was responsible for a student production of the medieval play *Everyman* – quite an accomplishment at a time when unsupervised student action was unusual, and a vote of confidence from her teachers, which was rewarded by success.

Though she was known even then for a quick, sharp tongue that militated against easy friendship, younger students such as Moira Curtain were struck by abruptly and awkwardly delivered small kindnesses. 'She took me aside and said: "You've got a big nose." Now, I was so relieved to hear this because I did have a big nose but everybody pretended I didn't. And I knew I did. She said: "So when you leave school you've got to do something about it." I knew I had to do something about it. And she said: "Make-up's your best bet." It was that theatrical background. She said: "Now, you've got to put darker make-up down here, and lighter make-up on the side, and you've got to watch how you have your hair." . . . And to me it was so liberating to have somebody say this, acknowledge something that everyone else pretended wasn't happening, and be constructive about it.'

By the middle of Germaine's high-school years, her resentment against Peggy and Reg was hardening and she became determined to leave home at the earliest opportunity. School friends were never invited home. Only a few had ever seen Peggy, usually when she was exercising at the beach. 'When all the other mothers were at school making cakes, and at the tuck shop, and in their nice polyester dresses with their white cardigans,' one former student recalls, 'Germaine's mother was in her leotards at the beach – and we couldn't believe that a mother would act like that. She stood out from the crowd. She didn't want to be like all the other mothers, and you can pass that on. It's obvious that Germaine doesn't feel like she needs to be like anybody else, either.' Another student remembered Peggy as rather elegant. Germaine saw her mother as eccentric, creating an 'unbourgeois and unworldly' lifestyle for the family.[34] Peggy dressed by choice in second-hand clothes and her own highly individual home-sewn ones. She did not play bridge or chatter over a hot cuppa with women friends: to Germaine, most of her mother's effort seemed to go into developing her tan.[35]

Despite her adolescent longing for conventional parents, like Peggy, Germaine was already going her own way with little concern for the views of others; and, as was the case with Reg, fantasy and role-playing were already a key part of her persona. She found a kindred spirit in a fellow student, Jennifer Midgley, now better known as the writer Jennifer Dabbs. Germaine and Jennifer were competitors at Holy Redeemer, the scholarship hothouse they attended before Star. They became close friends at their new school, where the scholarship girls tended to mix with each other. Four months older than Germaine and similarly sassy, Jennifer found her 'more interesting than the other girls there. She was eccentric, different.' There was much striking of attitudes from Germaine: 'She frightened a lot of people – they weren't game to extend friendship. She wasn't really aware of it, but she didn't care all that much anyway. She had this actor thing in her. She had to be noticed.'

Germaine had overtaken Jennifer academically at Holy Redeemer, but Jennifer was clearly the superior in one area her friend valued highly: music. A gifted singer and pianist, popular with other students, Jennifer shone at Star, and the nuns encouraged her musical talents with additional lessons and practice time. Germaine's voice was sweet and natural, but Jennifer's was brilliant; her exceptional ability was one of the attractions for her new friend. They were also drawn together by mutual mystification over the young Star girls' crushes on the senior students. 'It seemed odd to us,' Dabbs says in retrospect. 'We'd wonder, what's so wonderful about so-and-so? It turned us toward each other.'

Jennifer and Germaine were enthusiastic members of Star's choir. They held hands discreetly during rehearsals and performances, and sometimes even during Mass. They enjoyed student theater together too, Jennifer playing Marco Palmieri to Greer's Duke of Plaza-Toro in *The Gondoliers*. Germaine autographed Jennifer's copy of the program in precociously adult handwriting, 'Germaine Greer who belongs to JM.' After the operetta's performance at Caulfield Town Hall, Jennifer watched Germaine standing with Peggy and Reg Greer, 'all tall and rather striking.' Reg looked very proud of his daughter.

Germaine caused a panic at home by producing a copy of Radclyffe Hall's *The Well of Loneliness* at the height of her liaison with Jennifer.[36] The flowering of their friendship into grand passion was still playing on both women's minds well into adulthood. Fifteen years after the event, Greer guiltily recalled betraying the friend she considered her lover under pressure from her mother. In *The Female Eunuch* Greer describes a 'scene' where Peggy screamingly accused her of being unnatural after discovering a letter from Jennifer: '[To] stem her flow, I repeated what I had read in the Sunday Supplements, that it was an adolescent homosexual phase, and I was through it anyway. I expiated that pusillanimous, lying betrayal of myself and my love for weeks. After such knowledge, what forgiveness?'[37]

It also played on her schoolgirl lover's mind. Thirty years after their relationship ended, Dabbs told their story through the characters Kate Mitchell and Michaela Martin in *Beyond Redemption*, a *roman à clef* described by its publisher as a novel about rapturous love in the dark ages of the 1950s.[38] The pen portrait of Michaela is beautiful and strikingly recognizable. After the resolution of a fight between the friends, 'Immediately her face lost its severity and lit up with a beguiling smile. She wasn't what was considered to be "pretty"; there was far too much character in her face, and a vivacious intelligence shone out of her clear green eyes. Her hair was tawny and curlier than mine. It stood out around her head like a nimbus, complementing her clear creamy skin and contrasting with those startling eyes.'[39]

Forty years later the romance was still on Peggy Greer's mind, too: 'At Star of the Sea there was a girl, Jennifer. . . . They used to exchange love letters. They were always left around for me to read. . . . [Germaine] used to bait me, leaving love letters in her pockets addressed "My darling lover," after I'd told her to clean them out. I just tried to forget.'

In *Beyond Redemption* Dabbs paints a mixed picture of life at Star, called Stella Maris in the book. On one hand the ferocious consequences of transgressing the sexual morality of 1950s Catholicism are sharply etched – for example, when Kate fears she is pregnant in her matriculation year, after taking up with a touring Italian baritone in the wake of Michaela's rejection of her. On the other hand, the book acknowledges Star's capacity to nurture talent. Discovering Kate has perfect pitch, Sister Cecilia – Star's Sister Attracta – responds by arranging twice-weekly piano lessons and assigning the school annex as a practice room for her use after school: 'Then there was the singing, the wonderful high Masses, the Gregorian chant, the glorious songs of Pachelbel and Palestrina and standing in the choir loft looking down on the congregation and filling the church with music. We sang our hearts out. . . .'[40]

Neither girl was happy at home, though neither discussed it with the other. Instead they arrived at school as early as possible in order to be together, spent every break *à deux* and lingered for as long as possible after school, usually in the annex, a room crowded with abandoned furniture, ornaments and sideboards full of secrets, where Jennifer would practise the piano. 'She was very sure of herself,' Jennifer says of Germaine. 'She seemed to know how to get what she wanted. But there was this constant need for attention which I didn't have. I got attention, but I didn't seek it.'

There is a revealing moment in *Beyond Redemption* when Kate attracts the attention of an older, sophisticated student, Jude – in real life, the Star student Judy Richardson. Michaela, as usual, is with Kate while she practices piano in the annex. Jude admires Kate's playing and outshines Michaela's repartee, prompting Michaela to brag to Jude about her intellectual ability: 'Actually I came top of the state. It was in the papers. But then, I always come top. I have an IQ of genius level, you see.'[41]

When they were alone in the practice room, Germaine would pretend to be George Sand, writing slushy poetry in the back of her English book, while Jennifer, assuming the part of Chopin, played wistful nocturnes. They fantasized about an endlessly romantic, candle-lit life. At one stage they even planned to write an opera together, with Germaine responsible for the libretto.

The relationship was passionate, spiritual and romantic rather than genital, according to Jennifer. 'Germaine was the first person outside my family who loved me, and I realized: I love you. It was

21

unconditional, heady, unlike parental love, which was conditional. The sexual thing came later. It seemed very natural, the limited amount of sexual contact we had.'

Girls received mixed messages about the merits of achievement at Star, in Dabbs's view. The nuns relished their girls' success at matriculation and were proud of the school's high academic standards, but ambition had implicit limits. Dabbs was given special support and encouragement in music but not, she felt, with the aim of turning her into a top-flight soloist. She sensed that the nuns had more modest goals in mind: 'You weren't really supposed to stand out.' Religious devotion was still valued above academic prowess. In the school's prize lists, for example, the top student in 'Christian Doctrine' was listed ahead of the academic achiever of the year.

These conflicting signals concerning students' achievements were insignificant, however, compared to the teaching they received about relations between women and men. Dabbs's descriptions of the Christian Living classes given by 'Mother Julian' at the fictional Stella Maris illustrate the bizarre instruction given to the girls at the time. At a Christian Living class on the male reproductive system, Michaela provokes Mother Julian over the impending canonization of a young Italian woman, Maria Goretti, who had been stabbed to death while trying to resist rape. If she had struggled less, Michaela asks, wouldn't she still be alive? 'But wouldn't her soul still retain its purity and nobility even if she was raped and taken against her will, Mother? Why should *she* be considered impure when it was the *man* who was the aggressor. It was *his* crime. Not hers. And more to the point, why does the Church hold her up as an example to the rest of us? I think she was a fool.'[42]

Mother Julian splutters angrily at Michaela to sit down and continues the lesson, explaining that when a man forces his 'attentions' on a woman against her will, it is a grievous sin – one no decent Catholic man would contemplate. She goes on to inform the girls that, should they ever be overpowered and surrender to rape, it would be a most terrible sin for them, too, if they allowed themselves to enjoy it.

'We live in a civilized society and . . .'

'I suppose Maria Goretti thought that she lived in a civilized society too,' Michaela said, not quite under her breath. And Mother Julian finally lost her temper.

'You! Michaela Martin! Leave the room. *Immediately!* Go to my office and wait for me there.'[43]

Mother Julian goes on to explain to the girls – minus the disgraced Michaela – that while the act of intercourse gives 'a certain amount of pleasure' to men, who have a strong urge to procreate, it affords no such pleasure to 'women, *good* women.' A woman must never deny her husband's conjugal rights, says Mother Julian, but a well-brought-up Catholic man would be considerate of his wife's feelings in such matters.

Neither Germaine nor Jennifer doubted that they would later have relationships with men. They kept a booklet together into which they pasted pictures of their favorite film stars, and had a code word for their top six movie men – 'ROTASTGRALLAMEFECOWIMABR' covering the first two letters of the names of Robert Taylor, Stewart Granger, Alan Ladd, Mel Ferrer, Cornel Wilde and Marlon Brando. Ferrer and Brando were Germaine's particular favorites; Jennifer preferred Ladd and Wilde, while both girls liked Taylor and Granger. 'We imagined our long friendship could go on for ever at the same time as we pursued men,' says Dabbs. 'It couldn't be.'

'I remember waking up with a very light heart one morning,' Jennifer recalls of the moment she knew she loved Germaine. 'The realization was there. I couldn't wait to get to school and tell her. I did. She said: "I do, too." That's when the hand-holding started. Later we would kiss and caress, but that's all.' Neither had any concept of lesbianism at the time; Germaine, Dabbs says, was certainly sexually naive. Their first kiss took place on Jennifer's initiative after she had been on a date with the brother of another Star student. After seeing *The Student Prince* at the cinema, the young man had given her a big, wet, passionate kiss on the way home. Jennifer described the awful, sloppy kiss to Germaine and they wondered how either of them could ever do that with boys? Jennifer tried out an improved version on Germaine – warm, comforting, lips closed. 'We always kissed like that,' she says. 'For me, that was the first kiss. She was my first love.'

In *The Female Eunuch* Greer would write of schoolgirl love without naming Jennifer. Inseparable girls are often fascinated by each other, capable of deep spiritual and sexual, if not genital, relationships, she contended: 'Learning to dissemble these feelings, among the strongest and the most elevated that she will ever feel, is a squalid but inevitable business.'[44] Even the innocent caresses of such a love are necessarily furtive, Greer wrote, and the schoolgirl intuits from the beginning that the love will gradually come to be viewed in the light of prevailing social disapproval, ultimately to be ridiculed and disowned by the girl herself: 'Such loss is enormous, and brings her much further on the way to the feminine pattern of shallow response combined with deep reserve. From the frank sharing of another's being she turns to the teasing and titillation of dating, which all the world condones. I can remember a scene with my mother when she discovered a letter written by me to my lover at school, a girl who introduced me to Beethoven by playing his sonatas to me in a dingy annexe where we retreated at every spare moment, who held my hand while we sang harmonies of Palestrina and Pachelbel in the crack school choir, and pretended I was George Sand and she was Chopin, and vice versa.'[45]

Both women, writing as adults, recounted precisely the same details of their youthful affair – the annex setting, the songs they sang together, the role-playing as Chopin and Sand – and both explicitly acknowledged each other as lovers. The relationship was precious, making Germaine's retreat all the more dramatic a concession to conformity. According to Dabbs: 'She capitulated to her mother, didn't she? It's a strange caving-in for someone so headstrong and forthright. If she was true to form she'd have told her mother to get stuffed.' Perhaps worst of all, it came without warning. Germaine simply announced it was all over in 1955 when school resumed after the Christmas holidays, and gave no reason. It was their matriculation year. Jennifer dropped out to work in the theater, and did not complete her matriculation until years later, as an adult.

The 'squalid but inevitable business,' as Germaine referred to it, of dissembling over her feelings for Jennifer was done. Its 'inevitability' was never explained. Germaine turned her eyes to the University of Melbourne and her plans for leaving home.

Although she had rejected her girlfriend, boys did not figure significantly until Star was behind her. The first memorable male date of Greer's school years was with a painter she had encountered on a wharf during one of her meandering bicycle rides. She was sixteen and had never met the man before. She watched him painting a seascape and, after a long conversation about art, he asked her out. They went to the theater; Germaine wore her mother's high-heeled shoes, a pencil skirt and a batwing jacket. On the tram ride home a risqué conversation ensued. 'That struck me as strange,' recalls Greer. 'That's been the pattern ever since, the virgin who speaks in a risqué fashion.' His mannered gesture of kissing her hand when they reached her home struck her as ridiculous. She nearly hit him, and refused his subsequent invitations, claiming she had to study.[46]

Determined to be kissed properly by a man for the first time, Germaine went to a dance at the local town hall, dressed in white piqué and wearing a blue Coles bra underneath: 'I was no belle . . . I was the tall girl who played the men's parts in the school plays. I never got a date or a dance.' Except for the barn dance, when she attracted the attentions of a huge builder's laborer. They rode home in a cab, 'and there I sat all aquiver in my little white gloves and waited.' He grabbed her breast, squeezing it like a lemon, and split her lip with a kiss. It bled profusely and, terrified, she managed to get away. 'And when I stopped shaking I said to myself, "I won't muck about with *that* again." . . . It taught me something. That all the world pets and nobody loves.'[47]

She would, of course, muck about with that again – once she arrived at the University of Melbourne, her immediate goal. First Germaine had to sit her final exams in English, English Literature, History, French and German. She seems to have approached the year's study in a less than systematic way; her first-term result for English Literature was a poor 47 percent, for example, but she received first-class honors in the final exam.[48] Germaine visited the university during her final year at Star: 'I knew it was waiting for me, and I was waiting for it. I knew it was going to be mine.'[49] But bound up with going there was her drive to get away from home, from her aggressive, frustrated mother and her distant, condescending father, away from her better-loved siblings to territory she could make her own. If the conflict at home had been mighty during her school years, it was nothing compared with the collision waiting to occur when Greer's rebelliousness and emerging sexuality crashed headlong into the parental sensibilities of Peggy and Reg.

# 2

# Getting Away

Germaine arrived at the University of Melbourne in 1956, hungry for the life of intellect and adventure she craved at home. Yet the crucial elements shaping her life had already left their imprint by the time she arrived. Far from being a fresh start, the university and its environs were the stage on which she began to enact the consequences of her tension-riven childhood.

Since Reg had returned from the war, Germaine's family dynamic had consolidated itself as a vicious circle of anxiety, distrust, unhappiness and conflict. Desperate for love and affirmation, she was kept at arm's length by two adults struggling to come to terms with their own drastically changed personal circumstances. The more difficult and demanding the daughter became in her bid for parental warmth, the more explicit became the rejection by her father, in particular. The worse the cumulative rejection, the worse her behavior, reinforcing the apparently inescapable bind of the unloved and unlovable child. Long before she went to university she had come to believe that she was unloved and unwanted by her parents, who related far more easily to her younger siblings. There was also a deep cultural dissonance in the household between Germaine, who had swallowed a dictionary – as Australian argot would have it – and her parents, who had not. None of her intellectual efforts during her school years had won her mother's approval or elicited her father's attention and affection.

Germaine's low self-esteem did not preclude intellectual arrogance: she was a young woman with plenty of raw brainpower and something to prove. There was a broad streak of ambivalence about women in the making, rooted in her relationship with her mother, but there was a nascent feminism, too. Perhaps this was partly a reaction to her baby brother's favored treatment at home, and to her perception that girls in the Catholic education system received a lesser education than boys. Girls' lack of access to an elite Jesuit education would become a recurring theme for Greer, who failed to make the complementary observation that access to the superior teaching of the Jesuits was equally closed to the vast majority of Catholic boys who were also taught by less intellectual orders.

If the nuns who taught at Star of the Sea were not Jesuits, they provided positive female role models even while propagating a patriarchal religious message. The nuns' affirmation of Germaine as creative, talented and accomplished partly compensated for the lack of intellectual recognition and reinforcement she experienced at home. The negative influence of Catholicism on the formation of a feminist sense of self was outweighed by the positive impact of the nuns as powerful female role models whom she would remember with affection and respect.

Catholicism inculcated an intensity, a passion for definitive positions and a drive for the reconciliation of theory and practice within the positions Greer would adopt serially over time. That Catholic intensity imbued her thinking long after her faith collapsed in adolescence. When she arrived at university, burning to leave home and really live, this complicated personal and philosophical baggage accompanied her. The moral certainties dictated by Germaine's religion were gradually collapsing along with her faith, and a void was developing where a coherent belief system had once been. She was going to have to work out a replacement for herself.

'Germaine taught me a lot of lessons,' Peggy recalls. 'She used to use clear thinking on me as a kid. She would question my ideas. She'd slap an idea on the wall and start to tear it down. She said I was a muddled thinker.' According to Germaine, Peggy never admitted to anything and never denied anything either, 'and doesn't care whether statement A is at all compatible with statement B, because she uses language as a weapon, as a tool for manipulation.'[1] If Germaine was a clear thinker compared with Peggy, it was this same capacity for using language as a weapon, as a tool of influence, which would propel the younger Greer forward.

Persistence was another defining trait. Germaine was a great pesterer, according to her mother: 'She pestered Reg for a car. She said: "Mum's got one, why can't I?"' Reg remained unmoved on the car question, but Peggy used the same technique successfully to persuade him to buy their first, and last, family home. By the time Germaine started university, the Greers had moved into a clinker brick, Cape Cod–style house in Mentone, south of the bayside suburbs where the family had previously lived in rented flats. 'I pestered my husband until I got this house,' Peggy says. 'We got it so the kids could have friends stay over. Jane and Barry took advantage of it. Their friends would come over for coffee after school. We've been here since Germaine started uni. That was when the trouble started.'

The trouble had, of course, already existed for years, but university, financial independence and a burgeoning sexuality combined to ratchet up the household tensions until Germaine finally left.

Having matriculated well, Germaine won a teacher training scholarship with a generous living allowance. Even so, she found there was little left after paying for fares, stockings, underwear, stationery and the nominal rent her mother charged – 'meaningless to her, crippling to me.'[2] She bought shoes at sales, made her own skirts and knitted her own cardigans.

Peggy gives a different account of the household economy, in which none of the children was charged board. She blames Germaine's financial independence for breaking up the family: 'She wouldn't have gone without that Commonwealth scholarship and bursary for teaching.' Before Greer left home, Peggy went to the Department of Education looking for help. 'I said: "I've got this ungovernable uni student." I told them she wasn't studying, got all this money and wasn't dependent on me, and didn't take any notice of what we said. I was ushered into a room and I said to the man: "You give her this money and it's turning her into a tramp!"'

29

While 'Reg would be full of beer, snoring upstairs,' Peggy would lie awake waiting for Germaine to come home. 'I was worried about accidents. We were fighting. Reg'd wake up at night. She'd have come home with a boy, and he'd discover her in a clinch.' Remembering the spanners and screwdrivers her own father had thrown at her male visitors, Peggy says she did not want to tell Germaine not to bring boys home. 'Reg'd be shocked and worried. He'd bring it up at breakfast time. She'd come out with f . . . and c . . . and shit at the table! In front of the other children! She made those words popular.'

Germaine's retorts to her father were incendiary. The youth rebellion of the 1960s was not even a glimmer in the eye of 1950s teenagers; in middle-class Australia, politeness, twinsets and pearls still ruled, conservatism and sexism were the norm. Girls did not swear at their fathers, or at anyone else. According to Greer, she had learnt to swear at primary school: 'That's where I learnt all those four-letter words, because all the kids used them!'[3]

Tensions at home were exacerbated by the transition to university life, which held particular difficulties for women in the 1950s. Jeffrey Sher, then secretary of the Student Representative Council, welcomed new students in the pages of the student newspaper, *Farrago*. After a gentle homily on how success or failure at university rested almost entirely on one's own efforts, Sher was encouraging about life lounging round the University Union, known as the 'shop':

> For a few weeks, and only a few, you'll feel new and unsure of yourself. But it's surprising how little time it takes to get used to 'shop' life . . . You'll be able to recognise your fellow freshers. The men wear snazzy new sports coats, a tie, have creases in their pants; the women change daily, giggle and walk round in groups.
>
> On the other hand, the old hands among the men wear baggy strides, smoke continuously and walk around with an air of sublime indifference. The old hands among the women are seen to wear the same outfit as often as THREE days in a row.[4]

Rock-and-roll had not yet arrived. The campus Rhythm Club supplied the opening concert of the term: 'Freshers, freshettes . . . You are invited to attend the most super colossal, stupendous jazz show ever seen.' The star turns were Glen 'Butch' Prior leading the band on trumpet in a program of swing, modern and Dixieland jazz, and Brian Leonard, who had led the orchestra in the university revue the previous year: 'Brian will play a very sweet slush pump (trombone, peasants!!).' Featured songs included 'Golden Wedding,' 'Apple Honey' and 'When the Saints Come Marching In.'[5] The same issue of *Farrago* reviewed the efforts of young actors such as Barry Humphries, Noel Ferrier and Alan Hopgood, and carried poetry by Bruce Dawe.

The storm created by the publication of A. D. Hope's erotic verse *The Wandering Islands* the previous year was canvassed in *Farrago* later that month: 'Poet or Pornographer?,' the headline asked.[6] But the same issue ran the following advertisement, headed 'Female Linguists Wanted':

> Female arts students are urgently needed by final year electrical engineering students in connection with the translation of articles in foreign technical journals – these articles being required for the writing of theses. Close collaboration will be necessary.
>
> Qualifications: 1. Approx. 36-22-34 (depending on height). 2. Must have knowledge of one of the following: Russian, Sanskrit, Hebrew, Czechoslovakian, Japanese, French, German or English. 3. Need not have any previous experience. Freshers are particularly welcome.
>
> Payment: If necessary.

The attitudes underlying this specious notice were widespread in the 1950s. *Farrago* neatly conveyed the sexual ethos of the day early in 1956 when it advertised for a secretary, 'preferably female – redheads need not apply.'[7] 'Women weren't people,' one male former student recalls. 'They were minor social add-ons.' There were complaints when an all-male lounge became a 'mixed' facility after the reconstruction of the University Union.[8]

Germaine was miserable for the first few weeks, fretting about her height and whether she was dressed the right way. But the tall, smart, sharp fresher quickly became the object of male desire on campus. Before long she was table-hopping between friends in the Union cafeteria and throwing herself into student theater. By the middle of her first year she had drawn favorable notices for a vivid performance in the student revue *Up and Atom* along with fellow thespian Dick Pratt, later a multimillionaire packaging magnate. The production was described in campus reviews as the most unadulterated shambles in the memory of that generation of students; some cast members were so drunk they had to be sobered up before going on stage.[9] Yet the humorous exploration of the atomic age played to capacity houses for a week-long run, turning a profit and ensuring Germaine's early notoriety.

Theatrical success and plentiful male attention proceeded hand in hand: 'I started to get rushed, and I couldn't understand it.'[10] Frenetic activity notwithstanding, she was becoming severely depressed. Her sensible gabardine coat was stolen at the Union early in first term, and even the old Harris tweed coat purloined from her father left her shivering on the long train rides between Mentone and the university. She was racked by repeated bouts of bronchitis. A hectic social life and student theater on top of a solid academic workload wore her down, and she plumbed the depths of adolescent despair.

A melodramatic gesture at suicide while she was out walking on a windswept cliff-top was nearly fatal. Ignoring the signs and temporary barriers steering pedestrians away from the rain-weakened edge, Germaine stood on one of the more vulnerable spots and asked God to save her life if he considered it worthwhile. The edge gave way. She crashed down the cliff, the fall barely broken by a few scrubby bushes until she stopped dead – suspended, symbolically enough, by her father's tweed coat, which had caught on a stump. Then the cliff gave way again, tumbling Germaine on to rough beach sand at its base. She was catching her breath and reflecting on the idiocy of tempting fate when, as though God were rubbing it in, a dislodged stone bounced down the cliff and cracked her on the back of the head.[11]

At university Germaine alternately used and neglected her friends and admirers, pursuing a notion of love as wild, dangerous and mad – an idea she later ascribed to the reading of rubbishy books during adolescence. At its apogee during her first year, she became fixated on a fellow student actor. Germaine constantly thought and dreamed of him, even sang songs to him at night as though they could be transmitted through the dark from Mentone across to the other side of Melbourne where he lived. Driving her home one night from a rehearsal, the student stopped the car and, to her intense pleasure, began to kiss her. After becoming quite excited he suddenly, inexplicably, pushed her away and drove her home at high speed, apologizing as she alighted and declaring it would not happen again. The rejection devastated Germaine, who, oddly, blamed herself. He had stopped to kiss 'probably because I was unconsciously forcing the pace . . . Won't happen again! Those words destroyed me. For days I brooded over the way in which I had lost him.' Germaine's slide into depression became a headlong plunge. She broke down. The sound of loud bells filled her head, drowning her own voice during a British History tutorial. The breakdown was serious enough for her to be hospitalized, with a diagnosis of nervous exhaustion.[12]

Emerging from the hospital, Germaine was medicated to make the pain of the failed fixation bearable as the end-of-year exam crisis approached: 'I'd worked my butt off all year, had a break-down, been put on sedation but thrown the pills away and done the exams without them. The university environment was such a shock to my system and I had lost my balance.'[13] Germaine survived the episode and went on to second year, but there are various versions of the extent to which her grades were affected. In 1965 she is reported as saying she failed her first year because of emotional trauma,[14] an account with which her mother concurs. Writing later, however, Greer has the pain of rejection subsiding to a mere flicker when the exam results were released and she achieved first-class honors.[15] The loss of her student records from the Melbourne University archives makes it difficult to determine the matter conclusively.

The latter version casts Germaine as heroically overcoming the dire threat posed to her future by an unloving, insincere man – a man who, like her father, should have loved her but instead pushed her away: 'I was heavily sedated and as stupid as a fish. It looked as if my fixation on a man who really didn't love me was going to mess up my life for good, for if I didn't pass my exams, I could kiss my scholarship goodbye and go to the typing school that my parents had picked out for me.'[16] Germaine overcame the rejecting lover, Reg's symbolic successor, through the pursuit of education, the same route she would use repeatedly to ground herself during her life.

Back at home over the long vacation, Germaine resisted her parents' strictures. At the end of her first year the scholarship money dried up, with no prospect of more until the beginning of her second year apart from an advance book allowance for academic texts. Strapped for cash, Germaine was poking around the family refrigerator one summer day at the end of her first year and asked her mother whether she could have a banana. 'Those bananas are for my children,' Greer recalled her mother saying. 'You can't have anything to eat until you bring home some money for this house.' Germaine packed her briefcase with a nightie, a bottle of Schiaparelli 'Schocking,' a hairbrush and Ovid's *Metamorphoses*, went to the train station and was infused with happiness: 'I thought this is it. Life begins now.' She decamped to a house shared by three male friends and rang her father to tell him she was all right – 'those things that runaways say.' Not that it had the desired effect. 'Nobody gave a stuff whether I was all right or not actually,' she said later. 'That was the funniest thing.' After a friend told her that Peggy and Reg had reported her missing to the police – a serious matter, given that she was under age, without income and living with three men – Greer returned home 'rather than ending up in prison . . . I lay on my bed and my mother came in and said, "Who let all the flies in?" and I knew I was home.'[17]

A problem that had been growing throughout her first year became acute during the summer holidays. The long ride home with a boy more often than not included a parking session along the beach front or parkland. Germaine dreaded the ensuing struggle, during which she would draw a line short of sexual intercourse, but was disappointed if the pursuit did not occur at all: 'I was not frigid but I had a fierce sense of my own dignity.' The same 'squalid little battles' fought over and over again were a source of deepening gloom.[18]

Young Catholics commonly left the church because they felt it denied their drive for sexual expression, but in Greer's case the position was reversed: it was her waning faith that led her to reject the church's sexual strictures. 'One of the sources of conflict that was distressing me during my first year of university was the collapse of my Catholic faith and my unwilling arrival at the conclusion that there was no god,' she would recall. 'Once that had been decided, there were no rules about anything else either. I found myself thinking very hard about virginity and the morality of all that petting in parked cars. I decided that my behaviour was dishonest and cowardly and that either I was going to give up going out altogether or I had to accept my own sexuality and what was due to it.'[19]

She went to summer parties, warm and wild with everybody petting furiously, which intensified her inner conflict. Appalled to discover she was being described behind her back as a 'professional virgin' and a 'cockteaser,' she began to feel she would rather bear the consequences of full sexual engagement – being described as a whore or a slut. Ignoring the sexual pressure implied in the abuse was an option that did not seem to occur to her. Instead, at the beginning of her second year at university, she allowed it to drive her into a calculated decision to jettison her virginity.

Leon Fink was chosen for the task. The clever, rich, handsome son of a Jewish family in the upper-class Melbourne suburb of Toorak, Fink was a law student and head of the Jewish student society at Melbourne. He had been open about his desire for Germaine from the moment they had met on campus, but showed no interest in dating or petting. Although she believed him to be a hard man, especially in relation to women, Germaine found him 'upsettingly attractive.' So at the age of eighteen, a full twelve months after his original invitation, Germaine told Leon that his time had come. 'He looked at me with a bored expression. "When?" was all he said.'[20]

Fink, in fact, found Germaine thoroughly attractive. She was the second strong woman he had met at university, the first being a Jewish law student who went on to become a successful businesswoman. Leon considered Germaine much brighter than the rest of the students they mixed with, and admired her energy and vim. 'We were in a really flat period,' one male student friend of hers recalls, 'and this person bursts out of the woodwork, years younger than us, and charges ahead.'

It was a cool night in April, the middle of autumn – a day on which Germaine had worked out she was unlikely to be fertile. Leon collected her from the Union Theatre, where she was doing make-up for a student play, and they drove off in his Studebaker. Germaine was nervous but determined to proceed with the plan. 'He drove up into Studley Park and drew rugs out of the car,' she recalled. 'Then he did it. Just like that. It was a fearful anticlimax to all my cerebrations. I felt the tears running into my ears. Then he stood me up, turned me all round so I could see the illuminated city lying along the banks of the Yarra beneath us and asked, "Is anything different?" "No," I answered, "no." '[21]

The deed done, Germaine had no great desire to repeat it in a hurry. For a while she stopped going out, having resolved never to kiss a man on the lips again unless she was prepared to have sex with him. The connection with Fink continued for several months, constituting a few more sexual encounters rather than a love affair, before she moved on. Years later she wrote that she had loved Leon with all her heart.[22]

By her own account Germaine's eccentricity became more marked as her second year went on, with another unhappy summer looming at the end of 1957. She was experimenting broadly with life, dabbling in student politics, writing letters to *Farrago* and participating energetically in the campus drama scene. She began the year with a role in *Home Is the Hunted*, receiving a favorable notice for scoring lots of laughs in a production otherwise underproduced and insufficiently rehearsed.[23]

Soon afterward she became involved in a jocular but oddly telling exchange with a group calling itself the Society for the Confining of Immoral Impulses Amongst Engineering Students (SCIIAES). As part of a campaign to promote the segregation of the sexes on campus, SCIIAES members had defaced posters promoting a student comedy, *Venus Observed*, with the scrawled slogan 'BE PURE,' prompting Greer to protest in a letter to *Farrago*:

> I say, sirs, who are these upstart S.C.I.I.A.E.S.? Who are they who cry for segregation? Are they not a backward minority, sirs? Do they not attempt . . . to impose on others the cruel curbs which their own rapacious appetites so obviously need . . .
>
> Their only function is to introduce into non-sexarian meetings an element of pornography. This we can well do without. I cry to all students to put up with it no longer, but to take positive action against this snake we have nurtured in our bosom.[24]

The following month Hilton R. Brown of the SCIIAES responded with a letter declaring: 'I can say, quite frankly, that no member of the SCIIAES has felt this snake. Think again, G.G. BE PURE,

SUPPORT THE SCIIAES.' The same edition of *Farrago* carried several unusual classified advertisements: 'GERMAINE – Come back to me angel. Your loving husband Tojo,' for example, and 'GERMAINE – The children and I need you desperately. Lucky.'[25]

Another correspondent, J. Gavin Moore, writing 'to insult engineers, not to praise them,' claimed that the segregation of the sexes would create 'a race of automatons' on campus and subject 'all other men to eunuch-hood.'[26] Moore was at least drawing attention to the segregationist agenda of the SCIIAES engineers, even if he was less concerned with the consequences for women than with what he declared was the SCIIAES's true goal: the 'eunuch-hood' of other men.

In the same edition as Hilton Brown's letter, the paper ran an ostensibly humorous advertorial seeking a typist for the National Union of Australian University Students' office, headlined 'Are you pretty? Can you type? Then work for "The Firm."' 'Asked whether he preferred a blonde, a brunette or a redhead, Mr. Tak replied, "Yes,"' the advertorial went. 'At this stage Mr. Norman Geary, engineering appeal boss, interrupted: "She must be approved by the SCIIAES." This seemed to indicate that Miss Greer would not get the job. P.S: This is a serious advertisement.'[27]

The jibes between Germaine and the SCIIAES went on for weeks. One edition of *Farrago* featured a picture of a model in a black strapless dress, long black gloves and black hat, with the caption: 'This superb Dior model in black delustred satin was worn by Germaniac Queer at the SCIIAES Ball last night. Germaniac recently stole the show by nesting a viper in her bosom at the Mediterranean Fair Parade a few days ago.'[28]

Germaine's exchanges with the SCIIAES brought her attention, even notoriety, for what was essentially ersatz combat against conservative, sexist men. 'Her sort of rebellion wasn't earnest,' recalls the writer Beatrice Faust, a student contemporary. The charge would emerge again later, though when it did the male eunuch-hood cited by J. Gavin Moore would be transposed into the female eunuch-hood of Greer's first book.

The pages of *Farrago* repeatedly bore witness to the standard patronizing of women on campus. One *Farrago* correspondent rued the appearance of slacks on women students, and predicted the day would come when a young woman in a skirt was matter for comment: 'One of the attractions of this University used to be the nice sets of ankles which were available for the discerning observer to praise.'[29]

Germaine's still half-formed feminist consciousness was expressed intriguingly when she stood for the position of Women's General Representative in the 1957 Student Representative Council elections. On the one hand she said that as a woman she intended to represent women's interests actively; on the other, she expressly disavowed a belief in the equality of the sexes. A hairdresser for the Union building was the top priority of her election platform, followed by matters of concern to both women and men including parking, teaching standards and the failure rate. Germaine closed with a declaration that was entirely consistent with the 'special talents' thesis expounded by Mother Eymard at Star of the Sea: 'I do not believe in the equality of the sexes, but the superiority of women in those fields where their special talents are of most value.'[30]

There were five other candidates for the position. Felicity Anderson advocated the fostering of Australian-Asian relationships in university activities and espresso coffee for the Union, while Lillian Gill declared her priorities to be better community life among students, more organized women's sport and improved drainage outside the Law Library. Despite the compelling promise of a campus hairdresser, Germaine did not win.

Amid the politicking, the thespianism and the mock combat with the SCIIAES, Germaine was beginning to make her way in Melbourne's main bohemian subculture, the 'Drift.' Contemporaneous with the better-known Sydney 'Push,' the Drift was a refuge for the free-thinking and free-loving in the 1950s and early 1960s. The Drift and the Push had a lot, and little, in common. Both groups flouted conventional standards of behaviour; their members were sexually freewheeling and dismissive of prevailing social mores. The Drift was heavy with visual artists while, when it came to fine arts, most members of the Push had the aesthetic instincts of a bar-stool. Both had their share of philosophers, but the Drift's tended to be Wittgensteinian, while the Push's were Andersonian. The Drift had a distinctly Marxist streak, while the Push was conspicuously anarchist in complexion. Germaine came to know both groups intimately, but her initial contact was constrained by the fact that during her second year she was still living at home.

There was a sharp demarcation between those of Germaine's friends who were acquainted with her family situation and those who were not. With some, mostly women, she expanded at length on the problems at home – that her parents would not give her any money and, at one point, that she was not allowed to consort with her sister Jane because she was considered a corrupting influence. Others, mostly men, say it was almost as though she drew a shutter over life in Mentone. It was never mentioned; invitations to visit were rare, even when they were driving by the suburb on the way to beach houses or parties.

Bringing boys home was a risky business according to Germaine: 'Unless I was really sure of a young man's loyalty, I could not allow him to glimpse the bizarreness of my domestic reality. As like as not we would be assailed at the door by my mother wearing an old pair of underpants on her head, to protect her hair, and very little else, except for the suntan for which so much was sacrificed.'[31] Reg used to laugh at Germaine's scruffiness, when she wore his old tweed coat with her own sloppy-joe sweaters, and was unimpressed by the similar attire of the boys she did bring home.

'Germaine was no chic dresser – she featured bare feet quite a lot, which wasn't the go in the fifties,' recalls Rhyll Nance, a contemporary involved in the student drama scene. 'Pringle twin-sets and strings of pearls were still the go for some.' Germaine often went without make-up and wore odd combinations of clothes. Her style contrasted with that of Peggy, who still visited the campus for the odd dramatic production: 'Her mother was so dyed blonde, teetering on stiletto heels,' Nance remembers. 'The combination of the two was quite striking.' Germaine told Beatrice Faust that her mother encouraged her not to be around because it betrayed her own age: 'Her mother wanted her to be younger than she was, or not there at all.' For her part, Germaine was frustrated by her parents' failure to understand that the professionals of the future were not necessarily wandering around campus already kitted out in pinstripe suits – not that she was particularly interested in young men of that ilk anyway.

The summer at the end of Germaine's second year at university was as muddled and melancholy as the year before. Late in the academic year she had her first abortion. It cost the then mighty sum of £35. Soon afterward she met the first man with whom she could enjoy a reciprocal love, though he was not the type to impress her conventionally minded father. She had a job waitressing in a restaurant where a jazz band played. The drummer was a young Greek man her own age with huge hands – a star turn on the conga drums. Germaine's low morale lifted. He loved her and she loved him back: 'That was my first real love affair.'[32] His father was a wharfie who used to smoke the leaves of a tall bush growing in the backyard of their family home. Not yet familiar with marijuana, Germaine assumed it was cheap tobacco.

Germaine was with her young drummer for a year – working herself, or sitting listening to his music; they never danced together. He accepted a long work engagement interstate and, on his last night in the club, sang a blues song about his girlfriend 'ten foot tall.' It moved Germaine to tears. Then someone told him that she had been with another man. '[And] he just dropped me cold without another word,' she recalled later. 'Can you imagine that?'[33]

Germaine's scholarship money and the extra earnings from waitressing finally freed her from Mentone. She left home, with just one tragic final reprise with her parents yet to come. Life had, at last, really begun.

# 3

# *Drifting*

Superficially at least, there were few quieter places on earth in the 1950s than Melbourne, Australia. When Greer moved to Carlton at the age of nineteen, the world was full of promise. She was independent from her family with a little help from the state via her scholarship, and from local restaurateurs through the waitressing work they provided. She was the citizen of a country which had survived World War II and was enjoying unparalleled economic growth, fortified by a massive immigration program. The nuclear fallout shelters spawned in the northern hemisphere by the Cold War had no counterparts in the south; Washington and Moscow and their missile silos were thousands of miles away. Conservative governments were entrenched in Melbourne and Canberra.

In fact, momentous passages in history were unfolding at home and abroad. The Communist Party of Australia was in upheaval over the Soviet Union's brutal crushing of the Hungarian uprising. The Australian Labor Party was living with the immediate consequences of the infamous 'Split,' in which the Catholic, anti-communist 'groupers' of the Labor Right in Victoria and Queensland broke away to form the right-wing Democratic Labor Party (DLP). The DLP's informal alliance with the Liberal-Country Party coalition effectively delivered the balance of power in the Australian Senate to the conservative parties for the next two decades. DLP preferences helped to keep the conservatives in federal office for a record twenty-three-year run, until the election of the Whitlam Labor Government in 1972. Grouper sympathizers established a DLP Society at the University of Melbourne in 1957 and, according to *Farrago*, its launch attracted enthusiastic support.[1] Yet this was an aberration in a generally apathetic student body.

Even burning international issues like the arms race failed to ignite the passion of Melbourne University students at the time. A survey showed them divided, for example, over the banning of nuclear tests. Only a small minority felt strongly about the issue, and those who did mostly supported the continuation of the tests for the sake of scientific progress.[2] Academics such as Associate Professor of Physics C. B. C. Mohr were more active on the proliferation question, warning that if the superpowers were determined to have an arms race they must allow for the possibility that the Soviet Union might win.[3]

'Politically, We Just Could Not Care Less,' *Farrago* reported in August 1958. The year would not go down in the university annals as one of feverish political activity:

> It could never be said that this is due to the absence of contentious issues.
>
> The war clouds loom low over Lebanon, Irak, Jordan, and Cyprus.
>
> France has been alternatively in the throes of chaos and crisis.
>
> On the home front the Bolte Government has been returned with an increased majority, and the Menzies Government is faced with the same fate.
>
> Despite all this, our erstwhile politicians have not emerged from their long vacation hibernation.
>
> With nostalgia we recall the days when Casey, Calwell, Holt or Sharkey addressed student audiences in something like a grand-final atmosphere and faced their audiences with as much trepidation as a Christian in the Coliseum.[4]

Not all wars were fought with guns, however, and not all politics were federal, as Germaine was shortly to be instructed in an ugly and violent manner.

Just after moving to Carlton, she was raped. Twenty-five years later, and more than a decade after she published *The Female Eunuch*, she initially talked tough when discussing it. 'I had lots of adventures then,' she said of life after leaving home. 'I got raped and beaten up. I had affairs . . . I don't mind if you mention names. I believe in kicking ass and taking names, talking loud and drawing a crowd.'[5] To speak of rape in the same breath as 'adventures' and 'affairs' suggests a striking lack of feminist consciousness. The brittle bravado fell away as she recounted details of the attack – allegedly by a former student of the elite Xavier College, a footballer, 'just the sort of boy my mother would have liked me to marry.'[6]

Germaine and some male friends had gone to a party where they met up with some fellow undergraduates from the Melbourne University Football Club's barbecues and singalong drinking sessions. Germaine was a seasoned singer of bawdy songs, sometimes outdoing the young men by singing additional rude verses when their memories failed – a feat that slightly confused and embarrassed some of her young footballer friends.

One man at the party – a stranger to Germaine but known to some of her men friends there – insistently asked her to go outside. Germaine pointed out that everyone else at the party was kissing inside the house, in front of them, and asked why they could not do the same. He persisted. 'He wanted a light for his cigarette or I wanted a light for mine, who knows,' she recalled. 'How stupid we were in those days!' They went outside and ended up in front of the house, well away from the party at the back. He told her to come for a walk. 'It was too early to start screaming. People never understand these stories. You feel such a fool calling for help before there's any reason to call for help. But I knew I was in trouble.'

Greer remained passive in the face of intuitively sensed danger; she was drawn on even as she knew she should turn back. They walked down the street and he told her to get into a car. She did. He acted strangely, according to Germaine. She tried to get out, but he turned nasty and pulled the door shut against her head. Then he raped her. When she got out of the car she could not stand up and fell in a heap on the verge. Uncomprehending, he asked what was the matter. Germaine believed he must be insane to have no idea of the violence he had committed. 'He didn't break any of my teeth or blacken my eyes, but all the insides of my thighs were torn and bruised . . . [We] walked back towards the house and all I could think of was, "I've got to get home." All raped women have the same feeling, "I have to wash myself. I just have to get clean somehow." I'd fucked a few guys by that time. Sometimes it was a mistake and sometimes it wasn't. But when it was a mistake, it was my mistake. It wasn't forced on me. I really felt as if somebody had made me eat shit. I was certain that anyone who looked at me could tell what had happened to me. They could certainly tell that I was beaten up.'

According to Greer, everyone at the party was too drunk to notice. She went out to the back patio, where her friends stood around the keg drinking. They ignored her pleas to be taken home – 'in a minute,' 'sit in the car,' they said. Germaine sat in their car and went into shock; she vomited, her body temperature plummeted. Eventually she got out and flagged down a passing car. She explained that she had been raped and beaten, and the motorist took her home.

Her housemates found her on the bed almost unconscious. Some days later they brought the perpetrator home. Germaine nearly fainted: 'I thought, "They can't be doing this to me." But they brought him in and they said to me, "Is this him?" Apparently he had done this sort of thing before. He did it again, too.' They asked him whether he liked going to Portsea and Mount Buffalo – Victorian seaside and ski resorts respectively, where the affluent and their children holidayed. When he responded affirmatively they told him: 'Don't go there any more, because if we see you there we're going to kill you.' Greer described the informal process of peer trial and sentencing as a very Australian way of handling things. Even if this were true, it pales into insignificance next to her reliance on men to police their own, and her acceptance of their trivial sentence for a serious crime. Being banned from the playgrounds of the Melbourne elite hardly seems punishment proportionate to the trauma of rape – though at a time when a woman's sexual history was as much on trial as the alleged rapist, it was at least some penalty. 'He's still around and still swears I'm mistaken. Whenever I see this man I go cold, sort of stand there and say, "That's the man," and he says, "No, no . . . not me . . . it's someone else." '[7] She would return again to the subject in the 1990s.

From her second year at university, Germaine was frank about her sexuality at a time when women generally avoided the subject, no matter how many men they might have slept with. 'That was one of her breakthroughs – she was more open than even the men,' one former lover recalls. 'She was a super-bragger. She was categorizing men on her terms. A hand on the breast was a social disgrace at the time, yet Germaine would come into the Union Caf and announce who she'd laid the night before.' Yet, just as religion for Germaine was both a source of strength and a limitation, so it was with sex. 'She found out that sex was just about fucking,' according to one male friend. 'We got four or five fucks a year. She was getting twenty or thirty. Nobody could keep up with her.'

'She was looking for love,' another student lover observes, stating the obvious. But she pursued male partners with a gusto unparalleled among her female contemporaries, risking pregnancy in the process. As Germaine's planning for her defloration by Leon Fink showed, she was using the time-honored, reliably unreliable rhythm method, calculating the time when she was least likely to be fertile during a menstrual cycle. Other sexually active women on campus were using diaphragms; Germaine later relied on an IUD, the Graefenberg ring. 'You'd go to a doctor and the first question would be: Are you married?' recalls Rhyll Nance, who was something of a Union Caf confidante to Germaine and was concerned about her health. 'She appeared to have several abortions. I got concerned – there seemed to be too many. For a while she almost seemed to take a certain pride in it. She'd say: "I'm off to the phone-box to make an appointment." ' To Nance, the big-boned, worldly undergraduate Germaine came across as considerably older than her teenage years. Equable, stimulating and bright, she won a considerable reputation among students in her classes and with her forthright nature she sent shockwaves across campus. Her streak of eccentricity already made Greer quite unforgettable.

Some perceived a hard edge to her sexual persona. According to one former lover, she seemed driven, almost bent on a deliberate assault of her reproductive organs, such was her compelling pursuit of men. While Germaine's comments to Rhyll Nance almost certainly exaggerated her reliance on abortion – publicly, she later admitted to one termination – friends had the impression that her ability to conceive had been jeopardised. She told Nance that she doubted she would be able to have children. A former lover from Melbourne with whom she stayed in contact during her twenties was under the impression that her reproductive system was fundamentally compromised by the time she was twenty-five or twenty-six. Greer tried to conceive later in life, boosting her chances with various medical interventions; all hope was not lost, but her friends thought it at best faint.

The rape just before the beginning of her third year at university almost certainly contributed to a hardening in Germaine's relationships with men. By the end of her degree course, a certain disdain was obvious. 'She was contemptuous of how uninvolved men were,' recalls one student lover. 'She signaled it by her contemptuous treatment of men – she used them, then would give them the flick in public . . . Her contempt for men was really solidly in place. We blokes were all rejected. There was a really ugly, cold period when she rejected us all.' Having dismissed men as less than whole people, for a time she renewed her exploration of women, forming at least two intense attachments, though this did not affect her underlying heterosexual orientation.

At least one friend, Beatrice Faust, believed that Catholicism lay at the root of Germaine's behavior. 'She had the full convent syndrome – fucking like crazy, swearing, without being fully formed. . . . The way she talked about sex was morbid. She could swear about it, but not talk about it.' Yet for all the Catholicism embedded deep in her bones, Germaine projected herself as Jewish. She used to chatter in Yiddish as a party trick, and would speculate on the possibility of being caught up in the Holocaust. She became involved in a Jewish theater group. Germaine believed she might have been partly Jewish; for most of her adult life she was convinced that Reg, despite his anti-Semitism, was concealing his true Jewish identity. It was no accident that many of her lovers, including her first, were Jewish. Culturally, ethnically, if not in matters of religious belief, she always felt Jewish: 'I have this slim, long face. I wanted to be Jewish as a result of not wanting to have any part in the Holocaust. I like the way Jews saturate themselves in culture. Most men I went out with were Jewish. Jews are sensuous. White Anglo-Saxon males and Catholics are dead from the neck down. And I love people who love being rich.'[8]

The convent girl who flaunted an active sexual existence, the Catholic who fervently projected herself as Jewish, were obvious dichotomies. A subtler contradiction was hinted at in her voice, which occasionally revealed a certain fragility beneath the bravado. Greer had an almost childlike way of relating to people, according to Faust, and her two voices told the story. On the one hand Germaine could be bullying and obnoxious in argument, shouting people down; on the other, there was a palpable vulnerability. 'Her voice betrayed the vulnerability,' Faust says. 'She had an over-loud, theatrical voice. . . . She specialized in swearing in public, audibly across restaurants. When you got her normal voice on occasion, it was a little-girl voice sometimes saying vulnerable things.'

Faust experienced both sides of the Greer temperament. Germaine showed her some of the kindness and tenderness of which she was capable. At a time when Faust's relationship with her future husband had caused some jealousy and bitchiness among campus friends, for example, Greer took the initiative and intro-duced herself on a train with a friendly: 'Oh, you're going round with Clive Faust, aren't you?' As an engagement gift Germaine gave Beatrice a rolling-pin – made of china so that Beatrice would think twice before breaking it over Clive's head in a marital dispute. Rudeness and high-handedness, however, were more common. 'In between, you'd get these true moments,' according to Beatrice. 'You'd always hope the next time you'd get the true moment.' She was very testing of her friends: 'If you didn't put up with it, you weren't her friend, you didn't love her. She displayed brutality, indifference, the behavior of an isolate. But she wasn't manipula-tive.' On a certain level Faust believes Germaine displayed an almost helpless attitude toward her own life – aimless, directionless. It was an attitude that made the 'Drift' a natural destination.

The Drift gravitated around a few Melbourne pubs and restaurants and the artists' haunt of Eltham during the 1950s and early 1960s. It included some of Australia's leading post-war painters such as John Perceval, Leonard French, Clifton Pugh and Arthur Boyd, along with the left-wing historian Brian Fitzpatrick, the poet Chris Wallace-Crabbe, the writer Glen Tomasetti, philosopher David Armstrong, film-maker Tim Burstall and the activist Beatrice Faust. Germaine and her friend Ann Knappert, later Ann Polis, were among the youngest participants. A typical Drift might start with a meal at an Italian restaurant in Carlton's Lygon Street – the Del Capri or the Blue Grotto, perhaps – then proceed to the Swanston Family Hotel, the Drift's signature watering hole. The actor Barry Humphries, a Drift habitué, recalls the pub reeking of cigarette smoke, yeast, urine and some unidentifiable disinfectant, and containing the most interesting people in Australia: 'The noise was deafening, but the atmosphere was heady and as I stood in that packed throng of artists' models, academics, alkies, radio actors, poofs and ratbags, drinking large quantities of agonisingly cold beer, I felt as though my True Personality was coming into focus.'9

At closing time the gathered assembly often piled into cars and headed off drunkenly to Eltham, then a semi-rural town known for its mud-brick houses and studios, and its eclectic community of painters, potters and the occasional academic. 'Until the small hours the blaring gramophones filled the bush with the voices of Dylan Thomas, Lotte Lenya, Harry Belafonte and Bill Haley and his Comets,' Humphries remembers of the Drift parties at Eltham, 'frightening the wallabies and traumatising the kookaburras.'10

Many members of the Drift were to have an enduring social and cultural influence. There were those of superlative artistic achievement such as Boyd, while Brian Fitzpatrick was a beacon of radical intelligence in a sea of historians working from conservative and liberal perspectives. Tim Burstall was on the verge of making his first short film, and within a decade had produced the first feature film produced in Australia for years – *2000 Weeks*, a semi-autobiographical work following the frustrations of an artist in the then cultural wasteland of Australia who calculates he has two thousand weeks left to find fulfilment before he dies. Handicapped by exaggerated expectations, the film disappointed the critics; nevertheless, it demonstrated that feature film-making in Australia, though in a state of atrophy, was not extinct. Push film-makers Richard Brennan and Albie Thoms and producer Margaret Fink were part of the same film renaissance. Later, in the early 1970s, the Drift's Betty Burstall became the prime mover behind Melbourne's influential La Mama theater. Other Drift inspirations – Clifton

Pugh's encouragement of Barry Humphries' dabblings in the visual arts, for example – came to little, but not before 'a beautiful undergraduate in a cobalt-blue shift and provocatively laddered black stockings' named Germaine Greer had helped Humphries prepare an exhibition.[11]

'Because the sixties hadn't happened, there was a discernible need for bohemians,' argues Chris Wallace-Crabbe. There was an anarchistic 'let it all hang out' feel to the gatherings. In matters of language and sexual practice, women who were part of the Drift were already breaking the conventional female mold. Where the Drift differed from its more famous Sydney counterpart was in lacking a particular ideological base. 'Sexuality was in the air,' recalls Wallace-Crabbe. 'A lot of it was Lawrentian. He was a very big figure.'

Bill Collins, a member of the Drift who temporarily became a major figure in Germaine's life, evoked something of the game-keeper Mellors in the then-banned novel *Lady Chatterly's Lover*, according to Faust. Collins started out conventionally enough, studying agricultural science at university, before sliding into a somewhat affectedly rough existence as a slaughterman and gardener – a 'rough trade' archetype Greer would revisit repeatedly. Of middle height and slightly overweight, he had soft features and brown hair. Collins and Greer were lovers, and he remained devoted to her for years after she left Melbourne.

Collins recounted to a friend how he had returned home once during Germaine's Drift days to find her white, prostrate and hemorrhaging from an abortion – an expedient a number of Drift women were obliged to fall back on. While almost any procedure was better than none to a woman in a fix, the techniques could be rough-and-ready gynecological manipulations after which the women were effectively sent home to deal with the results themselves.

Greer was later dismissive of the Drift: 'It was a lifestyle, it represented a way of just hanging around. It was full of shit, I'm afraid. I always knew that. I knew it was second-rate.'[12] Yet it sustained her socially while she worked her way through her joint English-French honors degree course at university. In her final honors year in 1959 she was one of a fourth-year seminar group still remembered for its vigor and the high proportion of members who went on to academic careers. Known as the Poetry Seminar, it was the apogee of the English course, and compulsory for honors students. The seminar, covering English poetry from 1530 to 1760, was the focus of intense departmental attention – a forcing house where the big ideas were fought out in the faculty. The seminars were attended by anything from three or four academics to the entire English staff, including the towering Leavisite Sam Goldberg, then a senior lecturer and a critical influence on Greer's intellectual development. The intense, moralistic Goldberg was magnetic to the young student, only just turned twenty. 'She'd go into the seminars and tell the women, "This week I'm going to fuck Sam,"' recalls one fellow student. 'But he was too cagey to get involved with her.'

Melbourne University's English Department was in ferment at the time, as contending critical forces and personalities fore-shadowed a drama that would unfold into open warfare at Sydney University a few years later. The Melbourne department was headed by Professor Ian Maxwell, a vital, charismatic Scot whose interests ranged widely. A champion of modernism, Maxwell was also a great Burns enthusiast and became deeply interested in Old Norse. Under his pluralist policy of recruiting from a wide range of schools of critical thought, the English Department diversified dramatically. The result was a staff encompassing viewpoints from the intensely competitive Leavisite Goldberg to Vincent Buckley, a poet and academic whose passionate love of Irish literature heightened many students' consciousness of Australian writing and its Anglo-Celtic roots.

Within a few years, identification with 'Irishness' would provide others with some licence and rationale for the sort of flamboyant behavior adopted by Germaine. Without much in the way of Celtic heritage herself, though, she had little use for the pretext. 'She was much more like a young lady who had let her hair down completely,' one student recalls. Greer took little interest in Buckley's innovations – for example, in his path-breaking Australian literature course. 'She had no interest in Australian culture whatever,' according to Wallace-Crabbe. 'She was always very European in her orientation.'

This predisposition fitted in well with Goldberg's Leavisite approach, which he sought to make pre-eminent in Maxwell's pluralist department. Robin Grove, then a student and later an academic in the department, recalls that Maxwell approached Leavisism with 'suspicion and respect.' 'You could train the students to take part in Socratic debate rather than spoon-feed them – in that sense it was Leavisite,' Grove says of the department then. 'But the intellectual process was used without the content of the Leavisite approach.' That was not good enough for the Leavisites, whose tactics even occasionally included academic body-snatching. Faust recalls Goldberg pre-empting another lecturer with the announcement: 'The whole lecture you're about to hear is piffle. Come and listen to mine instead.'

Under Goldberg's influence, Germaine consciously trained as a Leavisite, absorbing Leavisism's characteristic moral seriousness, hostility to modern commercialism and harsh, exclusive view of what constituted superior English literature. Goldberg's Leavisite message was undoubtedly one of the two key secular influences on her intellectual development. It gave her a critical framework that reinforced and justified her intellectual temperament: prescriptive, dogmatic and intolerant of deviation. Leavisism supplied Greer's lifelong intellectual mode and contributed centrally to its content. Although Leavis himself was decidedly Protestant, his moralistic approach was deeply appealing to lapsed Catholics like Germaine with its unyielding dogma, its moral earnestness and its meta-physical preoccupations.

The son of an East Anglian piano dealer, Frank Raymond Leavis lived in Cambridge all his life, and for years endured a marginal existence on the fringe of university life. After holding a number of part-time positions, he was eventually appointed a fellow of Downing College. His wife, Queenie Dorothy Leavis, née Roth, was author of the seminal *Fiction and the Reading Public*.[13] For more than forty years, the couple pursued an intellectual mission which, despite his formal lack of academic recognition and reward, established F. R. Leavis among the most influential literary critics of the century.

*Scrutiny*, the quarterly review which F. R. Leavis founded and edited, was his principal avenue of influence, together with a number of books the best known of which were *The Great Tradition*

and *The Common Pursuit*.[14] Influenced initially by the poetry of
T. S. Eliot, Leavis considered English literature central to cultural
survival. There were great writers whose work he identified with
'Life' as opposed to the modern scourges of industrialism and the
crass values of mass culture – and there were the rest, whom he
dismissed. His core list of the great, adjusted somewhat over time,
included Jane Austen, George Eliot, Henry James, Joseph Conrad
and D. H. Lawrence. For Leavis great works of literature 'are
vessels in which humane values survive,' as Selden and
Widdowson put it, but they 'are also to be actively deployed in an
ethico-sociological cultural politics. Paradoxically then, and precisely because of this, Leavis's project is both elitist and culturally
pessimistic.'[15]

Deeply influenced by Queenie's work, Leavis was hostile to
modern commercialism. Their admiration for the organic strength
of pre-industrial cultures was as deep as their belief in the critic's
role to defend and preserve superior values against the
depredations of modern mass culture. In *Fiction and the Reading
Public*, Queenie proposed organized resistance to the social control
she believed was being exercised through advertising, entertainment and the mass media, influences that engendered passivity
and an unhealthy herd mentality in the general public. F. R. Leavis
drew heavily on her book for his work with Denys Thompson,
*Culture and Environment*[16] – a project of practical criticism designed
for use in schools by teachers, who were seen as potent agents of
cultural resistance. 'For Leavis, advertising is so powerful that it
can create personalities, or turn them into automata,' noted Chris
Baldick, analyzing the social mission of Leavisism. 'From the
evidence of advertising he suggests that there is a connection
"between standardisation of commodities and standardisation of
persons." '[17] This theme was later to be at the very heart of *The
Female Eunuch*.

Leavisism was strikingly authoritarian in its literary judgments;
furthermore, it lacked any developed theoretical justification of the
criteria for what made the canon and what did not. The Leavisites'
capacity to distinguish good 'poetic' qualities from bad 'poetical'
ones, Professor K. K. Ruthven commented, 'promises to be
extremely helpful until one discovers that there are no rules for

deciding which is which. What is claimed to be a formal distinction is in practice determined by feeling, with the result that one man's *simplicité* is another man's *simplesse*.'[18] The Leavisites' abhorrence of theory left them defenceless against the charge of arbitrariness in their literary pronouncements – not that it much affected the spread of their influence. Their thinking infused itself through the teaching of English, subsuming much that went before it and ultimately becoming an orthodoxy itself.

Goldberg's approach was almost more Leavisite than Leavis, according to John Docker, who studied in both the university English departments most affected by the Leavisite struggle in Australia – those of Melbourne and Sydney. As Leavis grew increasingly insistent that literature should be judged in terms of moral and metaphysical criteria, his Melbourne acolytes were almost out-pacing him in their rigor. 'The Melbourne Leavisites certainly bent Leavisism towards a preoccupation with the metaphysical in the fifties and sixties,' in Docker's view. 'They even felt Leavis himself hadn't gone far enough in this direction, and that this was one reason Leavis had never explored Shakespeare fully – the ultimate repository of metaphysical depths and truths.'[19]

Greer's adult writing, like the work of Leavis, on the surface denies theory. Greer's judgments rest on her 'feeling,' as Ruthven might put it. The lack of a theoretical framework is mysterious to readers approaching her work retrospectively from the standpoint of contemporary cultural theories. Greer did not have to repel a theoretical critique, as Leavis did in 1937 when the critic René Wellek famously challenged him to explain the theoretical basis of his work. Indeed, Leavis's success in flicking aside Wellek's challenge would undoubtedly have boosted Greer's confidence about doing the same should she find herself in such a situation. The example of Leavis, and the Leavisites' mode of analysis and operation, formed the rock-solid foundation of Greer's lifelong ability to assert her various positions as absolutely, incontestably correct. Wrestling with Catholicism had led her to hold strong views about the need to reconcile theory and practice; Leavisism gave her licence for dogmatism without theory. 'Melbourne turned her into a moralist critic,' according to Chris Wallace-Crabbe, 'into an anarchist with moral drive.'

The Poetry Seminar in which Goldberg was able to exert such influence was held on Thursday mornings. On Thursday nights the students would go to Germaine's loft, without the staff, and rehearse the seminar topic over flagons of wine, sometimes until the sun came up – an 'anti-seminar,' she called it: 'It wasn't because I thought my teachers were no good. It was because I thought my teachers were *very* good. It was important to maintain ideas that ran counter to theirs because they had a way of quenching us with rightness.'[20]

The loft was in a Carlton terrace on the corner of Barry and Grattan Streets, across the road from the university; the entry was via a cobbled lane at the back of the terraces. Its ambience tended to reflect Greer's state at the time. Simply furnished with a table, rugs and cushions, it already pointed to an interest in style. Visitors who called when she was depressed, malnourished or miserable, recall its bleakness – one even remembers slime on the walls. To the 'anti-seminar' visitors, however, it seemed cosy, lacking the usual student squalor. 'We were very good really,' Germaine recalled. 'I've never seen a group of students as gifted or hard-working as we were. I think that the English honours programme offered at Melbourne at that time was as good as that offered at any university in the world.'[21]

Germaine was the most exuberant, if not the most academic, of a remarkable group of students, according to Wallace-Crabbe, who also attended the seminars: 'It was far from true that she dominated the seminar. One sensed a very generous personality – enabling rather than crushing. While the Germaine of those days liked to shock, she wasn't hard and combative.'

At times her theatricality and salty language produced phenomenally effective shock tactics. On one occasion she walked into a Melbourne café and pronounced loudly: 'I'd like to wrap my big juicy cunt around . . . ,' naming the man who was her current object of desire. To say that this attracted attention in late 1950s Melbourne is a considerable understatement.

Already the more hedonistic climes of Sydney were calling. During her honors year Germaine visited the city after getting to know some Sydney people who had stayed at her loft on a trip to Melbourne; she dallied there, socializing with mates in the Push who urged her to drop out. The Sydney scene was much more sympathetic to her style. As one friend put it, Melbourne tolerated her but Sydney loved her.

Still she was reluctant to endanger the honors degree into which she had already put more than three years. 'At some stage, I think I must have thought to myself, "This is silly." Because the teaching at Melbourne University was the best I was going to get for the rest of my life.' Not because of her teachers, she added, but because of the great talent of her student peers.[22]

Greer's honors degree was jeopardized not only by the arguments of friends in the Push. Word filtered down to friends in Melbourne that she had suffered some gynecological catastrophe. The first Peggy and Reg Greer knew about it was when the long-absent Germaine turned up unexpectedly in Mentone. 'She came here and said: "I'm in trouble, physically," ' Peggy recalls.

> She was hemorrhaging. I told her I thought she had an ectopic pregnancy. Reg had just come home from work, was taking his coat off, washing his hands. I sent her up to him to tell him. 'Daddy told me to go back to where I came from,' she said afterward. It wasn't that he didn't love her, but she was so headstrong. Pushing him away from her.
>
> It was terrible when she was sick and went back to Sydney. But there was nothing I could do. She didn't tell me she was going to Sydney. . . . It would make anyone bitter. But it was self-inflicted. It was the times.
>
> Eventually there came a letter for Reg, not for me, but I read it. I was devastated at what had happened to her. She said she had an L-shaped scar on her abdomen to remind her always. He didn't write back. I did and blamed myself. I said: 'There must be something in me that made you profligate with your youth.' Mothers blame themselves. You ask: 'Why did that happen?'

Beatrice Faust ran into Germaine when she returned to Melbourne. 'I don't know what I'll do when I graduate,' Germaine told her. 'I might go back to the suburbs and have children.' Whatever the gynecological crisis had been, Faust was struck by the element of denial in Greer's speculative idyll.

Germaine sat the exams and graduated with second-class honors, upper division in English and French. Fellow students in the English Department had not expected her to top the year but were surprised that she failed to get a first-class degree. Poor results in French were to blame. 'I got involved in a stupid sexual blackmail situation with someone at the university,' Greer explained later. 'I was much too honourable to tell the professor about it; I just cut my classes. And as a result of cutting my classes, and going to Sydney, I didn't do very well in French.'[23] There were no laws let alone procedures in place to deal with such harassment at the time. Yet the language is telling. Instead of taking action against the perpetrator of sexual blackmail, Germaine put it to one side as a matter of 'honor,' to the detriment of her academic performance and future options. There is a marked quiescence and sense of sympathy for the aggressor – and this was not the comment of the pre-feminist Greer. It was made long after *The Female Eunuch* was published.

Germaine now had no chance of an academic job in the English Department. Her second-class degree may have been just the pretext some people in the Department were seeking in order not to give her a post. Glen Tomasetti recalls one of its associate professors, K. L. Macartney, remarking on Germaine's lifestyle: 'It is most ir-reg-u-lar, isn't it?' – implying that her way of life would make Germaine an unfit candidate for academia.

Greer did not go to the suburbs and have children, nor did she remain in Carlton. Instead, as Reg had earlier advised, she went back where she had most recently been: to Sydney and the Push. There the other crucial element in her intellectual armory was waiting for her. Already an anarchist and sexual libertarian in Melbourne, in Sydney she would acquire the theory to support her practices. While her principal works would later exemplify the Leavisites' tendency to apparently theory-free dogma, it would be Push libertarianism which formed their submerged theoretical core.

# 4

## *The Push*

---

When Germaine began visiting Sydney as an undergraduate it was not because of any animus toward her home town, but out of a sense of disappointment: 'I had no hostility towards Melbourne but I knew it was second rate.'[1] In Sydney the anarchist poet Harry Hooton was the first to give her some bohemian encouragement and cheer; seeing her striding around the streets of Sydney in a black dress and red stockings, he told her he admired her style. Her outfit provoked a different reaction from some of the local lads, who hung out of their car windows yelling, 'Who do you think you are?'[2]

Sydney's early post-war anarchists did not so much evoke the philosophy's traditional colors of red and black as the dreamy green and lavender-blue of the city's most famous tree – the lone jacaranda growing outside the Philosophy Department in the University of Sydney's main quadrangle. Under its spreading boughs, two philosophers would argue their line. One, the pessimistic libertarian Professor John Anderson, would capture Greer's intellect. The other – the rootless, broke but idealistic Harry Hooton – won an enduring place in Greer's affections.

Hooton was a minor cult figure, associated with the Push without being part of it. He had a small following of 'Hootonians' who would listen as he espoused his singular philosophy under the jacaranda tree when Anderson was not holding forth. 'There was never anything worthwhile made yet but by its own rules,' Hooton used to say. Greer found his philosophical line provocative: his devotion to freedom of the mind and spirit was absolute, his optimism about the innate perfection of human beings boundless. Hooton even had his own political theory – that things needed governing, not people, and that humanity would ultimately be liberated by technology.

When Greer met Hooton he was living with Margaret Elliott, who became prominent later as a film producer under her married name of Fink. Harry was forty-four when he took up with the nineteen-year-old Margaret; he was the great love of her life. Germaine was shortly to meet the love of hers, but unlike Hooton, with his boundless, big-hearted optimism, her great love was an intense exponent of the Push's 'anarchistic pessimism.' It was a relationship which proved to be the key influence on her philosophical development and the later work that made her name.

Margaret, then an art teacher, was a long-standing part of the Push, and she and Germaine socialized together, becoming firm friends against the backdrop of Germaine's affection and admiration for Harry. 'She just knocked on our door,' Fink says of their first meeting at the flat she and Harry shared in Wylde Street, Potts Point. 'I opened the door, and there was this phenomenal creature! I'm five feet four and she's six foot. I couldn't believe my eyes. She filled the door frame. Fabulous hair. Just a splendid creature!'

Hooton had a salon at Wylde Street on Sundays. Since his ability to publish was limited by their financial circumstances – one key work was produced only after Harry had a win at the races – direct, personal contact was vital for the transmission of his ideas. 'It was exciting, a bit dangerous because you didn't know who was going to knock on the door,' Fink recalls. 'Someone always did.'[3] Harry was tall, thin, dark, handsome, original, fascinating; there was never any shortage of female devotees. He was fervently Australian, loving Sydney, the bush and its archetypal poet, Henry Lawson; at the same time he was an internationalist, conducting lengthy exchanges with correspondents overseas. He was for a new world, his 'anarcho-technocracy' of the twenty-first century, and against the old. To Hooton, Europe was 'the cemetery.'[4]

It was in the Wylde Street flat and the Push pubs and parties that the bonds between Germaine and Margaret were cemented. They laughed, drank, danced and dallied in a bohemian enclave with a hard core of anarchist intellectuals – working-class in recreational style, but weighted with academics. 'If someone outside the university has an original idea, he's a crank,' Hooton used to say. 'If someone inside a university has an original idea, it'll be a miracle.' Even so, many Push members were, or would become, students and teachers of philosophy and psychology during a period when the ideas of Freud, Marx and their inheritors were being linked in potent new ways.

Barry Humphries' description of his first contact with the Push at the Assembly Hotel in the late 1950s is excoriating:

> ... a fraternity of middle-class desperates, journalists, dropout academics, gamblers and poets *manqués*, and their doxies.... These latter were mostly suburban girls; primary-school teachers and art students, who each night after working hours exchanged their irksome respectability for a little liberating profanity, drunkenness and sex.... The Push shunned me as well because I was actually doing something vaguely and peripherally artistic. If they had any unifying credo which was endemically Australian, it was a snobbish philistinism and a distrust of success. In the Assembly, for the first time I heard a commercial artist bad-mouthing the painter Sidney Nolan, who was in the early flush of his European fame. 'Course he's pulling the wool over the Poms' eyes,' he was saying to a rapt and convinced circle. 'The only reason he's doing well is he's hired a big public-relations firm. Trust old Sid, the cunning bastard!'[5]

Humphries' disdain partly reflected historical tensions between Sydney and Melbourne, in which cultural issues loom large; it is no accident that he emphasized the cultural divide between the Drift and its bohemian Sydney counterpart. There was no leading artist like Boyd or Pugh or even a vague equivalent at the center of the Push; if there had been, they would probably have been regarded suspiciously as soft and opportunist.

While Humphries identified the characteristically acid Push put-down, the account also betrays his own middle-class snobbery and sexism – an attitude that also became apparent during a passionate affair with Margaret Fink (then Elliott) in 1957. Since she was ostensibly visiting Melbourne on holidays, 'I didn't have to go home to Harry, so we were virtually living together. The first morning we woke up, Barry gave me an order for breakfast. I couldn't believe my ears!' Margaret made a gentle little speech in response: 'Well, I think it'd be more fun if we got up together and went somewhere and bought a grapefruit and came back and cut it together.'

Humphries' unselfconscious sexism was not unusual in the Drift. The women in it seldom openly criticized the men's more outrageous sexist statements. Glen Tomasetti recalls one Drift participant – a philosopher – drawing no protest when he pronounced categorically that Australia had six intellectuals, that he knew five of them and none were women. Tomasetti remembers Greer as one of the few women in the Drift prepared to challenge the men in such circumstances and cop the resulting put-down. On one occasion, the actor and theater producer Peter O'Shaughnessy launched into a monologue on the theme of incest in the work of Shakespeare when Germaine interjected, 'I've just finished a thesis on the subject.' After an exchange in which O'Shaughnessy offered to give Germaine his considered opinion if she showed the thesis to him, he declared dramatically that she and Tomasetti were suffering from that alleged Freudian malady, 'penis envy.'[6] Typically for Germaine, though, O'Shaughnessy – a considerable figure in Melbourne's cultural scene at that time – ended up inviting her for a bicycle ride around Kew.

Just as Humphries' breakfast order was not unusually sexist for a Drift man, neither was Margaret Fink's resistance an isolated response from a Push woman, except perhaps in its politeness. Strong Push women were not in the habit of playing housemaid to their partners. In the Newcastle Hotel one afternoon, when a woman begged off a party because she had to go and get her husband's dinner, Fink responded typically: 'Well, he can get his own fucking dinner!' Neither the language nor the sentiment was common among women in the wider community at the time.

The Push was not the only, or even the first, bohemian group in Sydney. A succession of culturally based nonconformist elites had existed in and around Sydney since the turn of the century, and a maverick precinct developed around Kings Cross between the wars. It was a 'city within the city, equivalent to Montmartre, Chelsea or Greenwich Village,' one observer in the 1940s claimed:

'Kings Cross has been taken straight out of Paris and dumped down in the middle of Sydney, including the artists and pseudo-artists in strange attire.'[7]

The Push had some superficial similarities with its precursors in Sydney, and even with its Melbourne counterpart. Conventional mores were flouted, alcohol flowed and no one appeared too concerned with status or advancement. Like the Drift, the Push was heavily pub-based. If the Swanston Family Hotel was the beating, boozy heart of the Drift, in Sydney, at the height of the Push, it was the Royal George and Newcastle hotels.

Yet the Push is rare, perhaps unique, in Australian social history as a bohemian enclave whose core members shared a passionate belief in the theories of an intellectual, and an academic philosopher at that. It was perverse that it should have happened in Sydney, legendarily a city of the senses and the sensual. The Push was not simply a clique loosely based on nebulous notions of social defiance, cultural superiority or pursuit of the muse. Its key figures embraced and propagated an all-encompassing and apparently rigorous theory – philosophical, political, social. Though there were 'careerists,' as Margaret Fink observes, the Push swallowed up the worldly ambitions of many of its devotees and subsumed them in the anarchist life – in some cases, for their whole lives.

Although it shared Hooton's anarchist bent, the Push was dismissive of his home-grown Utopian theory of 'anarcho-technocracy' – that 'man is God,' and that the material world is there to be enslaved by human beings for their use and pleasure. Where Hooton was an optimist, Push libertarians were determinedly pessimistic; they wanted no part of anarchism's historical tendency to chase Utopias. Not that they let it get in the way of having a good time. 'Harry and I mixed in the Push,' Fink says, 'because they were the only people around, really, who weren't respectable bores. But we didn't agree with their philosophy, which was steeped in Andersonianism.'[8]

Andersonianism was a specifically Sydney phenomenon. Its source was John Anderson, an intense Scot, who had studied and taught philosophy at the universities of Glasgow and Edinburgh before arriving in Australia in 1927, at the age of thirty-three, to become Sydney University's Challis Professor of Philosophy. He occupied the chair until 1958, during which time he held more than a generation of students in his thrall and regularly outraged wider Sydney society.

The son of a socialist school teacher in Glasgow, Anderson grew up in a radical household and remained true to his 'freethought' creed to the end of his days, incorporating an apparently conservative reinterpretation during his later years. Like some of his more prominent followers, Anderson migrated from youthful Marxism to alliance with conservative forces which opposed Communist totalitarianism during the Cold War. Against the thrust of much post-war education policy, he persistently championed the university as an institution for the disinterested pursuit of truth over narrow, instrumental purposes.

From early in his career it was clear that the wiry, fierce, black-eyed academic would be an iconoclast. His combative temperament emerged during his undergraduate days at the University of Glasgow at the time of the Great War. While the university authorities concentrated dwindling resources on the more utilitarian faculties of Science and Medicine, Anderson urged his fellow Arts students to shrug off their despair. They should 'shout, sing, kick up a row, get drunk, get locked up,' he wrote in the *Glasgow University Magazine*, 'do anything except creep about the quadrangles and the Union like "pale, forpyned ghosts," moving sluggishly from yesterday to tomorrow. You are not here for nothing. Your activities are necessarily restricted, but remember that you are alive, and let people know it.'[9]

Anderson's field was dominated at the time by idealists like the Welsh philosopher Sir Henry Jones, who taught Anderson at Glasgow. Freedom was a central theme for Jones, a prominent ally of the Liberal Party leader, Lloyd George. Active in religious and educational debate, Jones provided a model for the vigorous public role a philosopher might play. Anderson, however, came to doubt Jones' idealist approach, even as he was writing prize-winning essays reflecting his line; privately he condemned the idealists as 'state mongers,' and confided to a friend that his growing antipathy to idealism was bound up with his opposition to capitalism. As Anderson's philosophical approach developed, he concluded that an attitude of opposition in itself was effectively more important than opposition to anything *per se*. Anderson's background and rigidly contrarian nature suggest that this attitude was almost a temperamental imperative: he could no more have been an idealist than, say, Margaret Thatcher could have been a social democrat.

By 1918 Anderson was revealing his realist tendencies publicly. In one talk he canvassed the 'fallacy of optimism' and criticized notions of 'good' and 'progress.' Optimistic theories are based on the view that the ultimate nature of reality is good, he argued, or that good is more real than evil: 'But reality as such can be neither good nor bad.' A crucial influence on Anderson's disavowal of idealism was the Australian-born philosopher Samuel Alexander, an academic in Manchester who visited the University of Glasgow for several months in 1918. Alexander, a realist, drew boldly on Freud and Einstein in the course of his lectures. Anderson corresponded with him after Alexander's return to Manchester. Jones and his idealism looked ever less convincing.

Jones nevertheless left his mark in at least one crucial respect. As Brian Kennedy points out in his biography of Anderson, *A Passion to Oppose*, both Jones and Anderson held the conviction that philosophy is 'at every step, a way of life,' as Jones himself put it. It was a tenet Anderson transmitted vibrantly during his thirty-year tenure at Sydney.[10]

Anderson developed his own philosophical system of realism while maintaining an active interest in the tumultuous politics of the 1920s. Kennedy cites Anderson's political isolation at Edinburgh as a factor in his decision to seek the Sydney chair. In the 1926 general strike, for example, he sided with the militants and criticized students and colleagues for enlisting as special constables, winning himself few friends in the academy.[11] Anderson's views were similarly controversial after his migration to Australia, but their impact was infinitely greater. At Edinburgh he was a lecturer in the Department of Logic and Metaphysics; in Sydney, Australia's largest city, he was *the* professor of philosophy. Sydney was the only university in New South Wales with a philosophy chair during Anderson's tenure.

This fiery Scot dominated the intellectual life of Sydney for decades according to the philosopher David Armstrong, who studied as an undergraduate with Anderson, was part of the Push, and ultimately occupied Sydney's Challis Chair of Philosophy himself. Armstrong compares Anderson to Hegel in having a worked-out position on almost every conceivable philosophical and intellectual question, though Anderson never published a systematic exposition of his realist system. 'These views were very attractive to students,' Armstrong wrote in his own memoirs, 'not only because Anderson provided the latter with a ready-made world-system but also because the views were of a very uncompromising and dismissive sort.'

There was no atom of tender-mindedness in Anderson's thinking, Armstrong says, citing the poet James McAuley's quip that John Anderson had an answer to every conceivable question. It was 'No,' with the 'No' delivered in a strong Glasgow accent. With Anderson, every icon was to be smashed – God, immortality, free will, moralism, the common good of society, the lot: 'Anderson often seemed to go out of his way to be intellectually offensive. He once started a paper on Religion in Education by saying that the subject could be dealt with as briefly as that of the snakes in Iceland [*sic*, not Ireland]. It was all immensely attractive to young intellectuals.'[12] Anderson was not merely an iconoclast, in Armstrong's view – he was a meta-iconoclast, smashing the smashers of icons rather than creating new ones in their stead. Anderson wanted to be like Socrates, who had first asserted that the unexamined life is not worth living. 'No wonder we felt so superior to everybody else,' Armstrong reflects.

Andersonianism announced the essential independence of things, according to Peter Shrubb, a student and later an academic in Sydney's English Department: 'We wanted to hear that we were independent, that we were not what we were thought to be, and certainly not merely what we were desired to be. It was a doctrine of freedom, and it gave us freedom.'[13] Nearly a generation before the counterculture of the 1960s, young Andersonians were abandoning their family homes for city rooms where they could pursue freedom of thought, love and association. Therein lay the origins of the Push.

Anderson's quest for the life of critical inquiry, stripping away illusions and opposing transgressions on freedom, inspired a passionate following. Ironically, and perhaps all too predictably, Anderson expected his followers to toe his line. In his memoirs Armstrong describes the strong authoritarian streak in Anderson's personality which made him intolerant of dissent, preferring students to assimilate the contents of his lectures rather than challenge them critically. It must have jarred, at least subconsciously, in an intellectual set whose favorite pastime was demonstrating how thinkers fell into the very errors they had detected in others.[14]

In 1950 conflict within the university Freethought Society, the main organ of Anderson's wider influence on campus, precipitated the formation of the Libertarian Society, which the 'downtown Push' – as opposed to the uptown university freethinkers – would make its own. The Korean War had prompted the conservative Menzies government to propose the introduction of conscription, and a number of students formed an anti-conscription committee. In August Anderson addressed a Freethought Society meeting packed to the rafters to hear his view on the issue. Increasingly trenchant in his anti-communism, the ageing Anderson stunned the meeting by attacking the committee: opposing conscription, he said, meant fighting on multiple fronts instead of concentrating on the main battle for democrats, the containment of left totalitarianism. Not a single one of his 250-strong audience, on whom he could normally count for unequivocal support, appeared to agree. A few months later the Libertarian Society began meeting at the Ironworkers' Hall in Lower George Street. The downtown Push had formally begun. The breach within the Freethought Society widened the following year after Anderson supported the Menzies government's constitutional referendum which proposed to outlaw communism; the Freethought Society soon atrophied.'[15]

Anderson's theory of, essentially, permanent opposition made it unlikely that his band of freethinkers would remain unanimous in the long run. In any case, his creeping authoritarianism made some sort of reaction within their ranks inevitable: if not the Push, some other manifestation would have developed where libertarians unwilling to satisfy Anderson's new hierarchy of oppositions could coalesce. Even so, this influence was profound. While Andersonianism was not the only intellectual influence on Push libertarianism, it was its foundation and the core reason for its essential pessimism. It is no mere footnote to the history of the Australian intelligentsia. It is the reason why some of the best and brightest of the generation born from the Depression through to World War II in Sydney forsook the state as a site for positive action, rejecting the possibility as well as the desirability of reform.

At the same time the Push was consciously pluralist, even while the most committed libertarians at its center saw themselves as isolated in their bid to create a libertarian domain within, yet as far as possible disarticulated from, that cold monster, the state. While reformist progressives in other cities and other Western countries at the time saw the state as a vehicle through which reforms for the general good might be achieved, Andersonians argued that there was no such thing as a general 'good,' that the state was a malign force and that reform was, in any case, always doomed to fail.

Anderson laid down his core views on reform and the state in 'The Servile State,' an article published in 1943. Meliorism ignores the permanence of struggle, he wrote: 'The scientific student of society, then, will not be concerned with reform. What he will be concerned with is opposition – what he will be above all concerned to reject is "social unity." And he will reject it not merely as a description of present conditions but as a conception of a future society.'[16]

The scientific part of Marxism, according to Anderson, was its doctrine of history as struggle, while its notion of a classless society where contending historical forces resolved themselves in favor of the proletariat was Marxism's ignorantly Utopian 'servile part.' Servility was the most despised trait in the Andersonian constellation. 'The point,' wrote Anderson, 'is not merely the drabness that might result from attempts to eliminate social struggles, but the impossibility of eliminating them – and, therewith, the loss of independence and vigour that can result from the spreading of the *belief* that they can be eliminated.'[17]

Perpetual struggle was what mattered to Anderson. It was a delusion to believe that struggle could ever end because – in a standpoint familiar to Leavisites – authoritarian forces within society were too powerful to make lasting victory ever possible. Push libertarians implicitly accepted this view and set it at the heart of their own philosophical stance, augmenting it with notions of 'permanent protest' and 'permanent opposition' borrowed from other pessimistic anarchist philosophers and sociologists like the American anarchist writer Max Nomad. There are always authoritarian elites, according to Nomad – only the names change.[18] Freud and Wilhelm Reich were also key influences. Reich's view of the family as a microcosm of the authoritarian society was embraced enthusiastically by the Push from its inception. During Greer's intensive contact with the Push, up to her departure from Australia in 1964, Reich's assertion of the superiority of the so-called 'genital character,' engaging in 'natural' vaginal-penile sexual activity in preference to 'neurotic' clitoral sexual release, was adopted uncritically.

Whatever the supplementary influences, however, it was the pessimism of Anderson's realist philosophy that crucially informed Push thinking, underpinning countless thousands of hours of debate among the 'critical drinkers,' as one wit dubbed the group. A particular element not emphasized by Anderson himself but keenly seized on by the Push was his attitude to 'love.' In a journal article in 1941, Anderson argued that sexual repression had a central place in any repressive system, and 'that freedom in love is the condition of other freedoms, that while in itself it does not constitute culture, there can be no culture without it.'[19]

Sexual freedom was not merely a socially defiant recreational pursuit within the Push – according to the libertarians' reading of Anderson and Freud, supplemented by Reich, it was imperative if they were truly to live their theory. It was the duty of freethinkers to swear off jealousy and accept their partners partnering others without any tension at all. 'Everybody had a fuck here and there with everybody – that was just mandatory,' as one Push woman puts it.

Anderson had not himself turned Sydney University's Department of Philosophy into a center of free love in academe. The only remotely racy element of Anderson's self-conception was a vanity that he might be partly Romany in origin. His own sexual existence was conventional; even his infidelity took the conventional form of having a mistress. While Anderson returned at night to his wife ensconced in the leafy upper North Shore suburb of Turramurra, by day he pursued a long-term affair with Ruth Walker, a student who subsequently became an academic member of the Philosophy Department. Nor did Anderson particularly approve of what the Push was up to under its libertarian banner. He was critical of its members' sexual radicalism on the grounds that it was unlikely to help them to see through their sexual illusions – and seeing through illusions was the prime task for an Andersonian. Opposition to superstition was the best course for freethinkers, he contended: it was unnecessary 'to say that the holder of certain views must practise certain things. This itself is superstitious and makes it another religion.'[20]

Anderson's reservations held no sway in the Push at the time. While on the one hand the Push libertarians argued that their philosophy had 'no special claims' and that there was 'nothing in it to say that it must or should be followed,'[21] the group's equation of sexual repression with political authoritarianism was the basis for a dynamic in which free sex was the marker of the political progressive. The corollary was that anyone unwilling to be free sexually must be politically suspect. The libertarian belief in an intimate connection between freedom in one field and freedom in another was complemented by the conviction that authoritarianism and servility extended from one sector to another. A person who was, for example, 'credulous about religion, or who is sexually repressed will tend to be servile towards his employer, political bosses and so on, and is likely to have conservative political views.'[22] It was a profoundly Reichian extension of Anderson's philosophy. In a piece for Sydney University's student newspaper, *HONI SOIT*, one psychologist encapsulated the 'correct' libertarian line reliant on Freud and Reich:

> Contrary to the popular notion of free love as meaning simply promiscuous and indiscriminate sexual behaviour, what is important in free love is the absence of guilt feelings and compulsive tendencies. In turn, the absence of guilt feelings depends, partly at least, on seeing through the notion of sin and, consequently, on seeing through the moralists who put this sort of view forward. In an affair which is marked by the absence of guilt feelings, there will be an increase in sexual pleasure and satisfaction, leading to a lessening or disappearance of neurotic tensions and resulting in a straight-forward relationship: a relationship to which both partners will have an

objective, realistic approach. You would expect to see this sort of attitude carry over into other situations, into relations with one's family, with one's employer, etc. This suggests generally that free love, which includes seeing through sexual illusions, promotes, and is promoted by, seeing through illusions in other fields.[23]

The Push assumed a certain equality between the sexes, symbolized by its male and female participants' unconventional practice of drinking together in the bars of favored Sydney hotels. Custom at the time had it that the bars were the preserve of men, and women were restricted to the 'ladies' lounge,' with or without male friends. In contrast, the Push would only frequent pubs whose proprietors allowed *all* its members to drink at the bar. Push women also bought beers for the men as well as vice versa; according to some, the women tended to buy more often because they tended to be in paid jobs more often than Push men. Perhaps the most important symbol of sexual equality was acknowledgment of the fact that women had sexual appetites of their own, and were free to initiate liaisons with men instead of waiting to be asked. Women in the wider community who had lost their virginity generally pretended they had not. In the Push no one cared. Push women's horizons extended beyond being locked up in a suburb, married with children.

Push participants came and went; there were those who were more concerned with libertarian ideas and debate at the core, and those who simply enjoyed the lifestyle on the periphery. As anarchists, the Push's proponents acknowledged no leader, but any anthropologist wandering through the Royal George could hardly miss the dominant figures of Jim Baker, Darcy Waters and Roelof Smilde within the group. Jim Baker, then a lecturer in Sydney University's philosophy department, was the resident intellectual 'organizer,' the cerebral center of the libertarians within the Push. Darcy Waters and Roelof Smilde were the group's polemical and sexual focus – tagged later by others the 'princes of the Push' and the 'blond Adonises,' epithets tinged with a romanticism Push purists including Darcy and Roelof would disdain. During Germaine's heyday in the Push, Baker produced the group's publications and held forth intellectually in the back room of the Royal George, while Waters and Smilde cut a swathe from less formal academic positions.

Waters and Smilde were Andersonians who had dropped out of Sydney University and joined the Push at the outset with others disillusioned by the unholy alliances Anderson seemed to be making in his fight against communist totalitarianism. In their different ways, both were charismatic figures. Waters was tall, graceful, with a flowing blond mane and almost supernaturally good looks and charm into the bargain. He combined the bearing of a figure from Norse mythology with an unusually direct wit and playful appeal. Smilde had other assets: a scalpel-like intellect and penetrating gaze created a strong sense of connection in those with whom he conversed. For less obvious reasons, perhaps, than Waters, Smilde was a magnet for women. He was introduced to Margaret Fink at a party as 'the Lothario of the Push.'

As anarchists, Waters and Smilde would not have claimed or conceded their central role within the group, but the pattern of relations within the Push makes it clear that together they were first among equals, at the very least. To some outsiders, Waters and Smilde looked like two blond bulls bestowing their favors on an enthusiastic herd – a characterization vehemently rejected by insiders. What Push women readily concede retrospectively, though, is that there was a 'hierarchy of fucks,' and that Waters and Smilde were the prestige sexual partners. It was, as one woman recalls it, the Push equivalent of power-fucking.

Roelof Smilde was the intellectually gifted son of Dutch parents who emigrated to Australia on the eve of World War II. The Smildes had gone through hard times in Holland during the Depression, where Roelof's father worked intermittently as a truck driver. In Australia he joined the Royal Dutch Air Force, only to suffer an horrific accident in Darwin when he walked into the propeller of a plane. The accident blighted his life and psychologically scarred the entire family. 'He should've died, but he didn't,' Roelof says. Instead he lived another nine years, paralyzed down one side and barely able to speak: 'I had an horrendous adolescence because of my father.' The trauma surrounding the accident clouded Roelof's teenage years but did not suppress his academic and leadership capacities. He became captain of the selective North Sydney Boys' High School – doubtless a sign of things to come had not Andersonianism fatefully changed his course.

Smilde was an unlikely candidate for the role of quintessential Push man. Under other circumstances his qualities would have made him an obvious candidate for a career in public life. Instead his talents were deployed in top-level international bridge competition; he won multiple Australian bridge championships, and competed creditably in repeated Bermuda Bowls and world bridge Olympiads.

'In other times and other places, we would have been revolutionaries – we had the sort of political passion that would have made us revolutionaries,' Roelof says. 'In a different time and a different place, we'd have been up in the hills with Che Guevara, would have been anarchists in Russia in the early part of the century. But in this particular time, and this kind of place, with the sort of philosophic influence that we had on us, we became pessimistic non-revolutionary radicals who came to emphasize a way of life, who came to emphasize what the forces were against it and how you can try and form this way of life while recognizing what you were up against.'

A principal practitioner of the Push libertarians' anarchistic pessimism throughout the group's existence, Smilde considered one of the Push's defining features to be the correspondence between idea and action accepted and practiced by its members. This principle was most famously, or notoriously, applied to heterosexual activity. 'We saw what we thought was a correspondence between freedom in one area and freedom in another,' he says, echoing Reich, 'and we came to the view that sexual freedom was somehow central to all the others.'

While he liked a good time, Roelof was not a naturally easygoing carouser like his friend Darcy. His commitment to the philosophy and the life practices that were its corollary was uncompromisingly extreme. Roelof was 'closed, tight,' according to some Push confrères, with an intensity which sometimes crossed the border into mind-games. 'You can smell the moralist and the parson in him somehow,' says one.

The intensity, the whiff of moralism, were undoubtedly part of the attraction for Germaine. The scent of the strong, blond, intellectually well endowed young Smilde, home from his day job laboring on the Sydney waterfront, made it overwhelming. They met one weekend in the summer after her final year at Melbourne University; Germaine was nearly twenty-one, Roelof on his way to thirty. On holiday from Melbourne, she turned up at a Push pub one day clad uniformly in black – black hair, black mascara, black clothes, black stockings.

'She was vivacious, lively, a bundle of life,' recalls Smilde, 'thought she could do everything. Irrepressible. Women in those days were inhibited, shy, hanging back. She was such a natural, such a goer in herself – she just leapt in, wasn't inhibited or intimidated by the men. Germaine couldn't be intimidated. I thought: Jesus Christ!'

As the Push progressed that night from the pub to 'the Greeks,' Greer ended up sitting opposite Smilde at one of the restaurant's long trestle tables; they talked for well over an hour, mostly about libertarian ideas. When they met up again the same weekend at the rolling Push social gatherings, Germaine asked Roelof if it was all right if she came back to Sydney – not asking for permission, he believes, so much as looking for an affirmation of interest: 'I was a little bit startled. It was an unusual request. I don't remember having said anything, but she must've had the impression I was attracted to her. I said yeah, it would be all right.'

A month later, in early 1960, Roelof came home from a shift on the wharves to the small terraced house in North Sydney which he shared with a couple, to find that Germaine had moved in: 'I was told later she'd gone back to Melbourne and asked friends, "Who was that man? Tell me about that man."'

Though they did not discuss it – many Push members, particularly the men, tended to cut themselves off from their families – Germaine and Roelof had some common family territory. There was a shared European heritage – Roelof's Dutch parents, Germaine's Italian through her mother's side of the family. Both had serious difficulty relating to their fathers. Each had a parent who had performed a problematic communications role during the war: while Germaine's father decoded ciphers in a bunker deep below Malta, Roelof's mother was putting the blue pencil through letters in the war-time censorship office. The censor's blue pencil was the symbolic antithesis of her son's life, just as Germaine, the lover of acting, singing and dancing, could not have been further in spirit from the anorexic shadow of himself her father had been on return from war service overseas. 'We danced at parties,' Roelof recalls of life with the young, exuberant Germaine. 'In summertime we'd go to Nielsen Park [Beach] half-pissed, skinny-dipping.'

After some months sharing the house in North Sydney with others, Roelof and Germaine rented a place of their own – part of a rambling old mansion in Glebe Point Road, Glebe, not far from Sydney University. There was one big room, a kitchen and a bed-room; the flat was big enough to invite someone in for coffee, but not for entertaining the Push *en masse*. Germaine taught at schools in Sydney's inner western suburbs. Roelof quit the wharves and concentrated on playing bridge, working toward a new peak that would carry him to the world championships in New York in 1964. He drove cabs a few nights a week to supplement his winnings at the racetrack. They were fairly monogamous, particularly by Push standards; there was some fucking around but, according to Roelof, nothing of great note. 'Germaine was madly in love with him,' Margaret Fink recalls. 'She's been in love with a few people but I don't think the same way as she was with Roelof. . . . I think it was mutual. She was mad about him.'

To an extent she tried to live his life. Only love could explain Greer's informal apprenticeship to Smilde as a professional punter. He showed her the ropes, and remembers that Germaine 'threw herself into it in the way she threw herself into everything she did – she'd do it with her usual flair.' For a year she went to every metropolitan race meeting in Sydney with him, attending three tracks weekly to lay a uniform five-shilling stake on a single horse in each race; as the months ground on, the bet was upped to ten shillings. It was a disciplined regime designed to teach her how to make a living by gambling, but she found it so dull that she kept falling asleep over the form guide on Friday nights.[24]

To alleviate tedium at the track she gave several racing characters nicknames – one, for example, was dubbed 'The Scholar' because he was one of the few individuals she'd met at a racecourse who could actually put a sentence together. At the end of her year-long apprenticeship she had broken even, which according to Roelof was pretty good for a novice: 'I think she was captured by the color of it, but it didn't persist. It wasn't her.'

Was the Push? For Germaine, it provided a philosophy to confirm the attitude and lifestyle she had already acquired in Melbourne. She walked into the Royal George Hotel, into the throng talking themselves hoarse in a room stinking of stale beer and thick with cigarette smoke, and set out to follow the Push way of life – 'an intolerably difficult discipline which I forced myself to learn.' The Push struck her as completely different from the Melbourne intelligentsia she had engaged with in the Drift, 'who always talked about art and truth and beauty and argument *ad hominem*; instead, these people talked about truth and only truth, insisting that most of what we were exposed to during the day was ideology, which was a synonym for lies – or bullshit, as they called it.'[25] Her Damascus turned out to be the Royal George, and the Hume Highway was the road to it. 'I was already an anarchist,' she says. 'I just didn't know why I was an anarchist. They put me in touch with the basic texts and I found out what the internal logic was about how I felt and thought.'[26]

The Push libertarians, she implies, explained Germaine to herself. She absorbed the tenets of libertarianism wholesale; at last it gave her a theoretical foundation for her unorthodox lifestyle. Anarchistic pessimism was philosophical manna, filling a vacuum which had troubled her since she had lost her Catholic faith. Sam Goldberg's Leavisism, with its own cultural pessimism based on the belief that a crass mass culture could never be overcome, had been a peculiarly apt preparation for Germaine's reception of the anarchistic pessimism of the Push. Where Leavis considered superior English literature central to survival in the face of impending cultural doom, the Push prescribed permanent oppositionism and the freethinking life of inquiry where action matched ideas.

Leavisism was unabashedly elitist. The Push, conversely, was consciously pluralist – in theory. In practice, the libertarians at the Push's heart had their own special put-downs, 'authoritarian,' 'neurotic' and 'illogical' being the worst insults. Positions or behavior which did not meet expectations were condemned for 'inconsistency' – at least as loaded an epithet as 'servility,' the term applied to that worst of sins in the Andersonian universe. For the Push, whether or not one held to one's beliefs was the only real test for any way of life, for any view or personal endeavor. The inherent contradiction did not seem to occur to them: if their philosophy was truly pluralist, why should moments, or even a life, of inconsistency not be a perfectly legitimate choice?

Some in the Push harbored doubts about Greer's consistency. 'You knew she was there – she was a vibrant part of it,' Smilde says. 'Some people admired her and saw her as a positive force. Others were suspicious of her because she was so talented and wanting to do many different things. I think there was some sense on the part of some people that she wouldn't be consistent, that she couldn't be trusted. But I didn't have that sense.'

Push debate sometimes descended into bitter arguments but Germaine could hold her own, and then some, unlike many of the other women, who tended to be more subdued if they participated at all. Lynne Segal, later a noted feminist academic in Britain, was another exception. Apart from her deep friendship with Margaret Fink, Greer was not known for her closeness to other Push women. Their varying reactions to Germaine emerge in *Sex and Anarchy*, a history of the Push by Anne Coombs, who quotes Lynne Segal: 'Germaine was such a prima donna eccentric that you couldn't see her as a role model.'[27] Coombs also records a chance meeting in the 1980s between Germaine and an old Push confrère, Roseanne Bonney, who was with her second husband. 'My, your son has got to be a big boy, hasn't he,' Germaine commented. Bonney told Coombs that for Greer it was 'a typically bitchy thing to say.'[28] Then there is Judy McGuinness's famous encapsulation of Germaine's conversational excess: 'The thing about Germaine is that she never menstruates. She haemorrhages once a month and gives you a drip-by-drip description.'[29]

Germaine used to write frequently from Sydney to her friend Ann Polis in Melbourne, often addressing the letters in elegant calligraphic script. They were not always happy missives. When she felt miserable about Roelof, or when things had gone badly at the Royal George, she took refuge on the Sydney Harbour Bridge, with its big, broad metal girders and knuckle-sized studs: 'I used to run away to where the footpath was torn up on the bridge and climb down into the rigging underneath and sit waving my legs above the sea, where the wind called the southerly buster blew

75

away all the crossness and all the arguments.'[30]

Life with Roelof had begun ecstatically. She had sought and won the love of a man who on so many counts met her desire. Highly intelligent and the vigorous exponent of a philosophical system which seemed to solve the enigma of her life, Roelof was sufficiently cerebral for Germaine to feel engaged rather than alone in the higher reaches of the intellect. When it came to intensity, Roelof was well and truly her match. Strong and fit, he was physical without the muscular macho usually accompanying it. 'We were non-violent, rejected coercion,' he says of the Push. 'If a situation did look like turning violent we just tried to get away from it, and in some sense turn the other cheek like Christians rather than fight.'

For Germaine, it was not the fact that Smilde was mentor as well as lover which bedevilled the relationship. She was confronting the same problem she had encountered at Melbourne University: her feeling that her partners were less involved in the relationship than she. Germaine's commitment to Roelof was starved slowly by the lack of emotional sustenance he offered in return. Dialogue on anarchistic pessimism? Yes. Drinking shoulder to shoulder at the Royal George? Yes. Closely supervised punting tuition? Yes. Sex? Yes. Emotion? No. For her the relationship was denied the closeness, the intimacy on which it could have grown.

There were few fights. Roelof was happy with the way things were; Germaine, privately, was not. Roelof lived his life, lived the Push line, and in the process failed to give her the emotional succour she wanted from this man she loved so much. 'It would've been a lot more productive for her, and probably more productive for me, too,' Smilde reflects, 'if I'd yielded a bit more and listened to the sort of person that she was. . . . We didn't get together. We didn't correspond enough. I really think I didn't give her enough – it's not a question of room, not a question of space – I didn't give her enough in an emotional sense, I suppose.'

Germaine did not articulate the problem until right at the end. 'Maybe she couldn't,' he speculates. 'Maybe that was one of the things that was wrong. Maybe she couldn't. I think I got some sort of sense that she was unhappy, but it was not as though she ever had a go at me about it.' It burned slowly within Germaine until she found the situation untenable. Though she had been active in the making of the relationship, she was passive in its shaping – waiting, dissatisfied, and then leaving.

The problem was bigger than the relationship between Germaine and Roelof. It was the entire ethos of the Push, in which relationships were built entirely on masculine modes of behavior. In that respect, the Push reflected the mode of the wider society. As Elwyn Morris comments, analyzing her own years in the group, it would have been too much to expect the Push to be 'outside History,' to be the exception to the rule that even groups flouting conventional mores share some of the attitudes of the dominant culture.[31] In Anderson's words, 'what people are doing is very different from what they think they are doing.'[32]

Emotional denial was a key element of Push culture, considerably exaggerated from that already well entrenched in the masculinist culture of mainstream society. The explicit repression of jealousy, though imperfectly achieved, was essential to Push promiscuity. No emotion was allowed, no sign of shock, disappointment or distress permitted when one's lover sallied forth with another.

Renouncing possessiveness and transcending jealousy may have been noble goals in the context of Push theory, but in practice they worked in favor of the men. 'When Push men made women feel guilty about being "possessive," they were promoting their own interests,' according to Elwyn Morris. 'The Push ideology of "free love" obscured this conflict, at the expense of women.'[33]

The actual pattern of relations within the Push was at best a source of ambivalence for many, though not all, of the women involved. As Morris puts it, it took high rents to make the landladies of the 1950s and early 1960s forget their morals, so sex often occurred in less than salubrious settings: in cars, other people's bedrooms during parties, on the floor, on the ground. 'Tremendous social pressure was put on women to be available,' Morris recalls. 'Free love was free, in that men didn't have to pay, or even take a girl out, or buy her a beer; for a few of them, it was a new and loveless way of exploiting women. Promiscuity was a virtue, and possessiveness and jealousy cardinal sins.' Many of the men, in her view, were simply engaged in a typically male quest to notch up as many 'conquests' as possible: 'Those capable of love soon got involved in fairly monogamous relationships; the rest, because of neurosis, cultural conditioning or Push ideology, justified behaviour that was often cold, humiliating, and exploitative, as "non-moralistic." '34

Other 'enlightened' practices had their dark side, too. Push members always assumed collective financial responsibility for the financing of abortions, or 'scrapes' as they were known. No matter who the father was, and whether or not one was even distinguishable, the hat was passed around and everybody contributed. The flip-side, however, was that Push men, in line with mainstream mores, refused to share responsibility for contraception in the first place, considering it purely women's business. Many women had multiple abortions, far more than would have been necessary had Push men shared the responsibility for contraception. At a time when abortion was illegal and physically risky, it put the women's reproductive health in jeopardy. Nor were children welcomed in Push circles, which tended to revolve around alcohol at pubs and parties. Having children often led to effective withdrawal from Push social life for women; as mothers, they were perceived to have lost their sexual clout in the group.

Andersonianism was not in itself misogynous, and Anderson himself was a critic of the elevation of masculinist values. As early as 1930 he was asking, 'Has not the University as an institution something better to offer than the pitiful catalogue of the "manly virtues" which Rhodes considered requisite for the public man?'35 Wilhelm Reich was another matter. Push men enthusiastically adopted what from today's perspective looks like a bizarre claim by Reich for the superiority of vaginal over clitoral orgasm. Countless hours were spent discussing the issue in the pub instead of employing the tough-minded empiricism they prided themselves on to test the notion in bed with their partners – the ones who actually had the vagina and clitoris the blokes were pronouncing on so confidently.

A few of the men privately showed concern over whether their partners were sexually satisfied. Yet even one-to-one, without immediate risk of becoming the public targets of a libertarian diatribe, the women were loath to articulate and explain what they really were and were not feeling. The confidence simply was not there. The preconditions for women to begin forming opinions and analyses from their own perspective were only just beginning to fall into place. The gathering pace of women's participation in paid employment and higher education was crucial to this change.

While the libertarian men in the Push theorized endlessly about the hierarchical mechanics of the female orgasm, and their partners kept quiet, the warmth and depth and loving intimacy that many of the women really wanted went unfulfilled. Just as Germaine remained silent about it within her own relationship and within the group, so it was in the wider Push. 'I don't think she got what she wanted from the relationship,' Smilde admits, 'and I don't think she would've got it from anybody in the Push.'

After the unhappiness had simmered within for months, Germaine made plans to move out. 'I was happy to keep on going the way we were, but it didn't satisfy her,' Smilde recalls. 'And we didn't do the same things. I was interested in punting and bridge and the Push social life, and she was into acting and writing and teaching – she was a performer. So there are a lot of things we didn't do together. We spent a lot of time apart. And I think in that sense we just drifted apart.'

The Push reinforced the very elements of Germaine's childhood and adolescence which had hurt her the most. Just as Reg had loved her then kept her at arm's length, so it was in the Push. There could and would be some sort of connection with men, it underlined to her again, and it could even be intense – but it was without warmth, without comfort, without the loving intimacy for which she hungered.

Germaine loved Roelof and he loved her back, but strictly within accepted Push guidelines, and within the limitations of his own psychological and doctrinaire strictures. The depth, the emotion, the closeness were not there – and, like Reg, he was often not there at all. There was bridge to play and bets to lay and a certain amount of cab-driving to fit in, as well as the Push social life in which he was so pivotal. The emotional dissociation that went with loving a man in the Push, let alone one of its 'princes,' was everything her relationship with Reg had been, and traveled the same course: ecstatic hope, joy, then disappointment. In the end she followed the same escape route: the education system. In Melbourne she had thrown herself into school and then university life to assuage her pain at home; now she would do the same in Sydney. The university, after all, stood waiting a mile or so up Glebe Point Road, reminding her that there was another path to follow.

When Germaine Greer later looked back on her life in Sydney, it was Harry Hooton on whom she dwelt. Harry, the utopian anarchist who had admired her red stockings, who believed people were perfect and who was not weighed down by the tremendous forces of anarchistic pessimism that weighed heavily on her Push comrades. 'Alas, I understand him much better now,' she said twenty years later.[36] 'When I last saw him, he was dying, just a whisper of himself, but still enormous; the power of his soul filled the little room he lay in. And he called me to tell me that he had great faith in me, that he thought I was the woman of the twenty-first century. I didn't know what he meant then, but I think a lot of the things I've done since I've done out of a desire to please Harry Hooton. Too late . . .'

# 5

# *Byrony*

'After a while, I left Roelof and went to Sydney University to get my MA.'[1] Greer's return to the academic world from the Push was considerably more significant than her prosaic description years later betrayed. The Push life could engage people for years, sometimes decades. Once they were accepted in it, they could enjoy the seductively bohemian life for long periods, diverting themselves with endless variations in sexual partners in a self-contained, self-perpetuating realm of permanent protest. For Germaine, though, enrolling for a master's degree at the University of Sydney marked a renewal of her mainstream ambitions – a manifestation of the same forward momentum she had summoned since school days when faced with contrary pressures. Emotionally, the relationship with Smilde had proved a cul-de-sac. She took action: she moved on. She decided to revive her academic aspirations, to compensate for her upper second from Melbourne. A good Master of Arts in English from Sydney could restore her academic options.

Not that Germaine abandoned Push libertarianism – far from it. Sydney University was still a libertarian stronghold. The year she wrote her master's thesis, 1962, opened with a furor on campus over alleged depravities uttered by Dr. Peter Kenny, formerly of the university's Psychology Department, who was notorious for his Orientation Week speeches on sex. There was a complaint that Kenny had advocated 'an equal right to fornicate or not to fornicate; a rejection of "natural law"; a rejection of the word "ought"; a public marriage ceremony for homosexuals . . . [and] a special room in all homes for "solitary sexual practices"' – statements all freely conceded by Kenny. The attack, which linked Kenny obliquely to Sydney's Philosophy Department, was circulated to academics and civic leaders in Sydney.

Anderson's successor in the Philosophy Department, Professor A. K. Stout, retaliated by describing the premise of the attack as a 'thumping lie.' He pointed out that Kenny's doctorate was in psychology and he had not taken a single philosophy course, which hardly made the Philosophy Department responsible for Kenny's views. The complainant was undeterred, and replied that the Psychology Department acted as an annex of the Philosophy Department: 'The head of the department is an Andersonian, and so are the rest of his staff.'[2]

Whatever the philosophical inspiration, the university administration was not amused. The attack generated bad publicity, and some parents complained to the university's chancellor, Sir Charles Bickerton Blackburn. Blackburn told the Students' Representative Council there were to be no more sex symposia in Orientation Week. 'The Chancellor seemed so annoyed and distressed, and he took such a strong line that we were completely shocked,' one SRC member told *HONI SOIT*. 'We were so surprised that we couldn't make any reply.' After taking a couple of weeks to regroup, the SRC contested Blackburn's ultimatum – tellingly, in an Andersonian formulation: 'It is the duty of the University to encourage original thought, including nonconformist thought, and it is a breach of academic freedom for any element either within or without the University to attempt to suppress the same.'[3]

Professor Stout tried to play down the dispute, dismissing the attack as a crazy one-man vendetta against the Philosophy Department. It was not. The fact was that the Anderson-inspired Push had already given 'free love' a public profile and was beginning to generate a reaction accordingly. The Kenny dispute was a harbinger of the controversy which emerged later in the decade as sexual liberalism extended from bohemian communities into suburbia.

This friction at the juncture between the apparent moral

homogeneity of the 1950s and the heterogeneity of the later 1960s began earlier than is generally understood. Although Kenny's comments caused outrage among some people in 1962, others already found them passé. In an article in *HONI*, 'I knew Peter Kenny,' for example, Betty Arnold wrote that a ban on his sex symposia would be a pity, as they were great entertainment value, but suggested that a suitable replacement topic for debate might be 'Peter Kenny is outdated.'[4]

The territory was familiar to Germaine, too. She had been living her own personal sexual revolution since 1957 and had taken it to Sydney University with her – to her relationships and to her graduate work in the English Department. The defiance of sexual convention by George Gordon, Lord Byron, was a central element of her MA thesis, and a couple of years in the Push pubs had reinforced her own flamboyant personal style. Germaine was involved with men from Sydney's student theater scene. She was still leading with her lip, and quickly became renowned among the undergraduates for her liberal use of the word 'fuck' at a time when it still made most citizens blanch.

Yet Germaine had not returned to the university merely for a change of scenery. She was concerned to make a success of this academic reprise, and often opted for the library over parties or the pub. The subject she chose for her thesis was 'The Development of Byron's Satiric Mode' and on campus she carried a notebook inscribed 'Byrony.' How could Germaine, known for her razor-sharp ripostes, fail to delight in Byron's gift for inspired insult – his vitriolic attack, for example, on the conservative British politician and diplomat Castlereagh as an 'intellectual eunuch'?[5] The destination she would choose when finally leaving Sydney was decided by the poet-adventurer's own choice of university in Britain.

Byron was an unusual choice for a Leavisite, but then the Sydney English Department was not caught in the Leavisite grip Sam Goldberg was attempting to apply at Melbourne. It was clear from Germaine's cover page, before one even got to the body of the thesis, that Byron would emerge favorably from it. Below the title she quoted Elton: 'There has never been a sufficient reaction against the false censure of Byron.'[6]

Her choice of topic had resonances, real and prospective, with her locale and her life. Byron, whom she adored, and Sydney, the city with which she emotionally meshed, were creatures of the same era. Byron was born in London's Cavendish Square four days before Governor Arthur Phillip first ran up the Union Jack at Sydney Cove, the penal settlement from which the harbor city grew. After falling in love with Smilde and then leaving him, 'I fell in love with the city itself,' she said many years later. 'And of all my love affairs, this is the one that looks like it is going to last me the rest of my life.'[7] In true contrarian style, this has not stopped her from spending most of her time in Britain.

There was also a distinct similarity between the sort of literary figure Byron cut in the early nineteenth century and the role that Greer would play in the late twentieth. The cult of literary personality was launched in England with Byron. He achieved instant celebrity with the publication of the first two cantos of *Childe Harold's Pilgrimage* in 1812. 'Byron was certainly not the best poet of his generation, but as a candidate for contemporary fame he possessed an unbeatable combination of qualities,' in Norman Page's assessment. 'Snobbery, sexual attraction, an appetite for scandal . . . and the appeal of exoticism were all ingredients in the Byron craze. . . . [He] was an angry young man a century and a half before that phrase became a cliché. With his knack of making enemies by ridiculing fellow authors, allied to his photogenic qualities, he would have been a brilliant success as a television personality.'[8]

Even had Greer's reputation not preceded her, dozing examiners would have been awakened by the second sentence of her thesis, which broached the debate about whether Byron's suspected predilection for 'unnatural intercourse' explained his wife's decision 'to divorce her loving lord.' In an aside on Byron's treatment at the hands of literary historians, she also immediately raised his 'sarcastic encomia' on the adverse effect of biography on 'a great man's reputation' – in her view, well illustrated by Byron's case.[9] It was the germ of the hostility she would later turn on her own prospective biographers.

Germaine portrayed Byron as the poet of worldliness, commonsense and the pleasure principle. Parts of her analysis prefigured her later writing on relations between women and men. She noted, for example, Byron's observation that jealousy was infallibly exploitable as a manipulative tool, and his inference 'that coquetry is a weapon in the power struggle between the sexes.'[10] Byron, she argued, was aware of the existence of female sexuality and its demands, and understood the nature and causes of female 'hysteria' in the English 'bought wife.' According to Germaine, the plight of women in Byron's own society was a major theme of his epic *Don Juan*, which created 'the perfect picture of spontaneous love.'[11] Byron was already involved in a revolt against society's hollowness, absurdity and cant: 'It is not so much a political revolt – Byron was at best only palely and unsystematically agin the government – as a moral revolt, and, despite the carpings of contemporary critics, it did manage to establish some values of its own. They were realism, the promotion and enjoyment of pleasure, spontaneity, good humour, straightforwardness, generosity and freedom.'[12] Byron was, in short, the perfect Push man.

The fact that literary critics classified Byron as a Romantic – though not an unambiguous one – might have alerted Greer to the darker side of the Byronic hero. Previous treatments of the Don Juan legend had emphasized the calculating manipulativeness with which the hero extracted sexual favors. 'The traditional Don,' writes Professor Anne Barton, 'was, and remained, a demonic sensualist, deceiving women of all classes either with false promises of marriage or by pretending, under cover of darkness, to be someone else.'[13] If Byron dressed Don Juan's adventuring in less cynical and exploitative garb, it is difficult to support Greer's contention that the result was a model for modern relations between men and women. *Don Juan* is written from a male point of view; Don Juan's fictional female lovers, like those of Byron in real life, lacked a voice of comparable volume. Germaine's own experience of just this sort of sexual ethos in the Push had not prompted her to compare theory with reality.

Despite the ostensible anti-romance of Byron, and of the Push, much of the poetry of the former and the philosophy of the latter were essentially romantic in nature. While aspiring to realism, they idealized a kind of spontaneous sexual combustion as the acme of human connection. The reality was far more complicated, as Byron himself conceded in those much-quoted lines from *Don Juan*: 'Man's love is of man's life a thing apart;/'Tis woman's whole existence.'[14]

Germaine clung to her belief in 'the worldliness, commonsense and the pleasure principle' of Byron – and of the Push – long after second-wave feminists had begun to question the power relations underlying the new sexual freedoms of the counterculture and protest movements. Even as she was under Byron's spell in Sydney, another scholar overseas was preparing for publication the letters of Byron's friend and fellow poet Percy Bysshe Shelley, which threw a different light on her hero. 'Well, L[ord] B[yron] is familiar with the lowest sort of these women,' Shelley wrote, 'the people his gondolieri pick up in the streets. He allows fathers and mothers to bargain with him for their daughters, and though this is common enough in Italy, yet for an Englishman to encourage such sickening vice is a melancholy thing.'[15]

'She had this love of Byron,' recalls Albie Thoms, a student contemporary. 'She was constantly quoting him. She saw him as a romantic hero. She'd fallen for all the romantic male bullshit of the hero, the beautiful man. There was never any mention of Byron's treatment of women.' Given the man she most intimately associated with Byron, a critical analysis was not likely. 'She saw Roelof as a Lord Byron,' says Thoms. 'And Roelof was a very powerful figure, a very romantic figure.' Germaine might have left Smilde, but she had not forgotten him.

She was simply not alert to the cues which might have triggered a feminist response in her analysis, and little of what was happening at Sydney University was likely to speed up the process. Women appeared to have made little progress between Germaine's undergraduate days at Melbourne and her time as a graduate student at Sydney. Pictures of Miss University entrants, for example, still took pride of place in student newspapers.

Yet some women were beginning to question the nature of the exercise. 'The Miss University contest should not be simply a beauty contest,' Ruth de Berg (Miss Arts 1962) told *HONI SOIT*. 'It should choose a girl who has a combination of looks, personality and intelligence. I would be proud and pleased of a contest like that if it was based on something worthwhile,' she added, 'but at the moment it seems to be very superficial.'[16] Still, the accompanying photograph showed Miss de Berg with her frock slipping invitingly, if modestly, from one shoulder. The following year

*HONI* inadvertently underlined the tawdry truth about the fate of contest winners: 'Are you young? Are you beautiful? Are you an Arts student? Are *you* going to be Miss Arts? If you are then you will be crowned at the Arts Ball – and you will be well on the way to being Miss University . . . Miss Australia . . . Miss International Beauty . . . Mrs. Melvin Snurd.'[17]

*HONI* provided its readers with a steady diet of sexist jibes. The 'DEBBIE, miss freshette' comic strip, for example, featured captions such as: 'There was this wonderful Boy – But . . ./He read *Playboy*, so he was most disappointed when I wouldn't . . ./Unfold when he picked me up.'[18] *HONI* excelled itself with its first edition in 1964, which gave front-page coverage to a tongue-in-cheek article about 'Matrimony I' – a little-known course taken only by young women, the paper said, consisting of English I, Anthropology I and Psychology I. 'Matrimony is strictly a one-year course,' according to *HONI*. 'It should end at the nearest altar about December 1964. No examinations are necessary if proper precautions are taken throughout.'[19]

Germaine's feminist awareness was still constrained by Push thinking about women – which acknowledged female sexual desire and rejected the suburban stereotype, but was otherwise limited to largely symbolic positions such as the rejection of gender-segregated socializing. Rare critiques of the Push in *HONI SOIT* hinted rather than declared openly that in the process of trying to defeat conformism, the libertarians had created their own. One commentary on the Push in *HONI* used a series of notional, anonymous figures including a young, intelligent woman who had ultimately seen through the Push's 'negativeness':

> When she first came, they promised her freedom from the chains of middle-class banality, from the 9–5 drudge, from the pot-bellied male, from all that was common.
>
> But because she could disassociate and yet participate she could see beyond the pettiness of they who were enmeshed. She saw that in fact, they were more tightly bound than before, because of:
>
> poverty, boredom, habit, custom, dress, unconventionality; in fact all that they had rebelled against.[20]

The implications of Simone de Beauvoir's *The Second Sex*, of which Push women were aware at the time, had not given the group the mighty jolt Greer's own book would later. Neither the Push nor she herself were mainsprings of early feminist activism in Sydney.

Nor was she active in the embryonic Australian cultural renewal occurring at the time; she focused steadfastly on the European rather than the home-grown. Earlier in the century there had been an enthusiastic local market for Australian stories and characters, notably in a vigorous feature film-making industry before the Depression, but it withered later under adverse global economic and cultural pressures as well as the Anglophile snobbery of domestic opinion leaders. The post-war assertion of Australian cultural values defied the 'cultural cringe' which for years had elevated things British and belittled local achievement. This 'cringe' was aided and abetted by Anglophile political leaders like the conservative prime minister Robert Menzies, who had held power continuously since 1949. During a royal visit to Australia, Menzies summed up the establishment spirit of the time with a cloying recital to Elizabeth II of 'I did but see her passing by/And yet I love her till I die.' The cultural cringe was transmitted down the line through innumerable royal cover stories in the ubiquitous *Australian Women's Weekly*.

By 1962, however, a revival of Australian cultural life was under way. One landmark step was Sydney University's decision in September that year to establish the country's first full chair in Australian literature, appointing the English Department's Gerry Wilkes, thirty-four years old, to the position. Emblematic progress from above was mirrored by vigorous initiatives from below. For example, Robert Hughes, then an architecture student at Sydney University, took a break from study in the middle of 1962 to write *The Art of Australia*, one of the first titles commissioned by Penguin under its newly established Australian publishing program.[21]

A meeting between the youthful Hughes and Sir Allen Lane, head of Penguin Books, during his visit to Australia two months later caught the changing temper of the times and the social friction it was causing. Poets and Penguin consultants Geoffrey Dutton and Max Harris collected Hughes and took him to lunch with Lane at the Newport home of Lane's sister, Nora Bird, and her husband. The three writers quickly quaffed a bottle of red, and Hughes helped himself to another from the sideboard. 'After a couple of steps he caught his foot in the deep pile of the all-white carpet, and fell face down on the floor, the bottle of red glugging peacefully over the carpet,' Dutton recalls. ' "Fuck!" said Bob in a loud voice. Mr Bird jumped up. "Out! Out, the lot of you! I'm not having that sort of language in my house, in front of my wife!" We all got to our feet except Allen, who said genially "I made a fortune out of that word. I thought I'd reintroduced it to the English language with *Lady Chatterley!*" ' Mr. Bird's outrage dissipated and the three writers were allowed to stay.[22]

Hughes, who went on to become *Time* magazine's long-serving art critic, was one of a golden generation at Sydney University in and about 1962. Richard Walsh, a founder of the original *Oz* magazine and later chief of Kerry Packer's publishing empire, was sacked as *HONI* editor at the beginning of 1962 after offending the SRC. Walsh was reinstated, then resigned in protest at the principle of the matter, to be replaced by Laurie Oakes and Bob Ellis. 'Mr Oakes is in Arts II and can afford to repeat,' *HONI* reported. 'Mr Ellis is in Arts III, and can't.' Asked by a conservative SRC member to define *HONI*'s relationship to the student council, 'Mr Oakes did, but no one quite remembers how. It was perhaps the most noncommittal statement since Moses told the burning bush he stuttered.'[23] Oakes went on to become the doyen of the Canberra press gallery, Ellis to be the political gadfly of his generation.

Bruce Beresford, then making his first one-reel films – the beginning of a career which saw him decamp successfully to Hollywood – was flirting with poetry. Other poets included Lee Sonnino, who as Lee Cataldi went on to publish the memorable collection *Invitation to a Marxist Lesbian Party*,[24] and later became a translator of Aboriginal dreaming stories. The poet John Tranter was published prolifically in *HONI* – 'From the End or the Beginning,' for example, subtitled 'A brief and gentle explanation of why I forgot to pass the sugar, darling.'[25] Tranter went on to become one of Australia's leading poets, as did another young Sydney undergraduate at that time – Les Murray, commonly seen on campus with the shambolic Bob Ellis.

Geoffrey Lehmann, poet-cum-law-student, teased Robert Hughes about the profound debt Hughes appeared to owe others for some of the tyro critic's own paintings and poems. This unleashed a mock defence of Hughes in the *HONI* letters column by two correspondents: 'Our main concern is, quite simply, to ensure that Mr Hughes is not denounced as a charlatan in matters where he is not. It is our opinion that his drawing, "The Mad Emperor," 1958, is superior by every criterion to "Head of a Poet," by Leonard Baskin, 1955. We find that the poem "Odysseus," by Robert Hughes, 1957, is not as accomplished as "Mycennae," in the 1948 translation from George Seferis, nor would we expect it to be; yet on the other hand "Odysseus" is not without considerable artistic merit, when judged within its own terms.'[26]

The group with the most cachet on campus, however, was the foyer crowd, a loose association of student actors and their friends who hung about the Union Theatre foyer drinking coffee and talking about theater, films, books, music and each other. 'They like black coffee, Beckett, beards, gin, black clothes, sex, posters and themselves,' wrote one contemporary observer. 'They dislike ordinary people, milkshakes, inhibitions, football, parents, order, meals, the refectory, lectures and living.'[27]

There was some competition between the two main campus theater groups – Sydney University Dramatic Society (SUDS) and Players – although many student actors were involved in both. SUDS tended to prefer the modern, while Players concentrated on Shakespeare and the Jacobeans. John Bell was Players' great star, while Arthur Dignam was the lead at SUDS.

Dignam and Bell combined in some productions to startling effect, including *By Royal Command* off campus in 1964. Dignam's voice was 'limpid and mellifluous, like ripples in a bowl of mercury,' according to one reviewer, achieving 'an intimate love-match with the audience,' while Bell was like 'a statue of frozen cream, all sun-tanned cheekbones and marble body . . . half golden boy, half Jupiter.'[28]

'An explosion of awfully interesting people came out of those few years at Sydney University,' recalls Dignam. 'It was a totally European theatrical scene, but with a sense that you could do it yourself.'

Dignam had started out studying law before moving on to medicine and then to arts. He met Germaine after she had seen him in a Players production of John Ford's play *'Tis Pity She's a Whore*. The play was 'full of frightful goings on, very Catholic,' according to Dignam. It saw the young John Bell racing on to the stage with a heart on a dagger. Dignam, with his patrician looks, played the cardinal who says ' 'Tis pity she's a whore' at the end of the play.

All of a sudden, Germaine was part of the scene, Dignam says. 'She was incredibly funny – that was the first impression.' After seeing him in *'Tis Pity*, Germaine approached him one day at university. 'I was having a coffee with someone,' he recalls. 'She rushed up and said she was starting a salon, and would I come? There *was* no salon. She was just fantasizing. . . . But the salon was a great idea. The fact there wasn't one didn't seem to matter as much as the good idea in the first place.'

Dignam was part of the foyer crowd. 'We drank a lot, fucked a lot and had a good time,' he says of those who regularly congregated there. 'Mainly what you did was talk. You felt as though you were understanding something. It was a very optimistic sort of feeling, a very energized sort of time.'

Germaine's twin personae, the intellectual and the populist, were already evident to Dignam: 'She was ambitious, I guess. She knew she was entertaining, and it always seemed to be completely effortless. She had groups of people who kind of adored her, and she was naturally the center of attention. I'm very fond of her but I wouldn't want to live with her. She's a one-man show, basically, and I think I am too.'

Dignam was fascinated, not least by Germaine's sense of her body; clearly she was no run-of-the-mill ex-convent girl. He remembers her always dressing in the most comfortable yet stylish clothes. They became lovers, and at one stage holidayed together at Dignam's family home on Lord Howe Island. Dignam's parents were enchanted by his guest, as were some of the other islanders. One night Greer and Dignam went to a dance at the bowling club. When the dance ended at eleven o'clock they walked home by moonlight; there were no streetlights on the island. Germaine began telling Dignam a hilarious story about the royal family and they gradually became aware of a growing crowd of people walking behind them. When they got to the Dignams' house she stopped and finished the story for the benefit of the crowd. The locals said 'thanks very much' and went home.

'There was more than a hint of feminism in her at that time,'

Dignam recalls. 'She was the only woman we had met at that stage who could confidently, easily and amusingly put men down. We weren't used to it.'

Germaine was busy smashing icons. In 1962 she wandered into the Union Theatre one day where Albie Thoms, then a postgraduate drama student, was painting the backdrop for his production of *Ubu Roi*: giraffes frolicked on icefields and elephants lounged on beds in the surreal sets. Germaine offered a hand. 'She could paint!' Thoms recalls, impressed not only by her creative breadth but by her willingness to get dirty as well. Thoms, at the threshold of a considerable career as an avant-garde film maker, cast her in '. . . *it droppeth as the gentle rain*,' based on a Jacques Prévert ballet. Surrealist in style, the film was conceived in the shadow of the Bay of Pigs crisis when nuclear conflagration between the United States and Soviet Union seemed imminent. It was Thoms's first film, shot over a weekend in February 1963 at a house at St. Ives using actors drawn from SUDS and the Push. In a bourgeois cocktail-party setting, guests gaily sip champagne as storm clouds gather; eventually all is engulfed in the feces that fall from the threatening clouds.

Greer's early appeal is apparent in the film: fresh, statuesque and classically proportioned from the waist up, she towers gorgeously in her scoop-necklined dress over the other actors as they socialize, ignorant of the looming disaster. Thoms intended to show the film as part of *A Revue of the Absurd*, his production of short plays by Samuel Beckett, Eugene Ionesco, Alfred Jarry and Harold Pinter, among others, at the Union Theatre the following month. Germaine had roles in other parts of the revue, including Ionesco's *Maid to Marry* and Edward Albee's *The Sandbox*. An injunction banning the film's performance was delivered minutes before the curtain went up on the revue, however, because Gus Kelly, Chief Secretary for New South Wales, considered it in bad taste. 'It was banned because it featured such words as "shit" which, as we all know, policemen never use,' Laurie Oakes editorialized in *HONI*. 'I understood that the intellectuals from the NSW Constabulary who censored the production even came backstage and demanded to talk to Alf Jarry and Sam Becket [*sic*].'[29]

Thoms later took the revue to Melbourne University's Festival of the Absurd; it was a triumphal return for Germaine. 'She arrived in Sydney already a provocateur,' recalls Albie. 'When we went to Melbourne with *A Revue of the Absurd*, she was greeted as such – her legend had lived on. They were fascinated by her.'

As at Melbourne University, Germaine quickly established a theatrical reputation on campus at Sydney. 'She received early invaluable training in acting,' one *HONI* journalist wrote, 'for she was born an inveterate liar.' She liked the simple things in life, the piece continued: 'Good food, good wine, good music, good art, good books and bad people. She never attends formal functions, however, as she has neither the clothes or the manners. There are two men in her life, both castrated, one black called Gulliver and one brindle called Grimalkin. They tolerate each other, but are jealous of any intruder!'[30]

Germaine's absurdist sally was followed by a starring role in the university revue, *Drums Along the Tankstream*, with Paul Thom, John Gaden, Stefan Gryff, Vivienne Lincoln, Mary Patterson and a cast of thousands performing sketches by Clive James, among others. Wrote 'A. Tomcat' of Greer's 'Star of the Sea' skit in an *HONI* review, 'It is very hard on the sternum to watch German [sic] in nun's habit stripping sexily to appropriate music.'[31]

Not that she had altogether cut her ties with things Catholic. She enjoyed a close friendship with Peter Butler, a music student who composed the scores for *A Revue of the Absurd* and some of Bruce Beresford's early films. Greer and Butler sang with Butler's diplo-mat brother Richard and Richard's wife, Susan Ryan, in a choir at St. Joseph's Church in Newtown. Sunday Mass at St. Joseph's was given by a progressive priest from Sydney University, and the choir had been formed to sing the then-new liturgy. Like Germaine, Ryan – later a Labor senator – was Catholic born, bred and educated. Peter and Richard were converts. Susan and Richard, recent graduates from Sydney, were interested in church reform and hoped for further liberalization. 'We all went to Mass to sing in this modern choir,' Ryan says. 'Emotionally and culturally she was still Catholic, part of the whole scene.'

One morning, after going to an all-night party together, Greer and Butler were driving home when they passed the church of St. Mary Immaculate. It was Ash Wednesday, one of the most moving events in the Christian calendar, and early Mass was being said. On impulse they went inside. Tears began streaming down Germaine's face. Butler guessed that her grief flowed from the breach between Germaine and her faith rather than from the pathos of the Mass.

Greer's residual Catholicism arguably had other manifestations around that time. She told Peter Butler she wanted a child and was prepared to marry the first man who could impregnate her, adding sadly that problems with her Fallopian tubes made it highly unlikely she could conceive.

The schoolteaching with which she financed most of her years in Sydney provided an outlet for Germaine's maternal feelings. 'She was in love with the kids,' Albie Thoms recalls. 'She was a real mother hen, [so] clucky about these schoolgirls. "They're my babes," she'd keep saying.'

Catholicism's continuing resonance for Germaine did not moderate her generally flamboyant behavior. The Butlers had bought an old Jaguar XK-120, white with red leather upholstery, and taken it on their honeymoon. The newlyweds quickly realized they could not afford petrol for the car and sold it to Peter, who was making a little money managing jazz bands on the side. Sitting in a Kings Cross coffee shop after Mass one Sunday, Susan and Richard were startled when Peter roared up in the Jag. Germaine jumped out of the car, dressed all in black with long leather boots, and yelled: 'You sold him a heap of shit, didn't you!'

One weekend Peter took Germaine home for lunch with his family at Bondi. Things became tense after Germaine's arrival when Peter's younger brother Greg, then twelve years old, began bouncing a ball up against the pressed metal ceiling. 'Stop doing that!' snapped his father, Harold Butler, who then turned to Germaine and pronounced, 'This is the best ceiling in the world.' 'Oh, yeah,' she replied. 'It beats the Sistine Chapel.' Harold Butler years later made a point of seeing the Sistine Chapel and remarked: 'Yes, I can see what she means.'

After the Calvinistically intense Roelof Smilde, the complex actor-cum-philosopher Paul Thom was the most important lover of Germaine's Sydney years. 'Germaine's principal relationship, intellectually and physically, was with Paul,' Dignam recalls. 'He was sort of weedy and thin, but phenomenally intelligent, witty and mad about music. They were both very Jesuitical, with quite an awareness of being physically attractive.'

Thom was the comic hit of SUDS – 'a raving lunatic,' according to *HONI*, 'the funniest thing I have seen on or off the stage.'[32] Germaine had a perversely comic streak to match. Standing around drinking wine at a university party one night, one young man claimed Greer could never do anything to embarrass him. 'Here, hold this,' Germaine responded, handing him her glass. While he stood there, both hands full, she unzipped his fly and pulled his penis out for all to behold.

The relationship with Thom, however, brought out Germaine's hidden vulnerability as well as the braggadocio she generally sported. Don Anderson, then a student in Sydney's English Department, recalls the intensity of her feeling for Thom: 'She was desperately in love with him. She burst into tears at a party when she came across him cuddling someone else.' Anderson recalls visiting Germaine's bedside, along with Thom and some other SUDS figures, when she was hospitalized with another gynecological disaster – an occasion on which, understandably, 'she didn't look quite so indefatigable.'

From the beginning Greer aspired to a certain amount of fame, according to Albie Thoms. She always walked into a room in a way calculated to make an impact, he observed: 'She'd drop the word "fuck" at the earliest opportunity, talk loudly, laugh loudly, and often make derogatory comments.' Yet to him it seemed a facade, a performance she was giving off-stage. At rehearsals Germaine would sit knitting, making clothes, a picture of peaceful domesticity. 'I'm sure if someone was sick she'd take them some soup,' Thoms says. 'As a defence against her vulnerability, she created an intimidating persona.'

Germaine's power to overwhelm was a matter of physique as well as volume in Thoms's view: 'She intimidated people because of her size as well as her loud mouth. She was very physically imposing. Many of the women around were quite small and she'd just tower over them. . . . She frightened a lot of women on the scene.' Partly this flowed from Germaine's ready assumption of leadership in most situations: she was a natural leader, according to Thoms, and she provided leadership whether people wanted it or not. A thread of condescension toward other women was also perceptible, he says: 'There were many good women in the Push who just fucked because they wanted to – not because of any political theory. I think Germaine looked down on them.'

Vivienne Lincoln, a SUDS actor, remembers a less-than-armor-plated Germaine. 'She was always a star, but always incredibly vulnerable. Germaine was prickly though not malicious in those days – she had quite a soft center.' Once more her desire for Thom exposed the gap between Germaine's idealized model of sexual relations and the reality of their practice. A harborside party was held on Balmoral Beach at Sydney's Middle Head. A few people, including Germaine, went fishing on a little boat. Returning with two fish in hand, she found Lincoln sitting by the shore on Thom's lap. In retaliation she slapped Lincoln – unhappily rather than viciously – on the head with one of the fish. 'Paul was extremely clever, distant, a bit of a wimp,' says Lincoln of Thom. 'He protected her, I think. . . . He saw the hurt side of her.'

Another SUDS actor, Stefan Gryff, now married to Lincoln and working in British theater, took a different view of Germaine's relationship with Thom. He was 'a gentle soul' in Gryff's estimation: 'Paul Thom was a victim – he did what he was told. At the other extreme [for Germaine] it was truck drivers and road workers.'

> She was only alive, truly alive, when her ego had an erection . . . She was a master flirt – the eyes, the body language, little girl lost. She was a great actress. She's been acting all her life. . . .
>
> Germaine's talent is that she could express all facets of her personality. I think she was aware of her talents – [she was] a free instrument like all good actors should be. She could use any of the bits of her. It's a pity she didn't become an actor. She's a born actor. . . . She was a star. She was so good she almost seemed genuine in life – but I always thought she was acting. . . .
>
> She was *so* predatory. She bamboozled these guys. I told them. They didn't dare to reply. She was a queen – she was ruling this thing. . . . There's a little girl in there. It's all an act – but I admire the act!

Gryff found her 'men-oriented' and competitive toward women. There seemed to be considerable rivalry, for example, between Germaine and the intelligent, statuesque, strikingly blonde Danne Emerson, who moved in the same circles. In London a few years later, when Germaine and Danne unexpectedly ran into each other at a party in Notting Hill, tensions resumed where they had left off in Sydney over each woman's relationship with Roelof Smilde. Richard Neville, who accompanied Germaine to the party, recalls that the yelling match reduced the room to an astounded hush.[33]

'She is attractive,' Gryff says. 'The pity is she doesn't know it. . . . Any of her physical imperfections were obliterated by her spirit.' He adored acting with her: 'Whenever Germaine was on stage, you knew she was going to be good.' She had a wonderful sense of timing, sang well and had a great sense of humor. 'She was a brilliant, brilliant person,' he says. 'Nature has given her enormous abilities. But she was always on an ego trip – she was belligerent, confrontational, aggressive to men. . . . I always thought: You don't need to try so hard.'

'She was so articulate for her years,' Lincoln recalls, '[but] she used it as a weapon to beat people down.' Generally successful at cowing others in argument, Germaine made the mistake of provoking Gryff while sitting around with friends in the Union Theatre foyer one day. She began showing off, ridiculing Gryff's accent. Gryff responded in kind and, when the argument got nasty, he refused to give way. Greer burst into tears. 'She was a bully,' says Gryff. 'She'd run over people. She was fearless – she had enough balls for a hundred men. But if you're going to be a revolutionary, you don't buy houses in Italy.'

In August 1963, Greer and Gryff starred opposite each other in her major theatrical role at university: Brecht's *Mother Courage* in a Players production at the Union Theatre. Brecht began the first complete version of *Mother Courage and her Children* in 1939, the year World War II was declared – and the year Germaine was born. His goal was to demonstrate that war, 'which is a continuation of business by other means, makes the human virtues fatal even to their possessors,' and that 'no sacrifice is too great for the struggle against war.'[34] It was a theme with which Greer would have identified, given the consequences of war for her own childhood.

Mother Courage is a small-time commercial parasite on the Thirty Years' War (1618–48), dragging a canteen wagon around Europe with provisions for its soldiers. She is a paradigm of commercial pragmatism, changing sides twice during the hostilities, flying the flag of whichever side is winning at the time. In various ways her three children become victims of the war and her greed. In early productions of the play Courage's character was somewhat redeemed by a profound indomitability, but Brecht then altered the text to underline the triumph of Courage's commercial instincts over any motherly virtue.[35] 'She was fascinating,' Dignam says of Greer in the role. 'But she would've sorted out the Thirty Years' War *like that*, whereas Mother Courage is kind of a dumb woman.'

One of the poignant and frustrating features of the character is Mother Courage's inability to learn from her situation, despite being the repository of considerable experience and folk wisdom. 'She survives in a man's world because of her sense of humour, her shrewdness, her commonsense and her instinct for self-preservation,' Hugh Rorrison has observed. 'Courage sees through the system, and tries to play it, and that is where she fails. She does all she can but it is not enough. She is not the "hyaena of the battlefield" [she is accused] of being, but she is partly that, and she leaves us with mixed feelings.'[36]

Unlike her comic and satirical roles, Greer's Mother Courage was not a triumph – like the production as a whole, which *HONI* judged 'interesting' rather than a resounding success. Marie D'Arcy and Bobby Gledhill were praised, and Stefan Gryff and Paul Thom got honorable mentions, as did Peter Butler's score. Germaine was assigned the main burden of criticism.

> Germaine Greer failed to sustain the role of Mother Courage. She seemed intermittently to lose the character altogether. Her failure was aggravated by her difficult upper register. I am afraid Germaine could not convince me of her antiquity nor even of her maternity – she seemed disturbingly in the present – not surprising, as her personality all but swamped the character of Mother Courage. The spectators, instead of feeling morally superior to the hard-boiled peasant woman and her clever cut-throat mode of existence, were a little awed by the glib way in which Miss Greer carried off coup after coup. Needless to say, the theatrical effect was not that Brecht intended.[37]

After the opening night show a seminar was held on the play. Student theater and the student press were more than just diversions from the grind of student life in the early 1960s. They were well ahead of mainstream culture and university teaching in exploring the avant-garde and radical new directions in the arts and politics.

A few weeks after *Mother Courage* finished its run, the editors of Sydney's *Oz* magazine – the precursor of London *Oz* – were fined £20 each for producing an obscene publication. Richard Neville, then an arts student at the University of New South Wales, Richard Walsh, who was still studying medicine at Sydney, and Peter Grose, who by then was working as a *Sunday Mirror* journalist, were all university newspaper veterans. The police drew the magistrate's attention to two articles in *Oz* – an extract from the Queensland Parliamentary Hansard, and a history of chastity belts researched in Sydney's august Mitchell Library. The case revealed a bizarre distinction between the publication of libelous material from Hansard, which was legal, and obscene material, which was not. *Oz* had quoted from a debate among Queensland MPs about an article in the Queensland University Rationalist Society's magazine, *The Freethinker* – an article about a symposium speech by the irrepressible Dr. Peter Kenny, 'Are morals outdated?' After retiring for an hour to read the magazine, the magistrate said he was shocked that men with such good family backgrounds and the benefit of university education could publish such material. *Oz* in its Sydney and London incarnations would continue pushing out the boundaries of permissible publishing, in the process ensuring the limits were entirely redefined.

The student press, student theater and their offshoots were catalysts for academic change, as well. SUDS, *HONI SOIT* and magazines like *Hermes*, edited by Don Anderson, and *Arna* were drawing attention to issues and works that the English Department at Sydney would have considered not even remotely suitable for formal study. Don Anderson – 'We didn't sleep together: she was voracious, yes, omnivorous, no' – likens the department at the time to a big country town. 'Sydney was dull but liberal and pluralist,' he says, and 'the department was ripe for the entry of very bright, forceful personalities of whom Germaine was one.'

Sam Goldberg was another. In 1963 Goldberg took up a chair at Sydney and began to recruit more disciples for his version of Leavisism. According to Don Anderson, who was by then teaching in the department: 'He brought a breath of life which some of us inhaled and then rejected. . . . Bright, dapper, intellectually stimulating, Goldberg looked like Leopold Bloom – good-looking, Semitic, saturnine, and an elegant dresser. He used to smoke two types of cigarettes, saving the best for later in the evening.'

Goldberg's dedication to his subject could take extreme forms. Geoffrey Little, then a lecturer in the department, remembers a departmental meeting called by Goldberg to discuss examination questions: 'He didn't want open-ended questions, but rather ones with some point to them. The meeting went into the night, interrupted briefly by a phone call in the middle. We went for a beer, exhausted, afterwards. Someone asked him about the phone call. It was the hospital: his wife had had a baby.'

Little refutes accusations that the department was slow to adopt recent works for study, but concedes that Goldberg's appointment was welcomed by many who hoped he would challenge its 'monolithic tradition.' Concern mounted, though, when Goldberg began stacking the department with Leavisite colleagues from Melbourne. 'He thought many of us were suspicious of his intellectual standing,' Little recalls, 'but it was really just his abrasive manner. He thought only certain people were fit to teach certain things.'

Until Goldberg's arrival at Sydney, Germaine was free from stringent Leavisite scrutiny. Her thesis supervisor had been Derrick Marsh, fresh from imprisonment in South Africa for political agitation. Marsh had written his first book in prison; he dedicated it to the South African Minister for Justice for giving him the time to write. Occasionally Germaine would chat about Byron with Little. Then suddenly Goldberg was on the scene, complete with his Leavisite vocabulary, liberally using the body as metaphor: 'muscular' and 'sinewy' literary works were good, while the 'flaccid' were bad. Little remembers 'Goldberg talking one night, saying this is much the better vocabulary.'

Germaine's underlying literary stance might still have reflected Goldberg's muscular and sinewy imperatives, but her life in Sydney had not. In her thesis she had noted Byron's complaints about the dampening influence of cold weather on hedonistic pursuits. The harbor city, with its soft and sensuous climate, had the opposite effect. 'I was living in Cambridge Street, Paddington,' Don Anderson recalls. 'We had a party. The grass hadn't been cut for some time. Someone said: "I think Germaine has passed out in the back yard." We woke her up and she had a shower, thanked us and went home.'

Goldberg's arrival coincided with a heightening of Germaine's academic hopes and expectations. She was awarded first-class honors for her Master of Arts degree; after stumbling in Melbourne, she was back on the academic track. 'Sam Goldberg took over the English Department at Sydney just after I got my MA and I was appointed senior tutor in English,' she recalled. 'Goldberg told me I had to go to Cambridge to finish my training as a Leavisite, but unfortunately I went to Cambridge to become a Renaissance scholar instead.'[38]

'He may have considered her a bit of an impostor, going to Cambridge and doing a Renaissance topic,' Little says. But that was in the future. First there were her tutoring duties to discharge in her first academic job, though not her first teaching position. She had already taught in several Sydney schools to finance her life in the Push, so being responsible for students was no novelty. All of the vigor, high expectations and dictatorial demeanor she had displayed in the classroom came with her to the tutorial room.

The English Department was in the university's main building with its picturesque quadrangle, but burgeoning enrolments had forced the department to establish an outpost in the Carslaw Building near City Road, recently built to house various of the university's science departments. There Germaine had her office. She was dedicated, according to Professor Gerry Wilkes: 'She paid attention to the minutiae of teaching, writing long comments on work. She didn't want to be moved from her groups when other people went on leave.'

Carslaw faced west and was unbearably hot in late spring and summer. Germaine's office lacked a phone so she would use the phone in Carslaw's lift, riding up and down as she talked. Her attention and elevated expectations could be inspiring to students – if they could cope with the withering dark side to which they were spasmodically subject. While most academics would display a subdued censoriousness with erring students, Germaine was observed on occasion yelling banshee-like at teenage miscreants in the Carslaw corridor.

Her surviving tutorial records – page upon page of single-spaced typed notes on the students she taught English II in 1964 – provide a fascinating insight into Greer's attitudes as a twenty-five-year-old academic.[39] The reader is immediately struck by Greer's awesome confidence in her own judgment as well as by its powerful, often devastating, tenor. Her tendency to be dismissive about the intellectual capacities of students – especially her female students – was partly mitigated by a willingness to revise her opinion in the light of improved performance. The intensity of Germaine's judgments – mostly adverse – can seem extreme in view of the tender age of most of her charges. Her comments on one student's exercise revealed a rare glimmer of self-criticism: she hoped that her 'exhortations to discipline' had not been interpreted as 'recommendations for timidity,' and resolved to take corrective action.

Germaine frequently used denigratory, or at the very least condescending, diminutives when referring to her female students. Alleged 'schoolgirlisms' and signs of immaturity incurred a special ferocity. Even the more worldly young women were upbraided for 'brash vulgarity and iconoclastic confidence,' for rushing to judgment, or for importing 'imperfectly understood' ideas from other disciplines. Not all of her female students were judged harshly, but those who were praised – whether for their common-sense, their insight or their prose style, variously described as 'tough' and 'crisp' – stand out as real exceptions to the rule. A note from Goldberg to Greer concerning a student's possible transfer to the honors stream was signed familiarly: 'OK? Yrs, Sam.' It contrasted with the 'Miss Greer' Germaine had painstakingly typed next to 'TUTOR'S NAME' at the top of each student's record form. As in the army, where there were officers and others, at university Germaine drew a clear dividing line between academics and students.

Rather than criticizing her male students for schoolboyisms, childishness, silliness, superficiality or pert immaturity, she mainly complained that they were dull, boring and humorless. She appeared more willing to give young men than young women the benefit of the doubt. The onus of proof seemed to be reversed for male students: after an initial suspension of judgment, comments on their exercises tended to get worse as the year went on, while for young women Greer not infrequently had to soften her judgment after initially writing them off.

One young man, for example, began promisingly, only to have his subsequent work slammed as irrelevant and dishonest. Greer worried that another had been spoilt by her initial praise, as he was now producing 'highflown crap.' Then there was the male student who was yet to show his full potential in the first exercise, was criticized for banality and dullness by the second and became a 'pompous blatherskite' by the third.

One male student came in for particular favor. Though his work was careless, it was bouncy and honest; he mainly needed to settle down. Greer's sympathy for this young man lasted through to the next exercise: she welcomed his vitality and irreverence but lamented that he was not doing enough work, as he was too busy 'fooling around' at the *HONI* office and baiting the police.

The most poignant situations were those of young women who lacked confidence or were coping with difficult circumstances. One was not assured enough to state her observations cogently and pursue them to their logical conclusion; she needed 'more teaching than I can give,' Greer wrote after assessing the student's first exercise. The overstretching of English Department resources was probably a factor in the student's not getting more help, and predictably this young woman did not do well.

The most worrying case concerned a young woman from the country whose family opposed her going to university, and had only reluctantly agreed on condition that she assume responsibility for a younger sibling at school in Sydney This young woman was clearly under extraordinary pressure; she had been ill, and her scholarship prescribed that the degree had to be finished within the minimum three years. When Germaine assessed her first exercise, handed in after a deadline extension, she was favorably impressed by the student's intelligence and insight. The young woman had potential 'if she gets a grip on herself,' Germaine opined, incidentally locating the problem within the student rather than in her difficult circumstances. Germaine's subsequent comments evinced none of the compassion or generosity she occasionally showed other students. The young woman's work was criticized for pretentiousness and carelessness; some of it was 'the sheerest nonsense.' The tutorial records do not show whether the young woman passed English II and managed to keep her scholarship or not, but the tone of the assessment suggests it was far from certain.

By contrast, Germaine had got 'a grip on herself,' had righted herself after the fluctuating fortunes of Melbourne and of her first couple of years in Sydney. The indomitable John Anderson died while Germaine was writing her thesis on Byron. She was now literally as well as figuratively a post-Andersonian libertarian, as she would sometimes describe herself. As though announcing that libertarianism would never cease being a stormy, stirring presence in her life, it figured in a fresh controversy even as she was preparing to leave Sydney.

In June 1964 *HONI* carried a front-page story: 'Nazis claim 35 members in University.' This flagged a long interview on page three with Arthur Smith, leader of the National Socialist Party of Australia, by the paper's editor, Michael McDermott. The article was effectively an advertorial for Sydney's tiny band of fascists. Next to the interview *HONI* ran an article by the British Nazi Colin Jordan, 'The Great Lie of the 6,000,000,' containing the standard fascist disputation of the facts of the Holocaust.

The editorial on page two justified publishing the articles on free speech grounds: 'Particularly offensive have been the "standover tactics" used by Jewish groups, within and without the universities, to prevent the publication of Nazi policies in student newspapers.'[40] It went on to condemn an allegedly heavy-handed police raid on the Nazis' Sydney office the week before.

McDermott was a 'quasi-libertarian,' as one Push correspondent to *HONI*, Richard Brennan, described him – 'a position that I, for one, am a lot more "quasi" about than he is.'[41] McDermott was nevertheless deploying a standard libertarian line to defend his inflammatory actions, and the Push weighed in behind him.

Correspondents such as Brennan argued that there was a distinction between propagandizing and the dissemination of information. Yet McDermott's article on Arthur Smith and his National Socialist Party effectively conflated the two. McDermott wrote, without offering any contextual frame of reference at all, that if elected Smith's party intended to 'solve the Australian Jewish problem. What is this problem? A complete breakdown of moral, economic, religious and racial standards. How is this due to the Jews? They pursue policies deliberately directed towards these ends. The answer to the Jewish problem is deportation. A so-called "final solution" (i.e. by genocide) is not at all acceptable, and the Party denies that even Hitler carried out any such policy.' Smith's party, McDermott reported flatly as though relaying the latest rugby score, would 'work increasingly towards liberation of all nations under the Jewish-Communist yoke of tyranny.'[42]

After vigorous complaints and a heated SRC meeting debating whether the *HONI* editor had too much latitude, McDermott compounded his original offence with a lead story the following week attacking 'Jewish moves' to restrict the paper's editorial freedom.[43] Extraordinarily, page two – full of letters complaining about the Nazi propaganda – ran a three-column-wide banner headline declaring they were 'The Jewish Line,' while the facing page carried the headline, 'Gentile Letters to the Editor.'

Richard Walsh, who had pressing practical reasons to defend free speech at precisely that moment – he was about to be sentenced to a prison term on new obscenity changes against *Oz* – gently told McDermott to grow up and exercise some judgment. 'Society grants us a multitude of rights but that does not mean that we necessarily always exert them,' wrote Walsh. 'Granted you had the *right* to print this material, but was it a wise thing to do? . . . In exerting your right and in an endeavour to stimulate interest in Nazism, you have run the very real danger of fanning up indestructible prejudices. If freedom is important – and you claim it is – then you might have been charitable enough to spare one large section of our community the fear of having their freedoms curtailed.'[44]

McDermott was temporarily suspended as *HONI* editor at an SRC meeting in mid-July, despite the arguments of libertarians who attended.[45] SRC President Michael Kirby – later a High Court judge and a renowned human rights advocate – successfully moved that the use of issues concerning race, color or creed in *HONI* so as to incite hatred, ridicule or contempt was inconsistent with the principles and traditions of the paper. In August the pro-McDermott forces reoccupied *HONI*. The August 4 edition devoted a whole page to 'The SRC and *HONI SOIT*: the history of a struggle' by Tony Skillen, from a Libertarian Society paper presented the previous week. Two-thirds of that edition's front page was devoted to reprinting a libertarian broadsheet criticizing McDermott's suspension and the 'unprecedented restrictions' placed on the paper by Michael Kirby. The broadsheet article was by Roelof Smilde.

One of the striking features of the SRC meeting, wrote Smilde, was the abundance and diversity of objections to McDermott:

> It is obvious that McDermott has trodden on a lot of toes, hence the abundance of objections, but they have turned out to be predominantly SRC toes. Their dignity and their public image have suffered. And that, in these days of large SRC budgets . . . and good relations downtown, is a very serious matter.
>
> In a situation of conflict, it is not the amount of offence given but rather the reaction to that offence that is significant. The censorious, illiberal reaction of the SRC has gone a long way towards ensuring a dull, uncontroversial University paper in an establishment already stifled by respectability and a decline in intellectual, student activity.[46]

The trouble with libertarianism is that its indiscriminate pluralism meant one could end up in such unsavory company – willingly, sometimes even enthusiastically.

Smilde's article slid from the substance of the debate into what the Push considered was the higher libertarian principle of free speech. The real villain, as most drinkers at the Royal George at the time would have volunteered, was not the Nazi Arthur Smith and his virulent anti-Semitism; it was not McDermott, whose uncritical publication of the Australian Nazis' platform was at best idiotically naive. It was the SRC, with its 'big budgets' and its 'good relations downtown.' Libertarians, above all, had to be consistent; if being consistent meant defending the publication of virulently anti-Semitic propaganda against the strictures of people with positions in the system, then so be it.

The defining feature of libertarianism, whether of left or right, is its opposition to authoritarianism. The gap is small between this and a belief in the fundamentally pernicious nature of institutions – any institution and all institutions. As one exponent succinctly put it, 'the mere fact of being in a position of power leads to interests which are authoritarian rather than libertarian.'[47] It is not too difficult to discern the parallels with the 'I love my country but I fear my government' sentiments of the right-wing militia in the

United States. Thus the left libertarians of the Push were propelled to defend the dissemination of fascist propaganda in *HONI*, all in the name of consistency.

Perhaps John Anderson was awake to this when he asserted, in effect, a hierarchy of oppositions in the 1950s as the Cold War deepened. Perhaps Anderson was more the practical politician than his erstwhile followers had given him credit for. Could this explain why, when fascism was the principal threat to freedom in the Western world, he ran with the Marxists, and when left totalitarianism appeared the bigger threat in the 1950s, he threw his lot in with the Cold Warriors?

The Sydney libertarians in fact covered the entire political spectrum. For every Roelof Smilde the Push produced a right-wing intellectual like Peter Coleman, who became a conservative MP; for every left activist like Liz Fell it produced a conservative commentator like Paddy McGuinness. A philosophy that can encompass positions so diametrically opposed is of questionable use as a political paradigm. It helps to explain why, through her thirty years in public life, Greer adopted such a strange amalgam of progressive and conservative positions. Far from being a matter of inconsistency, her stance was often a result of her adherence to anarchistic pessimism – to the libertarianism of the Push – which provided a framework within which seemingly contrary positions could have their own internal consistency.

If there was one fault Greer found equally in the young women and men she taught at Sydney, it was their blindness to irony. As she looked north to Cambridge, she could not have been aware of the overwhelming irony to come: that she would become a celebrity feminist, acclaimed by the media as the high priestess of the women's movement, without any visible previous shred of interest in women's issues. Apart from her native bolshie spirit, nothing about Greer hinted at what was ahead. She was still caught up in the dogma and masculinist vocabulary of Leavisism. She was still bound up in the essentially romantic moral revolt of the Push and of Byron – the latest manifestation of the heroic male for whom she had been waiting since her father left for the war. Byrony, indeed.

# 6

# *The Untamed Shrew*

The young and bright, the creative, the dissatisfied, the ambitious – they were leaving, or had already left. The Australian migration overseas to the great metropolis of London and, later, New York, had been a familiar phenomenon since the British had first arrived with their convict boats, and would continue to be a compulsory step for ambitious *culturati* for another generation. They left in dribs and drabs with occasional backward glances to those they left behind. There was then a feeling of inevitability behind the exodus, that Australia was on the outer rim of nowhere and that the cultural epicenter of Life was irrevocably Atlantic. Barry Humphries had left in 1959. The 1960s exodus included Richard Neville and Martin Sharp of *Oz*, Clive James, Robert Hughes and Jenny Kee.

Expatriation had long been part of the subtext of much Australian writing, and had sometimes figured centrally. It could prove an enriching and a dislocating experience – and not always an improving one. The central character in Jessica Anderson's *Tirra Lirra by the River*, for example, is Nora Porteous, living in 1940s London, who occasionally runs into other expats. They talk of the harbor, the sun, the cicadas and the plane trees in Macleay Street, Potts Point – and, always, of who was going and who was staying. Nora appropriates the saying of one who declared: 'If you stay more than five years you become a pommiefied Aussie, than which there is no more pitiful creature on God's earth. Unless it's an aussiefied Pom, and that's how you feel when you try to go back.' For some the issues were simpler, Nora observes, and more physical: 'England was a nasty dank little country, they said, where the people were unfriendly, the sky low, and life was a misery for all but the rich.'[1] Existing between two worlds, even the most cosmopolitan of cultural refugees found that something stubbornly Australian survived.

Germaine Greer left in 1964 in the most favorable of circumstances; the sky might have seemed lower in Britain, but in relative terms her destination was a place in the sun. Germaine's first-class MA had secured her a Commonwealth scholarship to finance further studies at Cambridge. She had chosen Cambridge over Oxford because Byron – 'he's always been one of my heroes' – had gone there, she told a reporter the following year: 'Besides, Oxford had sent Shelley down which I thought was maybe indicative of something.'[2] She went to Cambridge as an affiliated student, a classification allowing graduates to earn a Bachelor of Arts in two years. 'I thought the one I had probably wasn't good enough,' Greer recalled. 'I was completely wrong. Cambridge offered an inferior version of the same thing. After the first term, I realised they were not going to teach me anything so I transferred to the Ph.D. programme.'[3]

Unlike Sydney University, Cambridge exists in splendid isolation from enticing urban diversions, marooned in the flat windswept fenlands of East Anglia. Greer had gone from a campus where she could drive downtown to the Royal George in five minutes to one where London was an hour away by train, and longer by car. One's chosen college acquires extra importance in such a milieu. Greer's destination, Newnham, assumed a particular, positive significance only much later in her life. When she arrived in 1964, she found it more a place for her to wet-nurse less worldly undergraduates than a source of scholarly succour.

Newnham, the second women's college at Cambridge, was founded shortly after Girton, both manifestations of nineteenth-century efforts to breach the male bastions of academic privilege. Girton was founded by the early feminists Emily Davies and Barbara Leigh Smith, better known under her married name, Madame Bodichon. It was part of the broader push for women's rights led by Bodichon, a cousin of Florence Nightingale and close friend of George Eliot, who believed that women's employment could not progress unless their educational attainment matched that of men. By contrast, the driving force behind the establishment of Newnham was Henry Sidgwick, a Cambridge don. While Sidgwick's emphasis was on admitting women to special university courses, Emily Davies at Girton opposed any academic compromise. 'Like Lilia in Tennyson's "Princess,"' wrote one historian of Cambridge, 'she would have the girls at her proposed college learn "all that men are taught".'[4] Their courses and examinations were to be identical to those of the men. Not that either the Girton or the Newnham path led to women earning degrees at the time; not until 1921 were they awarded even titular degrees, and women were not admitted to full membership of the university until 1948.

Muriel Bradbrook, the major academic influence on Greer at Cambridge, had first-hand experience of this situation. Bradbrook was fifty-five years old, a Reader in English and Vice-Mistress of Girton when Germaine arrived from Sydney. The following year she was awarded a chair, and later she followed in Emily Davies's footsteps, becoming Mistress of Girton. The Glasgow-born Bradbrook had entered the college to read English in 1927; in 1930 she received a certificate stating she had done all that would have entitled her to graduate as a Bachelor of Arts, if she were a man. There was 'no procession to the Senate House, no family parties in the Yard.'[5] The university simply mailed her a degree certificate on which the word 'titular' had been inserted by hand.

When Bradbrook was an undergraduate, women had to follow Union debates from the gallery because membership was closed to them. Though the musical societies admitted women, the dramatic societies did not – even when Germaine arrived, Cambridge's famous Footlights Club was still a male preserve. Despite the presence of Bradbrook and her fellow female students, one don, Sir Arthur Quiller-Couch, insisted on addressing his audiences as 'Gentlemen,' and refused to accept women in his evening classes on Aristotle's *Poetics*. Bradbrook recounts that Quiller-Couch was furious to discover on one occasion he had inadvertently awarded the Chancellor's Medal for English Verse to a Newnham student, Elsie Phare.[6]

The women's colleges refused to allow such open hostility to undermine the quality of education received by their students. Bradbrook was taught practical criticism and the modern period by F. R. Leavis, who would ride over on his bicycle 'with unbuttoned shirt and a knapsack full of books' to an old army hut where the classes were held. She was twenty-seven and had already written three books when Girton elected her to a teaching fellowship in 1936.

Bradbrook was widely traveled, an enormous enthusiast and a gifted scholar. Under her influence Greer embraced Renaissance scholarship and decided on Shakespeare as the subject of her thesis. 'That was unusual,' she explained later. 'You're not encouraged to do doctoral dissertations on Shakespeare because it's so hard to write anything new. You are warned that you have little chance of passing.' Germaine's command of French, German and Italian enabled her to overcome doubts about the proposal, which involved comparing Shakespeare's early comedies with their contemporary continental counterparts. A young American scholar, Dr. Anne Righter – later Professor Anne Barton – was her supervisor.

Righter, six years older than Greer, had graduated *summa cum laude* from Bryn Mawr, had lectured in art history at Ithaca College in New York, and had been awarded a doctorate from Cambridge herself in 1960. She shared Greer's interest in opera, art and travel, and even Byron was common territory. In 1968 Righter delivered the Nottingham Byron Lecture on 'Byron and the Mythology of Fact,' in which she cited C. Wilson Knight's proposition that Byron was a man continually trying to exact from life itself the qualities of great poetry. 'This, I think, is true,' she said. 'Byron needed to mythologise fact.'[7] She later published a book on *Don Juan*.

In an interesting development from Greer's MA in Sydney on Byron's moral revolt, she chose as the subject for her thesis 'The Ethic of Love and Marriage in Shakespeare's Early Comedies.' Love, marriage and sex were continuing preoccupations in both her personal and academic arenas. In relation to her academic work, the choice was deliberate. In her personal life, it was partly a function of the fact that she had had far more experience of the world than the students with whom she was thrown together.

There were shades, too, of Greer's sexual coaching of fellow students in the Star of the Sea school library – a continuing manifestation of her self-appointed role as roving sexual lecturer-at-large. 'When I first went there I wanted to be politically active, and socially lively,' she said later of the university. 'It's neither of those things. . . . I was twenty-five when I came to Cambridge, and I wound up as the great sexual counsellor. I was dreadfully older. English sexuality gave me the heebie-jeebies.'[8]

The site for much of the counseling was Newnham, which emitted a mixed aroma of floor polish, books and damp walls.[9] Public debate on the position of women was beginning once again to stir the year after publication of Betty Friedan's influential book *The Feminine Mystique*.[10] At Newnham, with its bluestocking heritage, Greer might have found herself at the cutting edge of feminism's second wave, perhaps helping to sharpen it herself, but at Cambridge feminist consciousness still existed more at the level of individual dissatisfaction than of organized analysis or action. One Newnham student's diary for the summer of 1966 records her anger after opening a dinner invitation to Christ's College addressed to her partner, which included a sherry reception for guests with their wives: 'Wives in for sherry only. Furious with rage and disappointment. What are wives supposed to do while hubs guzzle? Wander into street in glad rags, slink away to lonely restaurant meals, return to their hotels unescorted?'[11]

The outrages of patriarchy notwithstanding, Greer spent her time advising fellow students on modern contraceptive methods and sexually transmitted diseases, as she described graphically in the first London edition of *Oz* magazine. Richard Neville, editor of *Oz*, had first encountered Germaine at a party in Sydney. 'Aha, a male nipple,' she had said, taking hold of one of Neville's, which was visible through his open Hawaiian shirt. Germaine was oblivious to their fellow party-goers' fascinated gaze. 'See how it grows? Just like a dick.' Neville winced with pain. 'Nipples are a mass of erectile tissues. . . . You should learn to masturbate all your male parts,'[12] Germaine continued authoritatively.

To Neville, Germaine seemed bored and lonely at Cambridge. In his counterculture memoir *Hippie Hippie Shake*, he describes a visit Germaine paid him and his partner, Louise Ferrier, in London.

Most respectable in a cashmere twinset, tartan skirt, pearls and beehive hairdo, she complained about the locals' strange sexual peccadilloes and inadequate hygiene.

'Filthy and smelly,' she said, referring to the state of undergraduate underwear, 'like old dish-cloths.' Their sexual habits were no more gratifying. 'When I told one suitor to extend his variation of intercourse beyond *coitus interruptus*, you know what he called me? A strumpet!' She giggled . . .

Why didn't she extend her horizons beyond the campus?

'Don't be silly, Richard. It's no different. The poms all try to look like Michael Caine but it's a con. They're either queer or kinky.' She recounted how one London Lothario had wanted to squeeze her blackheads; and another had declined an amorous engagement on the grounds he only liked flat chests.

The last bloke she had met not only failed to achieve an erection, but insisted on stroking her [abdominal] scar . . .

I asked Germaine to write about her exploits for *Oz*.

'I'd love to. I've already got a title – "In Bed with the English." ' She rubbed her hands together. 'Isn't it great? You know what the last pom said to me?' She looked to the heavens. ' "Let's pretend you're dead." '[13]

'In Bed with the English,' faithfully recounting these experiences and more, was published without a byline in February 1967.[14] 'Darling,' it began, as though a private letter written to an intimate, going on to say that the author would love to provide a 'straight-talking McCarthy-Brophy rundown' on the English male. The invitation to write the piece was a compliment to her energy, enterprise and catholicity of taste, she wrote, and normally she would have thrown herself into in-depth fieldwork for it, but a vow that she would never sleep with an Englishman stood in the way.

The situation, Greer wrote, was dictated by circumstances which would appal those who knew how passionately she opposed sexual possessiveness: 'In Cambridge, where I live, there are (reputedly) eight men to every woman. It seems the ideal spot for a devoted practitioner of the arts of love, for nearly all the men are in the full flower of their potency, being between the ages of eighteen and twenty-two. When I arrived I was elated at the vastness of the opportunity for proselytising.' But for six months after her arrival the closest she had got to sex, she wrote – apart from endless discussions about contraception and venereal disease – was observing a few old flashers, scrawny and scrofulous, who derived some satisfaction from 'exposing to me their genitals, pallid and bluish in the frosty air.'

'In those six months I altered my image violently and constantly,' she wrote, 'but no real change in my fortunes resulted. I settled down to being bottom-wiper and information service about contraception and venereal disease and matters of the heart generally, and transferred my sexual hopes to the metropolis.'

Yet the metropolis yielded no better prospects. An architect who lived in the Fulham Road 'Michael Cained all over the kitchen in his cunning barbeque apron,' lighting candles, plumping cushions, burning incense, playing records but failing to look at her. In desperation she considered stripping, only rejecting the idea because of her pedestrian St. Michael's underwear. After dinner he prepared the spare bed, ran her a bath, lent her his toiletries and only then, when she was nearly asleep, crept into bed next to her and said 'ciao.' She went to sleep and made sure she never saw him again. This was the first of many such experiences: 'He is not always an architect. Sometimes he is a lawyer or a fledgling lawyer, or a baby stockbroker, or an accountant or in advertising. He is always *very nice*. He has an ideal of nice, gentle, restful, *uncomplicated sex*.'

In search of a beddable Englishman, our Donna Juanita resorted to the gentry, lolling about, playing tennis and going to the races with 'clear-eyed heavy-limbed young gentlemen with a desperate tendency to bray down one's earhole the most malicious gossip heard anywhere, generally on the theme of the *parvenu*, or the designing female who seeks to marry into the death duties class.' Alone at the end of a dinner party where the other guests had melted away one by one – conspiratorially, she surmised – the old-school-tied host slipped off his shoes and socks and made a hearty play for her. Taking advantage of his bare feet, she charged outside, sprinting across lawns, through a hedge and on to the neighboring cricket ground, where they struggled on the pitch in the moonlight. She lost a £15 earring and bawled him out for lack of loyalty to the cricket club, leaving him smoothing the ravaged wicket remorsefully.

The seductress then forayed into 'the wilds of Bohemia,' but with no better result. Her first quarry possessed 'so greasy a pallet presided over by underpants of so implacably tertiary a colour that I excused myself hurriedly and left.' Her second insisted that she run her fingers lightly over his 'moonscape back,' barely touching the skin. An hour later she fled, still fully dressed, arms stiff, and jumped on a bus. Her vow to avoid Englishmen followed: 'Ask me about Italians, Persians, Arabs, West Indians, Jews from anywhere, Irishmen, Welshmen, Africans, men from anywhere else but England and you've got yourself an article, but about the English lover, as you see, I know nothing.'[15]

A tragi-comic romp studded with floridly abject male characters, the piece exemplified Greer's outstanding comic writing ability: unless you were an Englishman, it was hilarious. At least one Englishman did take personal umbrage. In the letters column of the next *Oz*, one Rod Lake challenged Greer to sample his sexual prowess if, he said, she had the nerve. Lake announced that he was standing up for his fellow countrymen and was willing to have his name used if he failed to provide complete sexual satisfaction. 'The poor woman that wrote it must be pretty ugly, or a raving Nympho,' he wrote, or be 'trying too hard.'[16] Greer accepted the challenge, while reserving her right to refuse consummation upon inspection. She and Neville met the ostensibly presentable Lake at a pub. In a tight sweater and dark perm, Germaine looked like an ice-cream dipped in chocolate, according to Neville; she clutched his arm and demurred when Lake suggested they get on with it and repair to his bedsitter.

The mixture of sexual braggadocio and reticence was a recurring contradiction. One member of the Sydney University theater scene remembers Greer creating an inviting climate for seduction, for example, but expecting him to take the initiative. In Clive James's memoir of Cambridge, the character Romaine Rand – a gossamer-thin cover for Greer – displays great verve for the chase, but hesitates on the brink of liaison. James recalls how, after becoming acquainted with 'Romaine' in the Push, he received word that she had made a bet with the others that she could seduce the virginal Clive within twenty-four hours. As she strode 'like a Homeric goddess' through the door of Sydney University's Manning House cafeteria, he escaped through the side entrance and hid behind a large gum tree: 'The rumour that I hid *up* the tree was false but slow to die.'[17] Later, when a more experienced James wanted to seduce 'Romaine,' his most strenuous efforts failed.

Greer herself has attributed this contradiction to her emotional insecurity and 1950s upbringing. 'I need a bit more reassurance before embarking on a sexual encounter,' she explained. 'There have been complaints that I very seldom made advances, even in a relationship. Men have to court me and make the running. I have never rung up a man in my life. I realise how absurd that is. . . . I give out availability signals but if they don't pick it up I don't go any further. I grew up at a time when most men, if you blew in their ear, would follow you anywhere.'[18]

Given its theme of love and marriage in Shakespeare's early comedies, Greer's doctoral thesis could hardly fail to reveal her underlying stance on relations with men shortly before she wrote *The Female Eunuch*. The territory she chose, if not the precise topic, followed directly in Muriel Bradbrook's wake. In a rich, half-century-long academic career, Bradbrook had specialized in Elizabethan drama: Raymond Williams described her work on the history and analysis of dramatic forms and the conditions of their performance as 'defining and pre-eminent.'[19] Bradbrook had broadened her focus in the decade before Greer's arrival at Cambridge, publishing *The Growth and Structure of Elizabethan Comedy* in 1955 and *The Rise of the Common Player* in 1962.[20] Bradbrook's work on comedy contributed to an emerging stage history that was moving away from an exclusive focus on the play as text toward a broader understanding of performance and its cultural context. In her work on Elizabethan drama, she emphasized the ties between Elizabethan playwriting and popular festivals and revels – a connection she perceived as particularly close in the case of comedy, with its roots in homily and balladry. The greatness of the plays written at the time, Bradbrook argued, lay in the momentary fusion of the popular and learned traditions. Yet, compared with tragedy and history, the comedies of the period had been neglected by critics and literary historians, perhaps partly because of overconcentration on the text. 'Such comedy should not be read in terms merely verbal,' according to Bradbrook, but rather should 'be imagined as a living, complex, transitory performance.'[21]

Greer's thesis dealt with four of Shakespeare's comedies – *The Two Gentlemen of Verona*, *The Comedy of Errors*, *The Taming of the Shrew* and *Love's Labour's Lost* – which she presented as examples of Shakespeare's greatness as an experimental writer. Germaine's certainty was evident from the outset, as was the eye-catching hook, the colorful allusion, to make her examiners once again sit up and take notice. The first page of the introduction included a reference to 'mass masturbation [and] sex murders by infantile maniacs' on stage as examples of modern playwrights' experimentation with the basic rules of theatrical experience.[22]

Greer's claims for the dissertation itself were modest: 'All that I have striven to establish is that for the Elizabethans the marriage motif was not a commonplace, and above all that Shakespeare's interest in it was questing and intelligent. In the early comedies the relationships of lovers are explored deeply and imaginatively, in a way that cannot be explained by reference to established convention.'[23] This was certainly true, but there were signs that the journeying toward this conclusion had been more interesting, if wayward, than its endpoint suggested.

In the preface Greer thanked Professor Bradbrook for her great learning and unfailing enthusiasm with 'embryo Renaissance scholars' like herself, but her deepest thanks went to Dr. Righter for her 'gentle rigour.'[24] Greer had written thousands of words about the plays' cultural context, but had jettisoned most of them before the thesis was submitted. Dr. Righter, she said, had 'struggl[ed] through reams of ill-typed and presumptuous cultural anthropology, religious apologetics, and legal history, steadying my more riotous certainties, and perhaps she regrets more than I do that all that remains of it in this typescript is a bare page as well as a few hints in the Introductory section.'[25]

When Greer had asked the demographic historians what was known about the Elizabethan household, they 'gave me the choice of examining parish registers in remote districts for an indefinite period, until the computers should enable me to infer anything at all, and minding my own litterateur's business.' She had spent a great deal of time reading books printed in English in Shakespeare's lifetime, arguing that all were relevant when it came to recreating the intellectual climate. Her reading, however, was not exhaustive and might have been haphazard, she conceded, pleading she was 'at the mercy of capricious fate and the Elizabethan book-trade.'[26] As bids for examiners' sympathy go, it was tenuous. From a point of view strictly concerned with the doctoral candidacy, the disclaimer disclosed that a dreadful amount of time had been wasted.

Greer was on her firmest ground in evaluating the plays themselves, dismissing their relationship to continental models and emphasizing the originality of Shakespeare's formulations. Comedy affirms the logic of our existence, confirms us in the belief that all is for the best, she wrote. It induces satisfaction by exciting desires that it alone can gratify: 'Time and experience have proved that the most effective way of doing this is to create two people obviously meant for each other, and to bring them together after the pleasurable tension of confusions and delays. . . . It proves to be one of the most soothing and salutary gratifications fiction has to offer, the vicarious pleasure of watching the triumph of true love, even when it is insipid and especially when it is not.'[27]

She dismissed social history's contribution to understanding Shakespeare's concept of 'wedded love.' Shakespeare, she believed, was interested in 'love within society, not destructive passion, which must be . . . ritualised.'[28] The context was a new and more exalted attitude toward marriage than was taught by the Puritans and other reformers. It was a cause espoused in reaction to the champions of monasticism, who vilified marriage and put the married faithful in a state of guilt and fear. Greer noted in passing that Augustine and his fellow church fathers had taught that the married state, while not sinful in itself, was rarely free from sin. The church still taught that 'married folk enjoy one-third of the privileges of virgins in heaven,' she added, drawing on her first-hand experience of Catholicism.[29]

For Greer, coming from a Sydney milieu where marriage was considered the ultimate in reactionary retreat, it was a novel thing to contemplate it as a quasi-revolutionary cause in Elizabethan times. 'On the lips of Protestant martyrs,' she wrote, 'it became a part of the new mythology: Robert Barnes prayed to the boy king from the scaffold, "that he wyl se that matrymony be had in more reuerence than yt is, and that men . . . cast not of theyr wyues and lyue in auoutry and fornycacio."' Another manifestation of the crusading spirit was to be found in the 'frequently hyperbolic and irrational eulogies of marriage, which point forward to the development of the myth of living happily ever after' – for which she said the Elizabethans could not be blamed.[30]

Greer was circumspect about wading into the realms of social theory. 'At this stage in historico-sociological studies,' she wrote, 'it is impossible to give any accurate account of the ideology of marriage and its relation to general practice.' Although the rise of the modern nuclear family was associated with the decay of the feudal system, 'the change in ideology lagged far behind the event.' There was much more evidence of an intellectual ferment about marriage in the sixteenth century, she said, particularly in relation to legal and liturgical reform, 'but as it is beyond the scope of this study, and I am unskilled to interpret it, it must await another time, and probably another hand.'[31] As it turned out, however, Greer almost immediately cast aside her own doubts about her capacity for sociological analysis. She wrote *The Female Eunuch* just two years later.

Greer's treatment of *The Taming of the Shrew* is most interesting in this light. She saw the play's central concern as 'the equilibrium which must be established between man and wife, and the earning of love and loyalty within marriage considered as a *fait accompli*.'[32] The plot is recounted skilfully, and at length. Katherine, or Kate, is Shakespeare's shrew, Petruchio the character he created to tame her. Kate's fractiousness has succeeded in rendering her unsaleable as a wife: another character, Gremio, describes her as a fiend of hell. Yet from the outset Petruchio refuses to take her brawling seriously. 'When other men pale before her ineffectual rages,' the thesis recounts, 'Petruchio confidently expects to be able to ignore them: in describing them in terms of all the furies of nature, he suggests by contrast the real frailty of the single woman, and makes it clear that the battleground is his element. He speaks of her as of a worthy opponent whom he wishes to grapple with himself.'[33]

Petruchio's strategy is to baffle Kate, inducing her to shift ground by treating her as though she were behaving the way he would like her to be, rather than as her rages dictate. 'He will treat her well when she patently does not deserve it, so that the violent resentment that poisons her relationships may dissipate in wonderment and, eventually, trust,' Greer wrote. Kate finds herself 'cornered in embarrassing equivocations, which underline her sexual role. She reacts with childish violence, with blows and insults, but bit by bit, Petruchio gains the upper hand.'[34]

Bradbrook had published a journal article in 1958 on the play, locating the shrew in the general medieval tradition of bourgeois satire as well as folk tales.[35] She pointed out that according to tradition the shrew, the scolding woman, triumphed; if she was overcome, it was via theological argument or violence. With Petruchio and Kate, Shakespeare gave the traditional plot a novel twist. In conjunction with demonstrations of his 'natural' authority, Petruchio overpowers Kate by turning her own weapons – imperiousness, wildness, inconsistency and the withholding of the necessities of life, as Bradbrook described them – back on her. Kate is also the first in the shrew tradition, she observed, 'to be given a father, the first to be shewn as maid and bride; she is not seen merely in relation to a husband.'[36]

Feminists would later claim the term for their own purposes, based on a different interpretation altogether of the shrew's spirited resistance. In the 1970s a feminist journal in Australia even took *Shrew* as its name.

Greer followed Bradbrook down the path of the shrew tradition with an analysis she would shortly deploy in relation to modern marriage in *The Female Eunuch*. The archetypal shrew who reduced her husband to misery and penury, she explained, started out as a gay, brave and modest bride; her shrewish tendencies emerged as she began to exercise her will, 'even using the marriage bed as a pawn in her sordid bargaining with her husband.' This shrewishness, she wrote, was 'a cool prosecution of the battle of the sexes with neither pity nor respect for the opponent.' Such women were 'deeply and irrevocably self-interested, and always get their own way, using charms, threats, peevishness and violence indiscriminately: against this type there is no defence.' Conversely, Shakespeare's shrew, Kate, is 'energetic, full of fierce loyalties, and not at all dangerous to the man who knows how to profit by her extraordinary qualities.'[37] The most striking aspect of Greer's treatment of *The Taming of the Shrew*, the very heart of her thesis, is the almost total absence of feminist consciousness. Greer is generally careful not to endorse Petruchio's calculated 'taming' explicitly, nor to identify herself totally with Kate's ultimate point of view. One caution, for example, is a reference to 'what appeared to be a self-evident doctrine' to Kate, 'especially in the days of high mortality of infants and mothers, that women are the weaker sex, and need and want their husband's aid and protection.'[38] Such caveats, however, are few and far between, and in this case the qualification is followed by what could be read as an implicit endorsement of Kate's submission. Greer goes on to write that a husband's aid and protection cannot be won unless a wife acts in a way that encourages it: 'It is useless to resent dependence because women are incapable of attaining or enjoying independence: the extent to which they desire illusory freedom is the index of the extent to which they are incapable of achieving it.' Kate understands 'at last that her passionate pride was really the product of her fear and sense of inferiority, as we have already decided from an independent assessment of her behaviour.'[39]

The feminist reader encounters the uncomfortable possibility that Greer thought shrew-taming in the style of Petruchio and Kate could lead to happiness for women. That conclusion becomes harder to avoid as the examples of implicit sympathy for Shakespeare's plot mount:

> Marriage offered by Petruchio is a challenge, and an emancipation from an intolerable situation. Kate may take it without losing face. Petruchio brings her like a nervous colt to his side with caresses and cherishings, and then calms her girlish panic with a clear and uncompromising statement of his intentions, to which his wild-cat can find no smart rejoinder.
>
> For I am he am born to tame you, Kate, (II.i.270),
>
> rings like the greatest compliment he could pay her, and shows her a way to end her fruitless revolt; Petruchio vaunts like some hero who must ride a horse never before mastered, or draw an enchanted sword out of a rock.[40]

Shakespeare enacted in the play 'the new principle that a man gets the wife he deserves'; producers who highlight the slap and tickle 'have misunderstood the whole principle of Petruchio's taming, for nowhere is he required to offer Kate the least violence.'[41] Greer does not mention Petruchio's cunning subterfuge and conscious manipulation of Kate in the interests of achieving submission. To her, what set the play apart from the shrew tradition was that Kate had been 'persuaded to *want* to place her hand below [Petruchio's] foot,' symbolizing her surrender.[42] 'Surely, in the age that boasts Simone de Beauvoir, Mary McCarthy and Brigid Brophy, we cannot assume that the lesson of the play is so well-learned that there is no further need to teach it!'[43] And again: 'It is useless to repine at the ethics of Katherine's marriage; they are only too straightforward and clean.'[44]

Can Greer's apparent sympathy for Petruchio's scheme and Kate's submission be rationalized on historical grounds – that Greer believed it represented a better deal for women than others on offer in Shakespeare's time? Apparently not. Greer writes: 'There is hardly a woman alive who is not deeply attracted to the notion of a husband of the kind extolled by Kate: the difficulty is to find a man capable of assuming all this responsibility and exercising this kind of sexual and domestic dominion.'[45] How could it be? Why would Greer – highly intelligent, worldly, striking, striving – why would she of all people condone without disclaimer women's longing for men who are capable of exercising dominion over them?

An episode during the final stages of her work on the thesis highlights Greer's deep-seated passivity at the time, an almost perverse unwillingness to confront male abuse of power. She mentions it in passing as part of her account of the summer of 1967 when she went to a poor village in Southern Italy to polish the draft of her thesis.[46] Greer had arranged to meet her lover Emilio, a budding architect studying in Venice, and go south, but when she arrived in Venice to join him she found that he had fallen out of love with her. Stunned that this could have happened in her absence, she refused his hospitality and left on the next train down the Adriatic coast.

Emilio had arranged for the father of one of his friends to meet her at the other end. Greer did not care for the modern lodgings that had been organized, so she and Emilio's friend's father jammed back into his Fiat *cinquecento* and went looking for something she liked better. Every so often the man would groan and thrust his hand between her legs:

> For three days we searched, tears dripping off my face as I sat there, helpless, with the fat old man's hand between my thighs, unable to repulse him with sufficient violence because in my estimation the offence did not warrant real ferocity, although it compounded my desolation dreadfully. Besides, the old man was my only hope of finding anywhere to live, for I had neither licence nor sufficient money to hire a car of my own, supposing such a thing was to be had.[47]

It is difficult to imagine how a woman of even mild survival instincts, let alone feminist consciousness, could remain passive for so long in this situation, particularly when practical alternatives were at hand. Greer's Italian was good and she was an experienced traveler. She had at least a little money: she could have taken a train, or hitched a ride, somewhere else – to Rome, to Venice or even back to Cambridge. She could have sought help from other travelers, fellow students, or even from some of the counterculture tribe already wandering the continent. Consular assistance would not have been out of the question. There was, too, the option of reciprocation: planting her hand between *his* legs a few times, hard, fist clenched. She was articulate, capable, educated, experienced, multilingual, physically strapping, and yet apparently unable to deal with repeated sexual assault of a petty, sordid kind over three days in a car with a fat old man. What strange sense of justice made her decide, as tears streamed down her face, that 'the offence did not warrant real ferocity'? If not ferocity, why not, say, withdrawal from the situation?

Germaine was twenty-eight years old at the time. A couple of years earlier Nathan Silver, a young American teaching architecture at Cambridge when Greer was doing her doctorate, had already sensed a kind of impending doom in her. Silver had seen her perform in Footlights and was impressed. She was brilliant, witty, special, Nathan recalls, and very attractive. Combined with her naturally striking demeanor, Footlights had made her a notable figure on campus within a year of her arrival. Briefly, they were lovers.

Greer was billed as the first woman to achieve full membership of the previously all-male institution as a cast member of its 1965 revue, *My Girl Herbert*, which toured from Cambridge to Oxford, Bury St. Edmunds, Newark and Worcester before a three-week run at Hammersmith's Lyric Theatre. A former Newnham student had paved the way: the actress Eleanor Bron, who appeared in Footlights in the late 1950s.[48] Greer was compared to her in reviews of *My Girl Herbert* – 'that bit about me being a cross between Bron and Grenfell is FANTASTIC,' the *Sydney Morning Herald*'s London staff correspondent reported her enthusing.[49] In the same article a Sydney friend described Greer as a contemporary eccentric who 'will probably be to our generation what Isadora Duncan and Edith Sitwell were to theirs.' Not quite.

Greer had been invited to join Footlights after contributing a skit about what the English expected of expatriate Australians: 'The Australian is expected to bathe regularly several times a day, carolling loud snatches of "Tie Me Kangaroo Down Sport" and after bathing to spray on a large cloud of "Celui d'Herb Elliot" – our own special brand of four-minute sweat.'[50] Television offers followed the success of the Footlights revue – offers she would not accept, she said, if they interfered with her studies. Acting had to be in her spare time, for pin-money, since her ultimate ambition was to return to Australia and teach at the university. In her view, she was a better critic than creator anyway: 'I go on acting at the moment because I enjoy it. . . . I can't stop, in fact.' As one of the 'personalities' of Cambridge, she was never short of party invitations. 'Sometimes it's quite sickening,' Germaine told the *Herald*, 'realising you've been asked because of who you are rather than what you are.'[51]

In her memoir of undergraduate life, Eleanor Bron captured the Cambridge experience for many students at the time, at a particularly open moment of their lives, 'momentarily poised like passengers in an unusually well-appointed transit lounge.'[52] It had made her unfit to live with her family any more. 'I was too clever, my new friends were too clever,' Bron wrote. 'Even now I suspect that Cambridge has left me with, or encouraged, a drive towards cleverness for its own sake which is as difficult to throw off as a nervous tic. . . . My broadened mind could scarcely squeeze between the door-jambs.'[53] The same kind of intellectual immodesty endured with Greer. Nearly twenty years later, she described the awarding of her Ph.D. as 'possibly the only doctorate they have given for Shakespeare since the war. I'm not a little proud of it. Among the people who count, other Shakespearean scholars, I'm respected. It's just that I haven't written anything about Shakespeare for a long time.'[54]

In the preface to her doctorate, she had not hidden the fact that crafting her thesis from an inchoate mass of research had been a struggle; a sense of honest, if disorganized, intellectual toil induced by the scholarly strictures of the Bradbrooks and Righters of Cambridge, comes across clearly. More seductive influences, however, were at work: the notoriety, even the fame of Footlights, and the social popularity and reinforcement flowing from it. Greer had, in a small way, already become a star – and being even a small star in a place like Cambridge presaged the possibility of becoming a star in the greater world. What were the odds that intellectual rigor would win out over the lure of theatrical limelight, the media spotlight, and invitations to provide the provocative and seemingly authoritative, headline-grabbing quote?

The sense of impending doom Nathan Silver perceived in Greer was based on his feeling that she was more likely to be confined to the library than to secure a spot in the limelight. She was brilliant, witty and a thespian hit, yet to him Germaine still seemed quite unformed. Though she was approaching thirty, she was still caught in the transitional life of a graduate student, the cannon-fodder of the academy. Silver believed that Germaine's particular social and intellectual skills were specially geared to academic life – Cambridge's in particular – rather than to the outside world. Her 'worryingly open personality,' her lack of guile, made him doubt that she would cut it outside Cambridge's protective confines. Germaine was so forthcoming, so giving, according to Silver, that she was unusually receptive to other people: 'She would respond to everybody in their own terms in a way that generally happens with only weak people.' What happened next was crucial in ensuring that the limelight overwhelmed the library, overtaking academe, as Greer's primary sphere of activity for years to come.

When her doctorate was formally granted on 7 May 1968, the streets of Paris were seething with the students' revolt. At the graduation ceremony, Germaine conducted her own revolution

Cambridge-style by wearing an extreme mini-dress and black stockings with her academic gown. 'She looked fabulous,' Silver recalls. 'She looked like she wasn't wearing anything but sort of translucent tights under her gown, which was probably the case, actually. She looked great.'

Greer had already accepted an assistant lectureship in English at the University of Warwick, and had moved to Leamington Spa. 'I didn't belong anywhere,' she recalled later. 'I was miserable.'[55] She rented a bedsitter from a doctor who would not allow her to use her own furniture. One of the 'senior people' at the university took an interest in her: 'Not a very noble or elevated interest. I tried to set him up so I could blackmail him. I arranged to have one of my students catch him in my room. It passed the time. I think he knew what was going on.'[56] Life was only made bearable by her intense involvement in the process of teaching and by regular forays to London.

Walking through Portobello Road Market one Saturday morning, during a trip to London, Germaine was hailed by a friend, Derek Brook, who was lounging outside Finch's pub drinking with a man named Paul du Feu. Du Feu was intrigued by this tall stranger with 'frizzed-out soul-sister hair' who strode down the middle of the road like a gunslinger. Greer gave Brook an update on her progress – Byron was by-the-by, Shakespeare was her current interest and she had just delivered a doctoral thesis on his work. Then, du Feu recalls in his own detailed account of their relationship, Germaine launched into a monologue about 'a slip of a boy who had had the effrontery to lure her into a love affair and then knock her back, and how she needed to get well fucked to restore her normal mental clarity.'

Brook seemed to have heard it all before and turned to talk to another pavement drinker. At this point, du Feu wrote, 'Germaine's bold gaze zeroed in on me.'[57]

Taking du Feu's glass of Guinness from his hand and sipping it, Greer announced she had changed her mind about not having a drink and asked for a half-pint of the same. By the time du Feu returned with the Guinness, he perceived a marked change in body language: Germaine had adopted the relaxed but purposeful stance of someone receptive to getting 'laid.' After a couple more comments about the allegedly therapeutic properties of sex, she reached out and stroked his cheek, telling him he had an odd sort of beauty. Du Feu loved it. He was wearing work boots and concrete-spattered jeans, his skin weathered from working outdoors: he was the heterosexual equivalent of a rough trade fantasy come true. Du Feu made his living as a building worker; he was renovating a couple of houses in Derek Brook's street at the time. Germaine did not find out until later that he was also an occasional columnist and comic-strip writer with a good degree in English Literature himself. The heavy-drinking building worker, a few years older than her, was a man of words as well as work boots.

'What I saw was a strong, intelligent face under a halo of light brown hair,' du Feu said in an account reminiscent of Jennifer Dabbs's description of the schoolgirl Germaine, her tawny hair standing out around her head 'like a nimbus.' Du Feu observed a crackling energy in her, breaking through a 'patina of weariness':

> Changes of mood and feeling were vividly conveyed by slight shifts of expression. Like a face in a movie close-up. Her dress was a mixture of non-fashionable and hip. Above the waist she was hip, with a narrow-shouldered jacket and skinny sweater pulling up from her high waist. From the hips down, she wasn't hip. Her long legs were covered to the knee by a loose woollen skirt that would have been suitable attire for a middle-aged stallholder at a provincial church bazaar. Only the broad sexy hips *under* the skirt would have stirred a lot of un-devout lust at a church bazaar or anywhere else. Just then they were stirring a lot of lust in me.[58]

When last drinks were called, du Feu invited her to come to Brook's house for another one. She declined, citing an invitation to take tea with a member of the aristocracy that afternoon in Blenheim Crescent, not far away, but agreed to drop by Brook's place afterward.

By the time she arrived the sexual sparks flying outside Finch's pub had been extinguished by the torpid Saturday-afternoon atmosphere in Brook's living room. Germaine broke the impasse by picking up Brook's cat and pronouncing in detail on the finer points of feline copulation. Du Feu took the hint and, turning down an invitation to stay for dinner, repaired to drink whisky and Guinness chasers with her at a down-at-heel Notting Hill Gate pub.

They matched drink for drink the rest of the evening: 'Germaine talked and clowned and enchanted me. Christ, it's great to meet someone who entertains and gets you horny as hell.'[59]

They retired to Paul's dilapidated flat in Maryland Road, made love and talked, slept and then woke early to begin all over again. Germaine asked for a cup of tea; du Feu 'agreed in principle,' but got sidetracked. She asked for tea again, but again he got sidetracked. 'As I stretched back glowing, euphoric ... she propped herself up on an elbow, glared at me with her tough-guy expression and said, "Listen sport, I've asked twice for a cup of tea and all that happened was I got fucked. D'you reckon if I asked for a fuck I'd get a cup of tea?"'[60]

After the tea, they bought the Sunday papers and went to the local coffee shop for breakfast. Germaine provided an acid running commentary on the *Sunday Times* while du Feu dreamily ignored the *Observer* in front of him. 'The spring sunshine was shining in full on her face, highlighting the extraordinary beauty of her brows and cheekbones and nose as her head tilted and pivoted,' he recalled. 'At one moment she was pure pre-Raphaelite beauty – then a flick of her head transformed her into the wisecracking heroine of a thirties Hollywood comedy. . . . That morning I saw a brave and clever woman. I fell profoundly in love with her before I had finished my eggs, bacon, fried tomatoes and fried slice.'[61]

Germaine's line in loving breakfast patter was unusual. She commented first on du Feu's false teeth, asking whether they fitted badly and advising him to get new ones because of the way he favored one side of his mouth when he chewed; then she asked whether he knew he was suffering *arcus senilis*, revealed by the pale rim around his pupils and normally found in men of sixty or seventy. Paul told her he was hoping to keep his age a secret. He asked her to dinner at Brook's house that night. She had to return to Warwick that day, she said, but she could return on the train by eight to join him for dinner if he liked. A 200-mile round trip, it was evidence of interest, indeed.

Greer spent the following week working at Warwick. Du Feu discovered that over the weekend she had sounded out Derek Brook, asking him what du Feu was like, what he was *really* like. For his part, du Feu was nervous about plunging so deeply in love.

To prove to himself he was still in control of his feelings, he arranged to meet her at Finch's on Saturday, though she would arrive in London on Friday evening. At the appointed time he waited nervously for her to show up, scanning the street outside the pub. When she arrived they were shy with each other, but it turned into another 'sweet weekend.' Du Feu told Greer of his plans to take a working holiday cutting cane in Cuba; she sniffed that he was going to desert her already. Then, when he spontaneously canceled the booking during the week, she told him he should have stuck to his plan.

The next weekend he went to Warwick at Greer's invitation – the first of their disasters. She held a party for her students in the hunting lodge of the Earl of Warwick's estate. It rained, it was cold and the spit-roasted sucking pig was half-cooked; du Feu felt excluded as Germaine 'flirted around her students' and arranged for him to sleep the night on the floor of an undergraduate's bedsit while she counseled a suicidal young woman. At the party, du Feu had got 'drunk and mean.'

Greer asked what right he had to expect her to pay attention to him, and followed the challenge with a provocative: 'You're not going to put a band of gold round my finger, are you?' Paul thought about it for the rest of the week. When she returned to his flat the following Friday, he asked her to marry him. 'She wanted time to think. We'd made love and sipped scotch and talked the night away.... By the next morning, she had it clear. "You'll have to persuade me," she had said as we walked hand in hand along the shabby pavement.'[62]

Had du Feu known his Shakespeare better, or been to Cambridge University Library to read Greer's unpublished thesis, the challenge to 'persuade' her may have had greater resonance – or even sounded the alarm. At one point before the marriage she told du Feu he should read *The Taming of the Shrew* 'to pick up hints on how to deal with her.'[63] Foolishly, he did not bother re-reading it, he said later, because he had not particularly enjoyed it as a play. How much would he enjoy it as the model for their marriage? Germaine was casting Paul as Petruchio, playing to her Kate. He was being invited to a contest for domination – a contest that, for her to achieve happiness, he had to win. Du Feu had to win her submission by turning Greer's own qualities against her. It was a bizarre experiment in applying art to life, with consequences neither could foresee – not Germaine because, even though it was her experiment, experimental outcomes are never certain, nor Paul, who was unaware that an experiment was even being conducted.

Greer and du Feu went into a bar and ordered Guinness, which he arranged to be replenished at a steady rate. The Irish publican and the barmaid got involved in their discussion of marriage, urging Germaine to agree. For five drinks du Feu says he failed to rise to any of her baits – temporarily, unconsciously, deploying Petruchio's successful stratagem. 'I didn't feel like arguing that morning,' he wrote later. 'I just kept looking at her and loving her. Her face was fine drawn with controlled weariness.' Suddenly, she took his hand, kissed him and pronounced: 'I marry you.' Thus, they were married according to the old Anglo-Saxon law, joining hands in front of witnesses – the publican and the barmaid. The marriage was to be legally confirmed several days later, but in the meantime a mixture of elation and butterflies sent her into a state of high agitation.

Nathan Silver, himself recently married, was in London eating with his wife at a restaurant in the King's Road when Greer unexpectedly appeared and announced *she* was getting married. 'We were thunderstruck and said: Well, that's fantastic,' recalls Silver. 'She was obviously mad about this guy. We said, we have to meet him!' Then, the night before the wedding, a sobbing Germaine rang Richard Neville and told him what was to happen the next day. Neville asked if she was ill. Did she have a fever? Who was the guy? 'You don't know him,' she said; no one knew him, and no guests were being invited to the ceremony. She said she just had to tell someone. Neville tried unsuccessfully to get her to come over to his place. 'He's wild, he's wonderful,' she said of her betrothed before ringing off, still in tears.[64]

The wedding was at Paddington Register Office. It was a Thursday: Friday was out because Greer had an examiners' meeting at Warwick, and on Saturday the register office was fully booked. It was 1968, the climax of 1960s youth radicalism, perhaps the year least likely for someone like Greer – still a Push libertarian, who would shortly emerge as a counterculture figure as well – to commit herself to so conservative an institution as marriage. The £5 wedding ring was bought from the local pawnshop and given to du Feu's flat-mate, who was best man. When they were ushered in for the ceremony, the registrar remembered marrying du Feu for the first time twelve years earlier and insensitively asked him what had gone wrong. After the formalities were over, he wished him better luck this time.

They went for a wedding drink at the Dennis Club in Paddington, and abandoned their plans for a picnic in Hyde Park once they had settled into some serious drinking. Paul took exception when Germaine accepted an invitation to dance from one of the lesbians who hung out in the Dennis in the afternoons, prompting Germaine to rebuke him for high-handedness. 'Germaine was already straining at the bonds of matrimony and we were only two hours into it,' du Feu wrote. 'I was getting edgy by the time she caught an evening train back to Warwick.'[65]

She returned to London for the weekend, and they had another fight over lunch on Saturday with friends at an Italian restaurant in Pimlico. Greer charmed the Italian waiter, chose the wine and generally got up Paul's nose: 'She came on at the waiter like a Via Venetia bar girl owing the rent on a wet night, and terrified the fellow.'[66] Greer attacked du Feu's possessiveness. The row escalated when they met some other friends later that day: the angrier he got the more he drank, and the more he drank the angrier he got. Saturday ended with him telling Germaine to 'fuck off.' He stormed off to bed and she slept on the living-room floor.

Du Feu had a drinking problem, and Greer was keeping pace with him. 'She wasn't really in control much more than I was,' he said later; she may not even have been aware of the damage her 'viperish tongue' was doing.[67] He realized later, too, that he had underestimated the strength of her opposition to the institution of marriage. He had assumed she would wear her beliefs as lightly as other anarchist and assorted lefty friends of his who believed property was theft, for example, while acquiring houses and carefully monitoring the district's rate of capital appreciation.

Ignorant of the Petruchian strategy he was expected to use in response to Greer's petty provocations, du Feu felt he had been consigned the role of Patient Griselda from Chaucer's 'Clerkes Tale' – the poor, patient wife whose love is tested to the limits of her 'superhuman tolerance of bullshit.' The jousting had begun as soon as they had agreed to marry.

> She told me she had a standing engagement to go to a weekend party at Cambridge with some high-class people like architects (wow!). Obviously I could not be introduced to such exalted company, but she would go alone rather than break the date. She explained that at these weekend parties sooner or later drugs were often smoked (sensation!), and that while in the grip of *Reefer Madness* guests often indulged in uninhibited sexual congress, sometimes on a hearth rug in front of an open fire! (I'd been looking for that sort of dope for ten years.)
>
> I was also told that I must not be jealous or possessive. . . . I struggled to be tolerant and unpossessive but, of course, I WAS jealous and possessive and Germaine's posturing sickened me. . . . She told me she would like to have two or three children by different fathers (but none by me). . . .
>
> I had noted that her actions did not always tally with her flamboyant words. But her flash talk did upset me. For Christ's sake, I was in love with her. I was drinking more than usual, which meant I was drinking a lot. The anger and aggression I forced down when I was sober often spilled out when I was drunk. And when that happened, Germaine was always ready to add a well-phrased sanctimonious pacifist condemnation of the aggression she had provoked.[68]

One instance particularly riled du Feu. One of his friends, Michael Durnin, was being terrorized by a violent paranoiac whose estranged girlfriend had taken refuge at Durnin's. The man had chopped in a door with an axe trying to get to the woman at a previous address, and now, wrongly believing she was still at Durnin's, he kept ringing, saying he was coming round to get her.

Durnin, who was semi-invalided with kidney disease, called du Feu for help. When the stalker next rang, du Feu told him in colorful terms to come round – that Durnin had help. The stalker finally turned up at midnight, and du Feu chased him down Durnin's street wielding a wheel brace, only to fall into the stalker's diabolical trap. A police car's lights flicked on during the chase. Du Feu was arrested, charged with attempted grievous bodily harm and possession of an offensive weapon. Germaine was away at the time. When they spoke by phone nearly a day after the event, her reaction was, 'You fool. . . . Couldn't you have used your fists?' He could not be bothered trying to explain: 'She sounded like something out of *Tom Brown's Schooldays*, a prim pedagogue preaching muscular Christianity.'[69] To du Feu the episode illustrated a point Greer often made – that they came from different worlds.

One week she asked, in an ironic tone, if she was allowed to take tea with Lord Brooke at Warwick Castle. Du Feu responded, with equal irony, that tea seemed harmless; their conversation was beginning to sound like the 'crummy double entendres of a Restoration comedy,' he noted bitterly to himself. Greer then announced that du Feu had one advantage over Lord Brooke: the latter had never been to university. Du Feu was astounded by her 'elitist bullshit. . . . [It] had never occurred to me that my tertiary education redressed the disadvantage of my plebeian lineage. I don't think she realised how badly the concern for the niceties of social status she revealed squared with the anarchistic egalitarian creed she preached.'[70] A touch of Reg Greer's snobbery was beginning to show.

Given the short time Germaine and Paul were married, it was extraordinary how much conflict, active and passive, they managed to pack in. Du Feu went to Leamington Spa one weekend; Greer could not come down to London because she had exam papers to mark. They had a quiet evening: Germaine cooked steak and chips for dinner, they drank whiskey, and Germaine talked about the university. They went to bed, 'made love a little,' and then Germaine got out of bed to mark more exam papers. She spent the next day marking as well, and du Feu resolved not to go there again. He caught the train back to London, took a cab to a girlfriend's house in South Kensington, tucked into the bourbon and talked and made love with her the rest of the night: 'By the morning my depression had vanished.'[71]

Still, du Feu had not fallen out of love with his wife. She had told him she liked cooking and needed a kitchen as well as a stereo for listening to choral music. He rented a basement flat in Shepherd's Bush from a friend called Mortiboy. It was run-down but had a large garden; Paul reckoned he could fix it up in a few weeks. He arranged a few civilizing touches before Greer's first – and, as it turned out, last – stay. Flowers and a few vases were bought, along with new cooking and eating utensils. The fridge was stocked up. Derek Brook had been dispatched to choose a stereo system.

'I felt full of love for her as she stalked toward me along the platform at Euston Station,' du Feu recalls. Within two meters of him, however, she launched into a monologue about a faculty argument in which she was involved. It was punctuated, he says, by a brief kiss as they collided, and resumed without relief for the fifteen-minute taxi ride to Shepherd's Bush. When Paul pointed out it was not the subject closest to his heart, she rounded on him and accused him of heartlessness about the students whose fate hinged on the argument. The atmosphere was soured before they had even entered the flat.

Germaine sniffed disparagingly and told him he was paying too much for the flat. When she said she paid less than half the Shepherd's Bush rent for her place in Leamington Spa, Paul tried to point out that rents in Leamington were hardly on a par with central London. 'We rowed and got drunk till Monday morning, when I asked her to make me a cup of tea and use the fucking kitchen she had demanded,' du Feu wrote ruefully. 'She had been awake long before me and already done half a bottle of whiskey. She angrily refused to be made a domestic slave, packed her Gladstone and left for ever.'[72] He saw Greer three months later and asked her to try again, but she refused, telling him yet again that they came from different worlds. Du Feu concluded that she was right.

# 7

# *Catholicism and Counterculture*

'Caveat emptor' should have been printed on the top of the marriage certificate that Greer and du Feu signed at the register office that day in 1968. Paul decided he and Germaine were a couple of 'silly ninnies' who should never have married, but that was after the event. The mutual attraction was intense, and marriage, particularly for an anarchist, is a significant step. Just what this sweet-and-sour romantic melodrama signified to her, Greer refused to say. Though she has systematically mined the rest of her life experience for examples and anecdotes in three decades of book writing and journalism, her marriage has gone unanalyzed.

When Nathan Silver ran into Germaine a couple of months after the split she told him she had left du Feu because she had spent so much of the marriage crying, that she was crying all the time: 'He was treating me so badly, and I couldn't understand why he was so monstrous to me. I wasn't allowed to do anything.' Questions from outsiders, though, met deep resistance. Here was the dark heart of her internalized contradiction about relations between women and men. Rather than admitting it, exploring it and trying to draw lessons from it, she largely succeeded in surrounding the marriage with a wall of silence against which questioners tapped in vain.

A journalist from the *Australian Women's Weekly* received the full treatment when she inquired into the marriage a few years after the break-up. First Greer pulled faces to deter the questions, then she broke into an uncharacteristically broad Australian accent, and finally she exploded; a mixture of guilt, snobbery and defensiveness broke through in the comments that followed. 'From choice,' she shot back when asked whether it was true her husband was a laborer, adding that he had a better first degree than her, was as tall as her and built to match. She said she had liked him, and still did. She would give him a divorce if he really wanted one, but not if he insisted on 'coming the gentleman' and paying for it: '*He's* not the guilty party!'[1]

Sixteen years after the break-up, Greer's public comments reflected those she made to Silver at the time, but the defence of du Feu – that he was not the 'guilty party' – had disappeared. Marriage had made her realize the trouble women can get into, she told Clyde Packer: 'I was just not a free agent any more. Everything I did was criticised. He was really very destructive. . . . The English like to make a great story out of why I am a feminist and say that it is because Australian men are so dreadful. They've got to be kidding. I'd rather fuck an Australian than an Englishman any time. Any time.'[2]

The most depressing aspect of Greer's sparse public comments on the marriage was her explanation of why she did it. 'Because he asked me,' she said in 1972.[3] Twenty-one years after Greer left du Feu, she was only slightly more expansive. The additional comments confirmed the passivity and poor self-esteem suggested by her earlier minimalist explanation. 'We got married because he thought it was a good idea,' she told a reporter in 1989, 'and I thought he knew what he was doing. . . . I am a woman of the fifties, I wait to be asked. You must not have the notion that men were popping up out of the ground asking me to marry them.'[4] In another interview she even overlooked the fact she *had* been married: 'People say, why didn't you get married . . . as if I was being asked every hour on the hour by some perfectly acceptable person to marry him. I wasn't. I haven't exactly got blokes kicking the door down. They *will* take no for an answer.'[5]

At the most superficial level, the marriage failed because Paul expected it to change Germaine and Germaine expected it to change nothing. Germaine wanted to carry on with her flamboyant behavior unimpeded. This was an unrealistic expectation; the signs had been evident before their wedding, in du Feu's bad temper and excessive drinking during the wet weekend visit to Warwick. For Paul's part, there was no evidence at all to support his hope that marriage would smooth the edges from Germaine's more extreme positions: quite the reverse. Apart from the decision to marry, her idiosyncratic approach to life continued unchanged.

In any case, something more fundamental was involved. Paul du Feu was the culmination of the heterosexual rough trade fantasy Greer had been toying with since her first adolescent encounters with men. When the schoolgirl Germaine went in her white piqué dress, white gloves and blue Coles bra to a dance at the local town hall, determined to get her first proper kiss from a man, it was from a hefty builder's laborer that she accepted a cab ride home. Then there was her old Drift boyfriend Bill Collins, a slaughterman and gardener; and Roelof Smilde, who was working as a wharfie when she went to live with him. Smilde's status as a manual worker seemed to add some prized sweat and grit to their union. When Greer publicly referred to Smilde later in life, it was always as a wharfie, even though he had given up the job shortly after they got together. When Germaine went to Sydney University to get her master's degree she got involved with some gentle, compliant souls, as Stefan Gryff observed, but at the other extreme 'it was truck drivers and road workers.'

Paul du Feu fitted the pattern like a glove. On the rebound from a failed relationship, she saw him, stroked his cheek and this time walked down the aisle. He was like Smilde – fit, fair-haired, brawn with brains, and not the type to do what he was told. Where Smilde was a key figure in an established group, however, du Feu had only the front bar comrades of shabby Notting Hill pubs. While Roelof was living with a young Germaine, just turned twenty-one, simultaneously his lover and philosophical protégée, Paul was contending with a Germaine only a little younger than himself, intensely aware she was moving in 'a different world' – a Cambridge star with a prestigious doctorate under her belt and her own academic post at Warwick, she was mixing with dons and aristocrats while he was consorting with vagabonds, layabouts and East End low-lifes in his concrete-spattered jeans.

The heterosexual rough trade fantasy can be a straightforward, if exploitative, matter in women sufficiently unsure of themselves to want a sense of disproportionate power in their relationships. As with men who pursue 'bimbos,' one party exploits a power imbalance, using advantages of class, wealth, intellect and/or education to increase their sense of security and pleasure.

Germaine's conscious espousal of Shakespeare's Petruchio and Kate marriage model showed, however, that there was more to her stance than just a matter of liking beefcake and enjoying a sense of control. It revealed a hankering after male mastery at odds with the sexual equality she later preached. For Kate does not relate as an equal to Petruchio in *The Taming of the Shrew*. Nor does she marry him as an equal. She marries him *tamed*; as Greer put it in her doctoral dissertation, acceptance of Petruchio's offer of marriage ends Kate's 'fruitless revolt.' When Greer told du Feu he should read the play to pick up some hints on how to deal with her, he was being issued an invitation to outwit her, Petruchio-like, into submission. Not taking the cue, he cut his chances of fulfilling her fantasy, whether or not he had been inclined to try and do so.

The marriage of Greer and du Feu constituted a fleeting union of the mutually uncomprehending and aggrieved. Unlike Roelof Smilde, whose Push philosophy had given him long practice in negating the potent pulses of jealousy and possessiveness, du Feu had nothing to fall back on but alcohol when what he perceived as Germaine's wilful waywardness failed to abate. He doubted that it had even occurred to her that needling was not the best way to convert him to her simple faith in sexual promiscuity: 'I never really understood the theology of that faith anyway.'[6]

Interestingly, Greer had told du Feu a story which highlighted the social pressures in the Push to conform to its sexual ethos, about a couple who had lived together faithfully for several years until it all became too much for the man's libertarian conscience. He had betrayed his free-love principles for too long, he decided, and pressured his reluctant girlfriend to sleep with a friend. After some argument, she did so, but arrived home early the next morning to find her partner drunk and depressed, huddling in the corner of their lounge. He hated the situation he had forced them into for the sake of his libertarian beliefs. 'I never understood the moral to be drawn from *that* story,' du Feu said, 'unless it is that both of them were silly ninnies'; but then 'we were a pair of silly ninnies too, who should never have got married.'[7]

When Greer turned down his request to try again a few months after the break-up, she also told him he was an alcoholic. It turned him teetotal for a while. Germaine had already told him that a lover she had previously rejected had committed suicide, though when du Feu pushed her on the details it turned out he had died in a car crash rather than by his own hand. Should he meet with a drunken accident one night, du Feu decided, he was not going to give her the satisfaction of putting down his death to unrequited love. Depressed but determined, he was leaving nothing to chance.[8]

When he said he never understood the theology of Germaine's simple faith in promiscuity, du Feu perhaps came closer to identifying the source of the intensity of her sexual stance than he realized. As a teenager, she directly linked the collapse of her Catholic faith with the abandonment of conventional morality. Her unwilling arrival at the conclusion that there was no God during her first year at Melbourne University led her to conclude, equally, that there were no rules about anything else either.

The process of thinking this through was a source of distress to Germaine. While she abandoned God intellectually, the cultural background of religious rapture, intense devotion and ritual was not so easily jettisoned. The teenager who had collapsed on the church floor after hours of kneeling, arms outstretched, 'making love to this image . . . this person really' was hardly likely to expunge her spiritual thirst overnight, or perhaps ever.[9] The direct connection between her conclusion that there was no God and her decision to abandon petting and plunge into sex – 'to accept my own sexuality and what was due to it' – perhaps gave religion and sex a more dynamic and highly charged linkage in Greer than in most other people.

First, she pursued sexual plenty in Melbourne. Then the Push libertarians gave her a theory to explain, to rationalize, to make sense of the practice. She became a zealous exponent of the Push line, particularly, as du Feu found out, its emphasis on sexual freedom and opposition to monogamy.

When Germaine embraced the counterculture, what had previously been a mission became part of a holy war. Her journalism in

*Oz* on rock music and the underground took on mystical hues and, at times, almost a sense of religious ecstasy. Her conversion took a little while because, as she put it, 'I was very slow to turn on to pop.'[10] When it did happen, though, it was characteristically intense.

It was the combination of loneliness at the University of Warwick and a chance event at a Manchester television studio that exposed Greer to the emerging youth culture. She felt isolated, stuck in her bedsitter with little social life going on between faculty members. Her fellow academics were mostly male; they rarely invited her home to dine, and she felt she had little in common with their wives. This threw her into closer relationships with her students than might otherwise have been the case, and she was still young enough to be open to their influence.

Greer's varsity comedy success had also led to a role in the Granada Television comedy series *Nice Time* while she was teaching at Warwick. It did not make her happier – she said she did not really want the role – but it did incidentally expose her to rock music. She told Richard Neville she had seen a band play at the television studio in Manchester one day: 'The place was full of smoothies and groovers being cool, and this sweaty guy with his underpants showing, just blasted off. . . . His wailings blew out the crap – all the BBC gumshoes and bullshit – and I knew I was on his side.' In wardrobe, as she dressed for a sketch, the group admired her breasts, and Germaine suddenly realized 'groupiedom' was possible.[11]

Until then her musical interests had been broad – classical, contemporary, jazz, blues and folk – but did not include rock. She was converted overnight, and started taking in rock concerts by the score. She leased a flat in the King's Road as a restorative from the isolation of Warwick, and it became the base from which she established herself as a self-appointed authority on rock music and the underground scene. The post–du Feu period of her life was devoted to starfucking and proselytizing the promise of group sex: 'the highest ritual expression of our faith, but it must happen as a sort of special grace,' she wrote in *Oz*, sliding into an absurd quasi-religiosity.[12] Du Feu, had they remained together, would have had apoplexy or perhaps finally drunk himself to death.

Along with *IT*, *Oz* was the pre-eminent underground media outlet in 1960s London. Only a few years earlier, Sydney *Oz* had been the scourge of censorious local conservatives, but its style and preoccupations were essentially middle-class. The *DEBBIE* comic strip in *HONI SOIT* jibed in 1964: 'I read *OZ* you know/It's very satirical – especially about society and G.P.S. schools and the eastern suburbs and the north shore/But I suppose you can afford to be if you live there.'[13]

The anti-censorship cases that Sydney *Oz* fought in the early 1960s rested significantly on the argument that satire was entitled to greater latitude within existing censorship guidelines than other material. One Sydney University wit pointed out the path that had been opened up by the anti-censorship push: a cheesecake photograph of a naked woman appeared on *HONI*'s sports page, captioned, 'But I'm not obscene . . . I'm satirical!'[14] It was as sexist as any other cheesecake shot one might see, and aspiring oglers could see the opportunities ahead.

A comparison of Sydney *Oz* with the London *Oz* published from 1967 underlines the complete shift the counterculture accomplished in art, music and social mores in the space of a few short years. Martin Sharp created the perfect visual analogue for the 1960s underground in the artwork for Cream's *Disraeli Gears* album of 1967: it looked as if Sharp had managed to take a snapshot of his mind during a particularly fevered acid trip. After the first few editions, London *Oz* was drenched with Sharp's distinctive psychedelic artwork, and Neville had a sharp eye for catchy issues. Magpie-like, *Oz* provided a high-profile forum for the burgeoning array of nonconformist individuals and attitudes that emerged as the countercultural 'revolution' rolled on.

One thing the underground could never boast was sensitivity toward the grass-roots feminism stirring during the 1960s – and as with the underground, so it was with Greer. For the second edition of the London *Oz*, she penned a piece called 'British Breasts,' by-lined simply 'Germaine.' It certainly canvased revolution, but not a feminist revolution, let alone a socialist or anarchist one. She deployed several hundred words in a call for 'a full-scale revolution in the British bra industry.' The breast had been sorely neglected in England compared to the continent, she wrote, going into some depth on the difficulty of buying bras in Britain. 'The British manufacturer is convinced, possibly rightly, that the British breast is either meagre and knobby or big and floppy,' she contended. One glance at the women's magazines 'and any lass with boobs knows that fashion has passed her by'; the bosom was being driven out of Britain. The piece contained some arguably pre-feminist comment on how punishing some contemporary fashion was on women's bodies, but it was no call to feminist arms. 'The buttock went long ago, and the hip followed it,' Greer wrote, 'but surely we should make a stand about the bosom.' The magazine's editorial staff were right behind her, announcing 'The London *OZ* Beautiful Breasts Competition' on the same page.[15]

The magazine's fourth issue carried a picture of Germaine in sweater and pearls, sitting in a pub with Neville and Rod Lake, the Englishman whose sense of manhood had been offended by 'In Bed with the English.' The accompanying article provided a rundown of the sexual delights Lake claimed were in store for Germaine, as well as her rebuff – that his virtuosity would be motivated by patriotism, which could hardly constitute a motivation for her.[16]

To champion sexual revolution in the late 1960s was hardly to be part of the vanguard. The same *Oz* carrying the picture of Germaine in her pearls, for example, contained an article pointing out that even the English women's magazines were timidly suggesting marriage might be outdated. *Oz* criticized the 'exuberant avant-garde' for continuing to channel their love through register office ceremonies.[17]

While Greer had revealed no significant feminist instincts up to this point – indeed, her Petruchio-fetish suggested the reverse – contemplation of her cataclysmic marriage in 1968 might well have stimulated her to think and write about the position of women. Instead, her first major post-marriage piece for *Oz* was her ode to groupiedom and group sex, 'The Universal Tonguebath: A Groupie's Vision.' In retrospect it was one of the most pretentious and unintentionally hilarious pieces of journalism of the entire counterculture period, though at the time it caused a minor sensation.

The piece was the cover story in *Oz* 19 in early 1969. The cover showed Germaine and Vivian Stanshaw of the Bonzo Dog Band with the line, '*OZ* talks to Dr G – the only groupie with a Ph.D. in captivity.' Vivian Stanshaw has one arm wrapped around his waist, the other holding his chin, musing, eyebrows raised but looking serious. Germaine, hair shaggily permed, is reaching round from behind and unzipping his fly. In contrast to the sweater, pearls and perm look when pictured with patriotic Rod Lake, she was now grooviness personified, wearing textured flares and multiple hippy bracelets and rings. A photograph inside shows Greer sitting cross-legged, head bowed down to Stanshaw's feet with her back to the camera, while he stands poised, hands clasped at his waist, looking straight down at the lens with the utmost seriousness. In the first picture she appears poised to engage genitally a man whose attention has been given to the camera rather than her; in the second, her position is servile, prostrated in front of the man, who is still ignoring her.

The article involved Greer interviewing herself, as Neville later described it. She explained, via the medium of 'Dr G,' how she came to embrace groupiedom. She had 'pulled' her first pop star by accident at a ball in the country – 'the best scene for a calculated "hit".'[18] Disenchanted by her partner's spaced-out state, she sought out other amusements. Greer went on to present a dream idealization of spontaneously combustible, no-strings sex with male rock musicians.

'You recognise each other, and you play in tune. Because you meet that way there are no hang-ups, no ploys, well, no ways of exploiting each other. If you fuck, you do it with the carnal innocence of children or cats or something. . . . Usually you separate quite soon, because there are things to do, more things to have and do, and maybe it happens again a few times, maybe months apart. It's a bit like a jam session I suppose, or a supergroup. Maybe he's married or got an old lady: that's like his regular scene. He knows he can blow good things when he's with you, sometimes, things he can only blow with you, so you get together. That's how I like it. Monogamy is death for me.'

She's laughing but she means it. She explains that she's very promiscuous but out of the hundreds of guys that she's made, relatively few are popstars, but most of the popstars are names to conjure with.

'I guess I'm a starfucker really. You know it's a name I dig, because all the men who get inside me are stars. Even if they're plumbers, they're star plumbers. Another thing I dig is balling the greats before the rest of the world knows about them, before they get the big hype.'[19]

It reads like a parody of egotistical 1960s sexual liberalism, where sexual pleasure is heightened by the status of one's passing lover; the collective interests of women could not be further from mind. The reference to finding 'Englebert [Humperdinck] very horny-making' increases the suspicion that the piece is one of *Oz*'s more successful attempts at satire: 'He's so evil you know, getting all those lonely housewives to cream their jeans, with his tight highfronted shiny mohair trousers with just a touch of rubber hose. So fucking evil.'[20] But no, it was for real.

'Dr G' talks about having sex with a rock music figure high on heroin, wistfully commenting that she still feels very involved but doesn't see him any more – that he was getting sick, and had recently fallen off a stage. 'I guess it's unemancipated or something but I won't call him,' Greer wrote. 'I only hope if it gets really bad he'll think of me. . . . I love him you know, him and a thousand others as they say.'[21] The anachronistic passivity was still there.

Greer then adversely contrasts the gang rape of women – 'that's the fascist sort of homosexual kick' – with group sex in 'a loving sexual situation.' She had not often come across groups, she said, 'that were so together that they could make that scene.' The group MC5 were closest to it, according to the starry-eyed Dr G: 'I had to go to sleep in their hotel . . . and they slept two to a room with the doors open and everyone walked through. I found out I really *really* liked being able to hear other people balling very close to me while I was, and I was very pleased; you see, the group fuck is the highest ritual expression of our faith, but it must happen as a sort of special grace. Contrived it could be really terrible, like a dirty weekend with the Monkees.'[22]

The idea of a dirty weekend with the Monkees is so hilarious that it is again tempting to read the piece as satire. However, Germaine had relayed these precise views and anecdotes in all seriousness to Richard Neville before she wrote the piece. The quasi-religious elevation of group sex by 'Dr G' was preacher Greer in high sermon mode. 'I'd fuck Shakespeare, except that he specially asked that his bones not be disturbed,' she throws in for good measure. Then, as the piece ends and 'Dr G' gets ready to go and eat at a macrobiotic restaurant, 'Norman Mailer's penis blossoms in her head.'[23]

Norman Mailer's penis has probably often found its way into

places it should not have: the American feminist Gloria Steinem once weakened in the face of Mailer's persistent pleading, only to be saved by his detumescence.[24] But Greer, who, as author of the piece had total control over what appeared in the head of 'Dr G,' not only conjured up Mailer's penis but had it 'blossom' there. That taste for ersatz rough trade was rearing its head again. While Germaine was fantasizing about Mailer's member in London, the American feminist Kate Millett was minutely dissecting the misogyny of Mailer's writing for her doctoral thesis at New York's Columbia University.

The mainstream British press picked up the story from *Oz* and Germaine, with something of a public profile already from her cheeky *Nice Time* comedy role, gained considerable notoriety as the first groupie ever to give an interview. The University of Warwick was relaxed enough: academics had tenure, and it took more than promoting group sex and draping oneself around a bored-looking rock musician to force a resignation. Greer herself responded to the shock of publicity with a two-steps-forward, one-step-back strategy. The media coverage gave her a platform for her pet views, but she coyly parried questions about whether 'Dr G' was really her. 'I was really doing a send-up of the groupies, just portraying it as a way of life,' she told a reporter defensively. 'It's not necessarily me that's described in the article. My personal life is private.'[25]

Three years later there was no talk of its having been a send-up; Greer confirmed that it was, indeed, her own story. 'I wrote an article in *Oz* magazine in which I, as Germaine, interviewed a famous groupie called Dr G the day-tripper, who was also me,' she wrote in *Pol* magazine in 1972. 'In it I talked about the rock musicians I have known and loved, without mentioning their names, and the life led by people who are caught up in the rock culture.' Rock music was more frankly sexual than jazz, she declared, and this was 'a liberating influence for us all.'[26] Germaine claimed the term 'groupie' had not initially been pejorative. It was used first, she said, to describe the young women who were sought out by bored rock musicians on endless tours of middle America – 'funny girls, crazy girls, beautiful girls, who obeyed no rules but their own.' They were not into name-dropping: they had names of their own the musicians used to drop, she said.

Many musicians spoke nastily about these women, Greer conceded in this second article, despite the fact that the groupies had loved them, often dried them out, risked prison to procure drugs for them and got them safely through bad trips. It was their bad-mouthing, she said, that turned the word 'groupie' into an insult. Greer never came close to a feminist analysis of the phenomenon. In an elitist rationalization, she blamed the denigration of groupies on second-rate musicians, arguing that the top-drawer ones would never behave that way: 'Most of the musicians who did this were small-time types; you never heard Eric Clapton or Jimi Hendrix or Mick Jagger going on like that.'[27] She was saying, effectively, that the rock elite were 'gentlemen' and the rest were not – and this was two years after *The Female Eunuch* was published.

Until the run of *Nice Time* ended, her weekly routine was to spend two days a week in Manchester doing the show, two days a week in London at her King's Road flat, and three days at her Leamington Spa apartment while she taught. Together with semi-regular journalism for *Oz* and the partaking of the pleasures of the counterculture, her productivity was extraordinary.

Greer later characterized her critiques of the underground for *Oz* as Cassandra pieces which aggravated friends like Neville. They all added up to the same message, she said: 'You're full of shit.'[28] No reasonable reading of Greer's contributions to *Oz*, though, sustains that claim. Greer was trenchantly critical of individuals at times, and of hype generally, but she continued to idealize the counter-culture, the underground itself, even as its unattractive underside was becoming obvious. Her harshest criticisms were for those who had in some way betrayed revolutionary purity, and for those who lacked any sense of the spiritual dimension she herself perceived in the underground.

In mid-1969, for example, Greer attacked the British edition of *Rolling Stone* for allegedly differentiating itself from underground publications like *Oz* and *IT*, which were subject to immense censorship pressure at the time. 'It's better to print and be damned, because you'll be damned anyway,' she advised *Rolling Stone*, urging its editors not to backslide or compromise their editorial line.[29] Gene Mahon defended the magazine in the letters column of the next *Oz*: 'Dear Germaine, Revolution is a happening thing. Let's not be so *serious* about it. I hope you won't be stuck in your bag of defending "the underground". Like the man says, let's make it for the hell of it.'[30]

As a critic, Germaine could be lethal. She was particularly tough on those who in her view had not personally achieved the spiritual and sensual unleashing she felt the counterculture – particularly rock culture – was really all about. Her review of *Turning On* by Rosa Gustaitis, for example, shows a distinct lack of mercy.

> Up and down she went, turning on to everybody's thing, getting it right I suppose. Pretty, feminine, intelligent, moderately daring, the gurus dug her, especially when there was no other firm female flesh around, and through it all she took her notes. The best evidence that it didn't work, that *Turning On* is one thing she wasn't doing, is the book. Three hundred and twenty-six pages of well-rehearsed subjects and predicates, clauses, colons, phrases, epithets, reported conversation, paragraphs, parentheses and not a flash of freedom, brilliance, not a single verbal gesture more effective than a file card. Apart from the narcissism of the authoress, nothing comes through strong: not a kiss, not a blow, not a drug shifts this chick's cool and gets her prose off the ground.[31]

Nor did the rock musician Mick Farren welcome being told he could not sing and was incapable of being 'into his body.' In a piece that largely praised his analysis of the underground scene, Germaine told the world that the drugs Farren took for his chronic asthma had affected his potency. 'The machine gun that will rip open a policeman's chest and furnish Mick Farren with a satisfactory orgasm at last,' she wrote, 'is the weapon of the straights: to kill a man is simply murder; it is revolution to turn him on.'[32] The long-suffering Farren responded in a letter to the editor: 'Dear Richard, Having been presented as an asthmatic impotent, tone-deaf, sadist weird, I am now about to fall into the trap of writing a letter in reply to Germaine's piece.'[33]

Greer's other major journalistic enterprise in 1969 was to co-found and contribute to the European sex paper, *Suck*. Based in Amsterdam to evade the British censorship laws, *Suck* was conceived by two expatriate Americans – Jim Haynes and Bill Levy – who approached Germaine and Heathcote Williams, then a

London-based magazine editor, to come in on the original editorial group. A fervent exponent of sexual freedom, Haynes was a former *IT* editor and founder of the Arts Lab in London, a center for happenings and shows which ran underground movies; Levy had recent experience as editor of *IT*. The first mistake on *Suck*, according to Haynes, came at the initial meeting of the four, plus the model Jean Shrimpton, then Heathcote Williams's lover. All five of them should have stopped talking and gone and made love together; instead, it was only Williams and Shrimpton who broke off from the meeting for a while to have sex in an adjacent room.[34]

*Suck* was supposed to break the male heterosexual mold of pornographic publishing. The interests of women and homo-sexuals were to be represented, though how broadening the spread of sexual objectification was supposed to advance the interests of anyone apart from *Suck*'s publishers was hardly obvious. Factions soon formed, with Haynes, Greer and Williams on one side, want-ing to concentrate on the personal dimension, on sexual informa-tion and advice, while Levy and Willem de Ridder, the Dutch publisher from whose Amsterdam offices it was produced, were more interested in whatever was funny and shocking.[35]

Tom Wolfe met Greer and Haynes in London just after the first edition of *Suck* was published. He knew neither of them then, he said, but found Greer unforgettable: 'a thin, hard-looking woman with a tremendous curly electric hairdo and the most outrageous Naugahyde mouth I had ever heard on a woman.' As their dinner together proceeded at a restaurant on the King's Road, Germaine got bored and set fire to her hair. Two waiters ran over and flapped furiously at the flames with napkins, while Greer sat with a sublime smile on her face.[36]

While Germaine's hair blazed, Haynes explained to Wolfe what *Suck* was all about: sexual liberation, and through it, spiritual liberation. Wolfe scanned Haynes's face for a sign that he was having a little joke, only to realize he existed on a plane quite 'Beyond Irony.' Whatever it had once been to Haynes, Wolfe records, 'sex had now become a religion, and he had developed a theology in which the orgasm had become a form of spiritual ecstasy.'[37]

The journey from 'sexology to theology' was evident in the

United States, too, Wolfe observed, using a sex farm in the Santa Monica Mountains in California as an example. While sex was being had freely, prolifically, throughout its buildings and recreation areas, the conversational atmosphere was quite different. 'The air becomes humid with solemnity,' Wolfe recounts. 'Close your eyes, and you think you're at a nineteenth-century Wesleyan summer encampment and tent-meeting lecture series. It's the soul that gets a workout here, brethren.' Yet it was not a hypocritical cover-up:

> It is merely an example of how people in even the most secular manifestation of the Me decade – free-lance spread-'em ziggy-zig rutting – are likely to go through the usual stages. . . . Let's talk about Me . . . Let's find the Real Me . . . Let's get rid of all the hypocrisies and impediments and false modesties that obscure the Real Me . . . Ah! at the apex of my soul is a spark of the Divine . . . which I perceive in the pure moment of ecstasy (which your textbooks call 'the orgasm,' but which I know to be heaven).[38]

As a contributing editor for *Suck*, writing under the name 'Earth Rose,' Germaine did not restrict herself to fulfilling her missionary position on sex. She drew liberally on her friends' sex lives, peccadillos, limitations and diseases for column fodder – hardly a fair, let alone a friendly or feminist thing to do. When Wolfe read the first edition of *Suck*, he assumed that the names of the people whose sexual predilections were being detailed in Earth Rose's column were fictitious. Then he came to a snippet that read, 'Anyone who wants group sex in New York and likes fat girls, contact Lillian Roxon.' Roxon was one of Wolfe's friends.[39] What he did not know was that Roxon was supposed to be a friend of Germaine's, too, from the old Push days. Whereas Greer had left the Royal George for England, Roxon had gone to the United States to pursue her career as a journalist and rock expert. Richard Neville recalled some of Earth Rose's other choice moments in his sixties memoir. One concerned a well-known counterculture figure who had just recovered from a case of NSU. 'However, knowing his foreskin and disinclination to wash,' wrote Greer, 'he is still a risk.' The belt of a noted black actor and activist was 'once again whistling down the arched white thighs' of one of Germaine's old sexual rivals; and another one of her supposed friends 'does not like giving head, you have been warned. . . .'[40] All were named.

What did any of this have to do with feminism? Not much. Yet this same year, 1969, was the one in which Greer wrote *The Female Eunuch*. When her *Suck* colleagues were looking for her in between issues, they knew she could be found at the British Museum working on the book.

'I had this agent,' Greer said later, explaining the genesis of *The Female Eunuch*: 'Agents are responsible for a multitude of sins. I had finished the television show and one day I went to see her. She said, "Why don't you write a book?" She said that it was the fiftieth anniversary of female suffrage or some such bullshit. "You should write a book about why female suffrage failed." I remember losing my temper. I thought, "What are we talking about! Women didn't get the vote until there was nothing left worth voting for. And what do you think the vote accomplishes anyway?"'

Germaine stewed on the idea for a couple of days and then, quite incidentally, had lunch with Sonny Mehta, whom she knew from Cambridge. Mehta was by then a budding publisher. He told her he had not asked her to lunch to look into her eyes, Germaine recalled: he wanted some good book ideas. She rattled off a few and then told him how her 'dumb agent' had suggested she write a book about female suffrage. Germaine flew into a rage attacking the idea. When the rage had exhausted itself Mehta said to her, 'That's the book I want,' and suggested they go back to his office and sign a contract. 'Sonny, you'll never sell it,' Germaine protested. 'No, no, no!' he persisted, sealing the deal with a £750 advance, one-third of which she received on signature.[41]

'I showed the first chapters to Sonny and he said nothing,' Greer recalled. 'And I knew I hadn't done it. One day, I suddenly realized it had to be written in short chapters; otherwise nobody would read it because women don't have spare time and their concentration span is generally brief. So I began writing short chapters.' Sonny read them then gave them back 'speechless as usual. But I could tell by the look in his eyes that I was doing the right thing now. It was only a matter of weeks after that and it was finished.'[42] Thus Greer's 'dumb agent' and Sonny Mehta's canny commercial nose for a good controversial read combined to spark *The Female Eunuch*, which was shaped by Greer in response to the glimmers in Mehta's eyes. Until that point there is little evidence she had ever much considered the position of women other than in terms of Push libertarianism and, essentially, through the position of one woman: herself.

Testimonial feminism has an important and honorable role in the history of the women's movement, but extrapolating social theory from a statistical sample of one is a dangerous enterprise. For Greer, sexual plenty and spontaneity was a catchall, unisex solution to everyone's problems. She was not a part of the grass-roots feminism that gathered momentum in America, Australia and Britain as the 1960s rolled on. Rather she was part of the counterculture, whose 'free love' tenet coincided with her libertarian view of spontaneous sex as the universal balm. A reaction against men's exploitation of the counterculture's 'free love' ethos was, in fact, one of the sources of second-wave feminism's dramatic forward momentum.

Some of her work-in-progress was published in *Oz* 26 at the beginning of 1970. The issue appeared with the cover line 'Women's Liberation: A True Romance.' The cover showed a naked man with his hands on his hips, his genitalia liberally covered in medical adhesive tape, while the woman pictured next to him brandishes an axe in one hand and holds a strap-on dildo in the other, her mouth open in joyful exclamation. *Oz*'s castrating woman warrior wore a short floral dress and a beauty-queen-style sash reading 'Pussy Power.' Inside was Greer's piece 'The slagheap erupts,' by-lined simply 'Germaine.'

The *Oz* editors indulged their sexist sense of humor by following the article with a full-page illustration of an inflatable rubber torso, pictured from waist to knees, with a mock vagina rubber-welded in the obvious place. 'Men! Don't let women's liberation blackmail you,' it was captioned. 'Meet Wendy – *Oz*'s yum-yum rubber fun substitute – silent clean insatiable.'[43]

Greer herself attacked the very phenomenon of which she was about to position herself as champion. 'The 1969 second wave of women's liberation movements were very much a manifestation of those sinister forces in our society which we call the media,' she began. The newspapers were keeping up their circulation and thus their advertising revenue 'by inventing a new sensation – Women's

Liberation.' The media had created 'the fashion of female liberation,' she went on. She attacked Betty Friedan's efforts to get employment advertisements in the *New York Times* desegregated, and lambasted the martial arts classes run by Abbey Rockefeller and Roxanne Dunbar of the Boston Women's Liberation Movement. 'When nobody likes you, and you really don't much like yourself,' she wrote, 'the most common reaction is to turn nasty and attack first. Unfortunately any skinhead could tell Miss Rockefeller that cowardice and steel-tipped boots, broken bottles and safety in numbers, is better technique than any bloody karate which you can learn in debutante schools.'[44]

The real reason why women's liberation was a 'hot number' in the media, according to Greer, was because it 'smacks of lesbianism, female depravity, freakishness, perversion and solemn absurdity.'

> Many militant women show too plainly by their inefficiency, their obesity and their belligerence that they have not succeeded in finding any measure of liberation in their own company. They are still beset with middle-class sexual scruples, so that they cannot find any alternative to the phony concept of female sexuality as monogamy and child-bearing, except, as some extremists have advocated, masturbation, lesbianism or celibacy. These alternatives are more compulsive and repressive than the despised heterosexual confrontation, and the result must be to debilitate the movement, because repression consumes energy which might be used creatively. . . .
>
> Rather than increasing the possibilities in a revolutionary fashion, militant feminism is reducing them, imprisoning the new women in a wilderness of theory which grew itself out of a hopelessly distorted situation in which clear sight was [an] impossibility.[45]

Clear sight was impossible for women but not, apparently, for men. 'The bourgeois perversion of motherhood,' she went on, 'has been assailed by male psychologists and obstetricians: ought we not to listen to them?'

Greer attacked feminist activists across the spectrum – liberal feminists for their incorporation into the system, militant feminists for compulsive and repressive sexual practices and, extraordinarily, feminist self-defence practitioners for low self-esteem. Never mind which way your feminism leaned, if you were fat or belligerent, Greer argued, your lack of personal liberation showed. Sexual freedom – and, implicitly, sexual desirability – was her benchmark for personal liberation: 'A woman who cannot organise her sex life in her own best interest is hardly likely to transform society.' A woman's best interests meant junking monogamy and 'fucking for sex instead of ego and prestige.' An example was 'to mate down instead of up' since women 'automatically take on the class of their husbands' – preferable, she said, to typing, distributing leaflets and making tea for the men of the New Left.

Compared to feminist activists, men got a relatively light pummeling in the piece. They were the enemy, she said: they knew it and experienced the 'sex war' as an especially cold one. However, men had 'no perverse desire to remain enemies,' according to Greer. In liberating themselves, women would also 'free men of their neurotic dependence and the fearful inauthenticity of sexual relationships.' As many men as women hated brassieres and vaginal douches, she claimed, and some more so: 'They are as tired of guilt as women are of shame.'

Women's masochism had to be eradicated if male sadism was to become ineffectual, Greer wrote tellingly, but naively: it was a classic statement of a transformation that would be necessary but not sufficient to end the patriarchy. In a thundering conclusion, Greer wrote off the entire women's movement. 'There are signs that it is happening,' she said of her hopes for the wilting of male power, 'but slowly, and so far without prophetesses, but not in the workshops and chapters of the spasm misnamed the "Movement".'

In this rehearsal of her arguments for *The Female Eunuch*, careful readers were forewarned of the dark side of the book which would shortly follow. There was the negative, dismissive and derisory assessment of feminist activism of the day, whether liberal or radical in nature; there was an equation of certain physical appearances with lack of personal liberation; and there was a hegemonic heterosexuality that led her to condemn other forms of sexual expression as compulsive and oppressive.

Germaine was mounting her pulpit to proclaim the Push line on sexual freedom, via the counterculture, in the clothes of women's liberation. The simple faith in sexual promiscuity which so needled the uncomprehending Paul du Feu during their marriage was about to be writ large – first in the 'Cuntpower' edition of *Oz*, and then in *The Female Eunuch*. Greer had the youth, the charisma, the chutzpah and the media savvy to spread the word in a way no one had before. From those years of Catholicism, she knew a good sermon when she heard one. The woman the press would dub the 'high priestess' of women's liberation was about to deliver a sermon, not from the Mount but from the Mound of Venus. In the process she would change the course of her own life, and profoundly influence the lives of many thousands of other women as well.

# 8

# The Female Eunuch

The 'advocacy of delinquency' among women was Greer's chief purpose in *The Female Eunuch*.[1] We have to question the most basic assumptions about 'feminine normality,' she argued, when for so long female sexuality has been denied and misrepresented as passivity. 'The vagina is obliterated from the imagery of femininity in the same way that the signs of independence and vigour in the rest of her body are suppressed,' Greer wrote. 'The characteristics that are praised and rewarded are those of the castrate – timidity, plumpness, languor, delicacy and preciosity.' Physically and psychologically the suppression and deflection of women's energy had rendered them eunuchs in modern society. It was time to revolt.

Some women were already well along the path to liberation. Grass-roots feminist activism had emerged throughout the urbanized West as the 1960s progressed. Betty Friedan had articulated middle-class American women's dissatisfaction with their suburban lives as early as 1963 in *The Feminine Mystique*. In 1966 Friedan founded the National Organization for Women (NOW) to campaign for equal rights for women. At the same time many Western women were involved in the burgeoning array of activist movements that blossomed, intersected and overlapped in the 1960s – the civil rights and anti-war movements, the student protest movement, the New Left and the counterculture. Radical political groups and the counterculture proved fertile ground for feminism: small groups of women began meeting to discuss and analyze their unsatisfactory experiences *as women* in these movements and elsewhere. 'Men led the marches and made the speeches and expected their female comrades to lick envelopes and listen,' Anna Coote and Beatrix Campbell note in their history of the women's movement, *Sweet Freedom*. 'Women who were participating in the struggles to liberate Blacks and Vietnamese began to recognize that they themselves needed liberating – and they needed it now, not "after the revolution".'[2]

There was nothing new in women talking to each other, Coote and Campbell point out. What was different was that women were beginning to draw political conclusions from their experiences. At the same time, there were some isolated protest actions drawing attention to society's sexist foundations. In 1965 two women chained themselves to a public bar in Brisbane, protesting against the exclusion of women from front bars in Australian hotels.[3] In 1968 women demonstrated at the Miss America Pageant in Atlantic City, throwing bras and girdles into a bucket – without setting fire to them, contrary to media reports – to draw attention to the event's intrinsic sexism. Two years later a hundred British women would disrupt the Miss World competition at London's Albert Hall.

By 1969 the New York Radical Feminists and the New York Redstockings were publishing feminist manifestoes; Kate Millett was writing the doctoral thesis that would be published in 1970 as *Sexual Politics*;[4] and Gloria Steinem had given her first major speech, 'After Civil Rights – Women's Liberation,' to the Women's National Democratic Club in Washington. In Britain Juliet Mitchell was running a course on 'The role of women in society' at the 'Anti University' launched by radical academics. Sheila Rowbotham published *Women's Liberation and the New Politics*, linking housework with unequal rights at work, making explicit the objectification and silencing of women, and challenging Marxists to confront male hegemony.[5]

The new sexual orthodoxies accompanying the counterculture's 'free love' ethos were also being undermined. Feminists on both sides of the Atlantic were reading the Redstocking Anne Koedt's paper, 'The Myth of the Vaginal Orgasm,'[6] which identified the clitoris rather than the vagina as the center of women's specific sexual pleasure. In attacking the notion that the penis was the only possible – indeed, according to Reich, the only legitimate – source of sexual satisfaction, Koedt weakened the struts buttressing 1960s counterculture-style permissiveness which, as Coote and Campbell put it, 'kidnapped' women and 'carried them off as trophies' in the name of liberation. 'In the era of flower-power and love-ins, of doing-your-own-thing and not being hung up (especially about sex), "girls" were expected to *do it*, and impose no conditions. The more they did it, the more "liberated" they were deemed to be.' Young women were beginning to rebel against being set up 'in their mini-skirts and mascara, alongside the whole-foods and hippy beads and hallucinogens, in a gallery of new toys with which men were now free to play.'[7] The implication of Koedt's work was clear: when it came to women enjoying orgasms, men were an optional extra.

The industrial sphere was another key site for early second-wave action. In 1968 women machinists at Ford's Dagenham plant in Essex and the Halewood plant in Liverpool went on strike to have their work reclassified from unskilled to semi-skilled. The following year in Melbourne activist Zelda d'Aprano chained herself to a government building to protest against institutionalized pay discrimination. Women campaigning for equal pay boarded Melbourne trams and insisted on paying only 80 percent of the fare, in line with the lesser wages to which they were legally entitled.[8]

By the time *The Female Eunuch* was published in October 1970 the women's movement was rapidly gathering pace, its public forays often reported in the media. At the level of activism, though, the movement was still relatively small. In the course of their daily lives the mass of women did not often run across the paths being beaten through the patriarchal thicket by the early second-wave feminists. Others lacked a sense of commonality with the women in the movement's vanguard. Others again, many of them interested and potentially willing to embrace change, found feminist polemics too remote to move them.

Then came *The Female Eunuch*. Greer may have been 'last with the latest,' as Beatrice Faust puts it, but her book had the virtue of being magnificently accessible. It was bawdy, witty, provocative, dotted with intimate personal testimony and delectable historical titbits. Women *wanted* to read *The Female Eunuch*, relishing its daring and derring-do. 'I myself did not realize that the tissues of my vagina were quite normal until I saw a meticulously engraved dissection in an eighteenth-century anatomy textbook,' Germaine wrote, for example, at the beginning of a fascinating historical assemblage of snippets on women's genitalia in which she highlighted the fact that women had not always been so reluctant to discuss their sexuality.

Her approach was different. Many, many women responded to the book in a way they were not responding to other feminist literature – if, indeed, they had access to any at all.

Apart from anything else, Greer's language caused a sensation. The Australian feminist Anne Summers says it is hard today to describe the dimensions of the book's impact in the early 1970s. 'The [*Sydney Morning*] *Herald* had only just started using the word "pregnant" and "virgin,"' she recalls. There were no sexual references of any kind. 'In the underground press there would have been a bit of stuff around, and some of that was pretty confronting, but this was in a mainstream book – not something sold on street corners at midnight.' Women read Greer, listened, and noted her example well. Promoting the book in Australia, she mentioned she never wore underpants. 'So we all stopped wearing pants for a while,' says Summers. 'It was a bit breezy! We were all trying to be incredibly free. That was a much bigger deal than not wearing a bra, I can tell you.'

Greer's style was both a strength and a weakness. Structurally, there is little sense of a developing idea in the book, which is more a series of restatements of her core analysis from a variety of thematic vantage points. This is a quibble, though, when one considers the power with which she could cast common experiences in a shattering new light. Greer could really see, and Greer could really write. Take, for example, her compelling description of the dynamic of many miserable twentieth-century marriages:

> The real theatre of the sex war. . . . is the domestic hearth; there it is conducted unremittingly. . . . The housewife accepts vicarious life as her portion, and imagines that she will be a prop and mainstay to her

husband in his noble endeavours, but insidiously her unadmitted jealousy undermines her ability to appreciate what he tells her about his ambitions and his difficulties. She belittles him, half-knowingly disputes his difficult decisions, taunts him with his own fears of failure, until he stops telling her anything. Her questions about his 'day at the office' become a formality. She does not listen to his answers any more than he heeds her description of her dreary day. Eventually the discussion stops altogether. It just isn't worth it. He has no way of understanding her frustration – her life seems so easy. She likewise feels that he cannot know how awful her days can be. Conversation becomes a mere power struggle. She opposes through force of habit. Why should he be always right? Ever right?[9]

Another of *The Female Eunuch*'s strengths is its convincing revelation of the dark ambivalence of men toward women that is embedded in everyday social practices, many of which were taken for granted at the time of the book's publication, and to a significant extent still are. 'Because love has been so perverted, it has in many cases come to involve a measure of hatred,' Greer contended. In extreme cases it takes the form of loathing and disgust, manifesting itself in sadism and guilt, hideous crimes on the bodies of women, and abuse and ridicule through casual insult and facetiousness.[10]

At the same time, she argued that women had to stop collaborating in their own oppression. If women were to be better valued by men, they had to value themselves more highly: 'They must not scurry about from bed to bed in a self-deluding and pitiable search for love,' she wrote, 'but must do what they do deliberately, without false modesty, shame or emotional blackmail. As long as women consider themselves sexual objects they will continue to writhe under the voiced contempt of men and, worse, to think of themselves with shame and scorn.'[11] The belittling of women would not diminish until women stopped 'panhandling': 'In their clothes and mannerisms women caricature themselves, putting themselves across with silly names and deliberate flightiness, faking all kinds of pretty tricks that they will one day have to give up.'[12]

Greer made the clarion call to change in such emotionally appealing, idealistic terms that it was virtually irresistible. 'Sex must be rescued from the traffic between powerful and powerless, masterful and mastered, sexual and neutral,' she wrote, 'to become a form of communication between potent, gentle, tender people, which cannot be accomplished by a denial of heterosexual contact.'[13] She made the social 'delinquency' she sought to provoke so delectably inviting that few who read the book could fail to feel its attraction, in theory at least. 'The woman who realises that she is bound by a million Lilliputian threads in an attitude of impotence and hatred masquerading as tranquillity and love has no option but to run away, if she is not to be corrupted and extinguished utterly,' her argument ran. 'Liberty is terrifying but it is also exhilarating.'[14] The book closed with the confrontational question: 'What *will* you do?'[15]

*The Female Eunuch* triggered a shock of recognition in tens of thousands of Western women who read it, and in hundreds of thousands of women who received Greer's analysis via the media. It was feminism's smash-hit bestseller, generating scores of photographs, television and radio interviews and thousands of column-inches of newspaper and magazine copy, and making Greer popularly synonymous with women's liberation across the Western world. It prompted an untold number of women to rethink their self-perceptions, their relations with men, the entire basis of their existence. 'It changed my life' is the most common anecdotal response when the book is mentioned to women who read it in the early 1970s. Middle-class dinner parties broke up in bitter arguments on the book's contentious themes. Some women bought *The Female Eunuch* and hid it from their husbands, fearing the consequences of being found with such an inflammatory tract.

Gloria Steinem recalls the book's impact on two artist friends. While the woman artist's work was as good as her male partner's, he got the profile, the attention, and was generally taken more seriously. He returned home one day to find his partner reading *The Female Eunuch*, which suddenly came whistling through the air aimed at his head. The couple's professional and personal relativities were drastically reordered as a result.

Yet *The Female Eunuch*'s influence on the women's movement itself was in inverse relation to the book's popular impact. While it can still be readily bought from airport bookstands, it is essentially invisible on reading lists for women's studies' courses, hardly referred to in the annals of second-wave feminism and seldom rates even an isolated footnote in the vast literature generated by the women's movement. In later works that traverse similar territory, it gets such passing references that it might almost not exist at all. It is as though, as far as the women's movement is concerned, the book is lost in space.

MacGibbon & Kee published *The Female Eunuch* in 1970. The title was unmissable in bold block letters – dayglo pink on a white background. The blurb on the inside flap announced that the book would offend many, including conventional psychologists, economists, moralists and the 'conventional woman – the female parasite.' Women themselves were clearly going to be among the targets to whom Greer would assign blame. Quotes from the book on the back cover contained reader-grabbing hooks under such headings as 'Love,' 'Marriage,' 'Misery' and 'Revolt.' The first heading, 'Upbringing,' was followed by: 'What happens to the Jewish boy who never manages to escape the tyranny of his mother is exactly what happens to every girl whose upbringing is "normal." She is a female faggot.' Inside, Greer continues the comparison: 'Like the male faggots she lives her life in a pet about guest lists and sauce béarnaise.'[16] Greer never made clear in the book why she gave campery such a flogging, why homosexual men produced in her such obvious disdain.

Sales of the book began slowly, then took off. MacGibbon & Kee printed a second run in 1970, but by the beginning of 1971 there had to be monthly reprintings to keep up with demand. Paladin published the paperback version later that year. In the ensuing two decades it was the imprint's biggest and most consistent seller, reprinted a score of times and earning a twenty-first anniversary edition with a new foreword by Greer.

John Holmes's front cover illustration for the Paladin edition was one of the most intriguing and instantly recognizable images in post-war publishing. A naked, headless, legless mature female torso with a handle sprouting from each hip hangs by the shoulders on a pole like some fibreglass cast on an industrial production line. Holmes's first effort, never used, showed a naked woman from the abdomen up, breastless and faceless but unmistakably Germaine from her 'Universal Tonguebath' period, hair fashionably afrofrizzed, waist-deep in a pile of stylized breasts, presumably amputated in the creation of a 'female eunuch' based on an assumed equivalence of testicles and mammary glands.

*The Female Eunuch* is both exhilarating and exasperating to read. Greer's rhetoric soars, inspires; many insights are sharp, potent and motivating. Yet the book is so studded with political naiveties and passing shots at other women that it is difficult to reconcile as a whole. Its grand sweep, pacy prose and telling revelations encourage the reader to skate over the jagged edges and ride forward on Germaine's romantically anarchistic vision of assertive women in hot pursuit of pleasure, independence and spontaneity. In its popular consumption, this is precisely what happened.

*The Female Eunuch* contains six sections. Four of them – 'Body,' 'Soul,' 'Love' and 'Hate,' each containing numerous mini-chapters, some just two or three pages long – are sandwiched between two free-standing sections, 'Summary' at the beginning and 'Revolution' at the end. Germaine began by declaring *The Female Eunuch* part of the second feminist wave, gently deriding the first wave, whose evangelism she said had withered into eccentricity. The old suffragettes had served their prison terms and lived through the gradual admission of women 'into professions which they declined to follow, into parliamentary freedoms which they declined to exercise, into academies which they used more and more as shops where they could take out degrees while waiting to get married.' The cage door had been opened but the canary had refused to fly out, she claimed, going on to suggest that organizations such as the National Organization for Women (NOW) in the United States were the modern, and by implication equally ineffective, incarnations of the old suffragettes.[17]

Greer noted the daily exposure of women's liberation in the media: everyone was suddenly interested in women and their discontent. 'Women must prize this discontent as the first stirring of the demand for life; they have begun to speak out and to speak to each other,' she wrote. 'The sight of women talking together has always made men uneasy; nowadays it means rank subversion. "Right on!" '[18] Yet in the next breath she dismissed the likely impact of the 'organized liberationists,' who she said were a well-publicised minority, the same faces appearing every time a feminist issue is discussed. Thus, only a few pages into the book, Greer began the gratuitous trashing of activists and their practices that would all too often be a feature of her public forays. She devalued the grinding techniques for promoting grass-roots change, arguing that 'demonstrating, compiling reading lists and sitting on committees are not themselves liberating behaviour.' 'As a means of educating the people who must take action to liberate themselves,' Greer continued dismissively, 'their effectiveness is limited.'

There was an alternative for the woman alienated by conventional political methods: 'She could begin not by changing the world, but by re-assessing herself.'[19] Consciousness-raising was an important practice for the early second wavers: in 'CR' groups women shared their problems, experiences and insights *together* and drew conclusions accordingly. Right from the outset, however, Greer chose the risky course of encouraging women to locate the problem within themselves, without positioning the challenge in a wider framework. This was at best necessary but insufficient, at worst reactionary and individually destructive. For what could be less likely to wreak revolution than a series of individuals contemplating the problem *in them*, in the absence of a wider framework for change?

Some in the women's movement were more generous about Greer's book than she had been about the work of the movement and its prominent figures. Anna Coote and Beatrix Campbell later judged her book 'powerfully written and often wise ... widely publicised and wildly popular.' *The Female Eunuch* dug a channel, they argued, from the 'Love Generation' through to the women's movement, introducing many thousands of women to a new sense of self.[20] At the same time, Coote and Campbell drew attention to the reactionary potential of what they termed 'heterosexual chauvinism,' for which they considered Greer set the tone.

As well as developing fault lines over issues of class and political strategy, the women's movement was already beginning to be split by a futile disagreement about whether or not women should consort with men. Greer, herself becoming a public symbol of rampant heterosexuality, argued explicitly that sexual liberation could not be achieved 'by a denial of heterosexual contact.'[21] To be whole, to be liberated, was conditional on having active heterosexual relations. 'At its most glamorous and flamboyant, heterosexual chauvinism appeared like a revamped *femme fatale*,' according to Coote and Campbell. 'It was the kind of feminism men liked best. It slapped their knees for being sexual slobs and chastised women for being sexual slovens. Above all, it promised the superfuck.'[22]

Greer might have had faith in the socially disruptive possibilities of sexual liberation, Coote and Campbell argued, but *The Female Eunuch* was really protecting the conventions of heterosexuality rather than changing them. Greer's insistence that 'genuine gratification' must involve the vagina 'did not identify any difference between the vagina as *a* place of pleasure and *the* place; the hierarchy of sexual values remained intact.'[23]

Lynne Segal, originally a Push libertarian herself, acknowledges the book's widespread influence, but considers it 'surely a pre-feminist text or at the very least an unusual feminist text,' given its tenuous connection to the women's movement. 'Despite popular opinion,' Segal says, '*The Female Eunuch* is unrepresentative of women's liberation in its early days; the movement predominantly dismissed Greer's individualistic anarchism and dismissal of collective action.'[24]

*The Female Eunuch* is less a sermon from a high priestess than the call of the Siren's song – alluring provided one is prepared to accept her dictum that sexual liberation, which Greer used as a synonym for women's liberation, 'cannot be accomplished by a denial of heterosexual contact.' Nor did Germaine's book allow for the possibility that a lesbian could be liberated, for example, or that a celibate woman could be liberated, or that a woman content simply with self-pleasuring could be liberated. In this respect *The Female Eunuch* is one of the prescriptive extremes of second-wave feminism, every bit as wrong-headed as the other extreme dictating that only lesbians could consider themselves true feminists.

So was this all that liberation required – giving up one's panhandling ways, forsaking false modesty, shame and emotional blackmail, slashing away the ties that bind and pursuing potent, tender heterosexual relations? After Greer's pungent, meandering, often brilliantly written catalogue of insights into the position of women, the solution she prescribed was negated by a dose of empiricism about the sexual revolution. Germaine trounced her own Utopia by describing how the old malign forces had already adapted to the new sexual freedoms that had been brought by the contraceptive pill in conjunction with the 1960s protest movement, the counterculture and mass media.

> The permissive society has done much to neutralize sexual drives by containing them. Sex for many has become a sorry business, a mechanical release involving neither discovery nor triumph, stressing human isolation more dishearteningly than ever before. The orgies feared by the Puritans have not materialized on every street corner, although more girls permit more (joyless) liberties than they might have done before. Homosexuality in many forms, indeed any kind of sex which can escape the dead hand of the institution – group sex, criminal sex, child-violation, bondage and discipline – has flourished, while simple sexual energy seems to be steadily diffusing and dissipating. This is not because enlightenment is harmful, or because repression is a necessary goad to human impotence, but because sexual enlightenment happened under government subsidy, so that its discoveries were released in bad prose and clinical jargon upon the world. The permit to speak freely of sexuality has resulted only in the setting up of another shibboleth of sexual normality, gorged with dishonesty and kitsch.[25]

This analysis was typically Germaine, highlighting the intellectual influences which underpinned *The Female Eunuch*. There is the conjunction of the Push's anarchistic pessimism and Leavisism as she blames the bleakness of relations under the new social mores on her claim that sexual freedom had increased under 'government subsidy,' leading to 'bad prose.' Neither idea is explained, but the implication is clear: the state and inferior writing are doing their wicked damage again. There is the lumping in of homosexuality with the crime of pedophilia and undefined 'criminal' sex; and there is the Push's correct-line Reich, in which homosexuality is contrasted adversely with 'simple sexual energy,' for which read heterosexuality. There is the lack of interest, too, in reconciling key parts of the thesis she is developing with other parts of her analysis and conclusion – or even in acknowledging the gaps and disjunctures that exist in it.

Three other serious problems in *The Female Eunuch* were largely neglected at the time of its publication: its contradictory position on marriage, Greer's analysis of male violence and her treatment of her mother.

The book is premised on the Push's inherent disposition against marriage. Given the personal reflections and anecdotes dotted through *The Female Eunuch*, the chapter on 'The Middle-Class Myth of Love and Marriage' might have been expected to draw on Greer's tear-drenched three-week-long marriage to Paul du Feu. Instead it is the vehicle for what look suspiciously like off-cuts from her doctoral thesis. There is far more on the Renaissance and Shakespeare in the chapter than on modern matrimony and the tyranny of Mills and Boon.

The most significant element of the book's chapter on marriage is Greer's renewed endorsement of the Petruchio-Kate model from *The Taming of the Shrew*. Kate has the 'uncommon good fortune to find Petruchio who is man enough to know what he wants and how to get it,' she wrote in a reprise of her doctoral thesis. 'He wants her spirit and her energy because he wants a wife worth keeping. He tames her like he might a hawk or a highmettled horse, and she rewards him with strong sexual love and fierce loyalty.... The submission of a woman like Kate is genuine and exciting because she has something to lay down, her virgin pride and individuality.' She continued at length, giving legitimacy to Kate's defence of Christian monogamy on the grounds that 'It rests upon the role of a husband as protector and friend, and it is valid because Kate has a man who is capable of being both, for Petruchio is both gentle and strong.... The message is probably twofold: only Kates make good wives, and then only to Petruchios; for the rest, their cake is dough.'[26] Neither the thoroughly patriarchal nature of the Petruchio-Kate relationship, nor its contradiction of her call for women to slough off the Lilliputian ties that bind them to their men, emerged as a critical issue in the book's consumption. This conflict remained at the heart of Greer's life and subsequent work.

There was also a strange disjuncture between her insights into misogyny and her views on male violence, where she assigned the blame to women themselves. 'It is true that men use the threat of physical force, usually histrionically, to silence nagging wives: but it is almost always a sham,' she wrote. 'It is actually a game of nerves, and can be turned aside fairly easily.' Germaine claimed that she had lived with men of known violence, two of whom had convictions for it, but they did not subject her to violence 'because it was abundantly clear from my attitude that I was not impressed by it.' Most women are fascinated by violence, she argued: 'they act as spectators at fights, and dig the scenes of bloody violence in films. Women are always precipitating scenes of violence in pubs and dance-halls. Much goading of men is actually the female need for the thrill of violence.'[27]

To blame women for inciting male violence was at best naive and, arguably, something much worse. Lynne Segal cites Greer's view as encapsulating the 'nonchalance' of many liberals, and sexual radicals in particular, toward questions of male brutality – an expression of the denial and public tolerance of men's violence to women.[28] In Greer's case the stance was particularly strange given that she had been the victim of male violence herself. Surely she did not think *she* had incited her rape back in Melbourne in the 1950s? Or did she not consider rape a manifestation of male violence?

Greer's deep-seated antagonism toward her mother Peggy is the other striking aspect of the book. Not far into *The Female Eunuch*, Germaine presented her mother and grandmother literally trying to contain her. She recalled her grandmother begging her mother to corset her as a teenager on aesthetic and health grounds, to counteract her youthful ungainliness and support her back, which Liddy feared might not be able to bear Germaine's ultimate six-foot height. There was no sign that Peggy took the advice. She warned Germaine instead against emulating Australia's famous female swimmers, claiming their training regime produced broad shoulders and narrow hips.[29] This is the only neutral comment on Peggy in the book.

The first substantial discussion of mothering in *The Female Eunuch* comes in the chapter on 'Altruism.' As children, Greer wrote, we 'could see that our mothers blackmailed us with self-sacrifice, even if we did not know whether or not they might have been great opera stars or the toasts of the town if they had not borne us.'[30] Then in the chapter on 'Misery' comes damnation for women – specifically Peggy – pursuing education to overcome the unhappiness of their situation at home:

167

The idle wife girds her middle-aged loins and goes to school, fools with academic disciplines, too often absorbing knowledge the wrong way for the wrong reasons. My own mother, after nagging and badgering her eldest child into running away from home (a fact which she concealed for years by talking of her as if she were present, when she knew absolutely nothing of what she was doing), took up ballet dancing, despite the obvious futility of such an undertaking, studied accountancy, and failed obdurately year after year, sampled religion, took up skiing and finally learnt Italian. In fact she had long before lost the power of concentration required to read a novel or a newspaper. Every activity was an obsession for as long as it lasted – some lasted barely a month and those are too numerous to list.[31]

Peggy's efforts to educate herself were valiant attempts at just the sort of delinquency *The Female Eunuch* was supposed to be promoting. Yet in Peggy Germaine portrayed this behavior as pathological rather than liberating.

The chapter called 'Resentment' explores the use of children as weapons in domestic in-fighting at its most sinister. Greer depicted Peggy as more desperate than other mothers, muttering to Germaine as a child that Reg was a 'senile old goat.' Women promote their children's dependence as insurance against any attempt to disown them, according to Greer; they attack their husbands for ignorance of children's needs and are jealous of their children for enjoying more freedom than they themselves experience.[32] Without supporting evidence, Greer described it as 'very common' for mothers to enlist their sons in acts of violence against their fathers, especially in poorer families where the father's inadequacies can be 'ruthlessly underlined.' In Greer's argument, the son 'accepts mother's account of her suffering at the hands of his brutal father, and endeavours like Saturn to displace him in his own house.' Germaine claimed that her brother, as a three-year-old, was brutally deployed by her mother against her father in a 'less intense Oedipal' twist on the phenomenon: 'my mother knelt on my small brother's chest and beat his face with her fists in front of my father and was threatened with violent retaliation, the only instance of my father's rising to her bait that I can recall.'[33] She wrote of being beaten by her mother for giving away all her toys at the age of four when she no longer wanted them – probably a reference to the punishment that followed her giving her trike to the needy Pammy in Elwood.[34] Peggy's horror of the schoolgirl affair between Germaine and Jennifer Dabbs is graphically described, as is Germaine's capitulation.

The villain of *The Female Eunuch*, her portrait woven subtly through its pages, is Peggy Greer, depicted by Greer as physically brutal, manipulative, an emotional blackmailer and homophobe. Reg Greer, barely present in the text, has a bit part as victim. Without self-consciousness, Germaine nevertheless noted in the chapter 'Family' that when dealing with the difficulties of adjustment 'children seize upon their parents and their upbringing to serve as scapegoats.'[35]

How did she manage to elicit such interest and sympathy among general readers even as she did such unsympathetic things as attacking her mother, blaming women for male violence, and endorsing a patriarchal marriage model? Some clues to the power of Greer's book can be found in a paper by Rodney Miller subjecting *The Female Eunuch*'s last chapter, 'Revolution,' to a linguistic analysis.[36]

Miller reveals the traditional rhetorical ploys driving the verve and persuasiveness of Greer's writing. Germaine alternated between active and passive voice and welded the colloquial imaginatively into her prose. She created an ebb and flow by combining extremes of abstract and everyday language. 'This balance between extreme formalism and colloquialism can be seen in other public figures seeking a wide audience,' according to Miller, who also cites Bob Hawke's 'peculiar mix of extremely formal sentence structures with colloquialisms and a nasal almost "ocker" voice.'[37] Hawke went on to become Australia's longest-serving Labour prime minister. While still president of the Australian Council of Trade Unions (ACTU) in the 1970s, he bettered Greer in a television debate – virtually the only occasion in memory when she has come off second-best.

Greer also relied on rhetorical questions and parenthetical clauses to create a sense of cut-and-thrust in her writing. The question-and-answer form surges forward and then arrests the reader's attention. These rhetorical features often occur in the middle paragraphs, 'which to the casual reader may appear merely to be outlining matter that incorporates only a slight amount of rhetorical organization,' writes Miller. 'Although one must look more closely at certain paragraphs to observe their rhetorical components, the extensive occurrence of these features . . . reflects the constant presence of Germaine Greer as *rhetor*.'[38] The lasting power of *The Female Eunuch*'s final paragraph, according to Miller, comes from the close combination of emotional forcefulness with prescription, setting up Greer's ultimate rhetorical question: 'What *will* you do?'

But there was more to it all than appealing to reader emotion, deploying personal pronouns and the like. Miller notes that the higher the proportion of verbs to nouns and adjectives in a piece of prose, the more interesting and persuasive the writing is perceived to be. On this criterion, Greer's style is vigorous and highly verbal. 'Dr Greer's language is forceful and her argument is aggressively competent,' he concludes. 'Perhaps this is the most important model that she provides.' Greer's style, by Miller's analysis, represented a significant departure from the norm for women writers, who had often been associated with a more passive style, relying heavily on nouns and adjectives: 'By integrating language features once characteristic of males, Dr Greer is requiring readers to reassess how they view male and female.'[39] Ever the iconoclast, Germaine managed simultaneously to use traditional rhetorical techniques, to offend against them, and sometimes to transcend them altogether.

The conventions of rhetoric were originally developed in part to establish fair rules for discourse – to ensure, among other things, that speakers addressed each other's arguments rather than engaging in personal attacks. Greer used the techniques of traditional rhetoric to great effect in her polemic while breaching the form's *politesse*, attacking – as Australians put it – the player, not the ball. On top of this she incorporates intimate comment and stories, personalizing the polemic rather than confining it to the abstract space constructed by conventional rhetoric. Greer rooted her rhetoric in the body – through anecdote, often her own body.

Drawing on Plato's *Gorgias*, Iris Young points out the erotic dimension in communication, the fact that 'persuasion is partly seduction.' The most elegant and truthful argument may fail if it is boring: 'Humour, word play, images and figures of speech embody and colour the arguments, making the discussion pull on thought through desire.'[40] Greer understood this implicitly and used it brilliantly.

Her deployment of personal testimony – *with* the traditional tools of rhetoric rather than instead of them, as was the case with most other feminists using the testimonial form – created a massive multiplier effect, heightening the power of her prose. Her story-telling technique carried 'an inexhaustible latent shadow . . . that there is always more to be told,' as Iris Young describes it.[41] This lifted *The Female Eunuch* from earth and made it fly.

At the time of its publication, *The Female Eunuch* did not receive the close critical analysis it deserved. There were honorable exceptions – the English feminist Sheila Rowbotham, for example, and the Australian feminist Beatrice Faust – but they were confined to book reviews. Arianna Stassinopoulos, at Cambridge a little after Germaine, replied with the book-length work, *The Female Woman*,[42] but it was essentially a light-weight vehicle for anti-feminist backlash. Lynne Segal later took issue with Greer's flawed analysis of male violence. However, the only lengthy analysis to appear relatively close to the time of *The Female Eunuch*'s publication came from Juliet Mitchell in her book *Psychoanalysis and Feminism* – though even this was not much longer than a substantial book review.[43]

Mitchell was responsible for stimulating a re-examination of Freud among English-speaking feminists after his comprehensive trashing at the hands of Greer and Millett, among others. One need not agree with Mitchell's stance on Freud to recognize her insights into the lesser side of Greer's polemical style. Mitchell referred to Greer's 'disarmingly cavalier attitude' to mistakes in *The Female Eunuch*. 'She compounds many errors – with facility and wit,' says Mitchell. In the first paragraph of one chapter alone, Mitchell showed Greer referring without differentiation twice to psychoanalysis, six times to psychology and twice to psychiatry, before moving on to begin the next paragraph with: 'So much for the authority of psychoanalysis and the theory of personality.'[44]

Mitchell criticized Greer for setting up a false polarity in Freud between creation and destruction, aggressors and victims, Eros and death. She noted *The Female Eunuch*'s tendency to self-serving intellectual sloppiness as well as the combative implications of even Greer's most ostensibly peace-loving goals: 'If she accepts (and simplifies) Freud's notion of eternal Eros at war with his immortal adversary the death-drive, and then makes Eros (or rather Eros denied) equal women, and death equal men, so that the only way to save the world is for Eros-women to overcome death-men, then surely that accords a very aggressive role to Love?'[45]

One feminist had raised a warning flag about Germaine's warrior ways even before *The Female Eunuch* was published. In April 1970, *Oz* ran a piece written by 'Michelene' called 'Women on the Moon . . . Or the End of Servile Penitude, a Reply to the Slag Heap Erupts and particularly Germaine (Cunt Power) Greer.'[46] The piece responded to Germaine's anticipation of the imminent publication of an edition of *Oz* containing a 'positive statement of Cuntpower' which would expand on her view that the 'cunt must take the steel out of the cock.'[47] (The eventual edition was titled, much more satisfactorily from the censor's standpoint, 'Female Energy Oz.'[48]) Michelene took exception to Germaine's barely latent aggression, and objected that the women's movement did not want to replace 'penis-power by Cunt-power, or any generalised power.'

On the whole, in contrast with her strong public identification as a women's movement leader, Greer missed out on serious critical engagement with other feminists. Her loose logic and rhetorical excesses, her occasionally obvious impatience and condescension toward women who did not conform to her own notions, were not polished by critical interaction with informed peers. This set the pattern for her future work. It could be one reason why there is so little sense of growth and development in her later thinking and writing. In its absence, Greer would largely extrapolate in her writing from the particular life passage through which she was traveling at the time.

*Oz* unwittingly pointed to a key aspect of the way *The Female Eunuch* would be read in the two reviews it ran side by side. 'Reading *The Female Eunuch* I felt that there was not one Germaine Greer but several,' wrote Sheila Rowbotham. 'There was one I liked a lot, who had the defiance, the controlled, if sometimes desperate dignity, of revolutionary feminism. . . . But in the midst of the defiance and the irony there's a gawky, forlorn girl, miserably dragging sanitary towels about in her school satchel, uneasily moving into an unhappy adolescence, not liking her mother, self-conscious about being tall and dreaming of crushing her nose into a giant's tweed suit.' Rowbotham confessed that she had her own version of the tweed-suited giant fantasy – though in her case he was leather-clad and swept her off to the hills on his motorbike – but, like Michelene, she identified Germaine's general disconnectedness from the women's movement as a problem. Greer's analysis had 'an external quality,' Rowbotham argued; she lacked the passion and self-criticism of the women working within the movement. As a result she had missed out on learning from working alongside other women, being forced to re-examine preconceived notions, often painfully and painfully often.

'Oh wow it's been done before Germaine,' Rowbotham wrote:

> Ever heard of scarecrow radicals? They frighten the sparrows a bit at first until they get used to them. Scarecrows can look very impudent but they can't do anything. There have been lots of scarecrow feminists, lots of bold women who resisted the servile lot of other women, who made a great flurry and a show, and who ended up like George Sand rejecting the feminist socialist groups to perform for a male audience. You avoid the stiff tense humourless tightness you see as a feature both of feminism and of the revolutionary groups, and you suddenly find yourself becoming a sophisticated brand of titillation on the media. It's a trap that destroys people ruthlessly.[49]

Tim Harris in the accompanying *Oz* review argued that most people lacked the energy or capacity to live their lives in accordance with Greer's blueprint for freedom. Yet his reaction to *The Female Eunuch*'s essence echoed one that can still be heard today from women not involved in the movement recalling their first encounter with the book: 'suddenly one becomes conscious of a whole area of experience previously blinded by habitual response. To have altered our perceptions, enlarged our world, and amused us in the process, that is a brilliant feat.'[50]

In its inimitable style, *Oz* managed to capture the divergence in the review headlines: 'How to Get Your Man . . .' over Harris's review, and over Rowbotham's '. . . The Book That Men Love and Women Hate.' It was almost right. Many men did love the book, but so did many women. It was just that the less a woman had had to do with the women's movement at the time, the more likely it seemed she was to be impressed by *The Female Eunuch*. Women who were already active feminists read it with far more guile and could see the problems in it.

*The Female Eunuch* is arguably *the* book of the television age. It is not the most brilliant, the best-written, the best-selling or most insightful book; but it exemplifies so many key features of writing, publishing and reading in the mass-marketing era. If one had to choose just one book through which to illustrate the path post-war writing, publishing and popular thinking has traveled, this book would be a good choice. Take a great title, arresting cover artwork, a promotable, quotable author, add sex and install liberally in airport bookstands, stand back, enjoy the controversy and watch it sell its paperback cover off: it is a trite but true formula for modern publishing success. The book's author became a celebrity on three continents, and the man who contracted it eventually went on to New York to head one of the most prestigious publishing houses in the world.

Other elements also speak of its time. The style combines journalese and anecdote with the quasi-academic. It is studded with pull-out quotes, anticipating the drive to break up blocks of text as the march of computer graphics and MTV-length attention spans proceeds. It is a polemic of personal change whose influence attested to the powerful conjunction of ideas and the modern media; and it is an item designed for mass consumption. Its only atypical trait is, perhaps, its long shelf life. The book is still in print and widely available more than a quarter-century after publication.

Representing it like this in purely commercial formulaic terms is not meant to trivialize the book but rather to expose its business brilliance in pure, stripped-back form. *The Female Eunuch* is much, much more than the sum of its considerable commercial parts, more than a text tweaked into shape by the changing moods of Sonny Mehta's eyes. Its success in the marketplace and Greer's success as its author vastly expanded the scope and scale of her opportunities for 'delinquency' in Britain and abroad. Germaine Greer was launched. The world, for which read New York, was about to acclaim her the star that feminism was waiting for.

# 9

# *Celebrity Circuits*

Germaine Greer might have been fond of criticizing Freud, but they shared an attitude. Freud regarded repudiation of his ideas as a key indicator of their validity, as Juliet Mitchell observed; easy acceptance made him nervous. Because Freud was revealing the repressed unconscious, 'the revelation must by definition be unwelcome.' Yet he was also anxious to win adherents.[1] Greer shared this ambivalence. 'The more despised your course of action is, the more trouble you get into by following it, and the surer you can be it's the right one,' she said on the eve of *The Female Eunuch*'s publication.[2] The book was light on strategy and instructions, she added, because every woman is herself the expert and no ideology is as important as what she knows from her own experience. Why, then, did Greer think a book like hers – as ideological as any other polemic – was necessary? 'The only reason why I would ever have submitted to the commercialisation of Germaine Greer,' she said shortly after *The Female Eunuch* was published, 'was because I am convinced that the woman in the home is so alienated from her environment that nothing short of an earthquake will stir her to think that something is happening.'[3] She had cast herself in the role of significant seismic disturbance, and looked forward to the tremors she and her book would create.

If repudiation was to be her yardstick of success, the reaction to *The Female Eunuch* should have been cause for deep concern. The book created a huge stir, most of which took the form of long, laudatory profiles of the thirty-one-year-old academic, journalist and occasional actress. The attention took its toll on her nervous system. 'I keep going to the lavatory all the time, and I've lost my purse twice in a week,' she told a reporter shortly after the book's publication in Britain. The generosity of spirit Chris Wallace-Crabbe observed in Greer's younger days had waned, and the new flush of limelight did nothing to quell the tendency to scorn that was growing in its place. To the same reporter Greer went on to belittle an overweight boy who came into their view eating an ice cream, 'thus shortening his ugly little life even further.'[4]

The book was launched in October 1970 at a party attended by the *Oz* crowd, underground notables and a sprinkling of feminists. Germaine was one of the underground's own, and hip London knew where she was coming from: the counterculture, not a women's collective. A few months before *The Female Eunuch* appeared, she had published a spread on 'New Ways with Playclothes' in her incarnation as *Oz* magazine's 'Needlework Correspondent,' demonstrating original designs including the 'Phun City Bikini' and the 'Keep it Warm Cock Sock.'[5] At Germaine's suggestion, Richard Neville posed for photographs wearing her hand-knitted, multi-striped cock sock and scrotum pouch, which she said could be whipped up in an evening out of odds and ends of colored wool. Few feminist activists at that time were sitting around knitting – and cock socks tended not to be in the pattern books of those who were.

Once *The Female Eunuch* was published, Greer downed knitting needles and began the rounds of the press. In polite, restrained Britain her outspokenness was a gift for the media, which gave her an easy time and blanket coverage. At times the debate was almost genteel. 'From what do you wish to emancipate women?' asked one woman in a BBC Radio exchange. 'I was eighty yesterday,' the woman, a Mrs. Brander-Dunbar, went on. 'I've been a rural district councillor, played polo among men, hunted, run the village dancing classes and discussion groups, and for the last ten or twenty years run my house and home. I have never experienced any disadvantage in being a woman among men. Perhaps it is because I have always tried to act on my father's advice, which was:

They lived well in 1854

They knew good food and liked it—even as you and I. Certainly they used more home cooked food in those days, but there was one delicacy they always bought ready for use, Swallow & Ariell's Biscuits

They knew these could not be improved upon and they wanted the best — even as you and I

**SWALLOW & ARIELL LTD**
THE UNEEDA BAKERS

. Peggy Lafrank pictured in *Table Talk* magazine, February 1936, the year before she married Reg Greer

. Reg Greer, then a smartly turned-out newspaper advertising salesman on the way up, pictured several weeks earlier

. Star girls Jennifer and Germaine, at the height of their passionate friendship

4. Margaret and Leon Fink in 1961. Margaret and Germaine met through Harry Hooton, Margaret's first great love, and became firm friends. Margaret later married Leon, the man whom Germaine had chosen several years earlier to be her first lover

5. Roelof Smilde playing competitive bridge. 'Germaine was madly in love with him,' recalls Margaret Fink. 'She's been in love with a few people but I don't think the way she was with Roelof . . . I think it was mutual'

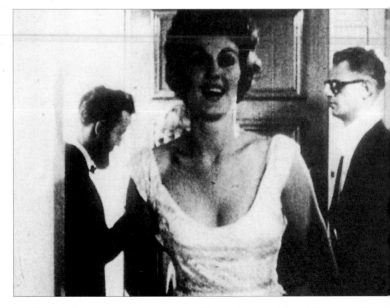

6. 'She's a born actor . . . a star.' Germaine in Albie Thoms' film ' . . . it droppeth as the gentle rain', 1963

7. Germaine takes an unscheduled fall during rehearsals for *My Girl Herbert*, the Cambridge Footlights 1965 revue. The cast included future Monty Python star, Eric Idle (far left). Next to him is Mervyn Riches and, on the far right, John Grillo

8. With patriotic Englishman Rod Lake, who offered to prove his sexual prowess personally to Germaine

OZ talks to DR G — the only groupie with a Ph.D in captivity.

Why the Press Council is a dangerous hoax.

Why Portugal — the poorest country in Europe — has a defence budget second only to the United States.

What the man who discovered that cannabis is non addictive said to Caroline Coon.

Millions are starving...Millions of pounds worth of food is dumped each year. Why?

You've never seen Ophelia looking like Marianne Faithful looking like this.

Led Zeppelin...Murray Roman...Everly Brothers...The Incredible String Band Two Virgins...BOB DYLAN

**Saucy Feminist That Even Men Like**

Germaine Greer

MAY 7 · 1971 · 50

9. 'I guess I'm just a starfucker really.' Germaine on the February 1969 cover of *Oz*, with Vivian Stanshaw from the Bonzo Dog Band

10. The *Life* cover encapsulating the mainstream media's embrace of Greer. 'I don't go for that whole pants and battledress routine,' Germaine told the magazine. 'It just puts men off . . .'

11. The Town Hall debate in New York, April 1971. Greer and Norman Mailer were a match made in media heaven: self-possessed, self-consciously potent and subterraneanly angry

12. Greer and Mike Willesee in 1973. Friends recall Germaine being so smitten she would beg off social invitations in order to wait by the phone in case Willesee called

13. Germaine in January 1972, sitting beneath a portrait of Queen Elizabeth II, at a press conference in Sydney to promote *The Female Eunuch*. 'Hard now, to recapture the excitement of Germaine's visit . . .' recalls Dennis Altman, 'more akin to a rebellious Royal tour than a book promotion.'

14. 'Germaine's bold gaze zeroed in on me,' wrote Paul du Feu, recalling the moment he met his future wife. He was fascinated by the tall stranger with 'frizzed-out soul-sister hair' who strode down the middle of the Portobello Road like a gunslinger

15. Reacting to a radio phone-in caller in December 1974

16. 'He's wild, he's wonderful,' Germaine said of Paul du Feu, in a late-night phone call to Richard Neville on the eve of her marriage. Du Feu was a building worker with a good degree in English literature. The marriage lasted three weeks

MS. GERMAINE GREER

17. At a meeting of writers, lawyers, scientists and politicians exchanging ideas in a dialogue marking international Women's Day, 1975, at the United Nations headquarters in New York

18. In Ethiopia: her enduring sympathy with the Third World was an increasingly powerful influence on her work

19 and 20. At Mill Farm, Greer settled into rural domesticity with characteristic determination, and began to enjoy what has probably been the most enduring contentment of her life

21. Sought-after critic, columnist and television presenter, Greer remains at the centre of London's literary circuit; seen here with Barry Humphries at the relaunch of *Punch* in 1996

always try to look like a woman and act like a man.'

'Mrs Brander-Dunbar, I really wish more women could tell the same story,' Germaine replied. 'It's true that women can do almost anything they want, they could probably play polo if they really wanted, they could probably be prime minister, although a good many people would have their noses put a bit out of joint. What I wrote the book about was why it is that so few women *want* to do those things ... so what I was talking about emancipating them from was first and foremost what I sometimes call an infirmity of will: a lack of desire to do things. Not everybody had your father, or your advantages, I'm afraid. It's not that the country is full of women sobbing and rending their garments and chafing against their imprisonment, but there are women who could do great things, who could be sources of enormous inspiration and help, who just aren't doing them.'[6]

The book's success in Britain preceded a commercial triumph in the United States. The American hardback rights reportedly sold for $30,000 and the paperback rights for the then-phenomenal sum of $135,000.[7] The advance publicity was compelling, and Greer's odd but effective mix of savvy and ingenuousness was amply evident when she came to promote her book in the United States. Her superficial acquaintance with the women's liberation movement in New York and somewhat further afield in America, had been enough for her to feel free to deride their approach and achievements in *The Female Eunuch*. While she was writing the book, the imminent prospect of visiting the American feminists' home ground was probably the furthest thing from her mind.

She also knew something of New York's cultural icons, having visited the city a few months before *The Female Eunuch* was conceived. On that occasion she had fallen out with her old Push friend Lillian Roxon. Roxon was in the middle of writing her *Rock Encyclopedia*,[8] had just developed the asthma which would kill her a few years later, had suddenly put on more than twenty-five pounds and was dealing with a cockroach infestation. Roxon cried off the standing invitation to Greer to stay with her, and booked her instead into a hotel with tariffs that suited Germaine's budget.

'She said, without a trace of compassion,' Roxon recounted, 'that it was all in my mind, and the love of a good man would solve everything, her usual solution but that's small comfort when your breath comes whistling out like a tea kettle and your publisher wants your manuscript fast.' When Lillian rang to see how Germaine was getting on, Greer, in her best Cambridge intonation, said she did not mind the junkies at the hotel, she did not even mind the transvestites or the prostitutes, but that she did object to the corpses in the lift. Unbeknown to Roxon, homicide was commonplace in the hotel's seedy neighborhood. The two women did not speak to each other for a year.

The next Roxon heard of Greer was when a journalist rang from London to tell her about the acidly affectionate dedication at the beginning of *The Female Eunuch*.[9] 'This book is dedicated to Lillian who lives with nobody but a colony of New York roaches, whose energy has never failed despite her anxieties and her asthma and her weight, who is always interested in everybody, often angry, sometimes bitchy, but always involved,' it began. 'Lillian, the abundant, the golden, the eloquent, the well and badly loved; Lillian the beautiful who thinks she is ugly, Lillian the indefatigable who thinks she is always tired.' Lillian hated it: 'I thought it was simply horrible.' Four other women were similarly honored.

New York was also partly familiar to Greer through the work of its writers and activists. When she arrived for her book tour, debate was raging over the contretemps between Norman Mailer and Kate Millett. Millett's book *Sexual Politics* had been published a few months before *The Female Eunuch* appeared in Britain. After Friedan's *The Feminine Mystique*, Millett's was the breakthrough book of second-wave feminism in the United States; *Sexual Politics* was radical feminism's high-water mark in mainstream publishing. Millett had exposed the deep, vicious misogyny that had been embedded in Western literature without comment for decades, using Mailer and Henry Miller as two of her prime examples. Mailer had recently retaliated with a piece entitled 'The Prisoner of Sex' in *Harper's* magazine, reasserting his chauvinist credentials and attacking Millett.

Most readers encountering Millett's dissection of Mailer's work experience an instant feminist conversion. Mailer, however, already had a very different place in Greer's psyche: during her earlier incarnation as *Oz* magazine's starfucking 'Dr G,' his penis had 'blossom[ed] in her head.'[10] Mailer was on her mind well before she began her American book tour, to say the very least.

Greer was also familiar with the work of the Black Panther Eldridge Cleaver. Her fundamental proposition – that men had enfeebled women, with their connivance, to serve male purposes – owed much to Cleaver's 'Allegory of the Black Eunuchs' in *Soul on Ice*, which she quotes in *The Female Eunuch*. 'The myth of the strong black woman is the other side of the coin of the myth of the beautiful dumb blonde,' wrote Cleaver. 'The white man turned the white woman into a weak-minded, weak-bodied, delicate freak, a sex pot, and placed her on a pedestal; he turned the black woman into a strong self-reliant Amazon and deposited her in his kitchen.'[11] Greer took Cleaver's weak white woman on the pedestal and made her the basis of a whole book.

Germaine's publisher, McGraw-Hill, had booked her into New York's Algonquin Hotel, the mid-town haunt of the literati. She checked instead into the Chelsea, hip rather than *haute*, the haunt of rock stars and artists, where another talented and unconventional antipodean, Australian painter Brett Whiteley, had recently been in residence. Suitably corrected, McGraw-Hill sent a gift basket of fruit up to her room to welcome her to New York. 'I guess they consider it inappropriate to send flowers to a female revolutionary,' she mused to the *Washington Post*.[12]

The spectrum of reactions to the book and its author within American society was as wide as the response within the American women's movement. *Life* magazine captured the mainstream media embrace of Germaine in its cover story, 'Saucy Feminist that Even Men Like.'[13] Inside, the magazine ran a startling five-deck quote in 36-point type before the piece even began: 'I don't go for that whole pants and battledress routine. It just puts men off . . .' The opening scene has Greer leading a graduate seminar on a Jacobean revenge tragedy at Warwick University when *Hamlet* strays into the discussion. A student queries why Hamlet lets Ophelia die. 'Because she's such a bore! That's why he lets her die,' Greer scorns. 'Because she's such an insipid and disloyal little bitch!' *Life* readers did not have to know anything about feminism to register the ambivalence about women underlying Greer's reaction. Then there were soothing words for men and a bizarre rewriting of the history of the struggle for female suffrage. 'They really want help,' Germaine said of men. 'They really want someone to share the responsibility. That's why men gave the vote to women in the first place. It was a cry for help.'

At the same time Germaine was constructively provocative on some feminist questions – notably that the women's movement's belief in the unilateral oppression of women by men was misleading and led nowhere, and that women had to see how they co-operated in their own oppression. 'It seems to me that if you go about shrieking, "Men must give us freedom!" then you endorse their mastery. What you have to shriek is: "Your time is up!"'

This restatement of one of *The Female Eunuch*'s core messages, along with a wholesale attack on marriage, was enough to stir middle America to action in *Life*'s letters column. 'We raise cattle,' wrote Mrs. Morris Larsen of Marsing, Idaho. 'When we find a cow with undesirable traits, she is taken from the breeding herd and sent to the butcher. How fortunate for future generations that Germaine Greer and her ilk are willingly removing themselves from motherhood.' Donald Petersen of Waterloo, Iowa, was more concise: 'Personally, I don't see how Germaine's husband lasted three weeks with her.'[14]

Almost as soon as she arrived in New York, Germaine started to back-pedal on her criticisms of the American women's movement and its key figures. 'I think I've been rather ungenerous,' she said. 'But it did seem to me that so much of what was happening was counter-productive. And everybody seems to get so uptight.'[15] Any amount of back-pedalling, however, was not going to be enough to neutralize the hostility she encountered from parts of the women's movement. The American feminist Claudia Dreifus penned one of the most astringent analyses of the book in which she declared that Greer was benefiting from being everything American feminists were not: 'pretty, predictable, aggressively heterosexual, media-wise, clever, foreign and exotic.' *The Female Eunuch* said all the right things about the economics of sexism, she conceded, and Greer's reading of female anatomy she considered brilliant. The book was nevertheless 'shallow, anti-woman, regressive [and] three steps backward to the world of false sexual liberation from which so many young women have fled.' Greer's problem, said Dreifus, was her attitude to her own kind – 'her inveterate dislike of women, her idiotic exhortations to revolution and nonviolence alike, and her passionate identification with all things male.

'Throughout history,' Dreifus continued, 'there have always been a few women who have been able to fight and seduce their way to the top of the patriarchy.' Greer was 'the closest thing we have to this old-world, old-style courtesan. Nor would she be offended by this description. By her own admission, she is a groupie, a supergroupie – which means that she is a sexual and intellectual consort to the royalty of rock music.'

> *The Female Eunuch* is designed to provide intellectual and sexual thrills to those men who would like to see a feminist revolution because it would take that *one* woman off their back and make a lot more women available to them. How nice to be told that women's liberation will mean the liberation of more women for bed service! One reading of *The Female Eunuch* suggested to me that it had been written to assuage the fears of jittery male chauvinists. A second reading convinced me that if Germaine Greer didn't exist, Norman Mailer would have had to invent her.[16]

Greer's relations with the movement were not improved when Christopher Lehmann-Haupt in the *New York Times* compared her book favorably with Millett's *Sexual Politics*: 'it is everything that Kate Millett's book is not . . . a book with personality, a book that knows the distinction between the self and the other, a book that combines the best of masculinity *and* femininity.'[17] Nor did it help that Greer's attacks on American activists, including Millett, had already been publicized in profiles before her arrival and the book's US publication.

The span of feminist opinion was, in fact, wide. There was Dreifus, with her open contempt. There were lesbian feminists like Jill Johnston, who saw the book as completely irrelevant. 'I tried to read her book,' recalls Johnston. 'It kind of threw me. I didn't know what the hell she was talking about, frankly . . . I don't think any of us were interested in her.' Kate Millett remembers *The Female Eunuch* as 'witty' and 'entertaining' – from a self-avowed revolutionary, potentially double-edged praise. Gloria Steinem gives her most latitude. '*The Female Eunuch* had the appeal that Germaine always has, which is daring, and just being out there,' says Steinem. 'And that's so rare in women because we're so trained to be concerned about approval that I just value it enormously in her. I think her downside and her upside are the same in a way, which is that incredible daring and certainty and willingness to do battle.'

Steinem experienced Greer's attention-grabbing social style in New York one day when they were dining with a couple of other women at a restaurant. Greer began discussing vaginal secretions, to the electrified attention of other diners, maintaining that secretions were to women what erections were to men. She had been having problems with her secretions and had gone to an unsympathetic physician who did not understand her view of them. 'But she found some solution,' says Steinem. 'I no longer remember what it was but I remember thinking it was a very valuable piece of information, being very grateful to her and wonderfully entertained at the same time. She was terrific.'

It was Greer's performance at what was to become one of the second wave's more infamous events, however, that cemented many American feminists' perceptions of her as a collaborator – 'a woman who was walking hand in hand with the enemy' as Jill Johnston puts it, evoking Ti-Grace Atkinson's metaphor for flirting with the patriarchy. The same star-studded event, where Greer was mixing and matching it with American literature's favorite unreconstructed brawler, cemented her nascent celebrity in America. It was what became known as the Town Hall Debate, held in New York on 30 April 1971.

A benefit for the Theater for Ideas, the debate was officially billed as 'A Dialogue On Women's Liberation with Norman Mailer, Germaine Greer, Diana Trilling, Jacqueline Ceballos, Jill Johnston.' Unofficially, there were expectations of an intellectual prizefight between Mailer and women's liberation. Documentary makers Chris Hegedus and D. A. Pennebaker recorded the event in their film *Town Bloody Hall*.

Mailer's central part in the line-up was inflammatory, and leading figures in the American women's movement had effectively boycotted the event. Steinem refused on principle to take part in debates: 'It always seemed to me a masculine form.' Ditto Millett: 'You don't debate human rights.' Millett felt the very idea of the debate with Mailer was a humiliation of feminism itself, but was happy for Jill Johnston to take her place. 'Jill made a wonderful performance art piece out of it,' says Millett. 'She wasn't going to debate anything.' Diana Trilling was a critic and establishment intellectual. Ceballos was president of NOW's New York chapter.

Greer was aware of the state of hostilities between Millett and Mailer. Sections of *Sexual Politics* had been published in journals before the book was even released, and her work had been referred to in the 'Female Energy' *Oz* edited by Greer in mid-1970. Mailer's response, 'The Prisoner of Sex,' had caused a sensation.[18] Germaine accepted the invitation to debate with him before having read 'The Prisoner of Sex,' and she had begun flirting with him before her plane had even left Heathrow. 'I'd really like to help that man,' she told a journalist from *The New York Times* in London.[19] Although she read 'The Prisoner of Sex' before the debate took place, she went ahead with the commitment nevertheless.

The Town Hall audience was glittering. New York's *cognoscenti* converged for the projected intellectual mud-wrestling match between Greer and Mailer; the excitement filled the Town Hall foyer with a Boeing-level hum. In the audience, tucked in among Manhattan's notables, were Greer's friends from St. Joseph's church choir in Sydney, Susan Ryan and Richard Butler – Butler was by then a junior diplomat in Australia's mission to the United Nations in New York. 'I'd read *The Female Eunuch* and had had fights all around New York at dinner parties,' Ryan recalls, 'including with my spouse at the time, I might say. I was saying: "Yes, she's right. This is right. This is the story." Richard was extremely hostile and said: "Please do not raise it in public. Please do not refer to it. This is intolerable behavior."' The book was kerosene on Ryan's new-found feminist fire.

'The whole event was fraught with fear and wildness,' Jill Johnston recalls. She had warmed up for it at the Algonquin with a couple of martinis among friends. When she arrived at the Town Hall, Mailer immediately confronted her without so much as a hello, demanding that Germaine be allowed to speak after Jill rather than before her, as originally agreed, 'because she's the star!' Johnston refused to give way. The line-up would be alphabetical: Ceballos, Greer, Johnston, Trilling.

Introducing proceedings, Mailer said at the outset that each of the 'ladies' would speak for ten minutes, followed by discussion and questions at the end. 'The evening was billed at one time as Norman Mailer versus the four ladies who are listed,' he told the audience. 'I may say that was done almost over my dead body. I may have vanity, but I do not have the vanity to think that one man can take on four women.'

Ceballos gave her speech: it was moderate, worthy. Then Mailer introduced what he considered, in conjunction with himself, the main event: 'The next speaker, who I suspect has done a great deal to fill this house, is that distinguished and young and formidable lady writer, Miss Germaine Greer from England.' The audience broke into cheers and applause as Germaine made her way to the podium.

'For me the significance of this moment,' she began, in an accent Roxon described as a cross between Queen Elizabeth and Vanessa Redgrave,[20] 'is that I am having to confront one of the most powerful figures in my own imagination – the being I think most privileged in male elitist society, namely, the masculine artist, the pinnacle of the masculine elite.' Mailer and the audience broke into exuberant laughter at what from a feminist should have been a high-grade insult but in the context of the evening seemed to be obvious flattery. 'Bred as I have been and educated as I have been,' Greer continued, 'most of my life has been most powerfully influenced by the culture for which he stands, so that I am caught in a basic conflict between inculcated cultural values and my own deep conception of an injustice.'

The literati often asked her in triumphant tones, she said, what had happened to Mozart's sister. She did not know and had to find out: 'And every attempt I make to find that answer leads me to believe that perhaps what we accept as a creative artist in our society is more a killer than a creator, aiming his ego ahead of lesser talents, drawing the focus of all eyes to his achievements, being read now by millions and paid in millions. One must ask oneself the question: in our society, can any painting be worth the total yearly income of a thousand families?' The crowd, a number of whose members' walls were no doubt richly adorned, applauded. 'And if we must answer that it is,' Germaine continued, 'and the auction reports tell us that, then I think we are forced to consider the possibility that the art on which we nourish ourselves is sapping our vitality and breaking our hearts.' The applause thundered.

Greer then quoted Freud on the nature of artists – that 'he,' the artist, longs to attain honor, power, riches, fame and the love of women, but lacks the means of achieving these gratifications. 'As an eccentric little girl who thought it might be worthwhile after all to be a poet, coming across these words for the first time was a severe check,' she said. 'The blandness of Freud's assumption that the artist was a man sent me back into myself to consider whether or not the proposition was reversible. Could a female artist be driven by the desire for riches, fame and the love of men? And all too soon it was very clear that the female artist's own achievements will disqualify her for the love of man. That no woman yet has been loved for her poetry. And we love men for their achievements all the time.'

Could it be a natural order that wasted so much power, she asked, that 'fretted a little girl's heart to pieces?' She said she lacked an answer and moved on to consider the function women had fulfilled in relation to art: 'We were either low sloppy creatures or menials, or we were goddesses, or worst of all we were meant to be both, which meant that we broke our hearts trying to keep our aprons clean.' Again, wild applause. In the future creativity 'will be the prerogative of all of us,' said Germaine, 'and we will do it as those artists did whom Freud understood not at all – the artists who made the cathedral of Chartres or the mosaics of Byzantium – the artists who had no ego and no name.'

The sentiments were exquisite, Mailer responded when Germaine sat down, but the remedy she proposed he dismissed briskly as 'diaper Marxism.' This did not stop him passing her a note inviting her to go out for a drink later. Susan Ryan recalls : 'She was good. She was just fantastic. . . . I was knocked out by it, and so was Richard. She was like what she had been, and I had been – a schoolgirl debater. . . . She came out in this amazing venue with Norman Mailer and all the crazed sort of New York trendiness, and she just stood in the middle of the stage, nice and straight . . . with no fuss and carry-on, and just delivered this homily to us. It was fantastic.'

Mailer introduced Jill Johnston as the *Village Voice*'s master of free associational prose. Pouncing on Mailer's introduction of Greer as hailing from England, Johnston immediately revealed her provincial origins. 'I think Germaine was born in Australia, and I was born in England,' she said. Turning to Germaine: 'Were you born in Australia?' Greer concurred. 'I was born in England,' continued the British-born but American-raised Johnston. 'I can't help it. That's just the first thing I thought of.' Johnston's niggle was the prelude to what would become the evening's real main event: Mailer versus Johnston.

'The title of this episode is "New Approach,"' Jill began. 'All women are lesbians except those who don't know it, naturally. They are but don't know it yet. I am a woman and therefore a lesbian. I am a woman who is a lesbian because I am a woman. . . .' There were gasps from the audience, a barely contained mixture of shock, disapproval and excitement. Piling on the provocation, Johnston lifted the audience with a witty exposition which went on to a sharp but humorous commentary on the Old Testament of fathers begetting sons, begetting sons, begetting sons with nary a daughter mentioned; then a mock White House media statement about a lesbian appointed to a cabinet post; and finally an awkwardly funny discussion between a married couple about a lesbian being invited home to dinner. Johnston had the audience laughing and squirming simultaneously until Mailer called time. Jill had already had fifteen minutes, he said, and it was not fair to the others: there would be no time left for debate.

A woman promptly jumped up from the audience on to the stage and started kissing Johnston passionately, to further gasps from the crowd. Another woman climbed up on to the stage yelling: 'Hey, Jill, what about me?' As all three rolled around the floor in a passionate embrace, Mailer barked: 'Hey, you know it's great that you pay twenty-five bucks to see three dirty overalls on the floor when you can see lots of cock and cunt for four dollars just down the street.' The comparison to the commercial titillation available in the Town Hall precinct did not throw Johnston, who asked Mailer if she could skip the discussion phase of the evening in exchange for being able to finish her piece.

'C'mon, either play with the team or pick up your marbles and get lost,' an angry Mailer snapped. 'C'mon. . . . C'mon Jill – be a lady.' Mailer said he really wanted to talk to her about lesbianism in the discussion period later, but his tone of voice was hardly enticing. Members of the audience began heckling. 'What's the matter, Mailer? You threatened because you've found a woman you can't fuck?' one woman shouted, infuriating Mailer, who replied: 'Hey, cunty, I've been threatened all my life, so take it easy.' The heckling continued. Mailer growled menacingly: 'What do you want to do, Jill? Skip to your last sentence and read it? Okay, we'll take a vote, but I'm going to do the counting. If you don't think that I've got enough fairness to do the count properly, then come and get this mike away from me.'

The confrontation was pure Mailer: sullen, bullying and blustering, culminating in a dubious vote. He went to the rostrum, conspicuously occupying the space to introduce Diana Trilling.[21] After a little more on-stage passion, Johnston and friends slipped out backstage. Apart from Mailer's short fuse and dictatorial temperament, the most telling feature of Johnston's banishment was her fellow panelists' pointed passivity: female eunuchs, indeed. 'I was betrayed by those women,' says Johnston. 'They didn't know what the fuck they were doing.'

With Johnston – the real bomb-thrower of the evening – out of the way, things settled down to a more conventional celebrity performance. Diana Trilling tangled with Greer after challenging her use of Freud, anticipating Juliet Mitchell's later criticism. 'If that is the way you are going to read Freud you will have to dismiss him as a fool, because he never said things like that,' Trilling said, to which Greer countered: 'I adopt the same attitude to Freud as you do. I quote him where it suits me and I don't where it doesn't.' Trilling was uncowed: 'I didn't say that I quote him where it suits me. I said I take from him that which suits me. I don't misquote him.' Germaine pulled a face and terminated the exchange, muttering to the audience: 'One of the characteristics of oppressed people is that they always fight among themselves.'

As it turned out, the only feistiness Mailer faced after Johnston's departure came from the floor. Betty Friedan, sitting near the stage, was handed the microphone at the opening of the discussion period. 'Be accurate, Betty!' Mailer yelled, invoking Friedan's implacable retort: 'Norman, I will define accuracy for myself. I don't need you!'

Susan Sontag extracted almost the only concession. 'I want to ask a very quiet question to Norman and Diana also,' she began. 'Norman, it is true that women find, with the best of will, the way you talk to them patronizing. One of the things is your use of the word "lady." . . . When you said, "Diana Trilling, foremost lady literary critic," if I was Diana I wouldn't like to be introduced that way and I would like to know how Diana feels about it. I don't like being called a lady writer, Norman. I know it seems like gallantry to you, but it doesn't feel right to us. It's a little better to be called a woman writer – I don't know why. But words count. We're all writers. We know that. . . . If you were introducing James Baldwin, you wouldn't say "our foremost Negro writer," and we certainly wouldn't say "a man writer." ' Trilling said she recognized Sontag's point; she permitted the description while not liking it. 'I think you ought to object to it,' pressed Sontag. Mailer capitulated: 'I will never use the word 'lady' in public again.'

For Greer and Mailer, the Town Hall debate was something of a love-in. Germaine, oddly chic in a full-length black gown and motley fox fur, and Norman, aggressive and charming by unpredictable turn through the events of the evening, were a match made in media heaven, with subtle body language to suit: sexual, self-possessed, self-consciously potent and subterraneanly angry. When Mailer's inevitable attack on *Sexual Politics* came, Greer met it honorably. Mailer griped that if Kate Millett was 'the one who's done the historical work which establishes that men control women in a political class system then we are all doomed.' She replied steadily: 'No-one would be more surprised than Kate to hear that she is being charged with having done this. . . . [We] have so many intricate problems involving each level of our society that it's absurd to demand of any woman at this stage that she show you the complete analysis or that she stands convicted of having made it.'

'I'm all for that,' continued Mailer. 'But I would ask then why do you women keep saying, without having done the analysis, why do you keep being so certain it's entirely the male's fault?' Greer now slid into a dodgy philosophical position that lent credence to the radical feminists' suspicions of her as collaborator. Her response let men, at that moment specifically Mailer, off the hook.

'I didn't know that any women were certain that it was entirely the male's fault,' she replied soothingly. 'That's precisely what we're trying to elicit. And if the fact is that men have been unconsciously tyrannical – and I think it probably is the case – then it's certain also that they were debauched by their own tyranny and degraded by it and confused by it almost as much as the people they tyrannized over.'

'We're in agreement on this,' affirmed Mailer, unsurprisingly. 'This is just old socialism when you get down to it.' Greer was Mailer's kind of feminist: good-looking, an intellectual pugilist in her own right, who disarmingly agreed it was not men's fault. Indeed, who said men might be victims of their own ascendancy!

Town Hall was a microcosm of social relations at the time. A man, and one of unabashed sexist complexion at that, was running the show – the star attraction, the center of attention. With nearly equal billing was the 'saucy feminist that even men like.' Their potential for congress – intellectual or, as the subtext had it, sexual – electrified the event. Two other women, lacking the stars' charisma and polemical vim, were heard politely. The real trouble-maker, challenging the crowd to the edge of the comfort zone even while getting laughs, was tossed out by the master of proceedings while her fellow female panelists looked on.

'Norman Mailer simply adored [Germaine] and couldn't take his eyes off her,' Roxon said. 'Everyone in that elegant audience . . . kept joking how that would indeed be the romance of the year.' Lillian quizzed Germaine: Had she gone home with him after the post-debate party in the Village? 'Please,' she snorted. 'I got into the cab to leave and there at the wheel was the man of my dreams.'[22]

The relief that Germaine gave men from the frontal assault of other feminists they felt threatened by was a major theme in the mainstream praise for *The Female Eunuch* in the United States. Max Lerner summed it up in the *New York Post*: 'Finally, a book . . . which one can read without feeling his intelligence assaulted by a shrill scold, a man-hating lesbian, or a dogma-shackled fanatic.'[23] *Time* noted that she seemed 'obsessed by sex,' and active sexuality for women was her 'triumphant answer to everything.' Greer wrote freely, the magazine said, 'of her pleasure in being a sort of supergroupie, and the sort of woman who can tame violent men. Indeed, there are a few passages in her book that make her sound more like a Helen Gurley Brown than a Kate Millett.'[24]

Greer also received a personal endorsement from Henry Miller, then eighty years old, who was the other prime example of literary misogyny targeted by Millett in *Sexual Politics*. 'I'd vote for Germaine as President if I could,' Miller said from his home in California. 'The one woman in the Women's Lib movement I'm in love with is Germaine. Oo-la-la! She is everybody's liberator and she writes like a man. Reading her is like reading *Tropic of Cancer*.'[25]

For a feminist, with endorsements like these, who needed enemies? Yet despite the dubious light they cast on Greer and her book, the fact remained that thousands of women enjoyed reading it and found it radicalizing in terms of their view of themselves and their relations with men. Sally Kempton, a member of New York Radical Feminists, perceived something important about *The Female Eunuch* that other reviewers, whether for or against, had missed. *The Female Eunuch* was a conglomeration of fact, speculation and polemic arranged in chapters, she said, with an almost poetic logic. The book was quirky, brilliantly written, full of bile and insight. Most of her insights were already available in the work of other feminist writers: de Beauvoir's *The Second Sex* was the definitive analysis, and no one since could claim originality except Millett. No matter, Kempton asserted: 'What [Greer] gives us instead is very like art.'[26]

Kempton's observation illuminates a key aspect of Greer's psychology that goes some way toward explaining its contra-dictory elements. At school Germaine loved art classes, was a passionate participant in Sister Attracta's choir, acted in plays, produced one herself and toyed with the idea of writing the libretto for her girlfriend's proposed opera. She maintained a lifelong interest in choral music, singing in choirs from St. Joseph's in Sydney's run-down inner-city Newtown to Cambridge's exquisite thirteenth-century Little St. Mary's Anglican Church. Her theatrical activities continued from school through Melbourne, Sydney and Cambridge universities and beyond into British television. Greer's dressmaking skills were renowned among women friends, who knew she could revamp ordinary clothes into something special.

She was equally handy with knitting needles and crochet hooks, as readers of *Oz*'s 'Female Energy' issue could testify. She aspired to write fiction. She and her Melbourne University friend, Anne Polis, had often talked of the novel Germaine planned to write. Later, in London in the mid-1960s, she began writing a 'potboiler,' as she described it to an old Sydney University colleague when they met on the steps of the British Museum. She told the Town Hall audience in New York of her childhood aspirations to become a poet. Her next book would be a weighty work on women artists. Greer's own artistic bent was too wide and persistent to be dismissed as merely a creative streak: it was part of the very foundation of her character.

Both Greer and Kate Millett were, in their ways, artist/scholars. In Millett the dual elements were more focused and formalized. She practised as a professional artist and had taught at Barnard and Columbia to pay the bills and put bread on the table: 'I'd been a downtown sculptor, a very serious visual artist, using my education to make a living. And I had to go to graduate school in order to keep the job. I had to get a doctorate.' *Sexual Politics* was the result. 'I was writing a Ph.D. thesis. I had to write a very different book [from Germaine's]. She had been a journalist and was writing a book of journalistic entertainment that was very well argued at the same time.' With Greer, the priorities were reversed. Her academic work had up to this point taken precedence over her various creative pursuits – most notably, acting. The theatre, television comedy, creative writing and singing all took a back seat to graduate study and university teaching. 'I need that,' Germaine said of teaching. 'Those students are my real family.'[27]

Millett had primary artistic outlets through sculpture and, later, autobiographical and creative writing. The scholar and the creator were more discernibly delineated in Millett than in Greer. In the absence of an alternative creative outlet, Greer's scholarly and, most importantly, her polemical works seem to have been suffused with her latent creative drive. In Greer the artist *manquée* often overwhelmed the intellectual. Hence her tendency to indulge in philosophical flights of fancy at odds with statements she had made elsewhere – sometimes even within the same work. When confronted with contradictions she would invoke a special licence, exercised through her sheer force of personality and consummate skill with words. The artistic temperament countered and some-times overwhelmed the scholarly instinct for internal consistency and the deeper development of ideas.

Germaine's obvious creativity and its lack of a satisfying, substantive outlet are almost certainly linked to one of her lifelong preoccupations: what she perceives as the historical failure of creative women to measure up. It is a theme to which she has persistently returned, and one that could explain what may amount to a creative block within her as much as an historical judgment about the works of creative women.

When *The Female Eunuch* was published in Britain, Germaine announced that she had already begun work on her second book – a 'more intellectual work' concerned with why there had been no female Mozart, on the limitations of female culture.[28] At the Town Hall debate she said she was often asked what had happened to Mozart's sister: that she did not know and had to find out. Nine years after *The Female Eunuch* came *The Obstacle Race*, a book about the fortunes of women painters and their work. 'There is then no female Leonardo, no female Titian, no female Poussin, but the reason does not lie in the fact that women have wombs, that they can have babies, that their brains are smaller, that they lack vigour, that they are not sensual,' she concluded. 'The reason is simply that you cannot make great artists out of egos that have been damaged, with wills that are defective, with libidos that have been driven out of reach and energy diverted into neurotic channels.'[29] More than a decade later, Camille Paglia retorted: 'That's absurd. All great art has come from mutilated egos,' citing Michelangelo and Beethoven as examples.[30] Nearly twenty years after *The Obstacle Race*, Greer's *Slip-Shod Sibyls* was published, in which she argued a similar case for women poets.

It was a view she personalized as well as generalized. At the London launch of *The Female Eunuch* she said she believed in thinking intelligently and feeling passionately – tenets she said she had violated when trying to write a novel: 'There were judicious observations on the part of the narrator and fatuous stupidities on the part of the characters.'[31] At the Town Hall debate she spoke of the withering impact on her, a young girl with creative aspirations, of Freud's casual assumption of the artist as male. When a former teacher asked if Star of the Sea could feature Germaine's schoolgirl painting of Our Lady of Guadeloupe in the school's 1983 centenary celebrations, Greer wrote: 'I'm astonished that you think it good enough for such an honour. . . .'[32] She was tremendously nervous about the reception of her first non-polemical book, *Daddy We Hardly Knew You*, the detective-style story of the search for her father's roots: 'It's the first I've written as a writer rather than arguing a case. I won't read the reviews. I'll cut them out and file them and look at them years later when I can read them without getting an upset tummy.'[33]

While so sure of herself in her polemical pronouncements, Germaine betrayed deep insecurity about her own creative talent. Unfortunately for the women whose creative work she discounted, Greer extrapolated her hypercritical self-perception into a view that the work of creative women generally – the painters and poets among them, at least – had never measured up to the best produced by men. Greer's extreme position on this is tenuous, though perhaps explicable given her own creative truncation and tendency to extrapolate universals from her own life.

One area where Germaine could safely be creative was that of her identity. Her tendency to self-aggrandizing fantasy was given free rein in New York, safe in the knowledge that Reg and Peggy were unlikely to contradict her from far-off Mentone. She later confessed she shared the trait with her father, and in New York she exercised it explicitly in relation to him. It centered mostly on Germaine's fantasy about being Jewish. The *New York Post* got the full treatment. 'A strange thing happened to me at the university,' she said of her Melbourne days. 'I began to gravitate towards the Jewish community, which was interesting because my father was an anti-Semite who found it embarrassing to do business with Jews. I spent all my time rapping with Jewish students, I learned Yiddish, I went out with nothing but Jewish boys, I joined a Jewish theatrical group. Finally, when I was twenty-one, the truth came out. My father told me he'd had a Jewish mother.'[34] She told the *New York Daily News* her father was of Jewish origin, and expanded on Reg's wartime traumas. After Malta he had been sent to Darjeeling, India, to recover but 'became worse because there was a twelve-year-old prostitute serving the whole camp.' No, he had not actually told her that: she had read it years later in a letter he had sent to her mother, which Peggy was throwing out.[35]

Greer had written a provocative book about women and men, and had come to New York to sell it. She told Lillian Roxon she felt it was the least she could do given the size of the advances she had been paid by her American publishers. Having come to New York to promote her book, why was she talking to American journalists about her father and the mysteries of her (imagined) Jewish heritage? Even stranger were her excursions into the romanticization of poverty. 'I find myself really caring about people,' she told the *New York Post* in a burst of cloying *noblesse oblige*: 'There's almost something erotic about it. I would rather walk on the Lower East Side and rap with winos and kids on the street, because something amazing is going on there, I would rather be there than here. It's something like a group grope, a way of getting together and really loving each other. . . . It's really like being in love with a drug addict because it's hopeless. That's what being in love with humanity is like. I feel some kind of spiritual growth, and that's what has happened to women in the movement. We're going beyond the individual libido to the collective libido.'[36] It dripped with an embarrassing romanticism only someone who had not known real poverty could display.

'There wasn't much personal consciousness,' Jill Johnston explains of the period. 'Political consciousness sort of included everything. . . . This was a moment, a very fierce moment. People, if they were anything like me, were being catapulted from obscurity into contradictions and strains on their ego that couldn't be handled. It invited self-indulgence, enormous self-indulgence, especially since so many of us were writers. The problems that are endemic to writers – the isolation, the need for affection, the desire to be more creative in your writing – the people I encountered, each one seemed to think that they had invented the movement. I'm sure Germaine thought that way, I know Kate thought that way and I know I felt that way. It was pathetic, really, when you come right down to it.'

Kate Millett was at the center of the storm. 'We were cresting, we were having a ball,' she recalls. 'It was tremendously exciting . . .

living high on the revolution. We were having, let's face it, an astonishing effect, given that there were so few of us and all that. And we were fresh meat for the media. Then it kind of became serious and they had to discredit us, cool this thing out, because I mean, there would've been real consequences. Bell Telephone would've had to pay its operators, you know. Equal salaries would've made a real big dent on economic life. Wives were talking back. Things were getting out of hand. So there was all this big backlash.'

Millett was the first target. Her portrait had been on the cover of *Time*, which drew criticism from radical feminists opposed to the creation of obvious leaders in the movement. The 'anti-leader' pressure grew partly from a distaste for power hierarchies, which were considered inherently masculine. There was also a feeling that if leaders were identifiable, they – and through them, the movement – would become vulnerable to manipulation from outside.

Millett had refused to sit for a cover photograph. *Time* solved its problem by commissioning a portrait of her, painted from a photograph taken when *Sexual Politics* was being reviewed. Millett was attacked by both sides. By the middle of 1971 she was having to defend herself inside the movement: 'I said: "Listen, I didn't let them take my picture. It's a painting!"' By Thanksgiving, the media had discovered Millett's lesbian relationships and the tone of *Time*'s previously glowing coverage went into reverse. 'They said: "Oh, my God, she's a bisexual! And her book doesn't make any sense,"' Millett remembers. 'The book now had a whole series of logical errors and stuff because I was a queer. Well, really! They blow up the balloon. They paint this little face on it and a name, and then they can bust it. It's extremely important for them to be able to control the culture heroes they create.'

Activists in the women's movement were caught in a double bind. Spreading the message widely to other women required publicity, by definition involving the media which, of course, was male-controlled. Media interest was hard to attract in the early days, according to Millett: 'We used to have to dress up for demonstrations and wear costumes so the bloody reporters and photographers would come. They didn't used to cover us. . . . So when *Sexual Politics* is making a hit we think: "Great, that will help feminism." Then, of course, you don't think it might be personally awkward or disconcerting.'

Millett was thirty-five and had hitherto lived an obscure life as a sculptor, scholar and, latterly, as a feminist; she had helped found Columbia Women's Liberation and was a member of Downtown Radical Feminists and Downtown Radical Lesbians. *Sexual Politics*'s overnight success was wonderful, Millett says, for a fortnight. After that it was a nightmare. 'Because of television,' she says. 'It makes you kind of crazy. You sort of lose your identity. . . . This is not really fame. This is just notoriety and celebrity, and they're really neurotic conditions. I had to make the same speech so many times I was nauseated at myself because I was just repeating myself. For a supposedly creative person, that's very humiliating. . . . I was imprisoned in this image. It went on for about a year and a half and I was just falling to pieces, so I started to write *Flying*[37] which was sort of how I righted myself. . . . When you're in that limelight you don't have time to do anything except get your hair washed and get your clothes together and get the car out. It absorbs you somehow, it eats you up.'

The use of Millett's sexuality to discredit her was an instance of a technique that was being widely deployed against women who tested the limits of patriarchal society. As Max Lerner had put it in the *Post*, men did not want their intelligence to be assaulted by 'a shrill scold, a man-hating lesbian, or a dogma-shackled fanatic.' That is, men preferred quiet, heterosexual women who did not worry themselves – or their men – with sexual politics. It was a potent line against women long conditioned to seeking male approval.

'The whole thing to intimidate the libbies was to make them queers,' says Millett. 'We answered this brilliantly by saying: "We support gay liberation. Of course, we agree on all these theoretical points." So we had all the right political answers. But, of course, back home in St. Paul my mother had a fit and so did everybody else's mother. . . . After I was, like, "dishonored" with this accusation of bisexuality, they took me right off the box and I've never been able to make a peep since, no matter what I want to say about political prisoners or anything else. So I got back my private life, and I really don't mind a lot not ever getting to talk on television because I've always been terribly frightened of television anyway. Poor Gloria, she got the job. She's good at the job, though. She's very, very good.'

A press conference was held to support Millett and express 'solidarity with the struggle of homosexuals to attain their liberation in a sexist society.' The formidable line-up alongside Millett included Gloria Steinem, Ti-Grace Atkinson, Flo Kennedy, Sally Kempton, Susan Brownmiller, Ivy Bottini and Dolores Alexander. NOW president Aileen Hernandez sent a statement attacking *Time*'s 'sexual McCarthyism.'[38]

NOW had its own lesbian-bashing element. Jill Johnston and Betty Friedan had clashed at a high-class fundraising event at Long Island in 1971, where Johnston had added some unplanned flair with a topless lap of the hosts' swimming pool. '[Friedan] was militantly opposed to the rise of lesbians within the ranks of the feminist movement,' Johnston says. 'She was scared to death it would turn off the women in the suburbs, and called us the lavender menace.' The generalized homophobia grew steadily worse. When Johnston was sent out on the road by Simon & Schuster two years later to promote her book *Lesbian Nation*,[39] 'the hostility was just wall to wall, there was no end to it. The insults were just heaped on. . . . The whole thing was imploding.' Johnston happened to flick through a magazine at an airport and came across a large picture loudly captioned 'People you should forget.' It was a picture of herself: 'Astonishing. The hostility was just universal.'

The issue began to undermine unity within the women's movement. What was supposed to be an inclusive milieu welcoming to women and accepting of difference became riven around divisive 'more feminist than thou' imperatives. There were divisions over class and political strategy, but sexuality was the storm center in the movement's internal tensions – to be or not be heterosexual or lesbian, and the consequences of that decision, became an overriding focus.[40] Coote and Campbell describe how early initiatives that might have led to a new sexual politics were crushed during the 1970s between the grindstones of these two unnecessarily opposing tendencies: a defensive 'heterosexual chauvinism' and a defeatist lesbian separatism. Neither broke with traditional categories; women were pressured to proclaim a sexual identity in polarized form: 'Both were shaped and defined by the values of patriarchal sex: "Do you fuck with men or don't you? Should you or shouldn't you?" For a time, these questions threatened to tear the movement apart.'[41]

A decade later it was a distant, bitter memory, but one which became a rationale for withdrawal from political activism by some women who had been energized and involved early in the second wave. From the vantage point of the mid-1980s, Sara Paretsky's fictional private investigator, V. I. Warshawski, evokes the divide when explaining her friendship with a murder victim to the Chicago police. The victim, Agnes, had emerged from the ashes of 1960s radicalism to become a hard-driving stockbroker.

> Anyway, Agnes and I were good friends at the University. And we stayed good friends. And in its way that was a small miracle. When our rap group followed the national trend and split between radical lesbians and, well, straights, she became a lesbian and I didn't. But we remained very good friends – an achievement for that era, when politics divided marriages and friends alike. It seems pointless now, but it was very real then.
>
> Like a lot of my friends, I'd resented suddenly being labeled straight because of my sexual preferences. After all, we'd been fighting the straights – the pro-war, anti-abortion, racist world. Now overnight we were straights, too? It all seems senseless now. The older I get, the less politics means to me. The only thing that seems to matter is friendship.[42]

'Everybody was threatened by everyone else, there's no question about it,' Johnston recalls. 'If there's that many people in such a great rage, and they're left to their own devices, obviously they're going to turn against each other.'

In her pre-second-wave existence, Johnston had been bound up in the art world as much as Millett. Her column of dance criticism in the *Village Voice* was evolving into free-associational prose of wider interest and she was enjoying life as a writer and card-carrying member of the New York avant-garde. Johnston had been almost completely insulated from politics: 'I didn't even know that we were run by men in Congress and the Senate. I was politically ignorant in the extreme.' Suddenly in 1969, when she was forty years old, feminism hit home. 'I had a huge reaction . . . like: "Oh my god, you mean all of those insults, all of that abuse, was because

I was a woman, and then on top of that a lesbian? I thought it was all personal. . . . My personal background intersecting with feminism was dynamite, and I was one of the angriest.'

The sense of rage was intimately bound up with the limited territory feminists had available to them because the vast bulk of resources – notably the media – were controlled by men. 'At that time the competition between women for the leadership was fierce and cruel, murderous,' Johnston says. 'It was just unbelievable. Of course, the men were putting the women up. Who published Germaine's book? Who gave Gloria the money for her magazine? It was all men deciding, really. They were doing it. The women didn't have the power or the money to project and put forth so-called leaders.

'So there was a rage really within the movement because of this virtually unexpressed problem. I don't remember any encounter with Germaine or Kate or anybody that wasn't fraught with this sense of the limited territory, and the contradictions involved, and the desire to lead . . . and the egos. . . . So what you had then was a lot of women suddenly in the limelight who were unequipped to deal with the attention, really. We all had problems, like Germaine, we all had incredible problems – as women, and because of our individual backgrounds.'

Gloria Steinem emerged as a kind of bridge between disparate elements of the movement. The concrete expression of this was *Ms.* magazine, which she co-founded as a forum for diverse feminist opinion. In her biography of Steinem, Carolyn Heilbrun notes that Gloria pointedly held Kate Millett's hand during the press conference defending Millett against *Time's* attack on her sexuality.[43] 'The lesbians all tended to like Gloria,' Johnston recalls. 'She was attractive. She represented the other side of the coin – the perfect daughter none of us were. And she was politically correct all the way down the line. She was appearing to embrace us, plus all the blacks and everybody, so she had the best profile of anyone. . . . She had the best persona for dealing with all different people.'

Steinem unsuccessfully sought contributions from Greer for *Ms.* As it turned out, the only Greer by-line ever in the magazine – 'Down With Panties'[44] – was reprinted from elsewhere. 'We wanted to publish her,' Gloria recalls. 'We were meant to be a forum of every possible feminist view, and I asked her a lot as I remember, or collectively we asked her a lot. . . . I just got the impression, rightly or wrongly, that it was too easy, that she wanted to go out and do battle. She wanted to do battle with male figures, and that's valuable because somebody's got to do it and it's not something that most women enjoy.'

The trouble was that Germaine tended to do as much damage with her attacks on other women and their efforts as she did in her combat with men; and in the war of attrition between feminists espousing 'heterosexual chauvinism' versus separatism, Greer was 'heterosexual chauvinism' personified.

Her interaction with Norman Mailer was an example. A few months after the Town Hall debate, she wrote 'My Mailer Problem' for *Esquire*.[45] In it she describes how she had accepted the invitation to debate before reading 'The Prisoner of Sex,' ignorant of several prominent American feminists' refusal to participate in the event. Before the first paragraph is through, she humiliates Kate Millett by repeating what she had heard – but said she did not believe – were the reasons for Kate's boycott of the debate: 'that Kate was afraid of Mailer, that she was gentle and shy, that she was exhausted and disgusted after being long enmeshed in the machinery of publicity.'[46] Millett, in fact, had specific philosophical reasons for rejecting the invitation, as did the other women whose rejections followed. After reading 'The Prisoner of Sex,' Greer says she could see there were legitimate reasons for not getting involved, yet remained so despite being asked by several New York women to withdraw. She then describes how she had planned a devastating attack on Mailer applying his own description of D. H. Lawrence – 'a middling male physique, not physically strong, of reasonable good looks, a pleasant-to-somewhat-seedy-looking man, no stud' – to Mailer himself in her speech. 'For all I knew he was a silvery maned bull of a man with electric blue eyes,' she writes, 'and yet I knew that the words would apply, for the tragedy of machismo is that a man is never quite man enough.'[47]

Greer pulled her punch. She had every intention of using the words against him in the debate, she says, having written them on a file-card in readiness, 'but when I saw how cruelly apt they were, my heart quailed with pity and I thrust the card to the bottom of the pile.'[48]

200

Mailer, as it turned out, wanted a one-to-one rematch with Greer on an American television talk show. According to her, as negotiations proceeded it emerged that Mailer had acquired the film and literary rights to the exchange without telling her. McGraw-Hill's lawyers stepped in to protect their author's interests: 'I remembered the warnings I had been given,' Germaine writes, 'by Abbie Hoffman and Gloria Steinem and others.'[49]

Her capacity for empathy with the enemy – and by any standard, that is what Mailer constituted for feminists at the time – seemed to know no bounds. After Mailer and Greer had discussed his putative deal on the phone, they went out for dinner. 'I was hectic and miserable,' Germaine writes, 'and Mailer twitted me for being less good-looking than at our former meeting. . . . And yet all the time I was struggling like a neglected and ugly daughter for my father's esteem. I was waiting for him to say he was sorry, to confess to a wounding and careless gamble, but he never did. He rallied me with minor unkindnesses until I recklessly spoke loving words to him like I might have to my own indifferent father, who only ever praised me to other people. "I love you," I kept saying, with the unsaid corollary, "so why do you treat me this way?" – the classic question of revolting women!'[50] Memories of Reg reverberating through her head, Germaine could not help reaching out and 'loving' Mailer – the ultimate heterosexual chauvinist, and a man who she believed was in the process of trying to steal her intellectual property. She sought his affection desperately.

Endlessly conciliatory towards Mailer, Greer was not prepared to extend the same generosity to the National Women's Political Caucus at the 1972 Democratic Convention in Miami. 'It was the first feminist presence really, in an electoral sense,' recalls Steinem. 'The National Women's Political Caucus had just formed that summer, and we were trying very hard – having in effect just sent out a signal and got back enormous response – to co-ordinate that response when most of us hadn't even met, and to look organized and have some kind of impact.'

*Harper's* sent Greer on assignment to cover the convention. The result was sharp, witty, insightful and, in some key respects, unfair. The 1968 Democratic Convention in Chicago had seen some of the worst official violence against the protest movement in 1960s

America when Chicago's Mayor Richard Daley loosed the Illinois National Guard and police wielding batons and tear-gas on protesters demonstrating against the Vietnam War.[51] Women and minorities had been on the outside looking in, and getting well beaten by the police for their trouble.

Four years later, at the 1972 convention in Miami, the picture was quite different. 'It's terrific, Gee,' the Yippie Abbie Hoffman told Germaine. 'We're inside the hall this time. All these women and blacks and young kids, it's terrific!'[52] Germaine, terminally jaded about the political process, looked at it all through gimlet eyes: '"Ah, come on, Geegee," he pleaded with me. "Don't be so down on everything! We gotta chance this time, Geegee!" "But Abbie," I replied faintly, "it can't work this way. What kind of bargaining power have these people got? Remember your Marx, man, and the nature of capitalism." "Aw Gee, I never read Marx, but Lenin woulda liked it." I realized with a guilty creak of the heart that Abbie was sick of trashing and being trashed. . . . Besides, he loved America.'[53]

The convention contained the usual blend of tokenism and boosterism, sincerity and syrup, but that did not make the visible emergence of women and minority interests any less significant. While it was a small start in terms of impact on the Democratic platform, it was a minor miracle compared to the bloody 1968 convention in Chicago.

For Germaine, however, it seemed a futile exercise. 'The women's caucus was not a caucus in any meaningful sense,' she said. 'They were in Miami as cards in McGovern's hand, to be led or discarded as he wished, not as players at the table. . . . Womanlike, they did not want to get tough with their man, and so, womanlike, they got screwed.' The Latin caucus, she complained, was 'muddled and bombastic. . . . None of the caucuses really existed as policy-making bodies or influential entities on the convention floor. A spurious leaderism ripped them all off and masqueraded as the collective voice. . . . Spokesman after spokesman claimed to have secured this or that, on a collateral of hot air, and the women's caucus was no exception.'[54]

As Steinem recalls: 'She just really condemned all of us for being in the electoral system at all, basically, and I think that was part of her more-left-than-feminist days. It was hurtful. I remember we were all quite depressed when we read the piece, but I can understand where she was coming from. It's just that if I had gone to another country I wouldn't have felt free to judge with that certainty what was going on in this other country.'

Gloria Steinem saw Germaine as like a comet that came and went through America: her fiery tail, whatever its hue at the time she passed by, always blazed and commanded attention. Given that it often contained rocky debris destined for the heads of other women, understanding Greer's position in the feminist movement as a whole was a matter of no small importance, if only to put her attacks into perspective. 'If by the movement we mean women supporting other women,' comments Steinem, 'then Germaine is not part of the movement because she has, as far as I know, not sought or given that kind of support. But if the movement is defined as "women moving" – as women "off our ass," so to speak – and the movement of ideas, then certainly she's been sometimes the furthest outpost and sometimes the rearguard, but always interesting and always influential.' It was part of her gift, and part of her problem.

# 10

# *Fame*

Rich and famous. The clingy little girl who had pined for her parents' love, who starred and stirred things up at her convent school, had made it. The young woman who lived an open sexual existence at university when her peers were still in twinsets and pearls, who celebrated Byron in Sydney and Shakespeare in Cambridge, who waxed lyrical about the divine attractions of rock stars and group sex, who married a building worker and took tea with the English aristocracy and who had recently written a book urging women to 'delinquency,' was now known throughout the Western world. Sporting identities aside, Germaine Greer with Rupert Murdoch was the only Australian popularly recognized on both sides of the Atlantic – and there were those who felt that, having given the 'Dirty Digger' *and* the 'High Priestess of Feminism' to the world, Melbourne had a lot to answer for. In another life, Germaine's brashness and bold tongue would have made her a perfect Murdoch tabloid editor in the 'Headless Body in Topless Bar' tradition. Fortunately, their professional paths never intersected in that way.

Success brought treats and tribulations. A woodcutter's cottage near Cortona in Tuscany was the prime possession acquired through her new riches, and it became a place where she entertained generously in a warm, earthy, domestic environment for years. She made the cottage a haven where she could cook, garden and reflect in peace, far from the maelstrom of public life. It also provided a refuge from her principal problem: British taxes. Greer took to tax exile with enthusiasm. Like many other wealthy Britons and British residents at the time, she cut her tax bill by spending large parts of the year elsewhere. When her old friend Richard Neville faced jail over an obscenity charge arising from the 'Schoolkids' edition of *Oz*, Greer was asked to give evidence in his support at the trial. It would not be possible, she told the *Oz* defence team: for tax reasons she simply could not return to London before the trial was over.[1] Meanwhile in New York, Lillian Roxon offered to sell posters and T-shirts in the street to help raise money for Neville's legal costs.[2]

Success brought another book advance, a long-running place on the lucrative American speakers' circuit and plentiful journalistic opportunities. In Britain Greer was assigned a regular column in *The Sunday Times*, then edited by Harold Evans, and contributed to American magazines such as *Esquire*, *Harper's* and *Playboy*. The odd crumb found its way into the feminist press, as when *Spare Rib* ran one of her columns on abortion after *The Sunday Times* rejected it.[3] Writing and the speakers' circuit left little time for teaching at Warwick University; after extended unpaid leave, she resigned her lectureship.

Some of her final articles for *Oz* threw into relief the twin elements of sex and confrontation, combining in the concept of potency, that dominated her persona at the time. In an obituary for Jimi Hendrix, for example, she described him in a jam session at the 'Speakeasy' in the early hours one morning not long before he died: 'He was at peace and potent.'[4] The adjective 'potent' was Greer's ultimate accolade. She feared that tolerance – of all things – was reducing the underground's potency. The underground's 'gestures had become louder and more rhetorical,' she wrote, 'more deadly serious than before, so that more than one power-player paused now and then to wonder whether he hadn't overshot somewhere and ended up nowhere. Our energy was all draining out into the void, meeting no obstruction, never bouncing back. Repressive tolerance was killing us.'[5] If it took the stimulus of intolerance to boost her energy levels, some of the reactions to her proselytizing on sexual freedom must have been galvanizing.

Much of the early work in the women's movement had been built around sexual issues. Anne Koedt's paper, 'The Myth of the Vaginal Orgasm,' constituted a critical moment in the development of second-wave thinking. Until Koedt's paper, the prevailing, male-constructed notion of the vaginal orgasm had gone largely unchallenged. Up to that point twentieth-century Western women had not debunked this myth, either publicly or, often, to themselves.

Gloria Steinem describes an electrifying moment, one 'when the light bulb goes on over your head,' while watching a television discussion between Betty Dodson, Flo Kennedy and Anne Koedt early in the second wave. Dodson was the most prominent activist on women's sexuality in the United States at the time, running workshops for women in which the participants examined their own genitalia and, as Steinem puts it, learnt how to masturbate with imagination and gusto. 'They were all talking about sex in a very open and frank way on television,' she recalls. 'I was absolutely stunned. I rang up the station and said: "Who are these women? I have to get in touch with them." '

Not too long afterward in Australia, similar revelatory sessions would be shown. In Sydney the 'Orgasm Meeting' was held at Women's Liberation House, where scores of women sat around frankly discussing their own experiences. 'There were as many orgasms as there were women there,' recalls Liz Fell who, with Wendy Bacon, was among the meeting's instigators. 'There was no way of neatly classifying them. It was revelatory for many women there, I think, that there was no right or wrong way.'

Steinem argues that feminism's fundamental energy cell was, and still is, to release women to be who they individually, uniquely are, including their sexuality. The impression that feminism and puritanism are entwined 'is a bum rap,' she says, 'because if you actually read the people it [puritanism] is supposed to be coming from, it's really not there.'

'It was exhilarating to see a woman who was claiming the right to be sexual without any qualms at all,' Steinem says of Greer. 'There actually was much more of that, and is much more of that. In this country at least, the anti-pornography movement has caused us to be seen as anti-sexual, which wasn't true at all. It's so interesting that I've gone from being called a slut to being called anti-sex in a mere decade. But I think in large part because the paradigm of sex is male-dominant, that if you're against male dominance then they think you're against sex, which isn't true. And Germaine's work helped a lot to say, "No, that isn't true," and to claim sexuality.'

Greer's flagrant flirting and aggressive sexuality delighted many men, while *The Female Eunuch* encouraged women to be more sexually assertive. Her heterosexuality was unambiguous and probably reassuring to women who were finding second-wave feminism enough of a challenge in itself without having to deal with questions of sexual preference at the same time. Many women were preoccupied with immediate problems centered on poverty, the sexual division of labor, reproductive issues and male violence rather than whether or not feminist principle demanded they become lesbian separatists. This could well have contributed to Germaine's popular reception among women in the general community, as opposed to those who were already involved in the movement.

While Greer stepped up her sexual proselytizing through the mass media, her involvement in *Suck* began to attract closer scrutiny. She was still a member of *Suck*'s editorial collective and was still writing pieces for the magazine, including her 'Earth Rose' column; but now that she had become an instant high-profile feminist, her involvement in *Suck* suddenly became contentious. The idea that pornography could have a positive political purpose – previously accepted as an article of faith in underground circles – was suddenly revealed to a more critical public. Greer was on the defensive.

'They want me to wear pants and be unavailable, and carry a jimmy to bash people over the head with if they feel my ass in the street,' she said of fellow feminists in an interview with the pornographic American publication *Screw*. 'They get mad at me for calling myself superwhore, supergroupie, and all that stuff. They think I'm cheapening myself, I'm allowing people to laugh at me, when the whole point is that if my body is sacred and mine to dispose of, then I don't have to build things around it like it was property that could be stolen. . . . Whore is a dirty word – so we'll call everybody whore and get people uptight; whereas really you've got to come out the other way around and make whore a sacred word, like it used to be and it still can be. That's why I use the word whore. My sisters won't allow it to be used. But I would prefer to be called a whore than a human being.'[6]

At best this constituted the far reaches of extravagance in Greer's sexual sermonizing, at worst a direct betrayal of what feminism was supposed to be about. Even as a pose for polemical purposes, it takes a truly eccentric and bizarre kind of feminism for one to identify as a prostitute – the complete commodification of a woman – other than to underline the sexual exploitation of women by men. In the context, this clearly was not Greer's purpose.

Typically, she managed to find a way in all this to sympathize, albeit condescendingly, with men. Trumping other women and showing solidarity and sympathy with men was becoming one of her keynotes. 'Anyone can have a fat old lady,' she told *Screw*, again revealing her instinctive contempt for women who did not fit the mold of feminine beauty. 'But young girls with clear eyes are not for the forty-year-old man who's been working as a packer or storeman all his life. So that when he sees her he snarls, mostly I think, because she's not available to him. She's a taunt, and yet another index of how the American dream is not his to have.

'I owe it to my poor brothers not to get uptight,' she continued. 'Because I am that, I am a woman they could never hope to ball, and in the back of my mind I reject them too. . . . A true revolutionary is guided by great feelings of love – I mean, that's really erotic. Ideally you've got to the stage where you really could ball everyone – the fat, the blind, the foolish, the impotent, the dishonest. We have to rescue people who are already dead . . . and that's not easy.'

While promoting sex with the figuratively dead, she was also blatantly writing about the sex lives of the living. After her American book tour, 'Earth Rose' shared with *Suck* readers Abbie Hoffman's attempts at sex with her in Central Park: 'I kept sliding out from under . . . because I've told Abbie I'll only ball him and Anita together, seeing as they boast of their togetherness, and he says Anita doesn't like me. Nevertheless it will be. Probably after the baby . . .'[7] Apparently without qualms about publishing other people's private lives, Greer would later demand absolute discretion in relation to her own.

*Suck* instigated two 'Wet Dream' film festivals in Amsterdam, where pornographic films were shown with some active audience participation and the odd 'happening.' Greer was a member of the judging panel for the first festival in 1970, along with Richard Neville, *Screw*'s editor Al Goldstein and others. Around this time her personal sexual menu was broadening; the old Push protocol that any sex other than heterosexual sex was neurotic and defective had given way, largely, it seems, as a by-product of her experience of group sex. 'The biggest problem in any group scene is that the girls get on very well together, because they don't rip each other off. . . . But men are really scared that some guy is going to fuck them. Now if the group thing is going to happen, that has to be a possibility.' She used an experience at one of the Wet Dream festivals as an illustration: 'I was kind of like a . . . tree with three sparrows perched in me, you know. And none of the guys was actually making off with a guy, which is really weird.'[8]

Any examination of the weight of Greer's views at and around the time of *The Female Eunuch*'s publication shows sexual revolution as her priority over women's revolution. She understood the link between them, but sex for Greer was the threshold issue. When the interviewer from *Screw* asked her how she would go about making erotic hard-core pornography, she replied: 'I don't know. It's a hard job. We have to use every power we have. We certainly can't do it every month or every week in a cheaply produced newspaper. We have to really get everybody at it. . . .' Other key feminists, by contrast, opposed pornography, and even those who did not usually had priorities above and beyond the creation of a pornography for women – a task Greer idealized as a core element of 'the revolution.'

The clash that led to her departure from *Suck* made it clear where Greer's priorities lay. The editorial collective had agreed to be photographed naked, and to run the pictures simultaneously in a future edition. Germaine threw herself into the task; according to *Suck* co-founder Jim Haynes, she commissioned a London photographer who was a friend of hers to take more than thirty photographs. She showed Haynes the photographs and posted a few of them to Bill Levy, another of *Suck*'s founders, in Amsterdam. Among those she sent to Levy was a shot taken in a pose worthy of an advanced yoga practitioner or circus contortionist. Greer's buttocks and vagina loom graphically in focus as she grins cheerfully at the camera, legs in the air with her head sticking out between them.

As Haynes points out, it was Greer who gave the picture to Levy: 'Germaine is an intelligent woman, an intelligent human being, and knowing Bill and giving him such a picture she should have known that he would publish it. Bill is a publisher and when he gets something like that it's a hot item and of course he's going to publish it. There was just confusion over how it was to be published.'[9]

When *Suck* 7 was published in 1972, the cover graphic showed a woman screaming as she is held aloft by one man and anally raped by another – a disturbingly violent image. Inside was the photograph of the naked, grinning Germaine occupying a full page. It was captioned 'Germaine Greer, A *Suck* Editor': no other naked editor was anywhere to be seen. *Suck* promoted its photographic scoop as '(In)Famous Germaine Shows Her Cunt.' The Australian film-maker Albie Thoms later included the picture as a single frame in the opening sequence of his film *Sunshine City*.[10]

Haynes then received 'this incredible letter from Germaine in which she completely blasted me, and I don't think there's anybody on earth who can blast as well as Germaine can blast.'[11] The next and final edition of *Suck* carried the letter in full.[12] Rather than resigning over the vicious rape depicted on the front cover, Greer launched into an assault on the other *Suck* editors over the bad faith she declared they had shown by running the naked picture of her without naked pictures of themselves as well. She described the sadistic content of the issue as disgusting, but her objection to it took up a mere five lines in an 85-line tirade focused almost entirely on the publication of her acrobatically posed nude photograph. The sick and violent content 'just aggravates the injury,' she wrote. She had only handed the pictures over in the first place because they 'were really rather good.'[13] Greer's overwhelming priority was her *amour propre*, followed by sexual revolution and, a poor third, women's liberation.

Even more confusingly, in her personal life she would regularly slide back into unreconstructed female masochism of the most lamentable kind. 'I rage, I melt, I burn,' she wailed over a new object of desire in 1972, 'I also simper and maunder and forget what I was saying. . . . My only interest in conversation is to nudge my interlocutors into some mention of him, which, achieved, I give the game away by grinning like a pike. I dog my unwitting beloved's steps and infest his environment. . . . No apologies at all of course to all those who have sought to deflect my obsession by bad-mouthing him. In the best masochist tradition I love him more the more others despise him. If you told me he was a wife-beater and a murderer I would probably devote the rest of my life to exonerating him.'[14]

It was a man, Frank Cauchi of London, Ontario, who unsuccessfully took Greer to task for her reversion to stereotype. 'After reading her brilliant and incisive dissertations against the male and specifically against marriage,' he wrote in a letter to *Time*, 'I cannot help feeling concerned over the conflicts that this high priestess has brought to untold thousands of monogamists all over the world. Where does she leave them now?'[15]

In celebrity orbit, one could survive for long stretches without having to bother about consistency. Greer was famous. 'She was a megastar, to use a Dame Edna Everage description,' recalls Susan Ryan. 'She was a megastar.' Sargent Shriver, soon to become the Democrats' nominee for the American vice-presidency, asked Greer out to dinner in New York after seeing her on a talk show, and later complained jocularly that more people had recognized her than him as they strolled through Greenwich Village afterward.[16] When *Harper's* assigned her to cover the Democratic Convention in Miami, the media covered Germaine covering the convention. *Time* photographed her chatting with Pierre Salinger and quoted her comment that the convention was 'a crock of s—.'[17] The *Wall Street Journal* ran an editorial on her criticisms of the convention.[18] In search of a prostitute to interview, Greer made a foray into Miami's 'Poodle Bar,' the haunt of hundred-dollar hookers and second home to many convention delegates – followed by a reporter from the *New York Post*, who recorded the exchange. 'But why do you dress like that?' the prostitute asked Greer. 'I make more money than you do,' Greer countered. 'You look terrible,' the prostitute persisted. 'Look,' Germaine said, her jaw firmer, 'I'm tired of this s—. I wear this, it feels good, it's got pockets and I carry lots of things and I've always had this haggard look and lots of people like it.'[19]

'The thing about being a celebrity,' one stellar friend of Greer's explained, 'is that you only ever meet other celebrities.' Even before her book was published, Greer moved in a special social stratum: the intersection of academia and the 1960s English underground. It set her apart from much of the subject matter of her writing. The most important insights and certainly the best writing in *The Female Eunuch* – as well as some of her most jarring comments – flowed from her own experience. In contrast, her discussion of the women's movement inevitably had an external quality, as Sheila Rowbotham detected when *The Female Eunuch* first appeared. That external tone became another keynote in her work. Whether she was emerging from the Chelsea to rap with the winos and street kids of New York's Lower East Side or searching out prostitutes in a Miami bar, there was a sense of the subject as object, as specimen. Greer was like an anthropologist venturing temporarily away from the air-conditioner and the mini-bar with field glasses strung around her neck, noble hand outstretched, sensibilities hypernaturally heightened. Her street tours and ghetto-crawls reeked of patronizing compassion and a romantic view of life at odds with her ostensibly tough-minded approach to the world.

Greer's fame spilled on to her husband, Paul du Feu. He became the first nude male centrefold for British *Cosmopolitan*, not only with his genitals artfully hidden but with his navel accidentally airbrushed out as well. He acquired a literary agent and a book contract with an advance larger than Sonny Mehta had given Germaine for *The Female Eunuch* in the first place. At a literary soirée in 1971 with his agent in London, du Feu met the woman who would become his third wife: the African-American writer and performer Maya Angelou.

Angelou was a phenomenon in her own right. Smart, statuesque, passionate, creative, direct – it was as though du Feu had set out deliberately to find another Germaine in terms of stature and strength of personality. Angelou cautiously checked out his bona fides with Sonia Orwell, George's widow, who described him as rather notorious and not exactly 'top drawer' – a 'working-class hero type.'[20] Du Feu asked Greer for a divorce. 'Why?' she responded. On being told the reason, she said she hoped Angelou knew what she was doing, and announced that a woman-to-woman talk was in order. She did not let the matter rest there, seeking out her successor in New York to dissuade her from marrying him. 'What's with her anyway?' Maya quizzed Paul. 'I think she wanted to have a woman-to-woman talk,' he replied. To which Maya exclaimed: 'Sheeit!'[21]

Amid the celebrity, the speeches, the interviews, the divorce, the multiple households and pursuit by the tax man, Greer's pre-occupation with potency remained constant. It was the link between the Greer of *The Female Eunuch* and the Greer of *Sex and Destiny*, which produced howls of dismay from feminists and charges of hypocrisy from all sides when it was published fourteen years later. Greer's appreciation of du Feu spoke eloquently of her taste in men. 'He's such a big, sexy guy – very handsome, very dishy,' she told *Playboy*. 'He's capable of busting his shirt straight down the back just by scratching his nose.'[22] She confirmed that she was transformed into a simpering wreck when she fell in love with such archetypal hunks: 'I become absolutely abject, utterly unscrupulous, totally dishonest, and I can do nothing about it. From being an interesting and independent woman, I just become a complete pain.'[23]

Some men were already evolving in response to the stimulus of feminism, but Germaine seemed unable to break free from the mold of her own habitual *modus operandi*. On a visit to Sydney shortly after *The Female Eunuch* was published, a young Sydney University student called Robert Tickner – later the Keating Government's Minister for Aboriginal Affairs – approached her outside the Fisher Library. 'I really admire your mind,' Tickner, a shy and idealistic country boy, volunteered. Germaine responded earnestly, slapping her rump: 'Yes, but what do you think of my body?'

The degree to which she had evolved personally was a matter for speculation among women friends during another of her visits to Sydney in the 1970s. A group of them, including Greer, set to drawing up lists of the men they considered their 'top ten fucks.' At the top of Greer's list was the legendarily well-endowed television journalist Mike Willesee. Some of the women were surprised at the overwhelmingly 'wham-bam' nature of the former lovers Greer had nominated – her list was heavy with men they considered among the most unreconstructed in Sydney circles.

Visiting Australia was as easy and familiar as putting on an old shoe. Greer returned several times during the 1970s to promote books and make television programs. There were still the old haunts to visit, and even the odd Push fling. The line of her old libertarian mates was much the same, except for the shuddering impact feminism had had on its masculinist predisposition, not least via *The Female Eunuch*.

Push women like Liz Fell and Wendy Bacon were central in challenging the meandering group's consciousness about sexual politics, and were at the forefront of new activist assaults elsewhere. Bacon came into the public eye with the publication of *Thorunka* – a racy variant on the University of New South Wales's student newspaper, *Tharunka* – which led to the most widely publicized Australian censorship case since Richard Neville and his fellow editors of *Oz* had faced court in 1963. Bacon pleaded not guilty to charges of selling an obscene publication and possessing indecent printed matter in the case, which was heard in February 1972 in front of an all-male jury. Greer lent support as a witness willing to testify to *Thorunka*'s literary value.

She was also on the stage, bottle of whisky to hand, when Liz Fell chaired a forum on sexual liberation at the Wallace Theatre, Sydney University, in January 1972. Gillian Leahy and Dennis Altman were the other panelists. This was the first public appearance of a gay liberation group in Australia, Altman told the audience, to joyous laughter and applause. Homosexual acts between men were still illegal, and discrimination and hostility were widespread; Altman underlined the risks the identifiable gay activists attending the forum were taking as a result. After some gentle chiding from Altman, Greer made up for some of *The Female Eunuch*'s short-comings by declaring gay liberation and women's liberation part of a continuum. In a defiant and defamatory act of gay solidarity, she went on to retail the widespread rumor that Australia's conservative prime minister, Billy McMahon, was gay: 'It's not a put-down saying he's a homosexual. That's the best thing about him.'[24]

Her rhetoric also tended to be more explicitly Marxist in Australia than to audiences elsewhere. 'Now the capitalist theory of libido leads to a development of a supply which is smaller than the demand so that you increase the value of the sex object,' she declared, for example, at the sexual liberation forum. She appeared in Albie Thoms's film *Sunshine City*, where she attacked what was then known as the European Common Market for intensifying the misery of the English proletariat. 'I feel really sorry for the people who can remember what it was like to be fighting for your life [who] suddenly now have got to start sucking arse to all these Germans,' she said, clad in a white T-shirt, sitting on a red chair in a sandstock brick courtyard in Sydney's eastern suburbs, cigarette in hand. 'Because it'll mean that the English working class – the same people who fight the wars for you – are going to go over and work in German mines and on German roads and in German steelworks as the lowest level of immigrant labour. It's the greatest indictment of war I've ever thought of.'

The high point of her fellow-traveling came in February 1972 during a discussion with Ian Turner, a Left historian, and the activist Chris Hector in Melbourne. 'I'm an anarchist still, but I'd say now I am an anarchist communist,' Greer clarified for their benefit.[25] She emphasized that, while she was concerned for the working class, she was not of it. 'I'm a middle-class revolutionary, a member of the alternative society. I f— all over the place, I have abortions, I don't get married, I do all those things. I don't wish to make myself completely irrelevant, but what I do want to do is to tell myself that if there is a revolutionary change in the working class, it's not along with me. It's for its own motives – because it seized power in its own way, because it commandeered the media for itself.'[26]

Greer's pseudo-Marxism was not a passing position. The class struggle and the feminist struggle are part of the same battle, she told ABC Radio seven years later: 'The whole point about women is that they're a sexual proletariat.'[27] But it was essentially a rhetorical gloss on what remained an anarchist position; and, as Beatrice Faust argues, Greer's position was finally an argument for the redistribution of women rather than the redistribution of wealth.[28] While she deployed socialist terminology, she never abandoned her Push training. 'I still am strongly influenced by the Andersonianism of the libertarians,' she told Fell in 1979. 'When I have to explain where I'm coming from to the English who see that I'm not a proper Marxist, or a proper Marcusian, or a proper Freudian or a proper anything else, then I have to invoke that kind of ad hoc training that used to be meted out to me in the beer-stained purlieus of the Royal George.'[29]

*The Female Eunuch*'s reception in her homeland underlined just how radical Greer had become in relation to mainstream Australia in the early 1970s. The *Sunday Telegraph* bought serial rights but the paper's owner, Sir Frank Packer – father of Clyde and Kerry – was outraged by the book's sexual content. He ordered the *Sunday Telegraph*'s editors to drop the excerpts they planned to run and replace them with tamer extracts. The ABC's management abruptly canceled filming for an ABC-TV *Four Corners* program which was to include coverage of a speech on abortion by Greer at Sydney Town Hall in March 1972. ABC's general manager Talbot Duckmanton declared that Greer had been 'over-exposed and now attracts little public interest.'[30] The then federal Labor Opposition leader, Gough Whitlam, asked in parliament whether the conservative McMahon Government itself was involved in getting the program stopped. The same month, in even more conservative New Zealand, Germaine was charged with using indecent language and obscene language during public lectures in Auckland. Hundreds of protesters chanted 'bullshit' in the court building when the charges were heard. The indecent language charge was dropped because there was no evidence that the word disgusted the public, but Greer was fined $40 for obscene language.[31] On her return to Sydney she attended the annual Women's Day march from Town Hall to Hyde Park. At its conclusion, as she and journalist Elisabeth Wynhausen repaired to the King's Head Hotel opposite the park, a young fascist wearing a swastika arm-band pelted her with eggs. She cheerfully posed for photographs in the bar showing her egg-smeared dress.

Greer's charisma and downright approach drew an enormous response from Australian women. '*The Female Eunuch* gave me a framework through which I could analyse the anger and boredom I felt about marriage and the feelings of lack of integration of myself,' the Melbourne left activist Edith Morgan recalled.[32] Journalist Ramona Koval described a kind of sisterly attitude developing in her toward the famous Aussie expatriate. For years Koval followed Germaine through newspaper articles, talk-show appearances and occasional visits: 'I was very familiar with Germaine Greer because she was one of us. Australian, feminist, outspoken, all things that I see in myself.'[33] Susan Ryan observed that Greer had a huge following among women who were not at all like her: 'Women who were housewives, who were pretty miserable, who read her book and decided to go and do a TAFE course or something like that – who just felt inspired by her book, and their life changed. They didn't become megastars, but they became a librarian or something. I've heard women say again and again when the subject of Germaine comes up: "Well, her book changed my life for the better." And they'll be modest women living pretty ordinary lives, but better lives.'

Germaine Greer was linked with numerous men on three continents during the 1970s, but as the decade progressed none of them provided what she decided she wanted most of all: a child. 'The question of being in the company of men is complicated by sex with men. . . . I'm pretty predatory,' she told the Australian journalist Claudia Wright on one of her post–*Female Eunuch* visits to Melbourne. The general impression among members of her old set in Melbourne and Sydney was that, even if she wanted to have a child, her troubled gynecological history would prevent it. But if she was sterile, as she told Wright, 'why would I be buying bloody contraceptives?' She had just been ordered off the pill, she confided, but having a child was still in the realm of theory: 'Look, I'm very rich and obviously I could have children in a perfect set-up. But it would be most dreadful and selfish of me to do this while other women are suffering to enjoy their children because of their circumstances.' During a large women's meeting in Melbourne, Wright observed Greer nursing a squalling child at the back so that the mother could concentrate on the proceedings.[34]

At the end of 1972 she discussed her maternal longings at some length with Margaret Whitlam, the wife of Australia's then newly elected Labor prime minister, during a visit to The Lodge. Greer described herself as a romantic and discussed wanting to have a baby without committing herself necessarily to one man. Whitlam told Greer it was a selfish proposition, but conceded that she probably had the resources to manage it. 'I have regular men all over the place,' Greer later told another woman, and went on to describe the female equivalent of the life of a sailor with women in every port. 'It's hard to explain this without boasting,' she continued, 'but I'm still friendly with – and close to – blokes that I've been making love to since I was eighteen and most of them would be delighted if I had their baby.'[35]

Greer was on the verge of thirty-four when her desire for a child sharply intensified. Meanwhile there were signs that her mode of living combined with her highly strung nature had taken a toll on her health. When she returned to Sydney after her visit to The Lodge she drank gin on an empty stomach, and became stricken overnight with projectile vomiting from pyloric spasm: 'Little do people know the long nights spent running in and out of bathrooms.'[36] A kidney complaint curtailed her participation in a rally after the annual women's liberation march in Sydney earlier that year.

By the middle of the decade, after several years of high living Greer was carrying some weight and showing the effects of having tippled a little too often. In early 1976 she went teetotal for a period to restore her physical balance: 'I think I was on the verge of alcoholism. I've always tended to use alcohol as a medicine – even as a girl. I like myself better, now I don't drink.'[37]

The desire to have a child grew stronger during her thirties as her biological clock ticked on. Nest-building, perhaps, she bought a large house in the fashionable London district of Kensington in 1973. She took out a court order to evict the dozen squatters living in it so that she could renovate, but not before the squatters and their sympathizers daubed it with slogans to prick her conscience. 'Germaine Greer (liberationist???) is trying to evict us,' the graffiti read. 'We are homeless.'[38]

She experienced some of the sensory pleasures of mothering through surrogate children, heightening her desire for a child of her own. In Sydney there was 'Bliss,' whose son Chapman became the object of Greer's concern and attention. Down on her luck, Bliss had found refuge with Liz Fell, who came to know Greer well when they worked together on a television series for an Australian production company in 1973. Greer took Bliss under her wing, providing financial assistance and helping to look after Chapman. On one occasion, Greer was observed putting Chapman to her own nipple in an attempt to suckle the child at her milkless breast.

When the Whitlam Government was dismissed in the constitutional crisis of 1975, Greer returned from Europe offering the Labor Party her assistance. Party officials suggested she could help most by keeping a low profile: the political atmosphere was already sufficiently charged without Greer throwing her own bombs into the mix as well. Her main, and most welcome, contribution to Labor's election effort turned out to be minding Susan Ryan's children in Canberra while Ryan campaigned as a Senate candidate for the Australian Capital Territory. Greer's erstwhile lover Paul Thom – by then living with Ryan – was there to keep her company.

In London there was Ruby, the daughter of a young English woman raising her single-handed. Germaine became godmother and, effectively, a surrogate parent to the little girl. Ruby was 'not a particularly brilliant baby,' according to Germaine, 'but she makes sense of everything because she's so lovable. When Ruby comes into this house it's like a fire going on in the grate. She's like Tinkerbelle in her little box. . . . I adore her. It's not like loving a man at all.'[39] She was smitten with the physical pleasure of mothering, telling one journalist of Ruby curling up with her for a nap. 'And I'll remember it all my life,' she said. 'She was between sleeping and waking, and there were these little fingers, curling and uncurling against my cheek. We have lost our physical pleasure in children. We no longer touch each other.'[40]

Nathan Silver and his family, including his young daughter Liberty – the same age as Ruby – once visited Greer in Cortona when Ruby and her mother were in residence. Greer took the two little girls under her wing, Nathan recalls: 'Germaine was a very hard parent. She demanded love and attention and a lot of respect, and she was punishing as well as loving – in a way that we real parents, either because we're such wimps or because we didn't act that way, never were. . . . This also had a stress on the two girls who loved each other, naturally. They started to compete with each other, which was not a terribly good sign.'

The American writer David Plante, who shared a cottage in the same part of Tuscany as Greer, recorded his impression of her mothering style in his book *Difficult Women*.[41] Plante arrived at the Cortona cottage with Greer in her car one day to find a child about a year and a half old playing with finger paint at a table under the fig tree. Green paint was being dolloped on to a piece of paper and all over the child's hands and wrists, with a few daubs on her face for good measure. In Plante's account, 'She was preoccupied and didn't see us until Germaine, standing over her, shouted, "That's not the way to use fucking finger paints!"' The toddler stared with a look of shocked awe at Greer, who tried to improve the child's technique while Plante entered the cottage where the baby's mother was reading a magazine. 'Germaine shouted to her from outside, "Where the fuck are you while your baby is making a fucking mess out of the fucking finger paints I paid fucking good money for?"'[42]

Greer's relationship with the Italian film director Federico Fellini around this time was emblematic of her situation. Creative, cosmopolitan and more stellar than Greer herself, Fellini literally brought light to her cottage at Cortona, donating a generator to the household. She told Fellini about her favorite fantasy – of working on a film set and finding an eminently adoptable lost girl asleep in a skip: 'We look high and low for her parents and then go out for dinner. I look up and the little girl is staring at me. She has chunks of brown hair which is crawling with ants. I feel real delight when I see that because I know the child is really abandoned.' Fellini interpreted the fantasy as being about work she had not done.[43]

One night when Fellini was staying with her in the cottage, an owl appeared at the bedroom window. It was an ill omen, symbolically evoking wisdom and, more notoriously death. The screeching of owls had been a portent of Caesar's assassination; Chaucer had written of 'the oule eek that of dethe the bode bringeth.'[44] The ancient symbolism was unmistakable to Fellini. He shrieked in horror and fled to the kitchen, where he spent the rest of the night huddled under a blanket.

It was as though that owl hovered over the rest of the decade, marring Greer's chances of happiness despite her good fortune in the public realm. She consulted a gynecologist in Australia who confirmed that the chances of conceiving were slight. Abortion, miscarriages and assorted gynecological problems had taken their toll. Greer had lived a free sexual life before feminism or fear of AIDS could help a young woman draw the line sexually when she wanted to – to say 'no' as well as 'yes' – and before the advent of modern contraceptive technology and safe, legal abortion. To some of her peers, her reproductive system seemed to be a casualty of her headlong quest for freedom.

Greer and Liz Fell swapped notes in Sydney one day about the abdominal scars they had both acquired in their youth. They were not from hysterectomies, contrary to the widespread impression among Greer's friends. A doctor known to several Push women had specialized in removing an ovary and Fallopian tube as the solution to nebulous gynecological problems – a procedure that drastically reduced the chances of successful conception. Fell had never conceived after the operation, despite an active sexual life without contraception.

In 1977, at the age of thirty-eight, with her chances of conceiving ebbing away, Greer had surgery at a Harley Street clinic in a bid to enhance her fertility. 'My uterus had been badly knocked about,' she told the writer Barbara Grizzuti Harrison. 'And they reconstructed it so it looked beautiful. One lovely tube and all the fibroids taken out. I had this middle-aged uterus ready to go. But it didn't go. I gave it a good shot, I spent four and one-half thousand pounds on it. That's it.'[45] Instead, at the end of the decade, another book was born. At the age of forty Greer rode the celebrity circuit again to sell *The Obstacle Race*. It was a tired, dispirited, resigned Germaine that Fell interviewed in 1979 on its publication in Australia.[46]

'My life since [*The Female Eunuch*] has been a disaster area and it's getting worse,' she told Fell. Financial problems were not the least of it. In Britain, the Inland Revenue was taking her to court for more than £20,000 in unpaid taxes on income Greer claimed she had never seen – money lost by people investing, she said, on her behalf: 'It's been a nightmare. . . . That leads to high tension all the time, and reduced capacity for work and having to mess about. . . . It's all very boring having conversations with tax lawyers.'

Fell questioned Greer about her relations with fellow feminists. 'One of the words that's often bandied around about you is that you're a superstar,' said Fell. 'That's the word that comes through a lot in the women's movement . . . that Germaine Greer's a superstar – she's quite isolated from the women's movement.'

'It's true I'm isolated but I always was,' Greer responded. 'I've been isolated, really, in every group I ever belonged to. As a libertarian I was pretty peculiar. As a member of the Push, I was a bit strange. I had my own bottle of Martell down at the Royal George. I mean it's always been a bit of a doing. I think I'm actually a crackpot.' Fell pressed on: 'Well, why are you so different?'

'Oh, I'm neurotic,' Greer volunteered unhesitatingly. 'Is there any doubt about that? I think it's a neurotic society. . . . I don't have any enduring relationships of any sort except with animals and plants. Human beings come and go. I seem to have gone through a goodly wedge of the world's population leaving it virtually unchanged, I think.'

Liz Fell was uniquely placed to probe the darker side of Germaine's otherwise glossy public image as liberated, successful and hedonist. As part of the Push, Fell had also become an exponent of its anarchic pessimism – but a critical exponent who had been part of the feminist revolution within the Push in the early 1970s. Fell's academic training had been in psychology: she had taught in the psychology department at Sydney University in the 1960s and was better versed in Reich and Freud than most of her Push peers. Germaine and Liz shared personal territory in the Push tradition, too; both had been lovers of Roelof Smilde, and each in her own very different way felt it was one of the most significant relationships of her life.

Greer had criticized efforts to promote non-sexist language as one of feminism's 'phoney struggles,' and in the interview Fell used this to open the way for Greer to articulate her ambivalent relationship with the women's movement. The hunt for scapegoats is a terrible waste of time, Germaine said: 'The identification of an enemy, so that you waste energy and aggression that you could be using just to kick free a space in which you can breathe and get something done. Lots of feminists . . . start off with a fundamentally damaged psyche from childhood which is geared to a certain subservient and self-denying way of life. And they then turn to feminism in exactly the same way as they might have turned to Catholicism or sadism and they make of it another rod just as tough as all the others. So in fact instead of developing energy and serenity, they get more and more fractured and more and more exhausted. I'm not going to name examples, but I can think of plenty of women who didn't even last in the feminist struggle because they made of it such a rocky road, they gave themselves such a hard time. I don't want feminism to be a religion – I want it first of all to be a support, a sisterhood, something that makes life easier, because most women have a hell of a bad time, and there's no point multiplying the contradictory pressures that lead to schizophrenia.'

'Well,' continued Fell, 'when you talk about enemies and scapegoating and so on, would you say that's happened to you in the past? Through standing out the front and writing *The Female Eunuch*, you got a lot of what you call misplaced energy and aggression and hostility?'

'Oh yes, but I'm not whining about that,' Greer responded. 'I always expected the feminists would attack me first, and it's the hardest attack to bear. It's the one that keeps me awake, or wakes me up at four o'clock in the morning trembling and sweating and all that stuff. I do, I just expect it. You know, the blacks expect it. They know their own people are going to be the ones to rip them down from any pedestal they manage to scramble up on to. I never wanted the pedestal in the first place so I don't really mind. I think I've usually deserved the criticism I get, by the way – that's why it hurts. But I can't see how I could have avoided it. . . . Because I'm a nutter. I just can't operate in certain circumstances.'

'Everything you've been saying suggests you're not very happy,' Fell continued carefully.

'Oh shit, why would I be happy? . . . What reason would I have to be happy? I mean, I'm happy enough, I've got me garden, got me cats.'

'Do you think you missed out on motherhood?'

'Yes, yes,' Greer confirmed. 'I don't doubt that at all. I certainly missed out on it. I've also missed out on all the anguish and misery that it entails. I can't complain about that either. I had my chances at motherhood and I happened to have chosen to destroy them at the time.' It was in this state of mind that Germaine began working on the bookend partner to *The Female Eunuch* – *Sex and Destiny*.[47]

While having a baby proved impossible, conceiving and delivering her third book was not, though the process was bloody and difficult. Germaine's own metaphor for writing was more scatological. She compared it to defecation: 'I have to write. It's a bit like shitting. It's quite nice. Especially if you do it nicely. You know, if a nice well-formed piece emerges. But if it's coming in dribs and drabs or not coming at all, or being forced out, if you're missing the rhythm somewhere, it's no pleasure at all. And yet sometimes there's an enormous pressure to do it. And not much pleasure when it's finished.'[48]

By the time Greer turned forty in 1979, her body of achievement looked somewhat uneven. In academic terms she had three degrees, a couple of years' experience as a university lecturer and had published two books. Of the books, *The Female Eunuch*, while drawing on some of her scholarly research, was popular in nature and would not have been much use as a credential for academic appointment. *The Obstacle Race*, which would be published that year, was the product of sustained original research, though not in Greer's own field – which was, of course, English literature. While she believed *The Obstacle Race* to be an important work and said she had written it as well as she could, she told Liz Fell she was apprehensive about its reception. 'The feminists are going to think I should have made higher claims for women painters,' she said. 'The art historians are going to think that I didn't know me arse from me elbow and that I didn't know the methodology of the discipline.'[49]

Greer's doubts about the work from an academic standpoint underlined the downside of the decade that saw her wildest success and notoriety. Germaine had spent most of the 1970s living high on the income from her book, journalism and the speakers' circuit. Given the uneven management of her investment and tax regimes, she occasionally endured some tight times as well – relative, at least, to the tide of money that washed over her upon publication of *The Female Eunuch*. Still, as her forties dawned, Greer found herself without a satisfactory professional niche. In 1979 she regained an academic toehold in the unlikely location of Tulsa, Oklahoma, becoming founding director of the Tulsa Center for the Study of Women's Literature at the University of Tulsa and Visiting Professor in its Graduate Faculty of Modern Letters.

The Tulsa Center was designed to train graduates with experience and interest in women's literature in what Greer described as the basic techniques of research and criticism, and offered bursaries, scholarships and fellowships to support scholars pursuing specific projects in the area. It was part of a huge undertaking, she said – the 'rehabilitation of women's literary history,' part of a wider female archaeology – in which the small, provincial University of Tulsa would now play a part. Greer, the avowed revolutionary, slipped briefly into that ultimate sin for Andersonians, meliorism: 'This may seem less challenging than attempting to overthrow [the academic] establishment but it has the merit of being more practicable. If we can help one feminist scholar to gain tenure we shall have made a concrete contribution towards change. If we can bring the face of one of our foremothers clearly out of the shadow we shall have made a greater change. It is by such gradualist measures that we shall eventually succeed in transforming our vision of the past, so that it can illuminate our understanding of the present and suggest the correct strategies for the future.'[50]

While Greer justified her meliorism at Tulsa, she continued to belittle the reformist attempts of others – persistently opposing, for example, American women's fight for an equal rights amendment (ERA) to the US constitution. 'Here in Oklahoma they think ERA means earned run average,' she told *People* magazine, arguing the proposal was merely window-dressing. 'People will think they have won something and they haven't.'[51] Her old anarchistic pessimism had not dimmed.

There was some mystification about why Greer had gone to the University of Tulsa, which had a modest profile in America's higher-education community. She had, in fact, been approached at a London dinner party the previous year by a university official who suggested she visit to teach a semester course. Betty Friedan, among others, thought Greer must have really needed a job.

Greer was facing financial problems at the time, and the salary did not go amiss. More than that, though, she revelled in Oklahoma's frontier atmosphere. It was the big, open West and it was full of unreconstructed men. 'Tulsa is the only place left to find the money – it's an oil state – and the freedom to do what you want,' she explained. 'And it's the last bastion of heterosexuality. It's wonderful.'[52]

In 1980 the visiting professorship was upgraded and until 1983 Greer was Professor of Modern Letters, spending nearly half the year in Tulsa and the rest in England and Italy. She acquired a patina of local color. Andrea Chambers, the reporter from *People* magazine who observed Greer at work and play in Tulsa in October 1979, noted her adoption of local exclamations like 'Yip!' and 'God damn,' as in Germaine's colorful classroom declaration, 'God damn. I'm sweating like a hog under this dress!' Her rented Mustang had a pint of Jack Daniels parked under the front seat; she was once again candid about her vulnerability to drink.

Chambers sat in on a few of Greer's classes. She commented on the high quality of her teaching, and recorded one priceless exchange. A student announced she was reading a book on nymphomania which mentioned one of the women poets under discussion in the class. 'I think nymphomania is a dubious term to apply to any human being,' sniffed Greer. 'Mary, please be selective, child.'[53] Chambers commented that when talking to her it was difficult to get her off the subject of sex and children. 'Let me advise any unhappy career girl in New York to hightail it down here,' she said of Tulsa. 'It's like Rome. Men follow you in the supermarkets. Back home [in] London, you can walk down Regent Street naked and no one would notice.' She explained she was telling her lovers that she was not using a contraceptive and that they might end up being a father. Using a sperm bank was not out of the question either, she told Chambers; she planned to consult her gynecologist in London about it.

While Greer was willing to contemplate anonymous sperm, she was still quite taken with the notion of herself as supergroupie to the rock aristocracy. 'I generally fuck my peers,' she said. 'I'm what you'd call a star fucker.' Her elitism was, if anything, intensifying, and her contempt for some other women was now unconcealed. 'They have to come to me,' she said, for example, of rock stars. 'I make a point of not being part of the slag heap, of meeting them from the audience side of the footlights.'

Andrea Chambers extracted from Greer in Tulsa one point that no one had before, which was an explicit statement of her consciously thespian approach to life, and her longstanding but unfulfilled creative aspirations. 'What I'm trying to do is entertain people,' she said. 'I grew up thinking there was one unpardonable sin – to be boring.' *People* used the quote to caption a photograph of Germaine in a bubble-filled hot tub, apparently biting her own toe – still exhibiting, at forty, the old flexibility evident in her infamous *Suck* shot. The real significance, however, lay in confirmation of what many had suspected all along: that the performer in Greer was the primary engine for much of her behavior and, probably, her wilder statements. A performer without an audience is a contradiction in terms; what had often looked like attention-seeking in Greer was precisely that. At forty years old, for example, she was continuing to retail ever more vivid accounts of her childhood to journalists. 'I used to go to school with black stockings to hide the bruises,' she told Chambers in Tulsa; at home, Greer said, she would cut her fingers with a razor blade to get attention.

Seeing a film version of *Il Trovatore* as a child with Peggy had provided her cue for the scale on which life should be lived. She told Chambers: 'I wanted to be a diva. . . . I was going to have thousands of lovers.' Her voice was good, but not good enough to make her a celebrated singer. Perhaps she would become a novelist instead. She had written one novel about a young girl in a convent school, she confided, but ripped it up. 'Isn't it boring that women write autobiographically?' she asked, apparently unaware of the fact that she had been writing her own life all her life, in episodes and anecdotes dotted through her various polemics and later underpinning entire books. She would write fiction again when she retired, she said, though it probably would not be published: 'My standards are too high.'

Greer's Tulsa revel finally soured – there was to be no baby and no renewal of her contract. Her graduate students were too thin on the ground. When the parting came, she dismissed Tulsa as a place of 'no hopery, small-time connery and pretentiousness' run 'like a banana republic.'[54] The familiarity and psychological security of Britain drew her back – a safe place to settle her reproductive struggle one way or the other and conduct the mid-life audit which would indirectly constitute her next book.

# 11

# Sex and Destiny

*Sex and Destiny* was the creation of Greer's child-dreaming years. Like *The Female Eunuch* before it and *The Change*, which was yet to come, it was a work in which she took her own personal experience and wrote it large. The old sexual libertarian, now irrefutably infertile, was revising her position in light of this saddening certainty. The book's main theme was evidence of her exhaustive research into her own problems. Chapter headings like 'The Importance of Fertility,' 'The Curse of Sterility,' 'Chastity is a Form of Birth Control,' 'Polymorphous Perversity,' 'The Short History of Contraception,' 'Abortion and Infanticide' and 'Changing Concepts of Sexuality' were practically an index to Greer's psyche at a time when she was dwelling on her childlessness and its relationship with her personal history.

There was a poignancy about this abstractly written commentary on matters obviously relating to her own predicament. 'Barrenness is by many peoples associated with sin, and particularly sexual sin,' she wrote, the observation bathed in the dim glow of her own dormant Catholicism. 'If children are the gift of God, the lack of them is God's punishment. . . . Where lechery is associated with barrenness, virginity and modesty are associated with fruitfulness. Women who flaunt their sexuality, driving men to squander their precious seed in barren wombs, are the personifications of death, disease and evil the world over.'[1] She went on to list the catalogue of complaints that, individually or cumulatively, could render a woman infertile:

> By no means all the women who find that when they wish to have a child they cannot, because of a tubal blockage, can remember an episode of acute pelvic pain and fever. Commoner even than infertility resulting from acute pelvic inflammatory disease may be fertility impairment as a consequence of chronic sub-acute infection, or from a series of insults to the reproductive system: abdominal surgery for any cause, including appendectomy in childhood, an abortion or two, induced or spontaneous, legal or illegal, a curettage or two, a couple of minor infections, insertion, rejection or removal of an IUD. To the consequences of these unremarkable events must be added those of alcohol intake, of smoking, radiation and medication, of stress and of ageing on the fertility of women who for cultural reasons tend to delay their child-bearing, to give a full picture of the commonest kind of infertility which causes disappointed women to besiege their doctors in the developed world.[2]

It was a catalogue with which Germaine would have identified, each factor potentially contributing to infertility – accidentally, unwittingly, erratically rather than systematically. Infertility is the risk a Western woman takes when opting for late child-bearing, Greer wrote: 'The factors that erode her fertility are all aspects of her chosen lifestyle, although she may well object that no one ever spelt out to her with any clarity what their cumulative effect upon her child-bearing potential would eventually be.'[3]

Greer now had to explain, rationalize and justify this suddenly discovered connection between the lifestyle she had proselytized extravagantly and the health risks involved. There is no doubt, she said, that the high frequency of pelvic disease in the West is related to the degree of sexual activity, and the number of partners most people expected to enjoy, especially in adolescence and early adulthood. 'To point out that this is so is not the same as to say that increased and freer sexual activity is wrong,' she continued, 'but it might suggest that the people who seek to suppress the expression of erotic desire because it conflicts with fertility are not simply irrationally puritanical in that their practice is justified by an actual connection between increased sexual activity and decreased fertility. Restrictive sexual mores could well be a response to the ever-present threat of extinction which many tribal societies have witnessed, if not in themselves then in neighbouring childless communities.'[4]

The old Push Germaine would have dismissed sexual restraint and its underlying cultural mores as a key element of authoritarian repression. Now, rather than attacking it, she explained it in almost Darwinian terms – that the very survival of tribal societies might have depended on it. This was speculation: while there is much ethnographic anecdote in *Sex and Destiny*, she does not cite empirical support for the thesis. But the book's significance lies not so much in the thesis itself as in Greer's abandonment of the core Reichian belief in the essentially conservative, authoritarian nature of sexual restraint. What Reich did not understand, she now agreed, was how far his concept of sexual revolution 'played into the hands of the consumer economy and the monopoly state.'[5]

> Reich's ideas were taken up by the avant-garde of the late fifties and became the unacknowledged morality of the late sixties. Their exponents had no political power, although they were extremely visible. Their ideas affected legislation and custom, not because they were in some sense correct but because they were eminently compatible with the perpetuation of the mechanisms of power in consumer society. . . . The promotion of sex which had begun with De Sade has reached its apogee in a civilisation which gives tangible expression to every form of human sexuality, every perversion, every paraphilia – except passion. The proper arena for these expressions is the bedroom of the sub-fertile monogamous couple: insofar as they prolong the survival of the consumer unit any elaborations of sexual congress are acceptable, even the mutual sin of condoned or shared adultery.[6]

Thus one of the leading proponents of the sexual revolution – one who had bathed group sex in quasi-religiosity, who called herself by preference 'whore,' and who had urged everyone to turn their energies to creating a new style of hard-core pornography – now criticized sex as the 'new opiate of the people.'[7] In a pointed reassertion of her Catholic roots, Greer once again linked sex and reproduction.

Like all religions, she contended, sex has its ritual observance – achievement of the perfect orgasm. Sexual catharsis has replaced all other rituals of purification: 'The blessed are laid-back, into their bodies, in touch with themselves. They shrink from no penetration, they feel no invasion of self, they fear nothing and regret nothing, they defy jealousy. The regular recurrence of orgasm provides the proof that they are in the state of grace.' To object that orgasm is itself inadequate to this high purpose is to expose oneself as orgastically impotent, for sex religion, like all others, relies upon self-fulfilling prophecies. To the faithful, Greer now said derisively, orgasm was a cure-all: 'Those who rise from orgasm sad or angry, disappointed or bored, are themselves at fault. They have held something back, harboured deep scepticism: they are the self-destructive.'[8] The pervasiveness of commodity sex, she concluded, had become absolute.[9]

Greer acknowledged that her attack on the ideology of sexual freedom could seem shocking coming from a sexual radical. It was galling, she said, to be lined up with the 'bigots and body-haters [in] opposition to contemporary sex religion.' However, our stupefied obsession with petty gratification is setting the scene for annihilation, making us 'dead to agony and ecstasy,' she continued. If it was merely the future of the West at stake it would not matter so much, but the spread of Western mores to the Third World threatened its very cultural survival: 'Young grinning couples grace hoardings among the intricate polycellular structures of villages full of families and their message is intensely seductive to the young and restless. The lineaments of gratified desire they see there will be theirs if they abandon the land, abandon the old, earn their own money and have fun. Having fun means having recreational sex: recreational sex means no fear of pregnancy, a wife who is always available and who is content with orgasms in place of land, family and children – orgasms and consumer durables.'[10]

Greer was now the poacher-turned-gamekeeper on the philosophy of sexual libertarianism. If her own infertility drove the reversal, it was not the only factor. Her love affair with the extended-family systems of traditional societies – the antithesis of the nuclear family she had grown up in – was the other motive force. This was particularly interesting in relation to Reich. His views on both sexual freedom and the nuclear family, as received by Greer in the Push, had been the absolute foundation of *The Female Eunuch*. Now Greer was explicitly abandoning Reich's attack on sexual restraint while retaining his antipathy to the nuclear family. Memories of her Mentone miseries – her father hunger and deep antipathy toward her mother – made it impossible to abandon.

Through friendships with other migrants from the countries of Britain's colonial past, and from her own visits to Italy, India and Africa, Germaine had much contact with traditional extended-family households. She liked them. The typical portrait she paints is of noise, love, squalor, shared concern, mutual obligation and multi-generational tolerance. Her work had shown an affection for such families from the outset. She used the Italian families she lived alongside while polishing her doctoral thesis in the summer of 1967 as the model for the communal child-rearing arrangements proposed in *The Female Eunuch*.

Greer's advocacy of the extended family model in *Sex and Destiny* typified another of her defining traits. Whatever she believed at a particular moment, she would take all the way to its purist conclusion, then several steps beyond. As a sexual libertarian she had charted a path so extreme – literally, personal salvation through sexual liberation – that she had to beat an obvious retreat in *Sex and Destiny* when its consequences caught up with her. Similarly, it was not enough to laud the positive attributes of traditional extended families in *Sex and Destiny*: Greer capitalized the 'f' in 'the Family' and claimed such implausibly extravagant virtues for it that even sympathetic readers became uneasy.

The patriarchal nature of 'the Family' she described was almost wholly ignored. Greer had, in effect, come to accept the family as given: since women were going to be part of this institution anyway, she argued, they might as well be in a kind of family where they could enjoy contact with other women rather than being isolated with one male partner: 'The Family offers the paradigm for the female collectivity; it shows us women cooperating to dignify their lives, to lighten each other's labour, and growing in real love and sisterhood, a word we use constantly without any idea of what it is.'[11] There was no attempt to envision a non-sexist version of the extended family structure as she had, in a way, in *The Female Eunuch* when sketching the possibilities for communal child-rearing. Nor was there any mention of the depredations suffered by women living in traditional extended families.

Did 'the Family' somehow magically eliminate the violence and petty humiliation so often found in the patriarchal family home, or the diversion of female energy to male ends? What of suttee, and the murder of dowry brides in India? Or the treatment of women in traditional societies who were outside such family structures? Or the higher value placed on male babies in several such societies, evidenced by the tendency to abort female fetuses, or let girl babies die? Such phenomena were ignored or glossed over in a book that constituted the greatest single leap backward by a high-profile feminist in the second wave.[12]

Germaine produced an apologia for the veil. 'One of the reasons for the success of Islam as a proselytising religion is that it rated the lowest and least prestigious groups as deserving of the same respect as the highest,' she wrote. '[It] covered their nakedness and veiled their women, conferring upon them a new kind of value and hence, self-respect. When the Shah of Persia outlawed the veil in 1937, he did not so much liberate his people as announce their dependency upon the West.'[13]

It was social theory by anecdote in a clutch of soft-focus vignettes of happy episodes in extended-family life. 'The Family' was the idealized family of Greer's dreams – as far from Peggy and Reg and Mentone as she could possibly imagine – shored up with scene upon scene of warm family encounters. Greer's paean to the wonders of the extended family shared much with the Olde Worlde homage to the noble savage. 'At times, I told her,' one commentator said, 'she reminded me of the old slave owners who used to say that since the darkies were always singing spirituals in the cotton fields, they were simple, happy folk who mustn't be freed by meddlesome outsiders.'[14]

Greer's argument in *Sex and Destiny* was diametrically opposed to the stance she had adopted at a Sydney sexual liberation forum twelve years earlier, where she had made several tough comments about the plight of women in the Third World. 'Having been in the Middle East and the Far East a little bit,' she said then, 'it seems to me perfectly obvious that even where women are deeply involved in production, and even where they are quite essential to [the] national economy, they are treated even worse than they are in capitalist societies, and their contribution to the quality of life is valued no more than the contribution of an ox.' And later during the same forum: 'I really am not interested in figuring out in terms of some psychic arithmetic whether an Indian woman working on the roads with ankle-irons this big is happier or unhappier than me. As far as I'm concerned, her liberation and my liberation are the same thing.'[15]

For all the failings of the extended family, its advantages are worth considering. The pity was that it was difficult to embark on a cool-headed appreciation of its virtues while Greer argued such an extreme case with so little feminist consciousness. For whatever reason – wilfulness, attention-seeking, or just plain bloody-mind-edness – it was as though she had an in-built mechanism to ensure revolt against her polemic, to sabotage its reception, despite whatever important observations and insights might be mixed up in the dross. Guaranteeing a good battle seemed to be more important than making a constructive, effective polemical intervention.

Greer's other theme in *Sex and Destiny* concerned her critique of fertility-control practices in both the developed and underdeveloped worlds. She argued that world overpopulation was a myth and that aid programs in the Third World were creating problems for individuals and communities alike by disrupting traditional fertility-control practices. Germaine's interest had been aroused in 1974 by her experience at the World Population Year conference in Bucharest, where she observed how pressure was being applied to Third World women to limit their number of children. Many women believed there were too many people in the world, she conceded; but the overpopulation case had not yet been proven, and even if it were it would not justify wholesale interference in the reproductive capacity and rights of individuals. No feminist can allow forced abortion or compulsory sterilization of women, she thundered in print after the Bucharest conference: 'The principle at stake, that of control over one's own body, is an integral and essential part of feminism. No act of faith in the oracles of demography can overrule it.'[16]

It was a timely counterweight to the tendency of the white West to impose its world view and policy prescriptions automatically on everyone else. Greer derided the 'phantasmagoric view of the future as universal Calcutta' which, she argued, underpinned a new fascism on fertility policy for the Third World – and all fascism, she pointed out, 'assumes a state of fictitious emergency, a threat of invasion, of civil war, of the black and yellow hordes taking over.'[17]

> Feminists cannot accept crude numerological analyses of the behaviour of women who have never spoken in the first person in their lives. They cannot permit the dissemination of a crude and misleading view of feminism as an ideology opposed to childbearing and the family. Within our own countries we are the unexplored, undeveloped, speechless population, systematically undeveloped by our conquista-dorial society. We are the 'Third World' at home; we must represent the alien population beyond the factitious boundaries of states; bamboozled, manipulated and exploited by the same forces that have held us face downwards over the lavatory bowl and the sink. That any superpower should give the name women's liberation to the boot that he is preparing to place upon the necks of Third World women, ought to call forth the most appalling exhibition of women's rage that the world has yet seen.[18]

Apart from sex, Germaine had not been so passionate about anything for years.

Greer's subsequent research for *Sex and Destiny* raised enough questions about the nature of the relationship between family size and Third World poverty to suggest that, at the very least, more micro-analysis was necessary before wholesale fertility-control programs were imposed from the outside. She emphasized the complex elements that combined to determine family size. High infant mortality rates motivated women to have more children than they might otherwise, to make up for likely losses; more children were needed to provide for their parents' old age than in developed nations with social security systems; and then there was the sheer pleasure children provided in otherwise relatively joyless circumstances. Greer also claimed that policy-makers had ignored and undervalued traditional fertility-control practices. This was an indictment of a most sensitive arm of public policy. While it might not have been news to practitioners and activists in the field, Greer's book had the potential to bring the issue to wide public attention.

Yet these ideas were swamped by her history and her revisionism. The interesting and potentially valuable parts of *Sex and Destiny* were overshadowed by Greer's romance with 'the Family' and her new stance on sexuality and contraception. Commentators focused on Greer as the libertine feminist who had suddenly discovered children and chastity. This apparent capitulation overshadowed the thoughtful and serious elements of the book – not least its critique of contraceptive practices in the West.

Those familiar with Greer's former proselytizing on sexual freedom could not resist chortling over the apparent hypocrisy of her new position as outlined in *Sex and Destiny*. How could they help it, when her declaratory stance as a 'whore' in the vanguard of sexual liberation had been transmuted in the 1980s to the view that it was fatally easy for Westerners who had themselves discarded chastity to believe it had no value for anyone else: 'At the same time as Californians try to re-invent "celibacy," by which they seem to mean perverse restraint, the rest of us call societies which place a high value on chastity "backward." . . . Instead of teaching reverence for the body we chose to teach callousness; instead of exploiting concern for children and the passionate desire for them to survive, we assumed that too many were surviving already. The chance to develop the human propensity for sexual restraint in the interests of the congested world has been missed.'[19]

Germaine Greer had created a major problem for herself – the problem of not being taken seriously. She had preached one thing with absolute certainty in her sexual prime. Now she preached the opposite without any attempt to reconcile the two or rationalize her shift – which she needed to do if people were to digest the two positions with minimal damage to her credibility. While it was true that she had consistently opposed 'commodity sex' through the 1970s and 1980s, in other obvious respects her position had changed sharply. Persistent belief in the face of contrary facts is stupidity, but serial certainty in the absence of a *mea culpa* is intellectual cupidity. She wanted the luxury of believing herself right, both then and now, and expected everyone else to believe it too.

This vanity caused perhaps the most interesting section of *Sex and Destiny* to sink with little trace. In the chapter 'Polymorphous Perversity,' Greer surveyed innumerable non-pharmacological contraceptive practices, including coitus interruptus, coitus reservatus, coitus obstructus, prophylactics and celibacy. Fourteen years earlier in *The Female Eunuch*, she had written disapprovingly of the prevalence of the condom as a contraceptive in 1960s Britain,[20] and argued that sexual liberation 'cannot be accomplished by a denial of heterosexual contact.'[21] Now she considered both options were respectable. Not only did the *volte face* make her a sitting target for criticism; the result was that a serious and substantial part of Greer's proposition was ignored – that it is perverse to promote sexual creativity exclusively for its own ends instead of for its obvious potential as a contraceptive technique as well; that some non-pharmacological techniques may have a useful role; and that the iron orthodoxy of male ejaculation into the vagina as the culmination of sexual congress hindered fresh thinking in the area.

> Our preference for mechanical and pharmacological agents of birth-control is irrational. Our position with regard to the function of sex is absurdly confused. . . . There is no logic in a conceptual system which holds that orgasm is always and everywhere good for you, that vaginal orgasm is impossible, that no moral opprobrium attaches to the expenditure of semen wherever it occurs, that considerable opprobrium attaches to the bearing of unwanted children, *and* at the same time insists that 'normal' heterosexual intercourse should always culminate in ejaculation within the vagina. These are the suppositions which underlie our eagerness to extend the use of modern contraceptives into every society on earth, regardless of its own set of cultural and moral priorities. As the basic premises of the position are incoherent, the position itself is absurd.
>
> Another name for this kind of mental chaos is *evil*.[22]

The final religious flourish betrayed *Sex and Destiny's* brimstone tinge. Suspicions that the book revealed the triumph of Catholicism over the counterculture in the struggle for Greer's soul were reinforced by her failure to consider the high failure rates of techniques like coitus interruptus, not to mention the cultural constraints that diminish women's power to ensure their effective use. To the extent that this could lull women into a false sense of security about such contraceptive practices, it was a serious flaw. Overall, however, the book made a significant contribution to debate about the implications of modern Western contraceptive practices.

Another of Greer's classic mixtures of the inspired, the

inconsistent and the insufficiently thought through, *Sex and Destiny* amply displayed her tendency to overstatement and romanticism. For example: 'I think I would rather be a hungry twelve-year-old in Pul Eliya than an obese twelve-year-old in Tulsa, Oklahoma.'[23] And similarly: 'Strange to relate, the poor get more opportunity to develop all these sides of themselves than do the rich, who are much the same the world over.'[24]

Where for the Greer of *The Female Eunuch* sex was the way to salvation, for the Greer of *Sex and Destiny* children were the road to happiness. They, not 'genital dabbling,' provide most of the pleasure in the world, she argued – in the Third World, at least. Women spent long, pleasurable hours cuddling their babies; men gossiped on their charpoys and under trees with their children standing between their legs: 'The eroticism of most of the world still includes the vast store of sensuality that radiates from children, whose deliciousness is more obvious to people grown old and gnarled prematurely by a life of bitter toil and hard rations than it is to our smooth-skinned, overfed selves.'[25]

Greer carried the crude 'east-west, good-bad' paradigm to extreme. Her psyche simply could not accommodate the possibility that a child born to a Western nuclear family had ever been loved and enjoyed. Her blinding insight about the potential pleasures of parenting relative to sex had come to her, she wrote, when observing her female cats, 'who wept piteously when it was time to undergo the gang rape which is feline intercourse, and purred continuously while in labour, even when the labour was obviously painful, and purred all through their suckling, not stopping till the kittens were weaned.' The tomcat may have enjoyed his brief pleasure, she said, but the females purred for a full two months after their kittens were born. 'My association with Italian peasants and with South Indian women and aborigines offered endless examples of the undemanding pleasure which children give to non-materialistic peoples,' she continued in full missionary mode, 'for whom they are the only entertainment and the reason for undergoing all the hardships which are their daily life.'[26]

'I think she would've been quite different if she had a child,' Peggy Greer says of her elder daughter. Until she had Germaine, Peggy reflected, 'maybe I was like that.'

'It made the women I knew who read it feel deserted, sad,' Gloria Steinem recalls of *Sex and Destiny*, observing that it was another instance of Greer looking at her own situation and writing it large. 'That makes sense, but you can overdo it. . . . Her apparent regret over not having children is something she expanded much too much to other people. So it came to seem as if the women's movements in various countries had advised women not to have children, which I don't think is the case – on the contrary, we were trying to talk about reproductive freedom. Or that all of us . . . that didn't have children regretted it, and that's not the case either. Certainly, I don't feel that.'

In the midst of plenty, of success, Greer was making hard work of her life. Infertility was a terrible blow to a woman like her who longed so much for a child, and who had tasted enough of mothering's pleasures at the periphery of her friends' lives to realize what she was missing.

But while most people just lived, sorted out the knots of their personal histories and got on with it, Greer had to live the drama, construct a theory and write a book about it. After extolling the large 'F' family in *Sex and Destiny*, what could be a more logical next step than searching for the patriarch? Reg had died before the book was published, but in another sense he was thoroughly alive. Superimposed on what was for Germaine the grimly remembered reality of his rejection of her was the ongoing fantasy Reg – the father, the man, of her dreams.

'At forty-four, Germaine Greer is a large, fraught woman whose face only truly relaxes with scorn,' Tina Brown observed when *Sex and Destiny* was published in 1984.[26] The din from the book still resonating, Greer sat in her woodcutter's cottage in Cortona and took out an old notebook in which she had jotted down ideas for *The Female Eunuch* so many years before. She turned the page, took out her pen and embarked on the final leg of the quest to lay her father-hunger to rest.

# 12

# Paterfamilias

'Here we go, Daddy, in at the deep end,' Greer began on the blank page of that old notebook. 'I discover, Papa, that I am like you in one thing at least. I hate remembering.'[1] Greer's symbolic linking of *The Female Eunuch* and the search for her father was no accident. The reflections that would become *Daddy, We Hardly Knew You* addressed a yawning gap in her first book. While Peggy Greer was dotted through *The Female Eunuch*, caricatured as the unpredictably violent, punishing mother, Reg was essentially absent, the merest hint of him here and there in the text. In *The Female Eunuch* he was not even the man sitting next to her in the dark, his faced turned away, as she evoked him in *Daddy*.

Reg had died, and in death was still ignoring his elder daughter. 'As I sat in the golden winter light of Tuscany, scribbling in my old notebook,' Germaine wrote, 'I did not know that my father being of sound mind had chosen not to mention me in his will. It never crossed my mind. I need never have seen the will, never have known that I was not even disowned, simply forgotten. Big enough and ugly enough to take care of herself. One look in the mirror is enough to prove to me that he can't disown me. Perhaps I have taken the hair off my face to expose his skull as a way of defying him: the cleft in the end of my nose, my receding hair-line, my lantern jaw, my large ears, my blunt fingers and my narrow chest are all he left me. They will have to do.'[2]

Greer was not the first feminist to quest after her father. One of her co-panellists in the Town Hall debate, Jill Johnston, had paved the way. Just as *The Female Eunuch* had been the book of Greer's sexual prime, so had *Lesbian Nation* been for Johnston. Several years older than Greer, Johnston had got to ruminating in print about her missing father earlier than the Australian, and in her case he was literally missing. Johnston was the illegitimate child of a well-connected Englishman and an American mother who constructed an elaborate story to cover the illegitimacy and explain her father's absence. Johnston grew up thinking, wrongly, that her glamorous and successful English dad was dead. This belief was dramatically demolished when her mother posted her an item clipped from *The New York Times* – his obituary – in order to avoid the possibility that Jill might see the article first. The fiction created by her mother, and unravelled by Johnston, became a key thread through her two-volume *Autobiography in Search of a Father*,[3] published several years before Greer's *Daddy, We Hardly Knew You*.

As a young woman Johnston was much taken with her father's glamorous aura, and reveled in a picture of him standing between King George V and Queen Mary. When she had a nervous breakdown in the 1960s, he was replaced in her psyche by the dead French poet and critic Apollinaire; she remained convinced Apollinaire was her father for some time afterward, and privately drew on his persona in her own work as a critic in New York.

The laying of fantasy flesh on the bones of absent fathers – one figuratively missing, one literally – is common to Greer and Johnston, but perhaps more neurotically so in Greer, whose father was, after all, still alive, still theoretically accessible, still physically a fact, when she was doing it. Identification with the missing father over the all-too-present, reviled mother is also common ground, as is the fantasy Jewish heritage each bestows on herself. They also put a similar weight on the father's role. 'The most important man for a girl is her father,' says Johnston. 'Men at large become comprehensible only by comparison.'[4] Similarly, for Greer, 'the great question about "did he love me?" I think is every woman's question. I haven't met very many women who were . . . confident of their relationship with their father.'[5]

Johnston came to believe that it was the fantasy father she had created who gave her the licence she enjoyed in the New York avant-garde during the late 1960s: 'He would allow me to jump [social] games completely, to be exceptional, to be free of the class and sex that bound me, to make work that broke all the rules, to be successfully antisocial, to become what "crime" had made of me, to join all the little kings in the art world who never grew up. . . . Later, in 1970, the rest of the world found me, and at last, at the age of forty, I left home, as it were – home where the father is primal, all-powerful, and never openly acknowledged.'[6]

Where Johnston evoked a mythical father, Greer's embroidering of fantasies was more direct. She had previously commented on at least one aspect of her identification with men. She had a 'masculinised form of libido,' she said not long after her father died. 'Because I tend to be more interested in something different. I mean I quite like periods of intense sexual excitement with men followed by a restoration of my privacy. I don't like waking up with stubble and breath and all that. I'd rather he went home.'[7] But in *Daddy* she morphs into Reg and wallows in paternal identification.

Germaine has 'his own longsighted eyes.'[8] Her hand is the 'exact replica' of his; during his physical decline she watches 'my own skull emerging through his transparent skin.'[9] She refers to 'my Greer face.'[10] The sedatives in her father's bathroom cupboard were 'his, not ours,' she remembers: 'Except when the hospital put me on the same ones, Tropinal, for nervous exhaustion, Daddy's own disease.'[11] She is 'left-handed like my father.'[12] 'My gut is painfully coiling and uncoiling upon itself' with an affliction inherited from Reg: "'Touchy tummy," Daddy called it.'[13] Then there is 'my tendency to aggrandising fantasy, that I had inherited from him and have tried all my life to inhibit and control.'[14] 'Like Daddy I'm claustrophobic,' she writes. 'Seriously claustrophobic. In a room without a window I can become dizzy, pass out or throw up. . . . Claustrophobia is hereditary.'[15] Both sang in church choirs, Reg as a reluctant schoolboy and Germaine right through her life. Not to mention that 'my hairline is identical to his.'[16] And where had it got her? She was left not even a trifle, she lamented – no cuff-link or fountain pen, or even a book with his name in it. Not even her name was in the will. Everything was left to Peggy or, if she predeceased him, to Germaine's siblings, Jane and Barry.[17]

243

As Reg's life slowly faded, Germaine filed away little chips against her better-loved sister and, more particularly, her brother, chilling the general warmth with which she referred to them in *Daddy*. When she and Jane visited Reg at the down-at-heel hostel he was living in, 'Jane wheeled and fled.'[18] Germaine scrutinized Reg's checkbook: 'The last stub showed that he had paid $2,500 to my brother and the balance was nil. He had been stripped and dumped in that awful place for me to find.'[19] Reflecting on things later, toward the end of her father-hunt, she added: 'Perhaps my brother was a lapdog and I was the kelpie.'[20]

Her truly bile-ridden blasts, however, were reserved for Peggy. Reg's alleged stripping and dumping was a 'smart move, and in every subtle and crazy detail the work of my mother.'[21] Jane had called Germaine in England to say that Reg wanted to see her. 'When I arrived I found that Mother had turned Daddy out of his own house' and committed him to a shabby weatherboard hostel full of derelicts, Greer wrote.[22] Peggy contests this. While Reg had been sick for a long time, she says, she wanted him to remain with her at home: 'I'm Catholic and I think you ought to stay together.'

Germaine was determined to keep Peggy in the villain's role of what was still for her the family's continuing suburban drama. 'Mother kept away from him, but he never ceased to ask for her,' she wrote in her reflections on Reg's decline. 'She treated him abominably, but he never uttered a disloyal word about her. He died in love with her, an achievement which she doubtless credits to herself.'[23] Greer not only portrayed Peggy as viciously motivated but hinted that she was mentally in disarray. 'Yes, no, yes . . .' she quotes Peggy beginning a sentence as they prepare to visit the beach. In short order, according to Germaine, Peggy produces a series of nonsensical verbal flourishes: 'No, yes, no . . . ,' a 'Yes, no . . . ,' and a 'Yes, no, yes . . .' follow at intervals.[24]

Greer derides her mother's appearance. 'She was wearing a skin-tight synthetic knit dress, striped green, yellow and white,' she wrote of Peggy's attire. 'It's nice, isn't it?' she archly quotes her mother.[25] Getting ready for the beach, 'Mother squeezed herself into a pair of pale-blue stubbies, out of which her tanned seventy-year-old legs oozed like Brown Windsor Soup sliding down a ladle.'[26] As their conversation at the beach degenerates, Germaine zeros in on the homosexual pick-ups occurring in front of them. 'You're a fag-hag,' she berates Peggy. 'You've sat us here right in the middle of the meat rack.' Peggy replies, 'They're not all queer, you know.' Germaine continues: 'Then I understood. Having found most of her life's necessities on a beach, Mother was now beachcombing for another husband.'[27]

'For Mother language is a weapon rather than a means of communication,' Greer declared, unconscious of the irony.[28] She amplified her view for anyone who would listen when the book came out. 'I treat my mother in the book as highly eccentric . . . and extremely dangerous, which she is. To me, especially,' one journalist was told. 'I mean, she can reduce me to complete trembling insecurity within seconds. . . . And then occasionally she just assails people. And it's very violent, and mad.'[29] Germaine told another: 'You mustn't think that my mother's sort of sitting, knitting, with tears in her eyes like Peer Gynt's mother, waiting for her bad girl to come home. My mother is not interested in this relationship and I'm not interested in it, either.'[30]

Greer was forty-four when Reg died and fifty when *Daddy* was published: old enough at least to have come to terms with her family life, if not to put its deleterious effects behind her. A fellow Star of the Sea student, Moira Curtain, who later taught at the school, recalls reading the book and discussing it with Mother Eymard. 'I'm really distressed by it,' Moira said. 'I'm distressed that a woman of fifty is still exorcising her ghosts. Especially that the Germaine I knew, with all that strength, was carrying around so much of her background that she hadn't exorcised. When you get to fifty you should be through that, you shouldn't still be hassled by it.' Eymard had not read the book, and Moira offered to lend her a copy. 'Don't lend it to me,' Eymard replied emphatically. 'I couldn't bear to think that Germaine is so sad. I couldn't bear to read that that wonderful girl is so sad.'

Why was Greer still so preoccupied with her parents? Perhaps partly because, as Barbara Grizzuti Harrison observed, 'she's about as introspective as a sweet potato';[31] and perhaps partly, too, because she had been so busy constructing the present that she had neglected the painful but necessary task of confronting her old demons, dealing with them and then moving on.

Barry Greer put his sister's father hunger in perspective. 'Germaine lost contact with Reg when she was about eighteen and never really established a rapport with him at all after that,' Barry said. 'When he started failing and his life started to ebb from him, she realised there was a whole lot of ground she needed to make up.'[32]

Their lost ground dated from Reg's return from the war. Yet Barry Greer's interpretation points to the gaps and irritants that, as Germaine grew to adulthood, became layered over the mutual hurt and pain she and her father had brought with them from early days. 'There were bad feelings between her and Reg when she went to Sydney to live,' Peggy Greer recalls. Later, when Germaine set her sights on further study overseas, it was clear the family breach would not be healed quickly. 'When Germaine left I was preoccupied, couldn't get it out of my head,' Peggy remembers. 'So I thought I'd do matriculation, by correspondence. This was 1963.' She was prompted by a friend down the street, who mentioned she was doing some study at home.

Out in the suburbs, on the example of a woman friend, Peggy Greer was taking things into her own hands, using the time-honored method of educational improvement – the one Germaine had used to lever herself out of Mentone in the first place. Peggy was a practical beneficiary of sisterhood in action. She studied part-time for years after that, eventually undertaking extensive tertiary language studies. 'I got my arts degree at Swinburne, majoring in literature and Italian, submajoring in Japanese,' she says. 'I'd like to do a master's or Ph.D. in languages. I'm thinking of doing French or Chinese now, but not at university.' From the time she burst into the public realm with *The Female Eunuch*, Greer poured scorn on Peggy's efforts and was still flaying her over her attempts at self-improvement when *Sex and Destiny* was published nearly a decade and a half later. 'Alive? Oh yes, she's *alive*,' Greer told Tina Brown when asked about her mother. 'She'll never die. She's now taking some ludicrous academic course. I do disapprove of the taxpayer's money going on educational programmes invented to keep old women off the streets.'[33]

Comments like these from a high-profile feminist appalled many in the women's movement. 'She enjoys what most women do not enjoy, and therefore it's valuable, which is going out and doing battle with men,' Gloria Steinem says of Greer. 'But she's not really that interested in women, nor does she get that much nurturing or support from women. And as I read what she had to say about her mother – she actually condemned the whole notion that women should be able to go back to school at a later age because her mother had done so – it was so devastating. Not only about her personal experience with her mother but [because] it generalized to others. I thought no wonder Germaine can't really get nurturing from women or feel close to women or feel joy in other women's success because there's this terrible knot there that hasn't been untied.'

Peggy and Reg did not see their elder daughter between her departure for England in 1964 and her return to promote *The Female Eunuch*. Germaine flew into Sydney in December 1971 and continued on to Melbourne the following month. But there was to be no reunion with Peggy then. When the book came out, Peggy took off on an extended European tour. 'I ran away, went overseas, to escape from the hoopla,' Peggy says. 'People were banging on our door, yelling: "Mrs. Greer, I know you're there!" '

Reg therefore constituted the entire parental welcoming party, and their reunion was not an unequivocal success. Reg looked suave, Germaine recalled later, decked out in a cream tussore suit for a restaurant meal with his now famous elder daughter: 'He told me later on the telephone that when lunch was over and the tension released, and he was walking back over Princes Bridge to where he had parked the car, he suffered a mass reflux and purged upwards and downwards all over his pale silk. I was aghast, but he chuckled ruefully and made light of my consternation. When I asked when I could come to see him again, though, he begged to be excused.'[34]

She expanded on the incident to Anthony Clare: 'That was just so horrible – the idea that for Daddy it was so much tension that he soiled himself. I couldn't bear that, to be responsible for that happening to my father. I just thought: This is impossible. I can't torture this man. It doesn't matter how much I need him, he can't stand me. Physically cannot bear it. For whatever reason, he just can't bear it, and in fact he asked me to stay away.'[35]

Whatever trauma Peggy and Reg had caused for Germaine during her childhood, wittingly or unwittingly, she could not now avoid facing the potent and terrible impact that she had on them. Peggy had fled, and close proximity had triggered a 'mass reflux' in Reg. However many degrees Germaine earned, no matter how sharp her rhetoric, no matter how big her international profile and bank balance might have become, the sad reality of her fractured parental relationships weighed heavily.

Greer drew parallels between her relationship with her father and her feelings for Australia. If she sometimes felt embattled by the intense media reception when she returned, she was, in her way, a classic Australian figure in a modernizing Australian landscape. Her style and language were unmistakably antipodean: forthright, without regard to the authority of entrenched institutions and their leaders, and manifesting a biting wit. Years after *The Female Eunuch*'s publication she described her pungent rhetorical style as 'a trick of Australian speech.' All Australians speak over-emphatically, she said: 'Just listen to any of them: listen to Barry Humphries, listen to Clive James, listen to Robert Hughes, they all have this "over the top" rhetorical power. It's one of the ways Australian language is spoken. I actually like it; I think it's rather good stuff. . . .'[36] In the 1990s the Labor Prime Minister Paul Keating epitomized the style, drawing on the rich, roistering Irish larrikinism and anti-authoritarianism streaked through Australian culture.

Greer's iconoclasm and anti-authoritarianism did not suddenly spring whole from her experience of the Push; they had deeper Australian roots, too. In terms of national identity, both can be traced back to the country's convict heritage – the 'us and them' of the jailed and the jailers, and later the British-born versus the 'currency lads and lasses,' not to mention the lingering subterranean rancour of the predominantly Celtic underclass versus the Anglo-Saxon establishment. As the journalist Elisabeth Wynhausen notes, it is probably no accident that three of the great liberation texts of the post-war period were written by Australians – Greer's great popularization of feminism with *The Female Eunuch*; Dennis Altman's path-breaking *Homosexual: Oppression and Liberation*;[37] and philosopher Peter Singer's internationally influential *Animal Liberation*.[38]

The fact that Greer visited Australia only intermittently was something her fellow antipodeans, used to their best and brightest living abroad for long periods, found unremarkable. Yet it loomed large for Germaine – apart from anything else, because Australians often asked her about it. She said she had planned her escape from the age of twelve: 'I think I decided that Australia and I were both deprived. . . . I used to walk down to Port Melbourne and watch the boats sail away, and I promised myself that I'd be on one just as soon as I could. It took me thirteen years to realise those plans. Once I'd gone, I knew I wasn't coming back.'[39] In her twenties she at least briefly entertained the idea of returning home some time to resume academic life in Australia. In her thirties, and particularly in her forties, she made a firm decision not to return despite the fierce core of unextinguished Australianness in her.

Remaining in Britain had a lot to do with money. In her early thirties, after *The Female Eunuch* was published, Greer argued that a population as small as Australia's could not support a media big or diverse enough to sustain someone like her.[40] In Australia again when she was nearing forty, she described her life in England as one of professional exile. '[There] I'm bankable: I can't earn a living in Australia,' she said. Not that her superior earning capacity and higher standard of living had softened her early impression of English men. 'The first time I ever saw Englishmen take off their clothes I couldn't believe the bodies I was looking at,' she recalled with undimmed, disgusted wonder. '[They] all looked like mildewed blancmange.'[41] At nearly fifty, she told the Australian journalist Lyndall Crisp she was earning £150,000 a year and believed she could not earn anything like that in Australia.[42]

Those who had dealings with her in the 1980s were left in no doubt about the importance Greer attached to money. When the ABC Women's Broadcasting Cooperative wrote in 1987 inviting her to comment on Andrea Dworkin's book *Intercourse* for a planned radio feature, she sent the letter back with the scribbled message: 'Please note, there is no short cut to getting me to work for you. I am a professional and expect to be paid: my time is paid for at terms negotiated by my agent. . . . Why is it that only Australians pull these stunts?'[43] Around the same time, in the run-up to the bicentenary of white Australian settlement, Greer began saying she would only come home for good if Aboriginal Australians wrote and asked her, since it was really their country.[44]

She could be brusque in her dismissal of questions concerning repatriation. 'Actually nowhere is home for me anymore, not even Australia,' she said in the mid-1980s. 'I think the idea of a home is a fantasy, something we create in our minds. I don't think it exists in reality. . . . I certainly wouldn't go to Australia for a book promotion tour. There are not enough people there, for a start, but the main problem is not enough of them can read.'[45] But for every patronizing slap like this, there were many gestures of sentimentality, intimately bound up with the closer ties Greer was developing with her siblings after her sister had called to tell her that Reg wished to see her.

With Jane, Germaine felt she had 'rediscovered my own sister'; they at last formed a satisfying relationship on the foundation of a friendly reacquaintance in the late 1970s.[46] 'I would do anything that Australia asked me to do, especially if there was a ticket thrown in because I have family here,' she said in the middle of her *Daddy* research. 'If I was asked to do a ground-breaking ceremony for a new brothel, I probably would.'[47] Around the same time she went to the races in Melbourne with a friend and was outraged when a hostile racecourse official took her to be English. Had she stood stubbornly clutching her Australian passport in the 'aliens' line at Heathrow all those years for nothing? 'Here was proof positive that I had no home, anywhere,' Germaine declared. 'The Australian passport I was so proud of . . . meant nothing if my countrymen took me for a foreigner.'[48]

Greer was beginning to sound like a wistful Aussie expat. 'Once a week, at least once a week, I dream about Sydney,' she said in 1981, telling the story of the adopted city of her young adulthood. 'I know it is a Sydney dream, first of all, because of the smells – the smell of the sea, the smell of the frangipani – because of the sounds – the sounds of the birds crying – and because of the feeling that the sky is so far away. In Europe, the sky sits on your head like a grey felt hat; in Australia, the sky is a million miles away and all that lies beneath it belongs to you.'[49] It was the light, above all, that transfixed her, 'the light that pours over everything, saturating everything, making even the most commonplace things seem beautiful.' When you live on the dark side of the world, she said, 'this light is something that haunts you, day in and day out.' It was Robert Hughes who suggested why such beauty might be abandoned in the first place: expatriation, he said, was about Oedipal revolt, 'about the feeling that if you're not going to kill your father, at least you're going to kill him symbolically by getting away from him. You find a new father.'[50]

Greer had not. There was no new father to be found in the wider world, nor did she find herself a great, heroic, Petruchio-like love. Not only had Reg failed her, but the tactical response – expatriation – had failed, too. It was little surprise that Greer conflated her father and her country. 'Well, it's a very funny thing,' she told Anthony Clare. 'It parallels my relationship with Australia, my relationship with my father. I left home when I was seventeen. I had to go back because I was too young to stay away, and I hadn't got enough money to live on or anywhere to live. I waited until I was eighteen, and then I left for good.' Reg, she said, 'made no attempt to stop me. I came back when I had enough money. You have to understand about going back to Australia. You have to have a lot of money. Finally, when I had the money, I went back to Australia, after *The Female Eunuch* was published, and that's when I saw my father again. And we went out to lunch, and that's when Daddy had the mass reflux on the way home.'

The details of Reg's gastric trauma and its drastic consequences for his silk suit were shared with Clare and his considerable BBC Radio audience. Pressed about her relationship with Australia, Greer responded: 'They don't write to me either.' In her eyes, she was not only a daughter of doubtful lovability but a citizen of doubtful lovability too. 'First of all, they make no overtures to me, and if I make overtures to them, I'm quite likely to get snubbed,' she said. 'Here's a perfect example. When Gough Whitlam was running for re-election after the disgraceful gerrymander that got him thrown out – the governor-general's interference in the affairs of parliament – I went to Australia and offered my services to the Australian Labor Party. And they asked me to kindly desist, and not to make any statements on their behalf. That's my relationship with Australia.' It was like her relationship with her father, Greer said: 'I may love them, and I may say so, but they don't love me. It's a fact.'[51]

A not uncommon complaint from Greer's generation of Australian expatriates concerned the dearth of invitations from Australian universities for visiting fellowships back home. It was one small facet of her complex about her country, like her father, not loving her. 'The Americans ask me to come and be a visiting professor all the time,' she boasted. 'Australia, never . . . forget it!'[52] So it was that her return to the academic world had been to a university in the United States, not Australia.

The loss of her academic perch at Tulsa in 1983 was followed by her father's death. When Reg died in April 1983, Greer had only recently been musing in print about men in Melbourne, though of younger vintage. 'The ambition of every Star girl was to be linked with a Xavier boy,' she wrote in an article commemorating Star of the Sea's centenary, 'for Xavier was the top Catholic boys' school, much grander than the humbler CBC which provided our usual dancing partners.'[53]

Just as the schoolgirl Germaine aspired to a Xavier boy over one of the humbler Christian Brothers crop, even as an adult she aspired for her father to be more than a war-damaged newspaper advertising salesman. 'That wasn't good enough for me,' she said, confronting her paternal fantasy in her mid-forties as she wrote *Daddy*. 'I had to tart up his image, had to turn him into a committed warrior against fascism; I needed my father to be a hero, exposing himself to all that death and danger dare. I don't approve of heroism, and yet I demanded heroism of my father, imposed it on him. Across the dark gulf of years a sharp thought leaps like a spark; perhaps I was Reg Greer's problem. The very idea makes my touchy tummy boil up under my ribs until I feel nauseated, my father's nausea in my stomach. (Oh, Papa, forgive me.)'[54]

Even when Greer embarked on 'this demented pilgrimage,'[55] as she called it, she managed to doubt the observable facts of her father's life while simultaneously continuing to exaggerate aspects of his persona. 'I am troubled by the nagging suspicion that the anxiety neurosis was a calculated performance,' she said, suggesting that her father may have been using his salesman's talent for role-playing, at which she believed he excelled. 'Reg Greer was not just a salesman,' she claimed, 'but a crack salesman.'[56]

Yet in literary terms, *Daddy* is by far Greer's most successful work. Constructed as a detective story in which the luckless but relentless Germaine runs her father's – and her own – lies to ground, its mixture of mystery, history, travelog and personal pain compel the reader to the final revelation. Greer sloughs off the prevarications and half-truths which Reg relied on and she herself spent a lifetime embellishing. The forward momentum is maintained in the face of two powerful contrary forces. The first is Germaine's own scepticism about the hunt's raw material, and the second the profound self-pity which punctuates an otherwise well-told tale.

Less than eighty pages from the start, she possesses strong evidence that Reg's family history as given to the military authorities and, when pressed, to the young Germaine was bunkum. Yet loyalty prevented her from entertaining such a suspicion: 'I scribbled the details in the margin of my notebook, and did my best to forget them.'[57] After a hundred pages, she notes that her father's habits yielded no evidence of the toff past he claimed: 'There was never any hint in my father's behaviour that he remembered a different way of life. He only drank fizzy Australian beer, and he drank it half-frozen.'[58] Toward the end of the book Greer acknowledged that for over a year she had known of a series of coincidences involving a family in Launceston by the name of Greeney.[59] 'I felt a cold fear that they would indeed be the end of the trail.'[60] The most telling hint came one-third of the way through the book in one of her brittle exchanges with her mother.

> 'I can't find your parents-in-law,' I said.
> Said Mother in a little girl voice, 'He told me he was an orphan.'
> 'Mother, if he told you he was an orphan, what are those names on the parish register at Saint Columba's?'
> 'What names?' asked Mother.
> 'Father: Robert Greer, journalist, and mother: Emma Rachel Wise.'
> 'Oh, those names,' said Mother.[61]

Peggy's disclosure so early on in the research that Reg had told her he was an orphan could not have been more clear, yet the awkward relations between Germaine and her mother, and the small matter of the publishing advance, got in the way. After all, had Germaine taken this as her research cue, *Daddy* might have been a short story not a book.

Greer was disarmingly open about the role of the publishing advance in the book's life. At first it is styled as merely a tool to deflect Peggy's opposition to the project. 'My mother asked me on Christmas Day why I wanted so much to know my father's background and early life,' Greer wrote. 'Looking for an answer she would not ridicule I said, "Hamish Hamilton have paid me a lot of money to write a book about him."' Peggy replied, 'Gee . . . I'm glad I don't have to do that to earn a crust.'[62] But as the going gets tough, her spirits falter and ill omens crowd in on her multicontinental research, money as a motive for finishing the book becomes explicit. 'Every day, in every way, it is demonstrated to me that there's nae luck about the house, but I cannot go backward. I've spent too much of the advance; I must struggle blindly forward. . . .'[63] As Greer says elsewhere in the book, 'I had kept an eye on the Greeneys; I knew exactly where to find them in the record, but I refused to look.'[64]

Finally she discovers the truth that she has suspected for so long: Reg and Germaine are not really Greers at all. Reg was an illegitimate child who had been fostered by the Greeneys, a provincial Tasmanian family. Barely educated, he had created a new persona at a careful distance from his poor, unpromising childhood circumstances. Then, during the war, his nerves had cracked, fracturing the identity he had invented for himself. Reg's role as a military cipher clerk had symbolized his shielded, encoded situation more acutely than his daughter had realized.

The other element working against the flow of Greer's family detective story is its deep seam of self-pity. Sometimes this is mitigated by a sense that her own exaggerated expectations of her parents have contributed to her problems, though her sharing of the blame tends to be spasmodic and short-lived. For example, Greer poses the question, in relation to Reg: 'Why do I demand that he be gallant and brave? I don't demand that my mother be gallant and brave, do I? But yes, I do. I want both of them to be tough, dinky-di, reliable, stalwart, straight. Both of them, in fact, in their different ways, are bounders. I am a bounders' child. The blood of bounders runs in my veins.'[65] More typical is the attribution of blame to Peggy and Reg without qualification, as in this recollection:

> When I came up to Cambridge my fellow-students were showing their parents around their rooms, the lecture theatres, the Backs, posing for pictures in the family album. The families beamed with pride and pleasure, shouted and ran about, gathering images of their successful children against the background of Erasmus' bridge and the Wren Library and the stone nougat of King's College. Nobody photographed me, not then, not when I knelt resplendent in medieval red and black with my hands joined in prayer within those of the Vice Chancellor, Germaine Greer Philosophiae Doctoris Cantabrigiensis. I collected my degree by myself. There was no victory supper, no champagne. I had worked all my life for love, done my best to please everybody, kept on going till I reached the top, looked about and found I was all alone. My parents were too ignorant even to appreciate what I had achieved. I thanked my lucky stars it was English poetry I studied, so that I had the charms and incantations to lay upon the wound in my soul. If I had chosen to study dentistry or computer science, I might never have won through to happiness.[66]

Practical considerations did not intrude into Greer's capacity to weep for herself in her historical family drama. She said herself that it took the financial windfall from *The Female Eunuch* to fund her first trip home to Australia seven years after first leaving to study in Cambridge. How were her parents, living on one middling income, supposed to finance a trip over to visit the Backs when she began her Cambridge study, let alone another for her graduation?

In her obsessional way, Greer speculated, she had become hypnotized by the father-daughter relationship.[67] 'Mothers carefully, diligently, constantly build the confidence of their sons,' she wrote. 'Fathers give only fitful testimony to the lovability of their daughters.'[68] Maybe so, but it did not stop Greer from fantasizing that Reg, old and frail, would finally let her come close to nurse him, bathe him, groom and feed him. He faded, however, his brain turning to 'soup,' too quickly for her to manage it.[69]

In *Daddy* she seized on every crumb of information hinting that Reg might have loved her after all. A public servant gave her access to Reg's war service medical records, which revealed he had

255

nightmares about cars rushing toward his daughter at high speed, threatening to run her over. 'A howl leapt out of my mouth before I could stifle it,' she said. 'I was literally winded by the sudden intimacy. I wanted to grab the man in shorts and tell him, "You see! He did! He loved me!" Instead I heaved and spluttered, like one choking on her own spit.'[70]

Not all the revelations were welcome. Greer rationalized Reg's fabricated family history as a lie uttered for her benefit, to provide a more secure and socially acceptable explanation of the family's background than he could otherwise provide: 'Now I know that in his description of his childhood and education there was not one word of truth, now I know that his wife and child were the only kin Reg Greer could ever call his own, I know that he was lying for me.'[71] It was more difficult to find benign explanations for the office philandering alleged by his old secretary, Joyce Bull, who thought he looked like Basil Rathbone.[72] 'Well, he was attractive,' said Joyce. 'Not that good-looking, but he was always beautifully dressed and he had a great line, great charm. He gave the impression of being quite well-educated, with the posh voice.' For once, Germaine sympathized with her mother: 'He had a flash job, flash clothes and a flash voice. He was a lounge lizard, a line-shooter, a larrikin, a jerk.'[73] By the end of her search, Germaine felt she was on the edge of losing her mind: 'All life seemed cruel and unbearable, senseless and empty. . . . Though I felt sad as hell, I did not feel merciful. I felt like hell, implacable, hard and bitter. My heart was wrung out, shrunken to a stone. I was exhausted without being sleepy, famished without appetite.'[74]

Nor was it so easy to rationalize her own role in extending Reg's lie and erecting new ones of her own about him. When she had set out on her father-hunt, it was with excitement and innocence as well as a Fury-like spirit of vengeance on those she believed had turned her father into the anorexic wreck he became in World War II. A year after his death Greer was still wedded to and working on her fantasy father. When the story of the wartime Enigma code-breaking project had come to light, Germaine told the *Washington Post*, she realized he had worked using an Ultra machine: 'She now believes that during those years "he was being debriefed by electro-convulsive therapy."' Her eyes narrow and the voice grows cold.

"They blew his mind away, and they're not going to get away with it." [75]

The truth turned out to be more prosaic. Reg had spent months deciphering codes in a hot, damp, dusty room tunneled twenty-four meters deep into the porous limestone of Malta during the prolonged bombing of the island. It was the strain of his subterranean vigil, intensified by his tendency to claustrophobia, that had broken him. While Germaine had compulsively embroidered this part of his life story, she had not known that, in relation to his parentage at least, the cloth itself was made up of lies in the first place. Not that Reg boasted. Again and again Germaine was driven to reflect on how hard she had pushed him on the details of a past he was so reluctant to remember or relate.

Reg's secretary, Joyce Bull, commented to Greer on how much Reg had seemed to fantasize. Reading the 'rubbish,' the 'farrago of errors,' she herself had perpetrated when interviewed by a writer for a book on leading figures in 1970s feminism, Greer confronted the hard evidence that she fantasized just as much: 'I made a myth about my father and I published it.' [76]

By the end of the search, she knew and understood far more about Reg and herself than when she set out, but the knowledge came at the price of lingering alienation and a deep sense of estrangement from her father. The book's denouement comes on a hot night in the bathroom of a Launceston hotel room; washing her sweaty face and neck, Greer catches sight of herself in the mirror and a furious dialogue begins. 'I hardly knew myself,' she writes. 'My face was set, my eyes staring, the pupils fixed as if suddenly grown insensitive to light. My brows had collapsed over them like a No mask of unutterable severity. My top lip was drawn down in a rictus with harsh wrinkles like hooks at the corners.' She tries to laugh at herself but it turns into a gruesome simper; her rigid features convulsed, then the hard-looking face, with eyes that looked as if they had never wept, returns.

'You're mad,' I said to myself.
The face answered, 'This is what you wanted, isn't it?'
'No, no, it isn't. It can't be,' I answered myself.
'Did you really think you'd find out that your father was a brilliant refined young man with a great future and distinguished connections

who just happened to lose touch with his family? You never really believed in him.'

'I did,' I wailed, trying to soften the cruel face staring at me, which didn't resemble Daddy's beloved face at all. 'I thought he was a prince in disguise.'

'That was just your own vanity. You knew he was illiterate. Jesus, you've been a teacher all your life. How could you not know the man could barely read and write? Why do you think he read his tabloid newspaper from cover to cover, because he'd rather have been reading the Tractatus? You knew he was a fraud. Dammit, you treated him as a fraud.'[77]

Greer returns to her bed and lies in the dark, reflecting on the traumatic conversation. Outside in the street the sounds of a drunken couple fighting assail her through the open window. A sleepless hour later she returns to the bathroom for a cool shower, to find the face still glaring at her. The face produces a string of accusations: it was Germaine herself who had locked her father into the lie about his ancestry; she had left home without a backward glance; and now she was returning to 'hunt him down,' not because she loved him, but because she hated him:

'You think you're so warm-hearted, so noble. You never gave the poor bugger a second thought. After you left home, you never wrote. You never called.'

'Oh, bullshit. All he had to do if he wanted to know where I was was call the University. He never bothered.'

'You sound like him.'

'There's a limit surely. I did my best at school. I did my best to be good. And there was never a word of encouragement. He never noticed anything I did. Perhaps I should have got polio or started sniffing petrol or something. Perhaps I would have been rewarded for being a fuck-up.'

'Oh, poor little genius you. Why don't you burst into tears or something?'

'You sound like my mother.'

'Who did you think I was?'[78]

Peggy. It always came back to Peggy – and, ultimately, to Germaine. 'Ms Greer duplicated her father's life of exile from his origins,' that other experienced father-hunter, Jill Johnston, observed on reading *Daddy*. 'Going back, rooting around, uncovering lies, his daughter found out what made her learn and what made her run.'[78] But would Greer's next move, as Johnston speculated, be to grow up to the point where she could forgive her parents? In practical terms, that would mean making peace with Peggy, or at least finally dissolving the knot between them that made Germaine so preoccupied with, and angry about, her mother.

# 13

## *Grounded*

Germaine felt no urgent need to pursue detente, with Peggy or anyone else. Yet finding peace of a particular kind now became an imperative.

She had fled the family home in Mentone as a teenager in the late 1950s, and spent the intervening thirty years putting it and its attendant trauma at as great a distance from her as possible. As an adult she had sought challenges and fulfilment on five continents, with widely varying degrees of satisfaction. As for peace, it was perhaps in the quiet of Cortona that she most completely found a haven. She returned repeatedly to cook, garden, read, write and entertain, often with great generosity, her hospitality extending to other expatriates living in the hills around her cottage as well as to visitors.

For all the benefits of the rustic life in Italy, though, not least the sense of renewal it conferred before the next round of high-voltage urban living, it was deficient in one important aspect. Cortona was far from the resources of the intellectual life, from the storehouses of literature which were the foundation of Greer's professional existence. For short visits this was not an insuperable problem, but it was a considerable practical barrier to making it a permanent home.

Germaine found what turned out to be the perfect compromise in the country which by then, more often than not, had been her home for twenty years. She made a patch of England hers: Mill Farm, a small acreage at Stump Cross near Saffron Walden in Essex which she bought in 1985, establishing her close to Cambridge and its superb library.

Mill Farm was, most immediately, a retreat from London, the appeal of which had waned in the wake of her recent acquaintance with Ethiopia – the latest in a long line of romances with developing nations. 'I just felt I needed dirt around me, not streets and street lights,' she said when she bought the farm. She wanted to put London at arm's length: 'I hate it all – the Café Pelican after the opera and everyone's there and the noise is awful and the food is pretentious and it's impossible to talk about anything sensible. . . . Since I got back from my first trip to Africa last December I'd show up in L'Escargot and they'd all say, "Oh, how waaas Ethiopia?" '[1]

At Stump Cross Greer settled into rural domesticity with characteristic determination, and began to enjoy what has probably been the most enduring contentment of her life. The township of Saffron Walden might be nearby and the motorway within earshot, offering speedy access to Cambridge, but the gently undulating Essex fields insulated Germaine and her three-and-a-half acres from the world at large. Her garden, dozens of apple trees of antique variety, two cats, a score of geese and assorted other animals, along with a floating population of lodger-employees, grounded her after years of urban distraction. She gave free rein to her passion for good food and gardening. Visitors comment on the thoroughly unbohemian industry and orderliness with which Mill Farm is imbued. Each animal in Greer's affectionately tended menagerie is known by name. The disciplined neatness of the orchard and gardens are typical of Mill Farm's carefully managed household economy; and inside the flint-knapped house Germaine's bottled preserves, medicinal herbs and accomplished cooking attest to an impressive domestic capability. 'She's just a clucky old Farmer Brown's wife really,' the gardening expert Jonathan Dawson said after visiting Greer's domain, departing loaded with root vegetables grown in that well-composted Essex earth.[2]

Greer also set up her own small press at the farm: Stump Cross Books, through which she has revived the work of women writers from the Restoration like Aphra Behn and Katherine Philips. The endeavor follows the spirit of Greer's work at Tulsa, which had earlier led to her editing a collection of seventeenth-century women's verse, *Kissing the Rod*.[3] Such work necessarily involves painstaking literary sleuthing to restore the integrity of texts corrupted by time and the manipulation of the woman poet's writing by her male patrons and publishers. Through such work Mill Farm generates enough of a buzz of activity to qualify as a hive, to provide a platform for her benevolent domestic dictatorship, without being so demanding as to make her hostage to the bucolic existence.

Through the second half of the 1980s, as Greer researched and wrote *Daddy*, she had gone through the menopause. Predictably for someone who to date had spent her whole life writing her life, spinning off a book from each of its key phases, Germaine set to work on a book about the experience. First she had written about sex in *The Female Eunuch*, then about its consequences in *Sex and Destiny*, then about death in *Daddy, We Hardly Knew You*. Now she moved on to what could reasonably be characterized in the continuum as sex-death with *The Change*.[4] The book was about the agonized joy of losing one's sexual clout – a surprising subject for someone who had seemed singularly unconscious before her own menopause began that such a woman could even exist.

Germaine began disengaging from sex in her middle forties. She related the shift to work fatigue and the machinations of her unsuccessful attempts to conceive. 'I have a bed in there as big as a ball park but nothing ever happens except I sleep in the swastika position, I think it's called,' she told one journalist. 'If I've been working like a train all day, I want to come home, eat, and watch TV. I really can't be bothered with it.' Referring to the five-hour operation she had endured in 1977 to repair her reproductive system, she added: 'I think that's one of the reasons I've gone off sex. It all got to be too much of a thing.'[5]

As she approached fifty, Greer hastened her philosophical retreat from sex, effectively denouncing it and belittling the movement for social change with which she had been identified in the 1960s and 1970s. 'I'm beginning to think sex is really disgusting and we should have nothing to do with it,' she said in 1986.[6] 'The 1960s social and sexual revolutions were, basically, a "wank,"' she said in a startling admission the following year. 'I was always very cynical about what was happening. We were just rich kids playing and were never really going to change anything – and not for women either.'[7] Then, on the threshold of fifty, she declared that 'maybe I've never been sexually awakened at all. . . .'[8]

The contrast with her earlier sexual politics was sharpened by the publication in 1986 of *The Madwoman's Underclothes,* a collection of Greer's essays since 1968. The collection not only highlighted the extent of Greer's departure from her previous advocacy of sexual libertarianism but exposed some of its retrogressive, masculinist elements as well.

The essays included 'A Groupie's Vision' – a retitled but otherwise undiluted reprint of her infamous 1969 article for *Oz,* 'The Universal Tonguebath: A Groupie's Vision.' Women's movement activists at the time of its original publication could analyze it as a prime example of Greer's embracing of sexual liberation on men's terms; with the benefit of hindsight, its republication meant that everyone else could, too.

In another essay from the collection, the previously unpublished 'One man's mutilation is another man's beautification,' written in 1983, Greer equated the wearing of nail polish, high heels and brassières by Western women with female circumcision in the developing world. This drew an anguished response from Donu Kogbara, a Nigerian writer, who reviewed the book. 'I felt abandoned and betrayed. . . .' she wrote.'Glamourising the Third World is a very common progression for disillusioned European liberals. These adherents to the myth of cultural relativism are to be pitied because Africa is not Utopia. And never will be.'[9]

Greer's earlier enthusiasm for sex was transmuted into a heightened delectation of food, a pleasure which she declared was infinitely variable: 'Sex is really not. It is one of the most banal and unrewarding experiences because, like housework, it's only to do again.'[10] Where this left the thousands of women who had been influenced by her views around the time of *The Female Eunuch,* Greer was not prepared to consider. She tended to duck responsibility for the consequences of her polemics, arguing – constant to her anarchist tenets – that 'it is axiomatic that one can only liberate oneself,' and that her work was designed to provoke thought and change, not to prescribe a course of action. She was now in the process of picking and choosing from her past, seeking to distance herself from the part for which she was best known – sexual liberation – and revive an element that could sustain her and provide intellectual comfort in the vacuum created by post-sexual existence. She turned back to the academy.

Greer's journey from proselytizer of sexual liberation to advocate of liberation from sex was not done without humor. 'I didn't renounce sex,' she observed candidly. 'Sex renounced me. I mean [there I was] pattering after it like a lost dog and it suddenly came to me that I wasn't looking any more.'[11] Her refreshing mutinousness remained, too, as she urged older women to be unapologetic, unique, extraordinary, to behave badly and be unpredictable – in short, to 'go out and be a batty old hag' along with her.[12]

*The Change* was the ultimate in Greer's tendency to universalize her own experience: her readiness, at each point in her life, to declare, 'I am, therefore it is.' To take just one instance: 'Once we are past menopause we are all oddballs.'[13] To which many women might well have replied: 'Speak for yourself!' On publication, Greer insisted she would see only women journalists to discuss a book on a subject she felt only women could understand.

*The Change* was Greer's characteristic rich amalgam of historical titbits and insights, fascinating personal anecdotes and bald-faced and sometimes poorly substantiated assertions, assembled in a well-written and highly marketable package. She reverted to her old ploy of planting an unmissable hook on the first page to seize the reader's attention. On this occasion it was a terrifying portrait of women's treatment by the medical profession in the name of 'eliminating menopause.' 'No sooner had they discovered electricity than they began thrusting electrified rods into the uterus ... [and] Marie Curie had not long discovered radium before radium rods were being inserted in the vagina.'[14] This set the historical scene for Greer's indictment of menopause management by modern medical professionals whose methods, Greer argued, belied the 'utter lack of understanding of what is going on.'[15]

Of equal importance, though, was Greer's premise that 'women are at least as interesting as men, and that ageing women are at least as interesting as younger women.'[16] Again, she was just catching up with what had long been truisms for feminists. Not that this undercut the book's worthwhile aspects. While menopause was not new as a subject in the literature of the women's movement, at the time there was a dearth of mainstream writing on the issue. Greer's *The Change* and Gail Sheehy's *The Silent Passage*[17] were the first popular non-fiction works to address the next big phase of life looming for the baby-boomers. It was therefore unsurprising, Barbara Ehrenreich suggested, that both books should be so 'morbid and alarmist.' 'An objective person, for example, would be forced to conclude from Sheehy and Greer,' Ehrenreich wrote, 'that it is unwise ever to hire a woman over forty-five – or forty, just to be safe. . . . A book titled *Menopause: No Big Deal* might better describe the experience of a generation of busy, high-achieving women. But it probably wouldn't leap off the shelves.'[18]

Yet Greer's book was valuable in drawing out the positive side, the 'peculiar satisfactions,' of growing older. Older women's writing on the subject of being older was invariably joyous in theme, she pointed out. What came as a shock to readers familiar with the Greer persona circa *The Female Eunuch* was her statement that before menopause she had never known such strong and durable joy. 'Before I felt less on greater provocation,' she writes in *The Change*. 'I lay in the arms of young men who loved me and felt less bliss than I do now. What I felt then was hope, fear, jealousy, desire, passion, a mixture of real pain, and real and fake pleasure, a mash of conflicting feelings, anything but this deep still joy. I needed my lovers too much to experience much joy in our travailed relationships. I was too much at their mercy to feel much in the way of tenderness; I can feel as much in a tiny compass now when I see a butterfly still damp and crinkled from the chrysalis taking a first flutter among the brambles.'[19] It was unsurprising enough in itself, perhaps, given the generation from which she hailed, but it was astounding from one who had hitherto had so much to say about relations between women and men. Had Greer merely kept this ambivalence from her listeners and readers as a thirty-something prophet of 'easy come, easy go' interaction between the sexes, or had she kept it from herself all those years too?

Any suggestion that menopause might have diminished Greer's taste for battle was negated in a court case which arose from *The Change*. Mary Anderson, a gynecologist, claimed that in the book

Greer portrayed her as uncaring, insensitive and unsympathetic; she sued and won substantial damages. It was the first time any victim of Greer's sometimes indiscriminate wrath had fought back through the law. But not even Anderson's court victory could subdue Greer, who promptly attacked the High Court judgment and sought to repeat the libel in Richard Ingrams's journal *The Oldie*. The former editor of *Private Eye* had worked with Greer for years; she had written gardening columns under the pseudonym 'Rose Blight' for *Private Eye*, and was now a columnist for *The Oldie*. Ingrams, no stranger to libel laws, refused to print Greer's column, which was an obvious invitation to a writ from Anderson's lawyers. Greer denounced him publicly and privately as a coward and claimed he had sacked her over the incident, which he strenuously denied.

While Greer was adjusting to life without sex, physically and philosophically, the academic life assumed a new appeal. She wanted a reconciliation with academia, and to a sufficiently satisfying extent got it at Cambridge. After she bought Mill Farm, Greer went to ask permission to use the Cambridge University Library and was told, 'Dr. Greer, it's your library.' She described it as the best moment of her life.[20] Symbolically, it was the welcome homecoming of which she had always felt so bitterly deprived at Mentone.

In 1989, aged fifty, Greer was made an unofficial fellow of her old college, Newnham. If the title implied that the appointment was in some sense marginal in character, for Greer it meant a good deal. In between her few years lecturing at Warwick as a newly qualified Cambridge Ph.D., and the brief sojourn at Tulsa in her forties, her academic career had been interrupted by long stretches of popular writing and media appearances. To the Wellington-boot-and-secateur respectability of Mill Farm could now be added the Cambridge seal of approval. She could also direct anyone who doubted her intellectual standing to a book produced for an academic publisher – *Shakespeare*, published in 1986 by Oxford University Press as part of its Past Masters series.[21]

That other great treasure, a child, almost came her way around the same time as her unofficial Newnham fellowship. She found out through mutual friends that Kate Fitzpatrick, an Australian actress who was a social acquaintance, had become pregnant by a French architect from whom she had separated almost immediately. Seven months pregnant, broke, partnerless and a long way from home, Fitzpatrick accepted the hospitality of Australia's Ambassador to Rome, Duncan Campbell, and his family. The residence's phone rang repeatedly: it was Greer trying to persuade Fitzpatrick to come for an extended stay at Mill Farm. They were hardly friends, yet the magnetic force of Greer's insistent representations led the straitened Kate to accept. She traveled from Rome to Stump Cross to endure what was to become a popular pregnancy horror story, widely circulated among the Sydney *culturati*.

Greer later commented that the common element in her floating population of men, women and animals at Mill Farm was that 'they are all under my thumb.'[22] No one felt it more acutely than Fitzpatrick, a striking woman of impeccable theatrical credentials who now found herself vulnerable in Greer's sometimes more despotic than benevolent milieu. It was winter. Without money or a car, Fitzpatrick was isolated on the farm, able to move only at the chatelaine's whim. It was cold. The heating at Mill Farm, visitors comment, tends to vary with the state of its owner's finances; Fitzpatrick's stay seems to have coincided with a fiscal tightening. There was some shivering that winter inside Mill Farm's flint walls. The cold, pregnant antipodean of a certain age also found she was expected to garden for her keep, like the other lodgers who had chores to perform as their contribution to the household. Greer also wanted the baby to be born in her room rather than Kate's own. Fitzpatrick covertly marshalled the help of sympathetic people in the vicinity and fled before her son was born. Germaine was left with the enduring sadness of her childlessness – though with the considerable compensation of more than a dozen godchildren, as well as several nieces and nephews, on whom to lavish maternal attention.

Through all this Mill Farm assumed a deepening importance as a source of succour in Greer's life. The drastically different nature of her birthday celebrations was one small symbol of changing priorities. At fifty the event was marked by a party in a Cambridge college and a photographic session for *Vogue* in which Snowdon portrayed Greer, clad in Missoni, astride a Harley Davidson motorcycle; at fifty-five it was spent carving a thirty-foot trench with a mechanical digger at Mill Farm.

Germaine's tendency to be dictatorial, disputatious and erratically flamboyant has if anything increased in proportion to her sense of security in the Essex countryside. In the 1990s she was at the center of a series of spats of varying public notoriety. A small one which she probably thought unlikely to reach the public realm concerned a librarian from the University of New South Wales, who wrote to ask for a copy of her doctoral thesis, which can only be consulted by going to Cambridge University Library. Greer put the librarian in what she considered her proper place. 'First-naming people you have never met, older than you, and possibly more distinguished than you,' Greer wrote, 'may be accepted practice in Australia, but in other parts of the world it is likely to reinforce the impression that Australians are a race of bumptious louts.'[23]

Other authors were a favorite target. She had refused to sign a petition in 1989 protesting against the Islamic *fatwa* against the author Salman Rushdie: 'I condemn evil. Evil is bad. But I won't sign the pious outcry against the problems that Salman has got himself into.'[24] By 1992 her position had hardened into tacit support for his persecutors. 'Salman thinks I approve of the behaviour of the Muslims, and in a way I do,' she said. 'These are poor people we are talking about, people with nothing but their honour to defend, the Pakistanis of Bradford; and they were organised by a fundamentalist mullah and they began having furious ranting speeches and burning things in the street. Well, why not?'[25]

She criticized David Malouf for his Booker-shortlisted novel, *Remembering Babylon*, arguing that its plot, in which a lost European rejoins colonial society after living for years among Australia's Aboriginals, was racially dubious. Hazel Rowley, author of an acclaimed literary biography of Christina Stead, wrote to Greer indicating interest in writing a biography of her, and received an excoriating reply. Biographical endeavor was parasitic, Greer raged; Rowley should at least wait until her subject was dead. Greer seemed unable to make a connection between her own propensity to comment in her work on living human beings, ranging from her mother to Mother Teresa, and that of writers like Rowley.

Richard Neville courteously sent the relevant parts of his book *Hippie Hippie Shake* off to Greer at Mill Farm, inviting her to set the facts straight before publication if he had made any factual errors. She sent it back unread with a threatening missive hinting darkly that terrible things happened to people who defied her will on matters such as uninvited biographical sketches. Neville, in passing, referred in the book to 'the hysterectomy scar on Germaine's abdomen,' reflecting the widespread but incorrect belief among her friends from Sydney and Melbourne that she had had a hysterectomy as a young woman. After ignoring the opportunity to correct the unpublished text, Greer loosed lawyers on Neville's publishers when the book was launched: they were forced to insert an erratum slip denying the hysterectomy in copies of the book's first print run distributed in Britain.

The dark forces Greer suggested she was capable of unleashing on Neville and others were, however, equally capable of rebounding on herself. When the journalist Suzanne Moore reflected on Greer's gynecological history and its significance after the publication of Neville's book, Greer attempted to use her column in the *Guardian* to vent a torrent of abuse against Moore. The *Guardian* had run at least one highly defamatory attack on a woman writer by Greer before.[26] The practice contrasted starkly with her claim in 1987 that 'I never attack other women.'[27] This time the paper refused to print the abuse. Greer and the *Guardian* parted company, but the attack circulated, and was reported widely anyway, so that Moore was unfairly but unforgettably associated with ample cleavage, birds' nest hair, 'fuck me' shoes and a lipstick-rotted brain.

In the 1990s Greer renewed her attack on the American feminists who had been the target of her ire in the early 1970s. Betty Friedan was 'crazy,' she told the visiting writer Barbara Grizzuti Harrison in 1992, before proceeding to make a bizarre attack on Gloria Steinem. Greer had not read Steinem's *Revolution from Within*, and did not intend to: 'I know what books not to read, I can tell you. . . . Gloria's a food-phobic. How can you be liberated and not eat? A lasting and always available pleasure, better than sex, surely. She's a naif. Doesn't have a clue. Never did. In 1972 she was thrilled to be in the smoke-filled rooms of the Democratic convention. Poor thing, she didn't have a card to deal with, no wonder she wound up in tears. I love her, of course. Well, better than I love Betty Friedan.'[28] Steinem had done what Greer had so far steadfastly refused to do – confronted and dealt with the internal demons that had trapped her into a certain way of living. Resistance to the idea of constructive introspection, as opposed to the self-dramatizing engagement with family history which Germaine retailed so publicly, was surely a significant element in her vituperative comments on Steinem.

What might be considered as the apogee of Greer's attacks on women and writers came with the publication in 1995 of *Slip-Shod Sibyls*, in which she announced that 'the dilemma of the student of poetry who is also passionately interested in women is that she has to find value in a mass of work that she knows to be inferior.'[29]

In her introduction Greer outlined what she calls the 'flying-pig or dancing-dog syndrome.' Historically, women daring to write verse had been as expectant of applause as Dr. Johnson's dancing dog, she wrote, but were also as likely to crash as a flying pig: 'The longer they were kept aloft by the wonder of the public, the more shattering the eventual crash.'[30] The male literary establishment had applied a double standard to women poets, she argued: by inflating the reputations of women who wrote second-rate poetry, they had reinforced the work's inherent mediocrity. The Cambridge academic Sir Arthur Quiller-Couch was one of the villains – not for excluding women from some of his lectures, as Muriel Bradbrook had recalled, but for applying the literary equivalent of affirmative action to women poets. Quiller-Couch perverted his revision of *The Oxford Book of English Verse* in 1939, according to Greer, by including a score of 'inferior' women poets. In 1972 when Professor Helen Gardner revised the anthology, twenty-one of the twenty-five women poets Quiller-Couch had included were dropped. This was proof, Greer argued, of a corrosive double aesthetic standard 'almost as damaging in its insidious operation as the double moral standard.' The essence of Greer's proposition was that Quiller-Couch's inclusion of 'inferior' women poets was both patronizing and destructive, while Gardner's culling was 'the honest exercise of a cultivated critical faculty'[31] – a debatable stance given the highly individual process of compiling an anthology.

'The more women adored poetry, the less able they were to write it,' Greer wrote. 'From being more or less practical and external, the obstacles in the path of the woman who wanted to write songs for others to sing became progressively internalised. It is less crucial for women to work out how men did this to women than it is to assess the extent to which women did this to themselves.'[32] As in *The Female Eunuch*, Germaine focused on the failures of women and their allegedly collaborationist tendencies. The theme harked back to *The Obstacle Race*, too, in which she had pointed to the lack of a female Leonardo, Titian or Poussin.

Greer dedicated the book to her old academic inspiration, Professor Muriel Bradbrook. Early in her career Bradbrook had been highly critical of Virginia Woolf in an article for the first issue of Leavis's journal *Scrutiny*.[33] 'She is young, Cambridge, ardent,' wrote Woolf in her diary afterward. 'And she says I'm a very bad writer. I shall be laughed at & pointed at.'[34] Nearly half a century later, Bradbrook revisited Woolf with considerably different results. Her evocation of the past is a triumph, Bradbrook wrote of *To the Lighthouse*, 'like a beautifully blended culinary master-piece.'[35] If Bradbrook's powers of perception had broadened and deepened over time, that of the young doctoral student she had taught all those years ago at Cambridge had not. With *Slip-Shod Sibyls*, Greer had in one swoop written off the work of women who wrote poetry in English before 1900 as essentially minor. Reviewers gave the book a mixed reception, some arguing that it was highly selective and a confusing mixture of recondite scholarship and sensationalism.

If women poets were a manifestation of the 'dancing dog or flying pig' phenomenon, why should not a similar case be made for women polemicists like Greer? The tragedy of *Slip-Shod Sibyls* is encoded in its damnation of the glitz, the acclaim, the enervating applause that major public success can bring – the factor, Greer argued, that prematurely threw off track the women poets she chose as examples, corroding their creativity and confining them forever to mediocrity. For this might well have been a description of herself, discounting and privately despairing of the tide of celebrity she met at full flood after *The Female Eunuch*'s publication, which carried her away from the rigor and measured demands of the academy. The book's dedication to Bradbrook was perhaps a gesture not only of admiration and respect but also of nostalgia and regret over what for Germaine might otherwise have been.

The siren lure of the electronic media has attracted Greer's thespian impulse ever since *The Female Eunuch* made her a celebrity. From guest-presenting The Dick Cavett Show in New York in 1971 to a regular place on the annual Booker Prize discussion panel, her BBC late-night, all-female chat show series *The Last Word* in 1994 and innumerable guest appearances in between, Greer has become a familiar television presence. Feminism, politics, literature, gardening, architecture are all grist to the mill for her salty comments and idiosyncratic mix of common sense, piercing insights and wildly extreme views, which have made her equally sought-after on radio.

The novelist and biographer Margaret Forster has observed some of the practiced techniques Greer deploys in her television performances. When other people are speaking, Forster notes, 'she puts on an expression of complete bewilderment even if the other person is talking complete sense so that the camera simply cannot keep off her; it is a look of pity.'[36] And as the journalist Polly Toynbee has commented, for Greer 'talking is a performance art of stories and ideas, turning the obvious inside out, taking nothing for granted, not even what she herself said five minutes ago.'[37] Backed up by her persistent, if erratically located, print media presence, Greer has acquired formidable clout with which to prosecute favored causes.

Often her polemic will be on the side of the angels, as with her recent denunciation of antiquarian book dealers who break up books to sell individual pages as decorative prints. 'If it is barbarous to burn a book, it is hardly less barbarous to dismember it,' she declared, calling for the European Parliament to ban the breaking up of antiquarian books.[38] The Antiquarian Booksellers' Association, which had commissioned Greer to write an introduction to the 1997 Antiquarian Book Fair catalogue, declined to publish her piece, construing it as an attack on some of its members. *The Times* immediately ran the article instead, drawing attention to an iniquitous but little-publicized problem.

Yet Greer equally often mounts her public pulpit to debate more dubious causes, as with her 'outing' of the Cambridge astrophysicist Dr. Rachel Padman as a transsexual. After Padman's appointment as a fellow of the all-female Newnham College, Greer told the BBC World Service and *The Times* that 'we have driven a coach and horses through our statutes and I can't believe we did it.'[39] Newnham's Principal, Dr. Onora O'Neill, and the college faculty had known from the time of Padman's recruitment about her sex change fifteen years earlier; it was not considered an issue. Yet Greer, in the spirit of biological determinism that had led her to write in a similar vein about Jan Morris in the 1980s, decided to make it an issue in the wider world – and with Greer this usually means publicity on at least three continents.

One of the odder episodes in Greer's unpredictable mix of do-gooding and cantankerousness was her grand gesture in 1994 of inviting the homeless, through an article in the *Big Issue*, to come and live with her at Mill Farm. Memories of the squatters evicted from Greer's newly acquired house in London twenty years earlier had faded. When Martin Hennessey, a journalist, masqueraded as homeless, wiled his way into Mill Farm and wrote the story for the *Mail on Sunday*, Greer was outraged and enjoyed widespread sympathy – and widespread media coverage. At best a gesture of latter-day *noblesse oblige*, the invitation was suspected of being intended primarily to slake Greer's thirst for the limelight.

While she seemed increasingly to revel in striking terror into the hearts of unsuspecting targets in the 1990s, there remained one relationship in which she could never, apparently, get the upper hand: that with her mother. The writing of *The Change* coincided with a brief diminution of her hostility toward her mother. Promoting the book in Australia, Greer told the *Australian Women's Weekly*: "She's terrific. And dreadful. She exhausts and depletes you. But she's really an amazing old woman.'[40] It was the nicest comment Greer had ever made publicly about her mother and, given the location and large circulation of the magazine, it was something Peggy, her family and friends would inevitably have seen.

Had Greer reached a point where she could forgive her parents? That was overstating the evolution. A few months later she had reverted to the mother demonology: 'She ate my father alive,' she told Barbara Grizzuti Harrison during her visit to Mill Farm. 'She was a bitch. Women like that have a lot to answer for.'[41]

Greer still had not made the link with the thought she articulated during the same visit that we have not yet learned to love the company of women. Besides, she had a young voice, Greer told Harrison on the phone around the same time. '[I] don't think I've ever grown up,' Germaine said.[42] Peggy Greer has a particular feeling for her elder daughter's voice. 'She's very like her father in many ways,' Peggy says, 'though when I hear her speak, I can't distinguish her voice from mine.'

# 14

## *Maverick*

---

Early in the fifteenth century the Chinese emperor Yung-le appointed the young Muslim-born Cheng Ho, who hailed from Yunnan, to lead a maritime expedition through Southeast Asia. On that first expedition, Cheng Ho sailed to Champa on the coast of Vietnam, then on to Java, Sumatra, Malacca, Ceylon and Calicut on the west coast of southern India. Between 1405 and 1433, at the instigation of Yung-le and his successor as emperor, Hsuan-te, Cheng Ho led a total of seven expeditions, each comprising several dozen large junks carrying more than 20,000 men. As well as South and Southeast Asia, his expeditions reached as far as the Middle East and the African coast – to Aden, Somaliland, the south coast of Arabia and Ormuz at the entrance to the Persian Gulf.

Cheng Ho's expeditions had a powerful effect. In the Javanese kingdom of Majapahit he intervened in the succession to the throne. In southeastern Sumatra he stepped in when there was a dispute between the local Palembang government and its resident Chinese colony, as well as involving himself in the internal affairs of the Samudra-Pasai sultanate in the island's northwest. Cheng Ho declared Calicut, Ceylon and Cochin vassals of the Ming empire, and defeated the royal army of Ceylon when it resisted his advance. As a result of Cheng Ho's voyages, China acquired enormous prestige and vastly expanded trade through East and Southeast Asia, and Cheng Ho became something of a cult figure in the region. Geographical works such as the *Treatise on the Barbarian Kingdoms of the Western Oceans* in 1434 and *Marvels Discovered by the Boat Bound for the Galaxy* in 1436 were based on the knowledge acquired through these heroic maritime ventures – all of which Cheng Ho undertook without testicles.

Cheng Ho had entered the gynaeceum of the Prince of Yen – later the emperor Yung-le – in Peking in 1382. A companion and fellow eunuch, Ma Huan, who went on the first, fourth and seventh expeditions, later wrote *Marvels of the Oceans* based on the journeys.[1] In imperial China, eunuchs were not only writers, military leaders and famous explorers; they constituted a bureaucracy which functioned in tandem with the civil service itself, and often enjoyed considerable advantage over the civil service by virtue of their privileged role in the life of the court. By the late fifteenth century more than 10,000 eunuchs were supported through the public purse, and by the time the Ming dynasty ended in the mid-seventeenth century some estimates put their number as high as 70,000.[2] While officially there was a ceiling on the level to which they could be promoted, the chief eunuchs were accepted as effectively equivalent of their civil-service counterparts in rank. At the high point of their role in the Ming dynasty eunuchs had extensive responsibility for the military, supervised the production of weapons, controlled most foreign trade under the tribute system, managed the imperial factories' production of silks, brocades and porcelain, procured the domestic products consumed by the court and managed many official building projects. Most significantly, they controlled the secret police.[3]

It was not only the eunuchs of the ancient East who acquired such power. In the West they found a similar role. As John Julius Norwich notes: 'For at least the four centuries since the age of Justinian . . . they had been highly respected members of society and holders of many of the most distinguished offices of Church and State' – though not, of course, the throne itself. This was the eunuch's key virtue from the ruler's standpoint – that 'never, however powerful he might be, could he make a bid for the throne.'[4] In practice, though, as keepers of the sacred bedchamber, eunuchs had intimate contact with the emperor and could play a critical gatekeeping role; some accumulated enormous riches from the bribes they extracted in exchange for access to the emperor. The wealth of the eunuch Theodore, for example, who had been *castrensis* responsible for Justinian's domestic staff, was calculated at well over 1500 pounds of gold on his retirement. According to A. H. M. Jones, 'in the reign of a weak emperor a eunuch might become virtual ruler of the empire.'[5]

When Germaine Greer wrote *The Female Eunuch*, it was not the rich, powerful, well-connected administrators and imperial gatekeepers she had in mind – it was more the servile, contemptible cipher that was *The Eunuch* of the Greek playwright Menander, as adapted by Terence in 161 BC.[6] Dorus, Terence's cringing, bullied eunuch, is shunted aside on his way to his new household so that a well-born young man can duplicitously enter the bedchamber of a young woman he desires. Dorus, almost without dialogue and barely present on the stage, has the supine, marginal character of Greer's 'female eunuch,' but not her looks. Greer's female eunuch is like a cross between the cringing Dorus and, say, the Roman *galli* – the castrated priests of *Magna Mater*, 'flamboyantly female in appearance, loud cross-dressers, "not-men." '[7]

The importance attached to testicles, and to keeping them attached to the body, lurks uneasily just beneath the surface of the modern Western male mind, preoccupied with exaggerated notions of genital potency. Germaine might have said as much, but did not, at the Town Hall debate in 1971 in response to a particularly interesting question from a member of the audience. The man began by quoting from Oscar Wilde's *The Importance of Being Earnest*: 'All women become like their mothers. That is their tragedy. No man does. That's his.' He then asked how 'the transformations that you envisage might result in a transformation of that.'

'I can only say in answer to that question that I do not resemble my mother at all,' Germaine retorted, bridling at the mention of the magic word 'mother' and missing the cue entirely. 'Not physically, if that's what you meant,' she continued, 'and not in any other respect as far as I can make out. It seems to be based on a false premise.'

It was another audience member, the writer Cynthia Ozick, who momentarily got the Town Hall debate – and Norman Mailer – by the balls. Ozick's question, she said, was her moment to live out a fantasy: 'Mr. Mailer, in *Advertisements for Myself* you said, quote: "A good novelist can do without everything but the remnant of his balls." For years and years I've been wondering, Mr Mailer: when you dip your balls in ink, what color ink is it?'

The panel and audience alike exploded with laughter at the patent absurdity of the quote. Luckily for Mailer, he recognized it himself. 'If I don't find an answer in a hurry, I think I'm going to have to agree the color is yellow,' he replied, triggering another wave of laughter. 'I will cede the round to you. I don't pretend I've never written an idiotic or stupid sentence in my life, and that's one of them.' There was applause.

Mailer on the back foot and graciously admitting wrong-headedness was, however, the exception that night, as it would be from men generally during the second wave. More typical was Mailer's reaction to interjections as he told the audience they must distinguish between his own views and his characters' views – that the novelist sets up characters he agrees with and ones with whom he does not. 'You're asking for a dialogue – here it is. This is my half of the dialogue. You can counter it.' There was another interjection, and he yelled back savagely:

> I'll teach you and you teach me. Fuck you. I want to teach you, too. I mean, fuck you, you know. I'm not going to sit here and let you harridans harangue me and say: 'Yessum. Yessum.' [Applause] When a man has sworn he won't strike a woman and the woman knows that and uses that, and uses it and uses it, then she comes to a point where she's literally killing that man, because the amount of violence that's being aroused in him is flooding his system and slowly killing him. So she's engaged at that point in an act of violence and murder, even though no blows are exchanged. Now, all I'm getting at is that this is the simple existential difficulty of the moment. The argument about the justice in this human relation is where is that point, because that's where there's absolutely never any agreement, whether it is the man or the woman who's playing with the point. But if you women are not willing to recognise that life is profoundly complex and that women as well as men bugger the living juices out of it, then we have nothing to talk about. Again.[8]

Mailer was articulating one of the central conflicts in relations between men and women, while at the same time personifying the violence that underpinned it. Thirty years after the second wave began, many men in unguarded conversation speak about this conflict in virtually the same way.

Just as Mailer explained the problem from the male point of view and displayed the violence at its heart, Greer perfectly encapsulated that night just what the problem was from a woman's point of view. 'It seems that sexual politics by and large has something to do with the act of fucking being to the advantage of the one who fucks,' she said, 'and to the disadvantage of the one who *is* fucked. And as far as I can see, the one who's fucked – be it male or female or a goat or a pig or a stone – is always characterized as female and inferior. And we all have an interest in changing the grammar of that verb, of opening it out to all its many, many possible permutations and getting our eyes off the retaliator for five minutes.'

The 'retaliator' was an allusion to the nickname one of Mailer's fictional characters gave to his penis: 'the avenger' had been given a workout earlier in the evening's debate. Just as the psychic violence inflicted verbally by women, as perceived by Mailer, remains an issue for men, the contempt for women expressed physically by men, as described by Greer, remains a central problem for her sex. On every criminal index one cares to consult, women form a tiny minority of offenders in the gross crimes of murder, assault and sexual abuse; overwhelmingly, it is still men offending violently against women. Violence remains the manifestation of many men's generalized fear and hatred of women, and the too-frequent failure of relations between them.

Did the second wave resolve nothing about these core problems facing women and men in their dealings with each other? In the old Marxist sense, the intensification of a revolutionary struggle would be expected to lead to an increase in repression as those with the upper hand sought to protect and reinforce their advantage.

It is only by looking at the sweep of recent women's history that the question can properly be answered. Women's rebellion was common to feminism's first and second waves. Muriel Bradbrook recalled of her own undergraduate days at Cambridge, for example, that there were women students who 'boldly smoked Turkish cigarettes, cut lectures, and read *Ulysses*. It was an age of literary and philosophic excitement.'[9] When Greer arrived nearly half a century later, in the first stirrings of feminism's second wave, her comments on the students of her college, Newnham, make it sound considerably less interesting than Bradbrook's Girton had been in the backwash of the first wave.

Women's assertion of their sexual agency is underrated common ground between first- and second-wave feminism, too – or more precisely, is part of an erratic sawtooth progression spanning the two, correlating roughly with wartime and economic boom. The relaxation of social mores accompanying periods of economic plenty and wartime dislocation – in the English-speaking West, at least – expanded women's scope for sexual expression, albeit generally on men's terms. In the Greer family household, when Reg went to war, it was the American soldiers on leave in Melbourne who showed Peggy what it meant to have a good time – so that, no matter what shape Reg had been in, he would have faced new challenges from an older and more worldly wife when he came home.

Even the 1950s, that decade mired in the cliché of oppressive suburban respectability, is undergoing a fresh analysis from the perspective of women's sexual agency. The historian Marilyn Lake suggests that the very stereotypes forced on women were part of a panicky reaction by men who were trying to contain women who had experienced an outbreak of full-blooded living during World War II. The 'changing structure of femininity and . . . the concomitant wartime stimulation of female desire had created havoc with traditional roles,' Lake writes. 'A restlessness had been unleashed that could not be easily assuaged.'[10] As Greer herself says of the period: 'It was still a blood sport, we got bruised. Sex in the 1950s was fun, but difficult: it always was, that's life.'[11]

So rebellion, actual and atmospheric, and the flowering of female libido in its widest sense, were manifest in the first and second waves of Western feminism. What distinguishes the two is the concrete changes wrought in each case. While the first feminist wave was about suffrage and establishing a beach-head for women in the education system, the second emphasized legal empowerment, where women strove to win recognition of their civil rights to defend their position and retaliate when the 'avenger' did them wrong. Supporting and complementing this drive was a flowering of self-help groups to promote women's health, provide refuge from male violence and address countless other specific needs, accompanied by a push to suffuse non-sexist thinking through the education system, the media and other critical sites. Just as the second wave was about achieving civil rights for women and cultivating a less discriminatory social environment, the third wave is now to a significant extent about reshaping gender relations by exercising those rights, building on the cultural gains already made.

On issues from rape to abortion, from marriage to employment, from harassment to discrimination in general, legal reforms achieved by the second wavers have transformed the landscape young women now enter. Exercising those rights can be daunting; barriers, both tangible and intangible, remain. Yet women today have a powerful menu of legal options to redress fundamental wrongs. Some critical problems like the feminization of poverty seem intractable; they are not amenable to solution by statute, and call for a different approach again. Yet those who are dismissive of the legal reforms of the second wave might reflect on how recently it is that a woman having an abortion was committing a criminal act; that female public servants had to resign from their jobs at marriage; that the state considered the man who raped his wife to be lawfully exercising, in effect, his property rights; and that a woman applying for a home loan would be shown the door rather than the current list of interest rates.

Second-wave reformers in Australia were perhaps the most successful of all their Western sisters in achieving progressive change, permeating government bureaucracies and pushing change from within and without public institutions. In her book *Inside Agitators: Australian Femocrats and the State*, Hester Eisenstein shows how the distinctive achievement of the Australian femocrats was based on a strong alliance between insiders in government and outsiders in the women's movement. 'A bureaucrat seeking social change?' Eisenstein wrote. 'To US ears this sounds like a contradiction in terms. Yet this generation of Australian feminist bureaucrats, along with many sisters and brothers who were their allies in grassroots organizations, trade unions, and political parties, helped to change the gender landscape of their country.'[12]

Both Greer's personality and her political philosophy sit oddly in relation to the distinguishing achievements of the second wave's insistence on the legal empowerment of women and its emphasis on collective action for grass-roots reformist change. At a time when the women's movement was most determinedly collective in its approach – often maddeningly so – Germaine was, in her own estimation, 'isolated,' 'pretty peculiar,' 'a bit strange,' 'a crackpot' and 'neurotic.'[13] Her Andersonian training ensured her intense, lifelong opposition to meliorism. To the anarchistic pessimists of the Sydney Push, the forces of oppression always adapted around reform, negating its impact; reform pointlessly took up precious energy and held out false hope of progress. This was the persistent subtext to the many otherwise puzzling statements in which Greer undermined the efforts of women striving for change; her opposition to the Equal Rights Amendment in the United States was a prime example. Her idiosyncratic individualism, anti-reformism and opposition to parliamentary politics removed her from the second wave's main game. This was not immutable; it was a matter of choice. When it came to the central reformist thrust of the second wave, however, the curious result was that Germaine became a eunuch herself.

As Cheng Ho and his ilk demonstrate, though, biological determinism is a flawed concept. Cheng Ho and many other eunuchs like him were questing, assertive and powerful, even if they lacked half the reproductive equipment with which they were born. It was a matter of culture, not genitalia, that precluded the possibility of a eunuch's becoming emperor – just as the anarchist Greer, according to her own philosophical dictates, could never be prime minister or president, nor centrally relevant to the concrete achievements of the second wave.

Greer was nevertheless a feminist, and an influential one. She was not *of* the women's movement, but this in itself is no sin. The problem was rather her deep, obvious ambivalence about women – that when she was being malign, mean-spirited, contemptuous and belittling about someone, it was as often as not a woman. She even framed her feminism in terms of an attack on women. Her feminist clarion call is not titled *The Bastard Male*, but *The Female Eunuch*, focusing attention on her view of women as weak, wheedling and flawed.

Gloria Steinem places Greer as part of the movement 'if the movement is defined as "women moving" – as women "off our ass," so to speak, and the movement of ideas.' This assessment is at the generous end of the spectrum of opinion about Greer in the women's movement. Compare it with Beatrice Faust's conclusion, reviewing the sweep of Germaine's work from *The Female Eunuch* to *The Change* and considering its relationship to the women's movement and women's health movement. 'Most other feminist works of that vintage . . . were written by women working with women for women,' Faust writes. 'Greer was working with men for anti-capitalist revolution through sexual liberation on men's terms. . . . Germaine Greer is a quisling to both movements and *The Change* must be seen as profoundly anti-woman.'[14]

The difficulty posed by Steinem's 'women off our ass' definition of what constitutes a feminist is that it can be so elastically applied that it covers the likes of Margaret Thatcher, too – a woman who undeniably got off her ass and achieved, though in a way inimical to the perceived interests of most women in the United Kingdom. Nor is it a coincidence that such a generous feminist catch-all can encompass both Greer and Thatcher. While Greer was at times highly critical of Thatcher, in libertarianism they in fact share philosophical roots. The libertarians inspired by John Anderson and his followers at Sydney University, and nurtured in the Push, drifted over time into two very different camps: left anarchism on the one hand, and the Hayek-style libertarianism exemplified by Thatcher on the other. As one former Push personality, now a successful businessman, remarked years later of Roelof Smilde: 'For Roelof libertarianism meant free love; for me it meant free markets.'[15] Even Push members of a leftist bent were not averse to having a beer with members of the exceptionally nasty end of the far right in the name of pluralism.

An extreme individualism underwrote the utter certainty expressed by both Greer and Thatcher, even in the face of incontrovertible facts, in their common 'this lady's not for turning' style. It could also be argued that, even when they take positions that are regressive from the standpoint of women at large – Greer's romanticization of extended families and the position of women in the Third World, for example, and Thatcher's opposition to state meliorism across the whole sweep of social and economic policy – they are still examples of assertive, powerful women in the world, expanding the range of role models available to other women.

While Greer was a Labour Party supporter and an habituée at Lady Antonia Fraser's soirées during the long years of Conservative government, it did not stop her praising the Iron Lady lavishly when Thatcher was finally pushed from the British prime ministership. Greer declared that she 'liked the cut of her jib' even while disliking Thatcher's policies. 'Women everywhere . . . salute her,' Germaine wrote. 'Because of her, every middle-aged woman waiting in the queue at the butcher's can tell herself that there may be a great statesperson sleeping within her, awaiting the call to greatness.'[16]

Greer and many other major second-wave feminist figures have been forgotten by 'Generation X.' This is a loss, since even Greer's dark side – her ambivalence about women, her quickness to criticize other feminists, her unacknowledged reversals of her own previously unequivocal positions – contains valuable pointers for the third wave. These are simple to express but, as the history of the women's movement shows, perhaps not so easy to remember and practice. Avoid trashing other women; be inclusive; advance on multiple fronts; and write and remember your history.

Greer's life also attests to the power of popularity. 'Greer succeeded as a celebrity,' observes Faust. 'The processes of celebrity gave her an influence disproportionate to her significance for feminism.'[17] It is a complaint most relevant for feminists in Greer's long-time home, Britain. As Shelagh Young comments, 'the media seem happy to repeatedly wheel out Germaine Greer in order to represent feminism to the masses.'[18]

Celebrity, or less pejoratively, popularity has its uses. If Greer's stance was flawed from a feminist perspective, she was arguably the most popularly influential feminist of the entire second wave, at least when it came to inspiring women's 'delinquency.' Among Western women born before 1960 Germaine has immense recognition, frequently accompanied by warmth and spirited regard. Her message might be mixed, her polemic often leading to practical cul-de-sacs rather than liberation, but Greer's in-your-face style and determination to lead her own flagrantly unconventional life to her *own* satisfaction have been an incendiary inspiration to the down-trodden of the domestic world. Even those who were not following Germaine's example could gain vicarious pleasure from it, and were just that much less likely to accept a handmaidenish existence.

However repellent she claimed to find the media, Greer's willingness to engage with them ensures that her views have been widely heard. Getting the message to more rather than fewer women and men is a goal that should not be pursued at the expense of prostituting the message, but neither is it one that should be ignored. 'The disappointment for me is that [*The Female Eunuch*] hasn't been superseded by a better book – it stays alone, embattled,' Greer has said. 'As far as intellectual feminists are concerned there have been lots of books, but that's not the point. At another level, the popularising, on-turning, fun-making, thinking book has not been written. There hasn't really been a book which has done the job of popularising the women's question in quite the same way.'[19]

Trivialization is the trap for willing media players. Chris Hegedus and D. A. Pennebaker bring it home subtly at the end of their documentary *Town Bloody Hall*. 'Thank you all for an incredible evening,' Norman Mailer says to the enraptured Town Hall audience, who reciprocate with applause. A photographer and cameraman appear on the stage. Germaine looks suddenly wrung out, and gazes lingeringly into Norman's eyes while they speak with one of the organizers in the midst of the media throng. The audience knots into discussion groups, leaving the hall in clusters, still debating the night's proceedings. Then, right at the end, a member of the audience – a man – yells up to the luminaries and hovering media on the stage, just audible: 'Will this get me on the news tomorrow?'

It was not so much trivialization, however, as optional adherence to the truth that accompanied Greer's migration to the celebrity zone. A journalist asked her in her later years, what makes you feel guilty? 'Lying,' she replied.[20] Around the same time she admitted her tendency to self-aggrandizing fantasy. The demands of fame, it seems, reinforced this tendency.

Greer's comments about physical abuse at the hands of her mother exemplify this. For more than twenty years Germaine rarely mentioned Peggy in her writing or in interviews without also recalling being hit by her as a child. Promoting *The Female Eunuch* in New York in 1971, she referred to 'lying on the floor being beaten savagely' as a girl.[21] She told psychiatrist Anthony Clare in 1987 that 'my mother did physically abuse me as a child. . . . She used a stick. And she used to hurt me pretty badly.'[22] Two years later in *Daddy, We Hardly Knew You*, Germaine continued: 'I was beaten and told I was a destructive child. I didn't need the beating, for I was crushed already.'[23] She was still raising it in 1992: 'I'm not so angelic that I can set aside that I was a small child being beaten and bashed,' she told the *Australian Women's Weekly*.[24]

These are only some of the many references Greer made over the years to physical abuse by her mother. 'I remember it so strongly,' she said, 'that if I sit next to my mother now, at Christmas dinner or something, I'm frightened. . . . I mean, my heart skips and trips and my palms sweat.'[25] Peggy Greer herself says in relation to disciplining defiant children: 'I can't see how you can get along without giving kids a whack.'

Yet in 1996 Greer flatly denied that it constituted abuse at all. She told the journalist Peter Ellingsen that Peggy's 'command module' was gone, that she was 'free-associating,' talking violently, and was likely to say that she had beaten Germaine as a child.[26] 'I was not abused by my mother,' Greer said. It was part of a pre-emptive strike against her mother's credibility. After attacking Peggy publicly for years, Greer now feared that Peggy might have spoken publicly about her. To undercut the impact of anything her mother might have said, Greer now hinted that Peggy was senile, adding a new item to her lifelong catalogue of attacks on her mother.

What made Greer believe she could get away with such obvious contradictions? 'When she left the University of Warwick after the heady success of *The Female Eunuch*, Greer and academe both lost,' according to Camille Paglia. 'Outside the discipline of the academic world, Greer's scholarly skills never developed. Her thinking is always stimulating but tends to dissipate itself in flashy spurts.'[27]

Greer herself identified the corrosive potential of success that comes too early and too easily, though she was referring to the women poets she examined in *Slip-Shod Sibyls* rather than to her own high-trajectory entry into public life. 'Systematic overestimation of an artist's work may have a worse effect upon her achievement in the long run,' Greer wrote, 'than unimaginative carping would have.'[28]

Paul Johnson's study of intellectuals suggests a more controversial possibility: self-serving deception. 'One thing which emerges strongly from any case-by-case study of intellectuals is their scant regard for veracity,' Johnson has argued. 'Anxious as they are to promote the redeeming, transcending Truth, the establishment of which they see as their mission on behalf of humanity, they have not much patience with the mundane, everyday truths represented by objective facts which get in the way of their arguments. These awkward, minor truths get brushed aside, doctored, reversed or are even deliberately suppressed.'[29] Not only deception but self-deception was a recurring theme in the lives of the intellectuals Johnson examined.

Greer's rape when she was an undergraduate at the University of Melbourne is a case in point. She publicly discussed it at length on two occasions – in a long interview with Clyde Packer in Santa Barbara in the early 1980s, and then in a column for the *Guardian* in 1995.[30] The experience was terrible enough as related to Packer. The additional details described in her column for the *Guardian* underlined the unpleasantness of the attack. The latter account gave importance to two aspects of the incident: the class identity of the rapist, and the reaction of the other men at the party where it occurred.

In her earlier account Greer said the rapist was a Xavier College graduate – 'just the sort of boy my mother would have liked me to marry.'[31] In the later account, she provided more detail about the rapist. This was crucial to her development of the story. The class identity of the rapist is intimately bound up with the reaction of the other men at the party, as described in Greer's piece for the *Guardian*. In Greer's earlier account, her male friends at the party were simply too drunk to notice her distress, too busy tossing down cold ones around the keg to respond to her pleas to be taken home. In Greer's later account, their inaction was due to upper-class male solidarity: there was no use reporting the attack to the police because the other men at the party would have closed ranks to save the rapist's hide.

One person was particularly upset when Greer's column was published in the *Guardian* in 1995. It was another man at the party – a University of Melbourne footballer and fellow undergraduate who had got to know Germaine at the football club barbecues and singalong drinking sessions. He considered her a kind of a mate. It was why, he says, he felt concerned when he saw Germaine gravitating toward the man who would later rape her.

Germaine's friend and another student had come to the party in the rapist's car. Far from being a Xavier boy, the rapist had dropped out of a state high school at the earliest opportunity and had worked his way up to the position of used-car salesman. Through his work he had acquired a superficial savoir faire, and had plentiful access to cars. There were a few undergraduates, including Germaine's friend, who used to get rides to parties with him. He had the transport; they knew where the parties were. Both the rapist and Germaine's friend played Australian rules football, though in Germaine's account for the *Guardian* they had been transformed into rugby players, with attendant upper-class implications.

The rapist had an air of unpredictability and latent violence about him, according to Germaine's friend. While the students were grateful for the rides, they were always wary of him. Greer's footballer friend recalls that at the party 'Germaine came up to me and said: "Introduce me to your friend." . . . I was a bit reluctant because I knew he had a bad reputation for being a wild man. He really was crazy. He was this big, strong sort of guy and he was pretty wild and had a bad reputation for losing self-control, wanting to fight people, so I was a bit reluctant to introduce them. She insisted, so I introduced her to him. Then he wandered off to get a beer or something and I said to her: "Listen, just be careful of him . . . don't go off with him." She just laughed.'

The party carried on and Germaine's friend lost track of where she was, what she was doing. Some time later he left the house via the front garden for a discreet leak. Walking along the footpath back to the party afterward, he heard crying coming from his wild friend's car. 'It kind of sobered me up,' he recalls, 'so I went over to see who was crying. I opened the door. It was Germaine. She was sobbing really uncontrollably, and I still remember it because it shocked me. It shocked me because to hear anybody cry is pretty shocking, but to hear Germaine crying, who up to now had always projected this tough, hard-bitten, loud-mouthed, foul-mouthed, match-it-with-the-guys image, confident, cocky, all that put together – and to see somebody like that sort of in this terrible state, I mean, really it still remains with me.'

He asked Germaine what had happened. 'She said: "— raped me." And I remember what I then said. I said: "Jesus, Germaine, I said not to go out with the bastard." I said: "Let me call the cops." And she said: "No, no, I don't want you to call the police." I said: "I must call the police. He's a bastard and we'll dob him in. . . . You know, bugger him – he's a bastard. I'll give evidence on your behalf." ' Germaine insisted he was not to call the police – a woman, she said, would never be believed. Germaine's friend then went inside and found her three housemates and told them what had happened; they comforted her as best they could, then sought out her attacker. Germaine's friend describes what happened next: 'These guys fronted this bloke and said: "What do you think you've been bloody doing? What's your story? What have you got to say for yourself?" And I remember his words. He said: "Oh, look, you know . . . I slapped her around a bit. I just tried to hustle her along a bit." '

The men were unimpressed: 'They wanted to call the coppers, too,' Germaine's friend recalls. 'They were prepared to dob him in. And she said: "No, no, I don't want you to. They won't believe me." ' He and his friends were outraged: as far as they were concerned, the assault had been on one of their own. The rapist was subsequently ostracized by them.

It was the unjust misrepresentation of his own and his friends' reaction that led him to speak out against Germaine's apparent rewriting of history. 'She's converted him into an upper-class bully with his rugby-playing mates backing him up,' he says, 'and she's now saying why she didn't report him was because his rugby mates would've said they'd had her, too – that they would've said: "Oh, we all had her." The reality of it was 180 degrees the other way. They, in fact, were prepared to dob him in to the police, as I was. . . . What sort of irked me about all that was the boys *didn't* behave like that. Now, the boys were no bloody angels, but they drew the line at brutality and bashing and rape. That really sickened them. And they were prepared to put that bastard in to the cops.' Germaine had every right not to let them call the police, he says. 'But the point is she can't now convert it into "all the blokes in together," into "all the rich boys ganging up." It just isn't true. . . . It just isn't bloody true.'

Is it, like the classic stare-down stalemate of many rape cases, a matter of one person's word against another? The only other time Germaine discussed the rape at any length was in an interview with *Playboy* in 1972, long before either the Packer interview or the *Guardian* column appeared. 'My men friends were more bitter than I was,' she said, lending credence to her footballer friend's recollection of events.[32]

'What happened to her that night profoundly shocked me,' he says now. 'I still haven't gotten over it. It was really just something you don't forget. All the things men say about women, you can trivialize them. But when you're confronted with the reality of it, it really brings you up very sharply against what you really believe in, what your values are, what's important to you.'

Do Greer's varying versions of events matter? 'If it comes to accuracy,' Germaine said in the Town Hall debate, 'it seems to me I won't mess about with matters of detail. But radical accuracy is important.' Quite so; passions are inflamed, action incited and not infrequently pain is caused by the quest for progressive change, and it needs to be done on the basis of reliable accounts of events, not versions that drift with the changing imperatives of the storyteller. Quite different conclusions are to be drawn, for example, from a situation where several men are prepared to testify for Greer in a bid to prosecute a rapist, and are urging her to do so, than from one where the men are showing post-attack solidarity with the attacker.

In 1995 Germaine used the account of her rape in the *Guardian* to argue for the outing of alleged rapists on the Internet in preference to prosecution through the justice system. The suggestion undermined a quarter of a century's hard work by feminists encouraging women to report what was a vastly underrated crime, and devalued the huge struggle to improve police and court procedures – not to mention the fact that 'outing' without trial is a fundamental betrayal of the concept of natural justice. Greer had scrapped any considerations derived from her own knowledge, articulated two decades earlier, that rape 'is a habitual crime . . . and any woman who decides not to prosecute ought to spare a little thought for the women who will be raped as a consequence of her decision.'[33]

Greer is right: radical accuracy is important. Her words have not always matched the deeds they purport to describe. This is far more damaging to her credibility than any media trivialization, yet has no apparent consequence in the accountability-free celebrity zone. Attempts to correct celebrity Kremlinizations of history when one is not a celebrity oneself can be all but impossible, as Germaine's university football club friend found out. He wrote a letter to a major Australian newspaper putting his recollections of the night of the rape on record, only to be told they would not run it: despite the slur against him and Germaine's other male friends at the party, the newspaper did not want to tangle with someone of Greer's stature. In a world increasingly conditioned by fanciful and routinely contradictory cover-lines in the popular press about the lives of even the modestly well-known, what hope truth?

'Some might say I am letting myself go,' Germaine said as her ageing become obvious. 'To a lifelong libertarian, that's a compliment. . . .'[34] A relentless commitment to truth and to free speech were the most admirable elements of the Push libertarianism to which Germaine subscribed all her life. In fact, she was a wavering exponent of both.

Greer subscribed to a kind of serial truth: her stories and philosophical line changed to fit with her needs at the time, without her attempting to admit or reconcile previous versions. Greer has been most strongly associated in the public mind with sexual freedom. 'For my generation it was important to say we had the right to make love and not to make love,' she said twenty years after *The Female Eunuch*'s publication. 'Now I say offhand to young women: be difficult, dangerous, inaccessible and demanding and don't care if it makes you unpopular.'[35]

It was the right to make love rather than the right not to make love, however, that Greer early and long emphasized, relentlessly promoting the notion of liberation through copious fornication. As Anna Coote and Beatrix Campbell note, Germaine gave the lead to the 'heterosexual chauvinist' wing of the women's movement when it was riven along sexuality lines in the 1970s. Greer 'made it plain that however many faults men had, they were indispensable when it came to sex, because penetration turned it into the Real Thing.'[36]

The trouble with the drastically different attitude to sex dating from her long, unsuccessful quest to conceive, and embodied in *Sex and Destiny*, is that Germaine refused to acknowledge the shift, let alone explain it. 'Her alleged discovery that no sex is better than bad sex is simply what the first feminist refugees from the Black Civil Rights movement, the Anti-Vietnam War campaign, and the so-called sexual revolution have been saying since the late 1960s,' Beatrice Faust pointed out, citing work as early as 1968 by feminists like Ti-Grace Atkinson, Dana Densmore, Anne Koedt, Susan Lydon and Anselma Dell'Olio on just this theme. 'In the pithy words of Jill Johnston,' Faust observed, ' "the love ethic that went to chicago [sic] and came out a fuck ethic was a fuck ethic to begin with." For "chicago," read London, Paris, Munich, Sunbury or Nimbin.'[37]

Frustratingly, Greer got halfway there, observing that Reich – the fount of the Push's sexual philosophy – had not understood how far his concept of sexual revolution 'played into the hands of the consumer economy and the monopoly state.'[38] At the same time she complained of being 'fed up with being told I've had this huge turnaround. I haven't. I've been saying the same thing for twenty years.'[39] Contrast this with Roelof Smilde's direct handling of an issue that was long at the heart of Push thinking:

> We did see this correspondence between idea and action, and we saw what we thought was a correspondence between freedom in one area and freedom in another, and we came to the view that sexual freedom was somehow central to all the others – which I don't think is true, actually. . . . [L]ooking at other societies and developments in our own society it just isn't true. You know, our model of the authoritarian world was sort of set by Orwell's *1984*. When I think about it, looking at society now, it seems to me that Aldous Huxley's *Brave New World* is much closer to what's happened than *1984*. Because there's a tremendous amount of personal freedom now compared to then – in mores, style of dress, sexual behaviour – and yet we're going

backwards. Politically, we're getting more and more centralised, there's less and less freedom. So this great liberalisation in mores and sexual behaviour, and the sort of thing people allow themselves, hasn't had any spin-off effect. . . .

I just think the view was too strongly put – the idea that somehow if you were orgastically potent and free, you would then be a sort of a free-living person who could take on anything. But it's turned out to be wrong. We didn't give enough countenance to what probably should've flowed from our own theory, that the forces opposing that are so strong that there isn't really a great deal of room to move.

This is not simply a matter of historical tidiness or intellectual honesty. These are current questions. Catharine Stimpson, for example, has encountered complicated attitudes toward the prevailing 'sex-saturated culture' among young women of the third wave. 'They are sexual libertarians,' she writes. 'Fewer of them support anti-pornography measures than one might think. . . . However, when they talk candidly, they say they are sick of being saturated with images of lousy sexuality – in pornography, movies and TV, advertisements. They are torn, because they do not want censorship, but they do not want the images of sexuality that surround them. They want to think through what a different culture of sexuality might be like.'[40]

Greer was the sexual libertarian *par excellence* of second-wave feminism who decided after menopause that sex was 'one of the most banal and unrewarding experiences'[41] – who felt more joy after the change than she had ever felt lying in the arms of young men during her years of sexual plenty.[42] After years of exhaustive field research, Greer is in a special position to reflect on what a different, a better, sexual culture might be like. Intellectual hubris, however, has stopped her acknowledging the reversal and finding a new path through the thicket of modern mores that can explain and reconcile her contradictory positions. Germaine may remedy this in her work-in-progress, *The Whole Woman*, planned for publication in 1999.

Toward the end of the Town Hall debate she got her biggest laugh of the evening in her put-down of Anatole Broyard's paraphrasing of Freud's famous question: what is it women want? 'I really don't know what women are asking for,' Broyard persisted. 'Now suppose I wanted to give it to them. . . .' To which Germaine replied smartly: 'Listen, you may as well relax because whatever it is they're asking for, honey, it's not from you.' She won the exchange but the question remains – not only in the minds of men but for women looking to Greer for some durable insight about it, too.

Greer's apparent splendid isolation within feminism, on a media stage all to herself, is one of the most striking aspects about her. Dennis Altman evokes something of its impact in his auto-biography, admitting he was more nervous meeting her for the first time than meeting Christopher Isherwood and James Baldwin. 'Hard, now, to recapture the excitement of Germaine's visit . . . more akin to a rebellious Royal tour than a book promotion,' Altman wrote of her return to Australia for *The Female Eunuch* in early 1972.[43] One of Beatrice Faust's most persistent criticisms of Greer is her lack of acknowledgement or even consciousness of the feminist scholarship that came before her works – not just *The Female Eunuch* but, more particularly, *Sex and Destiny* and *The Change* as well. The way she wrote was as though the path had never been trodden before her.

It was a trait Greer shared with the libertarians' mentor, John Anderson. Examining Anderson's work, Peter Shrubb noted, one might think that Anderson 'had invented his major views, and indeed as good as invented himself' – despite the fact that, if one started sleuthing, one could trace an obvious path from other philosophers to him. Reading Anderson, Shrubb felt he was in the presence of a mind dependent on separation, not connection, with others: 'We all clear space for ourselves by opposing, and it is an unusual article in any of the gentle fields of academe that does not wish to stake its claims through the heart of a vanquished opponent. But only one philosophical world comes real in these pages, and it is Anderson's; there is little sign I can see of any sense that it is one world amongst others, much less one state in a federation.'[44] What price splendid isolation? The work of both Anderson and Greer – in their times sensational, inspirational, to so many – too often peters out in an intellectual dead end.

Connectedness, intra- *and* intergenerational, is crucial if each new generation is not to expend precious energy reinventing the wheel or, worse, developing unworkable variations of it. Greer's old academic inspiration at Cambridge, Muriel Bradbrook, had a strong sense of modern feminism's antecedents. As an under-graduate at Girton in the 1920s, Bradbrook met one of the college's original students – Emily Gibson, subsequently Mrs. Townsend – who provided some valuable tips to her and the other Girton students. If any of them was hauled off to prison, the 80-year-old Emily said, she should take a change of underclothes so that the warders would know she was a lady, and claim vegetarianism because the food was better. The advice was well grounded: as a young woman she had spent a fortnight in Holloway jail in the cause of women's suffrage.[45]

In *The Female Eunuch* Greer was dismissive of the suffragettes. She was grotesquely dismissive of women academics, too. 'The prejudice that academic women are neurotic is justified in actual experience if not in theory,' she declares baldly.[46] It is no slip. She pursues the theme later in the book, commenting that: '[It is] true that in too many cases female intellectuals are arrogant, aggressive, compulsive and intense. They place too high a value on their dubious educational achievements, losing contact with more innocent recreations.'[47]

Greer admired Professor Bradbrook, though, whose scholarly sweep, integrity and enthusiasm had so fired young graduate students like Germaine. She would have drawn comfort, too, from Bradbrook's evocation of the female mavericks of the late eighteenth and nineteenth centuries.[48] Bradbrook cited, among others, Lady Hester Stanhope, who in 1810, grief-stricken over the death of an English general, decamped to Lebanon and 'exercised a despotism that quelled her visitors, and a power of conversation that sometimes caused them to faint of fatigue.' There were the Ladies of Llangollen, who in the late eighteenth century eloped together from Ireland to a Welsh valley, where they established a rural retreat and for half a century 'dressed like men, cultivated sensibility and forgot to pay their bills.' These women lived revolutionary existences without theorizing, Bradbrook declared, and their example could be more potent than exhortation.[49]

Bradbrook's maverick *par excellence* was Barbara Bodichon, née Leigh Smith – a young woman of independent income who earned a fortune of her own as a painter, having studied with Holman Hunt and worked in Corot's Paris studio. Bodichon, like Greer – both, coincidentally, milliners' daughters – had brains, money and beauty in abundance. Bradbrook described how in 1854 the twenty-five-year-old Bodichon caused a sensation with the publication of *A Brief Summary in Plain Language*, which comprehensively set out the discriminatory laws that submerged the married woman's legal identity: even her body belonged to her husband, who could enforce his conjugal rights by writ of habeas corpus. Bodichon agitated for married women's property rights, opened a school for the poor, co-founded the *Englishwomen's Journal*, was a leading figure in the first suffrage movement and was one of the founders of the college that would become Girton, to which she bequeathed £10,000. 'Barbara indeed in some ways resembled the noble eccentrics of a previous generation,' said Bradbrook. '[She] dressed unconventionally, she silenced the opposition with a masculine "Bosh!" and drove off visitors with "Devastators of the day, away, away!"'[50]

At the same time, Bodichon married a French doctor and spent half of each year with him in the then-French colony of Algiers. She lacked the single-mindedness of some of her feminist contemporaries, leading some to judge her an amateur. Not so Bradbrook, who believed Bodichon's lack of a single focus yielded a rare strength: 'She could be vigorous, masculine – Rossetti's "good fellow"; she could be deeply sympathetic, with the intuitive sympathies of the artist. The vitality which sustained her was fed directly into the work of her closest friend, George Eliot; thus her powers expressed themselves in what a modern poet has termed "nutrition of impulse.". . . In her determination not to forgo or suppress any side of her nature, she endured the conflict of interests that is more common today.'[51]

What is Barbara Bodichon, with 'face both sad and bright,'[52] to Germaine Greer with her countenance of bravura and pain? Here is the only possible place to make sense of Greer as a feminist – a feminist in the long tradition of maverick women.

Just as Lady Stanhope was despotic, the Ladies of Llangollen cross-dressed and Barbara Bodichon cried 'bosh' and banished 'devastators of the day,' so it is that a maverick like Greer's idiosyncrasies are indulged, her inconsistencies forgiven and the vitriolic side of her personality overlooked. If there is one thing about Germaine that is whispered fearfully in asides by people who are loath to provoke her, and that is nearly everyone, it is: 'We have to live with her.' As Altman comments, 'Germaine's temper tantrums were real,'[53] or, as Jim Haynes put it, 'I don't think there's anybody on earth who can blast as well as Germaine can blast.'[54] A heady mix of attraction, admiration and apprehension lies at the heart of many of her relationships. 'Any friendship with her has its downside,' in Albie Thoms's view. 'She turns on you at whim. She's always looking for a fight. She loves the fight!'

The curious thing is how Germaine can say the most unjust things, yet be so compelling, even winning. Muriel Bradbrook describes the same characteristic in Queenie Leavis: 'Queenie went in for straight tackling in the St Trinian's style, with such vigorous and well-aimed thumping and jumping that the enjoyment of her vitality was stronger than the thought of the victim's discomfiture.'[55] It is no compensation to the victims, of course, yet it helps explain why Germaine, like Queenie, has got away so lightly with her bitter attacks on others.

*The Female Eunuch* may have been the publishing equivalent of a tidal wave when it came to feminist books, but it was produced well into the swell of feminism's second wave; even its publisher bills it as a 'watershed' rather than a genuine trail-blazer. The sexual critique of *Sex and Destiny* was prefigured by the work of other feminists, as were aspects of *The Change*; and Jill Johnston was already pursuing the great father-hunt that would later be so successful for Germaine. It is eerie looking back at Cynthia Ozick's essay from early 1969, 'Previsions of the Demise of the Dancing Dog,' which anticipates several of the themes and motifs subsequently used by Greer. The most marked parallel is that with Greer's characterization of women – for Ozick woman's 'infantilism' reduced her to an 'it,' anticipating Greer's concept of the 'female eunuch.' Ozick wrote:

> Woman will cease solely to be man's muse . . . and will acquire muses of her own when she herself ceases to be bemused with gaudy daydreams and romances – with lies reinforcing lies – about her own

nature. She limits – she self-limits – her aspirations and her expectations. She joins the general mockery at her possibilities. I have heard her laughing at herself as though she were a dancing dog. . . . She surrounds herself with the devices and manipulations of an identity that is not an identity. . . . She lives among us like a docile captive; a consuming object; an accomplice; an It. She has even been successfully persuaded to work for and at her own imprisonment. No one can deny that imprisonment offers advantages, especially to the morally lazy. There have been slaves who have rejoiced in their slavery . . . and female infantilism is a kind of pleasurable slavishness. Dependency, the absence of decisions and responsibility, the avoidance of risk, the shutting-out of the gigantic toil of art – all these are the comforts of the condoning contented subject, and when these are combined, as they are in this country, with excessive leisure, it would almost seem that woman has a vested interest in her excluded role. If one were to bow to the tempting idea that her role has come about through a conspiracy (as it could not have, since custom is no plot), it would appear as though it were a conspiracy of sluggish women, and never of excluding men.[56]

The woman Ozick describes might easily be described, in fact, as a 'female eunuch'; the attributes Ozick identifies bear an uncanny resemblance to those later identified by Germaine. Ozick also explores the reasons why there have been no great women artists, drawing an analogy between women and Jews, asking where is the Jewish Michelangelo, the Jewish Rembrandt, the Jewish Rodin[57] – just as a decade later Greer explored why there is 'no female Leonardo, no female Titian, no female Poussin.'[58] Both deployed Dr Johnson's 'dancing dogs' remark, too – Ozick in relation to the attitude of American college students and academics to writing by women, and Greer in *Slip-Shod Sibyls* as part explanation of the dismal career dynamics of women poets. Originality is not, perhaps, Greer's outstanding virtue.

What Greer could indubitably do, though, and often do brilliantly, is write, perform and think fast on her feet. She writes powerfully, persuasively and affectingly. Parts of *The Female Eunuch* throw so fierce a light on the dynamics of sexism that, for those new to thinking about the position of women, it is difficult to believe that one could not see the phenomenon before her articulation of it. While parts of the book are dated, the most outstanding passages remain revelatory; progress has not been so great as to render them obsolete. Greer creates a genuine shock of recognition in showing us how fundamentally patriarchal relations have shaped women's lives; any woman who reads *The Female Eunuch* and continues her life unchanged becomes a witting rather than an unconscious partner in her own oppression. Against this has to be balanced the book's obvious ambivalence about women. One indication of how the contradictory elements balance out is, arguably, the number of copies that flew through the air aimed at a male partner's head, and the plethora of middle-class dinner parties disrupted by conflict over it. Most symbolic of all is perhaps the woman Anne Summers ran into in the women's lavatory during a break in a seminar at Sydney's Workers' Educational Association in 1972. The woman was reading *The Female Eunuch*. 'It had a brown paper cover around it,' recalls Summers. 'She used to hide it under her shoes because her husband had forbidden her to read it.'

Greer's other writing, particularly *Daddy*, often displays the same verve. One can only lament that her creative drive did not at some point overtake her polemical priorities. Some fine novels might have been the result.

Nor should the importance of Greer's thespian streak be underestimated. A good quip at the right time on the right platform can have more impact than a dozen books in this new, electronic media-driven era of the oral tradition. Two sallies stand out. At Washington's National Press Club in 1971, Greer put two of America's then-leading Casanovas into scathing perspective when asked about the relative stud merits of Senator Ted Kennedy and Norman Mailer: 'I've got a feeling that if breeding with either Ted Kennedy or Norman Mailer was the only future for the world, it might be as well that the world came to a halt immediately.' Twenty years later neither her mind nor her tongue was blunted. 'I have a great deal of difficulty with the idea of the ideal man,' she told a literary luncheon in the conservative Australian stronghold of Brisbane. 'As far as I'm concerned, men are the product of a damaged gene. They pretend to be normal but what they're doing sitting there with benign smiles on their faces is they're manufacturing sperm. They do it all the time. They never stop. I mean, we women pop one follicle every twenty-eight days, whereas they are producing 400 million sperm for each ejaculation

... I don't know that the ecosphere can tolerate it.'[59] In 1992 when Peter Butler, Germaine's old friend from Sydney University days, ran into her in New York it was, appropriately enough, at the Metropolitan Opera's performance of *Falstaff*: he saw her across the Met's dim foyer during the interval, standing alone, spotlit by the only beam of light in the room.

Greer's thespian talent gives her the ability to mask her pain, or massage it into a less publicly confronting visage. It is central to her persona that she most often chooses not to do so. Germaine has a limited capacity for forgiveness and, like her expenditure of empathy, it tends to be to the benefit of a man, not a woman. So it is that she can forgive and make an ally of her rapist's penis, its wilting synonymous with release from the attack,[60] but not make peace with her mother.

If there is a single practical message to be gleaned from the life of Germaine Greer it is this: ceasing to hate 'Mother' is as essential to a woman's happiness as giving up the futile search for a replacement father.

Much of Greer's animosity can be traced to her troubled relationship with her parents. When her war-ravaged father returned to find his marriage shaky and Peggy changed and that she had enjoyed her independence during the war, there was tension. '[And] in the middle of all of this is this brat,' recalled Germaine more than forty years later. 'This knowing brat! ... No confrontations with this child. Because this child will make the catastrophe happen.' That tension and Peggy's alleged declaration that Germaine was the only reason she had stayed with Reg led Germaine to see her childhood almost as a sacrifice on the altar of her parents' marriage.[61]

Still, Germaine volunteered, 'We flirted with our fathers and we flirt with every man we'll ever meet.'[62] Her relationship with Reg, she said, had made her unusually insecure in relationships. 'I'm a bolter,' she told Anthony Clare. 'A bolter. When things get difficult I bolt.... I've always had very high-intensity relationships, and once the intensity goes out of them I'm a bit confused. I don't know how to settle down to humdrumical things – I don't know what you do when you just sleep in the same bed as somebody.'[63] She never would find her Petruchio.

It was perhaps particularly unlucky that, against the backdrop of perceived paternal rejection, Germaine joined the cool anarchistic pessimists of the Sydney Push, where the emotional denial of her childhood was replicated and reinforced. 'I feel that we could've done better,' says Roelof Smilde in retrospect. 'We didn't have to make it as tough as it was, in maintaining a stance of anti-illusion, anti-romance. . . . In the course of fighting against illusion, trying to see through illusions, we denied romance, and while that's valuable, I don't think we should've been as tough about it as we were. There's room for a bit of intimate fun.'

'I knew that the chase was coming to an end,' said Germaine of her father-hunt in *Daddy, We Hardly Knew You*. 'We were closing in on our quarry.'[64] The book is an analogue for the discovery – usually made at a much younger age – that the perfect man does not exist, any more than the perfect woman does. During her quest Germaine accepted 'the dharma of a woman with neither father, husband nor son,'[65] but said nothing about mothers and daughters. A visitor to Mill Farm in the early 1990s found Greer constantly referring to things she needed to do in preparation for an apparently imminent visit from Peggy. The anxiety pervading the mother-daughter relationship was underlined when it emerged that the visit was still many months away.[66]

Greer has said that she sees the world 'astigmatically.'[67] The result is a vision that is by definition distorted, providing for her audience a view inspiring and infuriating in equal measure. As Nathan Silver put it, 'Germaine is brilliant, mad, wonderful, poisonous, and finally a great spirit of the age who deserves to be vastly honored by us and not more than very mildly singed by any of us.'

The fact remains that war is relative. Small domestic wars, wars in the home, can wreak as much mental and physical havoc in an individual as conflict between sovereign nations. The damage from military clashes can spill over, too, into the households and lives of third parties thousands of miles from the scene of battle, with insidious but devastating effect. Germaine Greer suffered collateral damage in two wars she had no role in starting: the world war in which her father fought, coming home damaged and unable to show her love, and battle on the home front between her parents, forever changed and chafing in the domestic sphere as a consequence of the larger conflict.

In Germaine Greer a deceptively simple, somewhat eccentric suburban upbringing brought forth scorn and insight, wit and intellectual waste, deep longings and lavish polemic. Greer's ruptured relations with her mother and father gave her the freedom to cut through the thicket of rules and expectations locking women into the traditionally confined role of suburban wife and mother.

Greer wrenched from her very guts a book that shook women into a new way of seeing their situation. Damaged by her childhood, despairing of her childlessness, partnership-shy, relentlessly holding up a public mirror to the psychic wounds she dare not contemplate in private, unrepentant – she is the maverick of mavericks, flawed, sometimes flailing, but always fighting.

This is the key to why she has been an inspiration to so many other women. She has never surrendered her sovereignty. Germaine Greer never was tamed.

# *Notes*

**Foreword**

1 Norman White, 'Pieties and Literary Biography' in John Batchelor (ed.), *The Art of Literary Biography* (Clarendon Press: Oxford, 1995), p. 214.

**Epigraphs**

1 Germaine Greer, *Daddy, We Hardly Knew You* (Penguin: London, 1990), p. 172.
2 Bertolt Brecht, *Mother Courage and her Children* (Methuen: London, 1983), p. 52.

**Chapter 1: Collateral Damage**

1 Greer, *Daddy*, pp. 112–3.
2 'The Forbidden Books of Youth,' *New York Times Book Review*, 6 June 1993, p. 13.
3 Greer, *Daddy*, p. 5.
4 Ibid., pp. 2–3.
5 Germaine Greer interviewed by Anthony Clare for the BBC Radio series, 'In the Psychiatrist's Chair,' August 1987.

6 Ramona Koval, *One to One* (ABC Enterprises: Sydney, 1992), p. 10.
7 Ibid., p. 14.
8 Clare, 'In the Psychiatrist's Chair.'
9 Koval, *One to One*, p. 15.
10 Greer: 'My mother tried to spike some doubt into that by saying that I didn't know if he was my father. Well, I do; he's my father, there's no question about that.' Ibid., p. 9; Greer, *Daddy*, p. 306.
11 Koval, ibid., p. 7.
12 Greer, *Daddy*, p. 12.
13 Koval, *One to One*, p. 9; Greer, *Daddy*, passim.
14 Clare, 'In the Psychiatrist's Chair.'
15 Greer, 'The Forbidden Books of Youth.'
16 The school now has a Social Justice Captain, in addition to the standard array covering sport and school leadership positions.
17 Germaine Greer in J. Bennett and R. Forgan (eds.), *There's Something About a Convent Girl* (Virago: London, 1991), p. 89.
18 *Who's Who of Australian Women* (Methuen: Sydney, 1982).

19 Address by Mother Eymard
   Temby, 'The Catholic Woman and
   her Christian Witness Today,' 26
   September 1967, Star of the Sea
   Archive.
20 Germaine Greer, *The Female Eunuch*
   (Paladin: London, 1991), p. 95; first
   published MacGibbon & Kee:
   London, 1970.
21 Note by Sister Josepha Dunlop, 13
   June 1990, Star of the Sea Archive.
22 Greer, *Daddy*, pp. 19–20.
23 Ibid., pp. 89–90, 101.
24 Clare, 'In the Psychiatrist's Chair.'
25 Gay Alcorn, 'This Greer Prefers
   Gardens to *Sex and Destiny*,' *Times
   on Sunday*, 20 December 1987.
26 Greer, *Daddy*, p. 219.
27 Ibid., p. 152.
28 Clare, 'In the Psychiatrist's Chair.'
29 Greer in Bennett and Forgan,
   *Convent Girl*, p. 90.
30 Ibid., pp. 90–1.
31 Clyde Packer, *No Return Ticket*
   (Angus & Robertson: Sydney,
   1984), p. 88.
32 Greer in Bennett and Forgan,
   *Convent Girl*, p. 89.
33 Greer, *Daddy*, p. 69.
34 Ibid., p. 20.
35 Ibid., p. 19.
36 Ibid., p. 236.
37 Greer, *Female Eunuch*, p. 95.
38 Jennifer Dabbs, *Beyond Redemption*
   (Mcphee Gribble: Ringwood, 1987).
39 Ibid., p. 139.
40 Ibid., pp. 141–2.
41 Ibid., p. 147.
42 Ibid., p. 165.
43 Ibid., pp. 165–6.
44 Greer, *Female Eunuch*, p. 94.
45 Ibid., pp. 94–5.
46 Packer, *No Return Ticket*, p. 89.
47 Kay Keavney, 'The Liberating of
   Germaine Greer,' *Australian
   Women's Weekly*, 2 February 1972,
   p. 5.

48 Archive note by Sister Josepha
   Dunlop.
49 Packer, *No Return Ticket*, p. 89.

**Chapter 2: Getting Away**

1 Clare, 'In the Psychiatrist's Chair.'
2 Greer, *Daddy*, p. 197.
3 Keavney, 'Liberating of Germaine
   Greer,' p. 4.
4 *Farrago*, 5 March 1956, p. 9.
5 Ibid., p. 3.
6 Ibid., 27 March 1956, p. 5.
7 Ibid., 5 March 1956, p. 1.
8 Ibid., 'Women in Men's Lounge,'
   25 June 1957, p. 2.
9 Ibid., 5 June 1956, p. 3.
10 Keavney, 'Liberating of Germaine
   Greer,' p. 5.
11 Greer, *Daddy*, p. 196.
12 Germaine Greer, 'Lovelife of
   Germaine Greer,' *Pol*, 4 (5), 1972,
   p. 8.
13 Packer, *No Return Ticket*, pp. 89–90.
14 'A Revue Star, but Feels She's a
   Better Academic,' *Sydney Morning
   Herald*, 2 September 1965, Women's
   Section, p. 5.
15 Greer in *Pol*, p. 9.
16 Ibid., pp. 8–9.
17 Packer, *No Return Ticket*, pp. 89–90.
18 Greer in *Pol*, p. 9.
19 Ibid.
20 Ibid.
21 Ibid., pp. 9–10.
22 Packer, *No Return Ticket*, p. 90.
23 *Farrago*, 2 April 1957, p. 5.
24 Ibid., 16 April 1957, p. 2.
25 Ibid., 1 May 1957, pp. 4–7 *passim*.
26 Ibid., 8 May 1957, p. 3.
27 Ibid., 1 May 1957, p. 2.
28 Ibid., 15 May 1957, p. 5.
29 Ibid., 2 July 1957, p. 5.
30 Ibid., 6 August 1957, p. 11.
31 Greer, *Daddy*, p. 198.
32 Greer in *Pol*, p. 10.
33 Greer, 'The Universal Tonguebath:

A Groupie's Vision,' *Oz* 19, February 1969, p. 31.

## Chapter 3: Drifting

1 *Farrago*, 6 August 1957, p. 4.
2 Ibid., 21 March 1958, p. 8.
3 Ibid., p. 5.
4 Ibid., 5 August 1958, p. 4.
5 Packer, *No Return Ticket*, p. 90. The account which follows is from *No Return Ticket*, pp. 90–3.
6 Ibid., p. 92.
7 Ibid., pp. 92–3.
8 Angela Levin, 'At Home with Germaine Greer,' *Mail On Sunday*, 23 March 1989, p. 96.
9 Barry Humphries, *More Please* (Penguin: Ringwood, 1992), p. 149.
10 Ibid., p. 176.
11 Ibid., p. 178.
12 Packer, *No Return Ticket*, p. 94.
13 Q. D. Leavis, *Fiction and the Reading Public* (Chatto & Windus: London, 1932).
14 F. R. Leavis, *The Great Tradition*, *The Common Pursuit* (both Chatto & Windus: London, 1949 and 1952).
15 Raman Selden and Peter Widdowson, *A Reader's Guide to Contemporary Literary Theory*, 3rd edition (Harvester Wheatsheaf: Hemel Hempstead, 1993), p. 23.
16 F. R. Leavis and Denys Thompson, *Culture and Environment: The Training of Critical Awareness* (Chatto & Windus: London, 1933).
17 Chris Baldick, *The Social Mission of English Criticism 1848–1932* (OUP: Oxford, 1983), pp. 188–9.
18 K. K. Ruthven, *Critical Assumptions* (CUP: Cambridge, 1979), pp. 46–7.
19 John Docker, *In a Critical Condition: Reading Australian Literature* (Penguin: Ringwood, 1984), p. 55.
20 Packer, *No Return Ticket*, p. 94.
21 Ibid., pp. 94–5.
22 Ibid., p. 94.
23 Ibid., p. 95.

## Chapter 4: The Push

1 Packer, *No Return Ticket*, p. 94.
2 'Germaine Greer's Sydney' in John McCreevy (ed.), *Cities* (Angus & Robertson: Sydney, 1981), p. 165.
3 From unedited transcript of Margaret Fink interview by Sasha Soldatow and Amanda Stewart, Sydney, 31 October 1988.
4 Ibid.
5 Humphries, *More Please*, p. 169.
6 Greer's honors thesis is missing from the Melbourne University English Department library, the repository for undergraduate theses.
7 Arnold Haskell, *Waltzing Matilda* (London, 1940) cited in Alan Birch and David S. Macmillan, *The Sydney Scene 1788–1960* (Hale & Iremonger: Sydney, 1982), p. 337.
8 Fink interview.
9 John Anderson in *Glasgow University Magazine*, 29 (4), 1918 cited in Brian Kennedy, *A Passion to Oppose: John Anderson, Philosopher* (MUP: Melbourne, 1995), p. 44.
10 Ibid., pp. 57–61 *passim*.
11 Ibid., p. 64.
12 D. M. Armstrong, 'An Intellectual Autobiography,' *Quadrant*, January–February 1983, p. 91.
13 Peter Shrubb, 'John Anderson as Literary Critic,' *Quadrant*, ibid., p. 44.
14 Armstrong, 'Intellectual Autobiography,' p. 91.
15 A. J. Baker, 'John Anderson and Freethought,' *Australian Quarterly*, December 1962, pp. 62–3; Anne Coombs, *Sex and Anarchy: The Life and Death of the Sydney Push* (Viking: Ringwood, 1996), pp. 11–13.

16 John Anderson, 'The Servile State,' *Australian Journal of Psychology and Philosophy*, XXI, 1943, p. 131.

17 Ibid.

18 John Docker, *Australian Cultural Elites: Intellectual Traditions in Sydney and Melbourne* (Angus & Robertson: Cremorne, 1974), p. 150.

19 John Anderson, 'Art and Morality,' in Janet Anderson, Graham Cullum and Kimon Lycos (eds.), *Art and Reality: John Anderson on Literature and Aesthetics* (Hale & Iremonger: Sydney, 1982), p. 90.

20 Anderson cited in Kennedy, *Passion to Oppose*, p. 167.

21 D. J. I., 'What Is This Libertarianism Anyway?' *HONI SOIT*, 30 September 1964, p. 5.

22 Ibid.

23 Ibid.

24 Greer in *Cities*, p. 156.

25 Ibid., p. 152.

26 Packer, *No Return Ticket*, p. 94.

27 Coombs, *Sex and Anarchy*, p. 204.

28 Ibid., p. 213.

29 Ibid., p. 113.

30 Greer in *Cities*, pp. 152–3.

31 Elwyn Morris, 'The Patriarchal Push,' *Quadrant*, January–February 1979, p. 75.

32 John Anderson, 'The Servile State,' p. 130.

33 Morris, 'Patriarchal Push,' p. 76.

34 Ibid., p. 75.

35 Baker, 'Anderson,' p. 52.

36 Greer in *Cities*, p. 165.

**Chapter 5: Byrony**

1 Packer, *No Return Ticket*, p. 95.

2 *HONI SOIT*, 27 March 1962, pp. 1–2.

3 Ibid., 5 July 1962, p. 1.

4 Ibid., 27 March 1962, p. 5.

5 George Gordon, Lord Byron, *Don Juan*, Canto I, dedication stanza xi.

6 Germaine Greer, 'The Development of Byron's Satiric Mode,' thesis submitted in partial fulfilment of the requirements for the Degree of Master of Arts (Honours) in the School of English Language and Literature at Sydney University, 1962 (unpublished).

7 Greer in *Cities*, p. 165.

8 Norman Page (ed.), *Byron: Interviews and Recollections* (Macmillan: Basingstoke, 1985), pp. xi–xii.

9 Greer, 'Byron's Satiric Mode,' pp. 1–2. Greer cites Byron's *Don Juan*, Canto III, stanzas xci–xcii:

Milton's the Prince of Poets – so we say;
  A little heavy; but no less divine:
An independent being in his day –
  Learn'd, pious, temperate in love and wine;
But his life falling into Johnson's way,
  We're told this high–priest of all the Nine,
Was whipt at college – harsh sire – odd spouse,
For the first Mrs. Milton left his house.

All these are, *certes*, entertaining facts,
  Like Shakespeare's stealing deer,
Lord Bacon's bribes;
  Like Titus' youth and Caesar's earliest acts;
Like Burns (whom Doctor Currie well describes);
Like Cromwell's ranks; – but although truth exacts
These amiable descriptions from the scribes,
As most essential to their hero's story,
They do not much contribute to his glory.

10 Ibid., p. 32.

11 Ibid., pp. 39–4.

12 Ibid., pp. 42–3.

13 Anne Barton, Byron: *Don Juan* (CUP: Cambridge, 1992), p. 3.

14 Recently, cf Susan Brownmiller,

*Femininity* (Ballantine: New York, 1984), p. 24; Harriett Hawkins, *Classics and Trash: Traditions and Taboos in High Literature and Popular Modern Genres* (Harvester Wheatsheaf: Hemel Hempstead, 1990), pp. 28, 36.

15 Percy Bysshe Shelley in Frederick L. Jones (ed.), *The Letters of Percy Bysshe Shelley* (Clarendon Press: Oxford, 1964) cited in Page, *Byron*, p. 52.

16 *HONI SOIT*, 19 June 1962, p. 1.

17 Ibid., 19 March 1963, p. 3.

18 Ibid., 25 June 1963, p. 9.

19 Ibid., 2 March 1964, p. 1.

20 Ron Weiner, 'Dynamics of the Push,' *HONI SOIT*, 25 June 1963, p. 9.

21 Robert Hughes, *The Art of Australia* (Penguin: Ringwood, 1966).

22 Geoffrey Dutton, *A Rare Bird: Penguin Books in Australia 1946–96* (Penguin: Ringwood, 1996), p. 51.

23 *HONI SOIT*, 3 July 1962, p. 3.

24 Lee Cataldi, *Invitation to a Marxist Lesbian Party* (Wild & Woolley: Glebe, 1978).

25 *HONI SOIT*, 18 September 1962, p. 6.

26 Ibid., 11 September 1962, p. 2.

27 Charlie L., 'I Hate the B......s!' ibid., 6 August 1963, p. 15.

28 'The Diminishing Monarchical Psychosis,' ibid., 7 July 1964, p. 12.

29 Laurie Oakes, 'Censorship Run Wild,' ibid., 23 April 1963, p. 2.

30 'Drums Along the Tank Stream,' ibid., 8 May 1963, p. 4.

31 A. Tomcat, 'The Drum on the Revue: More than Your Money's Worth,' ibid., 14 May 1963.

32 Ibid.

33 Richard Neville, *Hippie Hippie Shake* (Heinemann: Port Melbourne, 1995), p. 84.

34 Bertolt Brecht, *Mother Courage*, p. xvii.

35 Hugh Rorrison, commentary in ibid., pp. xxi–xxii.

36 Ibid., pp. xxiv–xxv.

37 Jason, 'Mother Courage,' *HONI SOIT*, 17 September 1963, p. 8.

38 Packer, *No Return Ticket*, p. 95.

39 Tutorial records (unpublished), Department of English, University of Sydney, 1964.

40 *HONI SOIT*, 30 June 1964, p. 2.

41 Richard Brennan, ibid., 30 September 1964, p. 2.

42 Ibid., 30 June 1964, p. 3.

43 Ibid., 7 July 1964, p. 1.

44 Ibid., p. 3.

45 Ibid., 21 July 1964, p. 1.

46 'Libertarian report on recent dispute between S.R.C. and "HONI,"' ibid., 4 August 1964, p. 1.

47 D. J. I., 'What is This Libertarianism Anyway?,' *HONI SOIT*, 30 September 1964, p. 5.

## Chapter 6: The Untamed Shrew

1 Jessica Anderson, *Tirra Lirra by the River* (Penguin: Ringwood, 1980), pp. 83–4.

2 'A Revue star, but Feels She's a Better Academic,' *Sydney Morning Herald*, 2 September 1965, 'Women's Section,' p. 5.

3 Packer, *No Return Ticket*, p. 95.

4 Bryan Little, *The Colleges of Cambridge 1286–1973* (Adams & Dart: Bath, 1973), pp. 147–8.

5 M. C. Bradbrook in Ronald Hayman (ed.), *My Cambridge* (Robson: London, 1977), pp. 39–40.

6 Ibid., pp. 43–4.

7 Anne Barton, 'Byron and the Mythology of Fact,' 38th Byron Foundation Lecture, University of Nottingham, 1 March 1968.

8 Packer, *No Return Ticket*, p. 96.

9 M. Matthews in Ann Phillips (ed.),

*A Newnham Anthology* (CUP: Cambridge, 1979), p. 263.

10  Betty Friedan, *The Feminine Mystique* (Norton: New York, 1963).

11  Extracts from the Diary of V. W. Grosvenor Myer, 15 June 1966, in Phillips, *Newnham Anthology*, p. 258.

12  Neville, *Hippie Hippie Shake*, p. 52.

13  Ibid., pp. 70–1.

14  'In Bed with the English,' *Oz* 1, February 1967, pp. 16–18.

15  Ibid., p. 18.

16  Rod C. B. Lake, letter in *Oz* 2, March 1967, p. 8.

17  Clive James, *May Week Was in June* (Picador: London, 1991), p. 23.

18  Levin, 'At Home with Germaine Greer.'

19  Raymond Williams in Marie Axton and Raymond Williams (eds.), *English Drama: Forms and Development – Essays in Honour of Muriel Clara Bradbrook* (CUP: London, 1977), p. ix.

20  M. C. Bradbrook, *The Growth and Structure of Elizabethan Comedy* (Chatto & Windus: London, 1955); *The Rise of the Common Player* (Chatto & Windus: London, 1962).

21  Bradbrook, *Elizabethan Comedy*, p. 7.

22  Germaine Greer, 'The Ethic of Love and Marriage in Shakespeare's Early Comedies,' Ph.D. Dissertation 6204, Cambridge University (unpublished), p. 2. Page 1 contains a single quote: 'May games and jests fill the World full of mirth/but the feeling of Grace fills the soule full of joy (Nicholas Breton, Wits private Wealth).' The thesis was submitted in 1967 and approved for the degree on 7 May 1968.

23  Ibid., p. 35.

24  Ibid., p. v.

25  Ibid., pp. ii–iii.

26  Ibid.

27  Ibid., p. 20.

28  Ibid., p. 27.

29  Ibid., p. 28.

30  Ibid., p. 29.

31  Ibid., pp. 34–5.

32  Ibid., p. 35.

33  Ibid., pp. 184–5.

34  Ibid., pp. 187–8.

35  M. C. Bradbrook, 'Dramatic Role as Social Image: A Study of *The Taming of the Shrew*,' 1958, reprinted in *The Artist and Society in Shakespeare's England: The Collected Papers of Muriel Bradbrook*, vol. 1 (Harvester: Brighton, 1982), p. 108.

36  Ibid., p. 111.

37  Greer, 'Shakespeare's Early Comedies,' pp. 203–4.

38  Ibid., p. 208.

39  Ibid., pp. 208–9.

40  Ibid., pp. 191–2.

41  Ibid., p. 210.

42  Ibid., p. 211.

43  Ibid.

44  Ibid., p. 212.

45  Ibid., p. 209.

46  Germaine Greer, *The Madwoman's Underclothes: Essays and Occasional Writings 1968–85* (Picador: London, 1986), pp. ix–x.

47  Ibid., p. ix.

48  'I was not the first girl to appear in the Footlights (though I was the first to be in a Footlights Smoker, a claim to fame that I owe to Bamber Gascoigne who didn't know the rule about women in Smokers and wrote a part for me into one sketch); but it was still not their policy.' Eleanor Bron in Hayman, *My Cambridge*, pp. 185–6.

49  'A Revue Star, but Feels She's a Better Academic,' *Sydney Morning Herald*, 2 September 1965.

50  Ibid.

51 Ibid.
52 Bron in Hayman, *My Cambridge*, pp. 186–7.
53 Ibid., p. 175.
54 Packer, *No Return Ticket*, p. 95.
55 Ibid., p. 96.
56 Ibid., p. 96.
57 Paul du Feu, *Let's Hear It for the Long-Legged Women* (Putnam: New York, 1973), p. 112 *et passim*.
58 Ibid., p. 113.
59 Ibid., p. 117.
60 Ibid., p. 118.
61 Ibid., pp. 118–9.
62 Ibid., p. 122.
63 Ibid., p. 126.
64 Neville, *Hippie Hippie Shake*, p. 171.
65 Du Feu, *Let's Hear It*, p. 125.
66 Ibid.
67 Ibid., p. 129.
68 Ibid., pp. 126–7.
69 Ibid., pp. 135–6.
70 Ibid., pp. 129–130.
71 Ibid., p. 136.
72 Ibid., p. 138.

**Chapter 7: Catholicism and Counterculture**

1 Keavney, 'Liberating of Germaine Greer.'
2 Packer, *No Return Ticket*, pp. 96, 98.
3 Keavney, 'Liberating of Germaine Greer.'
4 Levin, 'At Home with Germaine Greer.'
5 Bruce Wilson, 'Life Without Father,' *Melbourne Herald*, 7 April 1989.
6 Du Feu, *Let's Hear It*, p. 130.
7 Ibid.
8 Ibid., p. 140.
9 Greer in Bennett and Forgan, *Convent Girl*, p. 90.
10 Germaine Greer, 'The Universal Tonguebath,' p. 31.
11 Neville, *Hippie Hippie Shake*, p. 146.
12 Greer, 'Universal Tonguebath,' p. 33.
13 'DEBBIE,' *HONI SOIT*, 21 July 1964, p. 2.
14 Ibid., 10 March 1964, p. 8.
15 Germaine Greer, 'British Breasts,' *Oz* 2, 1967, pp. 10–11.
16 *Oz* 4, 1967, p. 4.
17 Ibid., p. 11.
18 Greer, 'Universal Tonguebath,' p. 32.
19 Ibid.
20 Ibid., p. 33.
21 Ibid.
22 Ibid.
23 Ibid., pp. 33, 47.
24 Carolyn Heilbrun, *The Education of a Woman* (Dial: New York, 1995), p. 178.
25 Richard Mound, 'She's a Way–out Ph.D. from Aussie,' *People*, 27 August 1969, p. 7.
26 Greer in *Pol*, p. 10.
27 Ibid.
28 Greer, *Madwoman's Underclothes*, p. xxv.
29 Germaine Greer, 'The $1,000,000 Underground,' *Oz* 22, July 1969, p. 4.
30 *Oz* 23, August/September 1969, p. 6.
31 Ibid., pp. 30–1.
32 Germaine Greer, 'Mozic and the Revolution,' *Oz* 24, October 1969, pp. 27–8.
33 Mick Farren, 'Kill for Love,' *Oz* 25, December 1969, p. 45.
34 Jim Haynes, *Thanks for Coming!* (Faber & Faber: London, 1984), p. 218.
35 Ibid., p. 228.
36 Tom Wolfe, *The Purple Decades* (Penguin: Harmondsworth, 1984), p. 287.
37 Ibid., p. 288.
38 Ibid.
39 Ibid., pp. 287–8.

40 Neville, *Hippie Hippie Shake*, p. 170.
41 Packer, *No Return Ticket*, p. 98.
42 Ibid.
43 *Oz* 26, February/March 1970, p. 20.
44 Germaine Greer, 'The Slag–heap Erupts,' ibid., pp. 18–19.
45 Ibid, p. 19.

**Chapter 8: The Female Eunuch**

1 Greer, *Female Eunuch*, p. 25.
2 Anna Coote and Beatrix Campbell, *Sweet Freedom*, 2nd edition (Basil Blackwell: Oxford, 1987), p. 5.
3 Gisela Kaplan, *The Meagre Harvest: The Australian Women's Movement 1950s–1990s* (Allen & Unwin: Sydney, 1996), p. 32.
4 Kate Millett, *Sexual Politics* (Touchstone: New York, 1990, first published 1970).
5 Sheila Rowbotham, *Women's Liberation and the New Politics* (Spokesman: London, 1969), pamphlet no. 17.
6 Anne Koedt, 'The Myth of the Vaginal Orgasm,' paper presented to the Women's Liberation Conference in Chicago, Thanksgiving 1968, reprinted in *Notes from the Second Year* (Radical Feminism: New York, 1970).
7 Ibid., pp. 11–12.
8 Kaplan, *Meagre Harvest*, p. 32.
9 Greer, *Female Eunuch*, pp. 322–3.
10 Ibid., p. 20.
11 Ibid., p. 300.
12 Ibid., p. 304.
13 Ibid., p. 21.
14 Ibid., p. 22.
15 Ibid., p. 371.
16 Ibid., p. 86.
17 Ibid., pp. 13–14.
18 Ibid., p. 15.
19 Ibid., p. 16.
20 Coote and Campbell, *Sweet Freedom*, p. 12.
21 Greer, *Female Eunuch*, p. 21.
22 Coote and Campbell, *Sweet Freedom*, p. 240.
23 Ibid., p. 241.
24 Lynne Segal, *Is the Future Female? Troubled Thoughts on Contemporary Feminism*, 2nd edition (Virago: London, 1994), p. 88.
25 Greer, *Female Eunuch*, pp. 50–1.
26 Ibid., p. 234.
27 Ibid., pp. 354–5.
28 Segal, *Is the Future Female?*, pp. 84–5.
29 Greer, *Female Eunuch*, p. 36.
30 Ibid., p. 169.
31 Ibid., p. 316.
32 Ibid., p. 324.
33 Ibid., p. 325.
34 Ibid., p. 364.
35 Ibid., p. 266.
36 Rodney G. Miller, 'After the Evolution? Language for Social Comment in Germaine Greer's Book, *The Female Eunuch*,' a paper delivered at the 4th National Congress of the Applied Linguistics Association of Australia, University of Sydney, 27 August 1979, p. 3.
37 Ibid., p. 11.
38 Ibid., p. 12.
39 Ibid., pp. 20–1.
40 Iris Young, 'Communication and the Other: Beyond Deliberative Democracy,' in Margaret Wilson and Anna Yeatman (eds.), *Justice and Identity: Antipodean Perspectives* (Allen & Unwin, Sydney, 1995), pp. 146–7.
41 Ibid., p. 147.
42 Arianna Stassinopoulos, *The Female Woman* (Davis–Poynter: London, 1973).
43 Juliet Mitchell, *Psychoanalysis and Feminism* (Penguin: Harmondsworth, 1990), first published 1974.

44  Ibid., p. 340.
45  Ibid., p. 345.
46  *Oz* 27, April 1970, pp. 18–19.
47  Greer, 'The Slagheap Erupts,' p. 19.
48  *Oz* 29, July 1970.
49  Sheila Rowbotham, '. . . the book that men love and women hate,' *Oz* 31, November–December 1970, p. 18.
50  Tim Harris, 'How to Get Your Man . . . ,' ibid.

**Chapter 9: Celebrity Circuits**

1  Mitchell, *Psychoanalysis and Feminism*, pp. 295–6.
2  Camilla Beach, 'Are Australian Women Really So Frigid?' *Sunday Telegraph*, 21 June 1970.
3  'Women's Lib vs. the Press: Germaine Greer addresses the National Press Club,' Washington (Center for Cassette Studies: Hollywood, 1971).
4  Ray Connolly, 'The Strange and Eccentric Worlds of Dr. Greer,' *Melbourne Herald*, 14 October 1970.
5  *Oz* 29, July 1970, p. 5.
6  From a BBC Radio discussion reproduced in the *Australian*, 6 March 1971.
7  Lillian Roxon, 'Germaine Greer: That Female Phenomenon,' *Woman's Day*, 24 May 1971, p. 5.
8  Lillian Roxon, *Rock Encyclopedia* (Grosset & Dunlap: New York, 1969).
9  Roxon, 'Germaine Greer.'
10  Greer, 'Universal Tonguebath,' pp. 33, 47.
11  Eldridge Cleaver, *Soul on Ice* (Rampart: New York, 1968), quoted in Greer, *Female Eunuch*, p. 67.
12  Tom Zito, 'The Greer Career,' *Washington Post*, 22 April 1971.
13  Jordan Bonfante, 'Germaine Greer,' *Life*, 7 May 1971.

14  *Life*, 28 May 1971.
15  Helen Dudar, 'Woman in the News: Germaine Greer – Female, But Not Feminine,' *New York Post*, 10 April 1971.
16  Claudia Dreifus, 'The Selling of a Feminist' in Anne Koedt, Ellen Levine and Anita Rapone (eds.), *Radical Feminism* (Quadrangle: New York, 1973), p. 361; first appeared in 1971 in *Nation*.
17  Christopher Lehmann-Haupt, 'The Best Feminist Book So Far,' *The New York Times*, 20 April 1971.
18  Norman Mailer, 'The Prisoner of Sex,' *Harper's Monthly*, subsequently *The Prisoner of Sex* (Weidenfeld & Nicolson: London, 1971).
19  Judith Weinraub, 'Germaine Greer – Opinions That May Shock the Faithful,' *The New York Times*, 22 March 1971.
20  Lillian Roxon, 'Germaine Greer.'
21  According to Mailer biographer Carl Rollyson, Trilling hissed at Mailer as he crossed the stage, 'Don't touch them!,' fearing he would try to pull the three entwined women apart; see Carl Rollyson, *The Lives of Norman Mailer: A Biography* (Paragon House: New York, 1991), p. 340.
22  Roxon, 'Germaine Greer.'
23  Max Lerner, 'The Prisoner of Non-Sex,' *New York Post*, 28 April 1971.
24  'Sex and the Super-Groupie,' *Time*, 12 April 1971.
25  'Germaine for President,' *Daily Mirror*, 6 March 1972.
26  Sally Kempton, 'The Female Eunuch, by Germaine Greer,' *The New York Times Book Review*, 25 April 1971.
27  Dudar, 'Woman in the News.'
28  Connolly, 'The Strange and Eccentric Worlds of Dr. Greer.'

29 Germaine Greer, *The Obstacle Race: The Fortunes of Women Painters and their Work* (Picador: London, 1981), p. 327; first published 1979.

30 James Wolcott, 'Paglia's Power Trip,' *Vanity Fair*, September 1992, p. 301.

31 'Liberating Party,' *Evening Standard*, 13 October 1970.

32 Letter from Greer to Sister Raymonde, 5 March 1983, Star of the Sea Archive.

33 Angela Levin, 'A Libber at 50: Germaine Greer Seeks out her Dad,' *Sunday Telegraph*, 2 April 1989.

34 Dudar, 'Woman in the News.'

35 Sidney Fields, 'Cry of Rebellion,' *New York Daily News*, 21 April 1971.

36 Dudar, 'Woman in the News.'

37 Kate Millett, *Flying* (Knopf: New York, 1974).

38 Toni Carabillo, Judith Meuli and June Bundy Csida, *Feminist Chronicles 1953–1993* (Women's Graphics: Los Angeles, 1993), p. 57.

39 Jill Johnston, *Lesbian Nation: The Feminist Solution* (Simon & Schuster: New York, 1973).

40 Cf Carolyn Heilbrun, *The Education of a Woman: The Life of Gloria Steinem* (Dial: New York, 1995), pp. 164–7 and 'Trashing' chapter, pp. 276–309; Barbara Ryan, *Feminism and the Women's Movement: Dynamics of Change in Social Movement, Ideology and Activism* (Routledge: New York, 1992), chapter 4, 'Ideological Purity: Divisions, Splits, and Trashing,' pp. 53–64; and Coote and Campbell, *Sweet Freedom*, pp. 240–6.

41 Coote and Campbell, ibid., p. 240.

42 Sara Paretsky; *Killing Orders* (Penguin: London, 1987), p. 78.

43 Heilbrun, *Education of a Woman*, p. 165.

44 Germaine Greer, 'Down With Panties,' *Ms*, July 1972, p. 8; originally 'Going without,' *The Sunday Times*, 19 September 1971.

45 Germaine Greer, 'My Mailer Problem,' *Esquire*, September 1971, reprinted in Greer, *Madwoman's Underclothes*.

46 Ibid., p. 78.

47 Ibid., pp. 80–1.

48 Ibid., p. 81.

49 Ibid., p. 88.

50 Ibid., p. 88.

51 Cf Terry H. Anderson, *The Movement and The Sixties* (OUP: New York, 1995), pp. 214–26.

52 Germaine Greer, 'The Big Tease,' *Harper's Monthly*, October 1972, reprinted in Greer, *Madwoman's Underclothes*, p. 129.

53 Ibid.

54 Ibid., p. 134.

**Chapter 10: Fame**

1 Neville, *Hippie Hippie Shake*, p. 271.

2 Ibid., p. 343.

3 Germaine Greer, 'Killing No Murder,' *Spare Rib*, July 1972, reprinted in *Madwoman's Underclothes*, pp. 117–9.

4 Germaine Greer, 'Hey, Jimi, Where you Gonna Run to Now?,' *Oz*, October 1970, reprinted in ibid., pp. 41–4.

5 Germaine Greer, 'Welcome the Shit–storm,' *Oz*, January 1971, reprinted in ibid., pp. 45–6.

6 Germaine Greer, 'I Am a Whore,' *Suck*, 6, October 1971 (excerpts from 'An Intimate Interview with Germaine Greer,' *Screw: the Sex Review*, May 1971).

7 Ibid.

8 Ibid.

9 Haynes, *Thanks for Coming*, p. 230.

10  Albie Thoms, *Sunshine City*, 1973.

11  Haynes, *Thanks for Coming*.

12  *Suck*, 8, June 1974.

13  Haynes, *Thanks for Coming*, pp. 231–2.

14  Germaine Greer, 'Germaine . . . Now She Says She's in Love,' *Sun-Herald*, 9 July 1972, reprinted from *The Sunday Times*.

15  *Time*, 14 August 1972, p. 8.

16  Lillian Roxon, 'Germaine's Night on the Town,' *Sydney Morning Herald*, 17 August 1971.

17  'The Media Mob,' *Time*, 24 July 1972, p. 45.

18  'The Heart of Women's Lib,' *Wall Street Journal*, 4 October 1972.

19  John Lang, 'Ms. & Mr. Meet a Madam,' *New York Post*, 10 July 1972, p. 2.

20  Paul du Feu, *In Good Company: A Story in Black and White* (Mainstream: Edinburgh, 1991), pp. 9, 11.

21  Ibid., p. 87.

22  'Playboy Interview: Germaine Greer – a Candid Conversation with the Ballsy Author of "The Female Eunuch,"' *Playboy*, January 1972, pp. 74–6.

23  Ibid., p. 68.

24  Greer at Sexual Liberation Forum, Wallace Theatre, University of Sydney, 19 January 1972, unpublished transcript.

25  'Greer on Revolution; Germaine on Love – a Discussion,' *Overland* 51, Autumn 1972, p. 44.

26  Ibid., p. 48.

27  Liz Fell interview with Greer for ABC Radio, *The Coming Out Show*, 9 June 1984.

28  Beatrice Faust, *Apprenticeship in Liberty* (Angus & Robertson: North Ryde, 1991), p. 341.

29  Fell interview with Greer for *The Coming Out Show*.

30  ABC Puts Ban on ' "Over Exposed" Germaine,' *Australian*, 19 March 1972.

31  'Germaine Greer Fined: Battle Outside Court,' *Sydney Morning Herald*, 11 March 1972.

32  Edith Morgan, 'A Strong Commitment' in Jocelynne A. Scutt (ed.), *Living Generously: Women Mentoring Women* (Artemis: Melbourne, 1996), p. 163.

33  Koval, *One to One*, p. 4.

34  Claudia Wright, 'Big Mumma Watches her Girls in Action,' *Melbourne Herald*, 17 February 1972.

35  Sally Brompton, 'How the most deeply feminine of instincts caught up with the most liberated of women – and what kind of man will she choose to make her dream of a baby come true,' *Daily Mail*, 3 February 1976.

36  Ian Moffitt, 'Ms Germaine Greer Revisited,' *Australian*, 27 December 1972.

37  Brompton in *Daily Mail*.

38  'Squatters in Greer House Threaten Violence,' *Sydney Morning Herald*, 25 August 1973; see also 'Squatters Defy Quit Order,' *Daily Telegraph*, 23 August 1973, 'Germaine Kicks out Fifteen Hippies,' *Daily Mirror*, 5 September 1973.

39  Brompton in *Daily Mail*.

40  Frances Cairncross, 'Feminism in the Pink, with Certain Purple Patches,' the *Guardian*, 4 September 1982.

41  David Plante, *Difficult Women: A Memoir of Three* (Victor Gollancz: London, 1983).

42  Ibid., pp. 105–6.

43  Tina Brown, 'Germaine Is Still Battling to Get Away from Mum,' *Sydney Morning Herald*, 11 February 1984.

44  Ad de Vries, *Dictionary of Symbols*

*and Imagery*, 2nd edition (North–Holland: London, 1976), p. 353.

45 Barbara Grizzuti Harrison, 'Germaine Greer: After the Change,' *Mirabella*, September 1992, p. 90. She later told Jeremy Isaacs that a particular IUD, the Graefenberg ring, was to blame for her infertility. (*Face to Face*: Jeremy Isaacs speaks to Germaine Greer, BBC, 1995.)

46 Liz Fell interview with Germaine Greer for ABC Radio, *The Coming Out Show*, 25 January 1979.

47 Germaine Greer, *Sex and Destiny: The Politics of Human Fertility* (Secker & Warburg: London, 1984).

48 *Playboy* interview.

49 Fell interview with Greer, 1979.

50 Germaine Greer, 'The Tulsa Center for the Study of Women's Literature: What We Are Doing and Why We Are Doing It,' *Tulsa Studies in Women's Literature*, vol. 1, no. 1, p. 24.

51 'Witty, raunchy and nobody's eunuch, Germaine Greer is teaching Tulsa a thing or two,' *People*, 17 December 1979.

52 Judy Foreman, 'The Subject Is Germaine,' *Boston Globe*, 17 November 1979.

53 Andrea Chambers, unpublished reporter's file (20 October 1979) to *People* magazine.

54 'Germaine Jets in to Look up Old Pals,' *Daily Telegraph*, 30 August 1983.

### Chapter 11: Sex and Destiny

1 Greer, *Sex and Destiny*, pp. 50–1.

2 Ibid., p. 61.

3 Ibid., p. 62.

4 Ibid.

5 Ibid., p. 198.

6 Ibid., pp. 198–9.

7 Ibid., p. 199.

8 Ibid.

9 Ibid., p. 217.

10 Ibid., pp. 217–18.

11 Ibid., p. 241.

12 A useful corrective to Greer's romanticism is Lynne Brydon and Sylvia Chant (eds.), *Women in the Third World: Gender Issues in Rural and Urban Areas* (Edward Elgar: Aldershot, 1989).

13 Greer, *Sex and Destiny*, p. 104.

14 Ann Leslie, 'The Germaine Feminists Hate,' *Melbourne Herald*, 21 January 1984.

15 Greer at Sexual Liberation Forum, 1972.

16 Germaine Greer, 'On Population and Women's Right to Choose,' *Spare Rib*, March 1975, reprinted in *Madwoman's Underclothes*, p. 192.

17 Ibid., p. 193.

18 Ibid., p. 194.

19 Greer, *Sex and Destiny*, pp. 105–6.

20 'It is appalling to reflect that the most popular form of contraception in England is still the sheath.' – Greer, *Female Eunuch*, p. 314.

21 Ibid., p. 21.

22 *Sex and Destiny*, pp. 128–9.

23 Ibid., p. 252.

24 Ibid., p. 417.

25 Ibid., pp. 217–18.

26 Tina Brown in *Sydney Morning Herald*.

### Chapter 12: Paterfamilias

1 Greer, *Daddy*, p. 15.

2 Ibid., p. 21.

3 Jill Johnston, *Autobiography in Search of a Father, Volume I: Mother Bound* (Knopf: New York, 1983); *Volume II: Paper Daughter* (Knopf: New York, 1985).

4 Ibid., vol. II, p. 102.

5 Koval, *One to One*, p. 8.
6 Johnston, *Autobiography*, vol. II, p. 103.
7 Fell interview with Greer for *The Coming Out Show*, 1984.
8 Greer, *Daddy*, p. 3.
9 Ibid., p. 14.
10 Ibid., p. 16.
11 Ibid.
12 Ibid., p. 71.
13 Ibid., p. 81.
14 Ibid., p. 150.
15 Ibid., p. 177.
16 Ibid., p. 300.
17 Ibid., p. 20.
18 Ibid., p. 3.
19 Ibid., p. 4.
20 Ibid., p. 219.
21 Ibid., p. 4.
22 Ibid., p. 3.
23 Ibid., p. 12.
24 Ibid., pp. 304–6.
25 Ibid., p. 304.
26 Ibid., p. 305.
27 Ibid., p. 308–9.
28 Ibid., p. 12.
29 Gordon Burn, 'My Father My Self,' *Telegraph Weekend Magazine* (London), 25 March 1989.
30 Koval, *One to One*, pp. 16–17.
31 Harrison, 'Germaine Greer: After the Change,' p. 88.
32 Gay Alcorn, 'This Greer Prefers Gardens to *Sex and Destiny*.'
33 Tina Brown in *Sydney Morning Herald*.
34 Greer, *Daddy*, pp. 5–6.
35 Clare, 'In the Psychiatrist's Chair.'
36 Koval, *One to One*, p. 15.
37 Dennis Altman, *Homosexual: Oppression and Liberation* (Outerbridge & Dienstfrey: New York, 1971).
38 Peter Singer, *Animal Liberation* (Cape: London, 1976).
39 Packer, *No Return Ticket*, p. 99.
40 Germaine Greer, 'Why I Won't Live in Australia,' *Sunday Australian*, 23 January 1972.
41 Ben Sandilands, ' "Physical" Sydney, as seen by Germaine Greer,' *Sydney Morning Herald*, 30 December 1978.
42 Lyndall Crisp, 'Ms Greer's Back – and Still Firing,' *Times on Sunday*, 29 November 1987.
43 Liz Fell and Carolin Wenzel (eds.), *The Coming Out Show: Twenty Years of Feminist ABC Radio* (ABC Books: Sydney, 1995), p. 72.
44 Crisp, 'Ms Greer's Back.'
45 Caroline Wilson, 'Greer puts Thatcher Through the Wash,' *Melbourne Herald*, 12 August 1985.
46 Greer interviewed by Fell, 9 June 1984.
47 Crisp, 'Ms Greer's Back.'
48 Greer, *Daddy*, p. 31.
49 Greer in *Cities*, p. 149.
50 Packer, *No Return Ticket*, p. 20.
51 Clare, 'In the Psychiatrist's Chair.'
52 Packer, *No Return Ticket*, p. 99.
53 Germaine Greer, 'Star Girl,' *The Sunday Times*, 3 April 1983.
54 Greer, *Daddy*, p. 127.
55 Ibid., p. 224.
56 Ibid., p. 193.
57 Ibid., p. 78.
58 Ibid., pp. 105–6.
59 Ibid., p. 239.
60 Ibid., p. 242.
61 Ibid., pp. 110–11.
62 Ibid., p. 17.
63 Ibid., p. 107.
64 Ibid., p. 230.
65 Ibid., p. 180.
66 Ibid., p. 152.
67 Ibid., p. 81.
68 Ibid., p. 83.
69 Duncan Fallowell, 'Greer: A Woman of Substance,' *Times on Sunday*, 24 January 1988, and Greer, *Daddy*, p. 67.
70 Greer, ibid., p. 66.

71 Ibid., p. 192.
72 Ibid., p. 232.
73 Ibid., p. 235.
74 Ibid., pp. 240–1.
75 Curt Suplee, 'Germaine Greer, Insistently,' *Washington Post*, 1 May 1984.
76 Greer, *Daddy*, p. 301.
77 Ibid., pp. 245–6.
78 Ibid., pp. 247–8.
79 Jill Johnston, 'Liar! Liar! Liar!,' *The New York Times Book Review*, 28 January 1990.

**Chapter 13: Grounded**

1 'Germaine Gets into the Dirt,' *Sun-Herald*, 29 September 1985.
2 John Hind, 'The Jury's Out on Germaine,' *Cosmopolitan*, July 1995, p. 51.
3 Germaine Greer (ed.), *Kissing the Road* (Virago: London, 1988).
4 Germaine Greer, *The Change: Women, Ageing and the Menopause* (Penguin: London, 1992; first published Hamish Hamilton: London, 1991).
5 Christena Appleyard, 'No Sex Please, I'm Bored,' *Sun*, 1 June 1983.
6 Germaine Greer, A Life in the Day of Germaine Greer,' *The Sunday Times*, 3 August 1986.
7 Yvette Steinhauer, 'The Cross Words Churn on Greer's Harbour Cruise,' *Sydney Morning Herald*, 30 November 1987.
8 Fallowell, 'Greer: Woman of Substance.'
9 Donu Kogbara, 'Twisted Sister,' *Girl About Town*, 17 November 1986.
10 Valerie Grove, 'Batty Hags Are Beautiful OK?,' *The Times*, 14 October 1991.
11 Germaine Greer to Phillip Adams

in Jane Fraser, 'Sex, Orgasm – and a Little Death,' *Australian*, 13 November 1991.
12 Grove, 'Batty Hags.'
13 Greer, *The Change*, p. 437.
14 Ibid., p. 1.
15 Ibid., p. 15.
16 Ibid., p. 35.
17 Gail Sheehy, *The Silent Passage* (Random House: New York, 1992).
18 Barbara Ehrenreich, 'Chronicling The Change,' *Time*, 26 October 1992.
19 Greer, *The Change*, pp. 433–4.
20 Greer, 'A Life in the Day of Germaine Greer.'
21 Germaine Greer, *Shakespeare* (OUP: Oxford, 1986).
22 Greer to Sarah Boxer, *The New York Times Book Review*, 11 October 1992.
23 'Germ warfare hits the campus,' *Sydney Morning Herald*, 2 May 1991.
24 Burn, 'My Father, My Self,' p. 32.
25 Harrison, 'Germaine Greer: After the Change,' p. 92.
26 On this author, for example, who was described inter alia as an 'amoeba,' a 'dung-beetle,' 'intestinal flora' and a 'brain-dead hack' in Greer's column in the *Guardian* of 31 October 1994. In attacks designed as a pre-emptive strike against this book, she continued to denigrate it as exclusively concerned with her sexual partners. Greer did not consider the possibility that her intellectual roots might be more interesting.
27 Steinhauer, 'Cross Words.'
28 Harrison, 'Germaine Greer: After the Change,' p. 87.
29 Germaine Greer, *Slip-Shod Sibyls: Recognition, Rejection and the Woman Poet* (Viking: London, 1995).
30 Ibid., p. xxi.
31 Ibid., pp. xx–xxi.

32 Ibid., p. xiii.
33 M. C. Bradbrook, 'Notes on the Style of Virginia Woolf' reproduced in *Women and Literature 1779–1982: The Collected Papers of Muriel Bradbrook*, vol. 2 (Harvester: Brighton, 1982).
34 Ibid., p. 157.
35 M. C. Bradbrook, 'To the Light-house' reproduced in ibid., p. 163.
36 Vicky Ward (ed.), 'Encounters with Germaine,' the *Guardian*, 21 October 1994.
37 Polly Toynbee, 'Ironing in the Soul,' the *Guardian*, 19 May 1988.
38 Germaine Greer, 'Books and Barbarism,' *The Times*, 10 June 1997.
39 Clare Longrigg, 'A Sister with no Fellow Feeling,' *Guardian*, 25 June 1997.
40 Hickson, 'Could This Really be Germaine Greer?' *Australian Women's Weekly*, February 1992.
41 Harrison, 'Germaine Greer: After the Change,' p. 93.
42 Ibid., p. 86.

**Chapter 14: Maverick**

1 Jacques Gernet, *A History of Chinese Civilization* (CUP: Cambridge, 1996), 2nd edition, pp. 401–2; first published in English, 1982. Originally published in French as *Le Monde Chinois* (Librairie Armand Cohn: Paris, 1972).
2 Frederick W. Mote, 'The Ch'eng–hua and Hung–chih reigns, 1465–1505' in Frederick W. Mote and Denis Twitchett (eds.), *The Cambridge History of China, volume 7: The Ming Dynasty 1368–1644*, p. 365.
3 Ibid., p. 366.
4 John Julius Norwich, *Byzantium: The Apogee* (Penguin: London, 1993), pp. 129–30; first published Viking: London, 1991.
5 A. H. M. Jones, *The Decline of the Ancient World* (Longman: Harlow, 1966), pp. 201–2.
6 'The Eunuch' in *Terence*, vol. 1, translated by John Sargeaunt (Harvard University Press: Cambridge, Massachusetts, 1912).
7 Mary Beard, 'Re-reading (Vestal) Virginity' in Richard Hawley and Barbara Levick (eds.), *Women in Antiquity: New Assessments* (Routledge: London, 1995), p. 170.
8 Hegedus Pennebaker Films Inc., *Town Bloody Hall* (1979).
9 M. C. Bradbrook, *'That Infidel Place': A Short History of Girton College 1869–1969* (Chatto & Windus: London, 1969), pp. 116–17.
10 Marilyn Lake, 'Female Desires: The Meaning of World War II' in Joy Damousi and Marilyn Lake (eds.), *Gender and War: Australians at War in the Twentieth Century* (CUP, Melbourne, 1995), p. 75.
11 Grove, 'Batty Hags.'
12 Hester Eisenstein, *Inside Agitators: Australian Femocrats and the State* (Allen & Unwin: St Leonards, 1996), p. xi.
13 Fell interview with Greer, 1979.
14 Beatrice Faust, 'Greer's Cassandriad sends Women into Retreat,' Melbourne *Age*, 9 November 1991.
15 Recounted by Melbourne writer Jenny Lee.
16 Germaine Greer, 'A Black Day for Every Woman,' *Daily Mail*, 24 November 1990.
17 Faust, *Apprenticeship in Liberty*, p. 340.
18 Shelagh Young, 'Feminism and the Politics of Power: Whose Gaze Is it Anyway?' in Lorraine Gamman and Margaret Marshment (eds.), *The Female Gaze: Women as Viewers of Popular Culture* (Real Comet

Press: Seattle, 1989), p. 174.

19 Daisy Waugh, 'The Eunuch's Bequest – Did this Book Change Women's Lives?' *Sunday Correspondent*, 22 April 1990.

20 Fallowell, 'Greer: Woman of Substance.'

21 Dudar, 'Woman in the News.'

22 Clare, 'In the Psychiatrist's Chair.'

23 Greer, *Daddy*, p. 311.

24 Hickson, 'Could This Really Be Germaine Greer?'

25 Clare, 'In the Psychiatrist's Chair.'

26 Peter Ellingsen, 'Germs' Warfare on Biographer,' Melbourne *Age*, 7 June 1996.

27 Camille Paglia, *People*, 30 November 1992.

28 Greer, *Slip-Shod Sibyls*, p. xxi.

29 Paul Johnson, *Intellectuals* (Harper & Row: New York, 1988), p. 169.

30 *Guardian*, 21 March 1995.

31 Packer, *No Return Ticket*, p. 92.

32 *Playboy* interview, p. 66.

33 Germaine Greer, 'Seduction Is a Four Letter Word,' *Playboy*, January 1973, p. 64.

34 'Germaine Greer on facing up to 50,' *Australian Women's Weekly*, August 1986, p. 129.

35 Daisy Waugh, 'The Eunuch's Bequest.'

36 Coote and Campbell, *Sweet Freedom*, pp 241–2.

37 Beatrice Faust, 'A Contaminated View,' *Age Monthly Review*, 4 May 1984.

38 Greer, *Sex and Destiny*, p. 198.

39 Geneva Collins, 'Germaine Takes off Panties to Progress,' *Australian*, 9 November 1987.

40 Catharine R. Stimpson, ' "Wild Boars and Such Things": Pains, Gains and the Education of Women,' *Furman Studies*, vol. 36, June 1994, pp. 23–4.

41 Grove, 'Batty Hags.'

42 Greer, *The Change*, pp. 433–4.

43 Dennis Altman, *Defying Gravity: A Political Life* (Allen & Unwin: Sydney, 1997), p. 71.

44 Shrubb, 'John Anderson as Literary Critic,' p. 44.

45 Bradbrook in *My Cambridge*, p. 40.

46 Greer, *The Female Eunuch*, p. 150.

47 Ibid., p. 357.

48 *The James Bryce Memorial Lecture delivered in the Wolfson Hall of Somer-ville College, Oxford on 6 March 1975 by Professor M. C. Bradbrook, Litt.D. Cantab, Mistress of Girton College* (Holywell Press: Oxford, 1975).

49 Ibid., p. 2.

50 Ibid., p. 4.

51 Ibid., p. 6.

52 Ibid., p. 16.

53 Altman, *Defying Gravity*, p. 71.

54 Haynes, *Thanks for Coming*, p. 230.

55 M. C. Bradbrook, 'Queenie Leavis: The Dynamics of Rejection' in *Women and Literature*, p. 127.

56 Cynthia Ozick, 'Previsions of the Demise of the Dancing Dog,' *Motive* 29, March–April 1969, pp. 7–16, reprinted in *Art and Ardor* (Knopf: New York, 1983), p. 281.

57 Ibid., p. 278.

58 Greer, *The Obstacle Race*, p. 327.

59 Greer to a literary lunch in Brisbane, reported by Adrian McGregor, 'Greer mocks men's misses,' *Sydney Morning Herald*, 14 November 1991.

60 *Guardian*, 21 March 1995.

61 Clare, 'In the Psychiatrist's Chair.'

62 Fell interview with Greer, 1984.

63 Clare, 'In the Psychiatrist's Chair.'

64 Greer, *Daddy*, p. 239.

65 Ibid., p. 98.

66 Harrison, 'Germaine Greer: After the Change.'

67 Clare, 'In the Psychiatrist's Chair.'

# Select Bibliography

**Works by Germaine Greer**

Greer, Germaine *The Change: Women, Ageing and the Menopause*, Penguin, London, 1992.

*Daddy, We Hardly Knew You*, Penguin, London, 1990.

*The Female Eunuch*, Paladin, London, 1991.

(ed.) *Kissing the Rod*, Virago, London, 1988.

*The Madwoman's Underclothes: Essays and Occasional Writings 1968-85*, Picador, London, 1986.

*The Obstacle Race: The Fortunes of Women Painters and their Work*, Picador, London, 1981.

*Sex and Destiny: The Politics of Human Fertility*, Secker & Warburg, London, 1984.

*Shakespeare*, OUP, Oxford, 1986.

*Slip-Shod Sibyls: Recognition, Rejection and the Woman Poet*, Viking, London, 1995.

'The Development of Byron's Satiric Mode,' Unpublished Thesis, Sydney University, 1962.

'The Ethic of Love and Marriage in Shakespeare's Early Comedies,' Unpublished Ph.D. Dissertation 6204, Cambridge University, 1967.

**General**

Altman, Dennis *Defying Gravity: A Political Life*, Allen & Unwin, Sydney, 1997

—— *Homosexual: Oppression and Liberation*, Outerbridge & Dienstfrey, New York, 1971.

Anderson, Janet, Cullum, Graham and Lycos, Kimon (eds.) *Art and Reality: John Anderson on Literature and Aesthetics*, Hale & Iremonger, Sydney, 1982.

Anderson, Jessica *Tirra Lirra by the River*, Penguin, Ringwood, 1980.

Anderson, Terry H. *The Movement and The Sixties*, OUP, New York, 1995.

Axton, Marie and Williams, Raymond (eds.) *English Drama: Forms and Development – Essays in Honour of Muriel Clara Bradbrook*, CUP, London, 1977.

Baldick, Chris *The Social Mission of English Criticism 1848–1932*, OUP, Oxford, 1983.

Barton, Anne *Byron: Don Juan*, CUP, Cambridge, 1992.

Batchelor, John (ed.) *The Art of Literary Biography*, Clarendon Press, Oxford, 1995.

Bennett, J. and Forgan, R. (eds.) *There's Something About a Convent Girl*, Virago, London, 1991.

Birch, Alan and Macmillan, D. S. *The Sydney Scene 1788–1960*, Hale & Iremonger, Sydney, 1982.

Bradbrook, M. C. *The Artist and Society in Shakespeare's England: The Collected Papers of Muriel Bradbrook*, vol. 1, Harvester, Brighton, 1982.

—— *The Growth and Structure of Elizabethan Comedy*, Chatto & Windus, London, 1955.

—— *The Rise of the Common Player*, Chatto & Windus, London, 1962.

—— *'That Infidel Place': A Short History of Girton College 1869–1969*, Chatto & Windus, 1969.

—— *Women in Literature 1779–1982: The Collected Papers of Muriel Bradbrook*, vol. 2, Harvester, Brighton, 1982

Brownmiller, Susan *Femininity*, Ballantine, New York, 1984.

Carabillo, Toni, Meuli, Judith and Bundy Csida, June *Feminist Chronicles 1953–1993*, Women's Graphics, Los Angeles, 1993.

Cataldi, Lee *Invitation to a Marxist Lesbian Party*, Wild & Woolley, Glebe, 1978.

Coombs, Anne *Sex and Anarchy: The Life and Death of the Sydney Push*, Viking, Ringwood, 1996.

Coote, Anna and Campbell, Beatrix *Sweet Freedom*, 2nd edition, Basil Blackwell, Oxford, 1987.

Dabbs, Jennifer *Beyond Redemption*, McPhee Gribble, Ringwood, 1987.

Damousi, Joy and Lake, Marilyn (eds.) *Gender and War: Australians at War in the Twentieth Century*, CUP, Melbourne, 1995.

Docker, John *Australian Cultural Elites: Intellectual Traditions in Sydney and Melbourne*, Angus & Robertson, Cremorne, 1974

—— *In a Critical Condition: Reading Australian Literature*, Penguin, Ringwood, 1984

Dutton, Geoffrey *A Rare Bird: Penguin Books in Australia 1946–96*, Penguin, Ringwood, 1996.

Eisenstein, Hester *Inside Agitators: Australian Femocrats and the State*, Allen & Unwin, St Leonards, 1996.

Faust, Beatrice *Apprenticeship in Liberty*, Angus & Robertson, North Ryde, 1991.

Fell, Liz and Wenzel, Carolin (eds.) *The Coming Out Show: Twenty Years of Feminist ABC Radio*, ABC Books, Sydney, 1995.

du Feu, Paul *Let's Hear It for the Long-Legged Women*, Putnam, New York, 1973.

—— *In Good Company: A Story in Black and White*, Mainstream, Edinburgh, 1991.

Friedan, Betty *The Feminine Mystique*, Norton, New York, 1963.

Gamman, Lorraine and Marshment, Margaret (eds.) *The Female Gaze: Women as Viewers of Popular Culture*, Real Comet Press, Seattle, 1989.

Gernet, Jacques *A History of Chinese Civilization*, 2nd edition, CUP, Cambridge, 1996.

Hawkins, Harriett *Classics and Trash: Traditions and Taboos in High Literature and Popular Modern Genres*, Harvester Wheatsheaf, Hemel Hempstead, 1990.

Hawley, Richard and Levick, Barbara (eds.) *Women in Antiquity: New Assessments*, Routledge, London, 1995.

Hayman, Ronald (ed.) *My Cambridge*, Robson, London, 1977.

Haynes, Jim *Thanks for Coming!*, Faber & Faber, London, 1984.

Heilbrun, Carolyn *The Education of a Woman: The Life of Gloria Steinem*, Dial, New York, 1995.

Hughes, Robert *The Art of Australia*, Penguin, Ringwood, 1966.

Humphries, Barry *More Please*, Penguin, Ringwood, 1992.

James, Clive *May Week Was in June*, Picador, London, 1991.

Johnson, Paul *Intellectuals*, Harper & Row, New York, 1988.

Johnston, Jill *Autobiography in Search of a Father, Volume I: Mother Bound* Knopf, New York, 1983.

—— *Autobiography, Volume II: Paper Daughter*, Knopf, New York, 1985.

—— *Lesbian Nation: The Feminist Solution*, Simon & Schuster: New York, 1973.

Jones, A. H. M. *The Decline of the Ancient World*, Longman, Harlow, 1966.

Kaplan, Gisela *The Meagre Harvest: The Australian Women's Movement 1950s–1990s*, Allen & Unwin, Sydney, 1996.

Kennedy, Brian *A Passion to Oppose: John Anderson, Philosopher*, MUP, Melbourne, 1995.

Koedt, Anne, Levine, Ellen and Rapone, Anita (eds.), *Radical Feminism*, Quadrangle, New York, 1973.

Koval, R. *One to One*, ABC Enterprises, Sydney, 1992.

Leavis, F. R. *The Great Tradition*, Chatto & Windus, London, 1949.

—— *The Common Pursuit*, Chatto & Windus, London, 1952.

Leavis, F. R. and Denys Thompson, *Culture and Environment: The Training of Critical Awareness*, Chatto & Windus, London, 1933.

Leavis, Q. D. *Fiction and the Reading Public*, Chatto & Windus, London, 1932.

Little, Bryan *The Colleges of Cambridge 1286–1973*, Adams & Dart, Bath, 1973.

McGreevy, John (ed.) *Cities*, Angus & Robertson, Sydney, 1981.

Millett, Kate, *Flying*, Knopf, New York, 1974.

—— *Sexual Politics*, Touchstone, New York, 1990.

Mitchell, Juliet, *Psychoanalysis and Feminism*, Penguin, Hardmondsworth, 1990.

Neville, Richard *Hippie Hippie Shake*, Heinemann, Port Melbourne, 1995.

Norwich, John Julius *Byzantium: The Apogee*, Penguin, London, 1993.

Ozick, Cynthia *Art and Ardor*, Knopf, New York, 1983.

Packer, Clyde, *No Return Ticket*, Angus & Robertson, Sydney, 1984.

Page, Norman (ed.) *Byron: Interviews and Recollections*, Macmillan, Basingstoke, 1985.

Paretsky, Sara *Killing Orders*, Penguin, London, 1987.

Phillips, Ann (ed.) *A Newnham Anthology*, CUP, Cambridge, 1979.

Plante, David *Difficult Women: A Memoir of Three*, Victor Gollancz, London, 1983.

Rollyson, Carl, *The Lives of Norman Mailer: A Biography*, Paragon House, New York, 1991.

Rowbotham, Sheila *Women's Liberation and the New Politics*, Spokesman, London, 1969.

Roxon, Lillian *Rock Encyclopedia*, Grosset & Dunlap, New York, 1969.

Ruthven, K. K. *Critical Assumptions*, CUP, Cambridge, 1979.

Ryan, Barbara, *Feminism and the Women's Movement: Dynamics of Change in Social Movement, Ideology and Activism*, Routledge, New York, 1992.

Scutt, Jocelynne A. (ed.) *Living Generously: Women Mentoring Women*, Artemis, Melbourne, 1996.

Segal, Lynne *Is the Future Female? Troubled Thoughts on Contemporary Feminism*, 2nd edition , Virago, London, 1994.

Selden, Raman and Widdowson, Peter *A Reader's Guide to Contemporary Literary Theory*, 3rd edition, Harvester Wheatsheaf, Hemel Hempstead, 1993.

Sheehy, Gail *The Silent Passage*, Random House, New York, 1992.

Singer, Peter *Animal Liberation*, Cape, London, 1976.

Stassinopoulos, Arianna *The Female Woman*, Davis-Poynter, London, 1973.

Thoms, Albie *Sunshine City*, 1973.

Wilson, Margaret and Yeatman, Anna (eds.) *Justice and Identity: Antipodean Perspectives*, Allen & Unwin, Sydney, 1995.

Wolfe, Tom *The Purple Decades*, Penguin, Harmondsworth, 1984.

**Journals, Periodicals and Newspapers**

*Age Monthly Review, Australian, Australian Journal of Psychology and Philosophy, Australian Quarterly, Australian Women's Weekly, Boston Globe, Cosmopolitan, Daily Mail, Daily Mirror, Daily Telegraph, Esquire, Evening Standard, Farrago, Furman Studies, Girl About Town, Guardian, Harper's Monthly, HONI SOIT, Life, Mail on Sunday, Melbourne Herald, Mirabella, Ms, New York Daily News, New York Post, New York Times Book Review, Overland, Oz, People, Playboy, Pol, Quadrant, Spare Rib, Suck, Sun, The Sunday Times, Sunday Telegraph, Sun-Herald, Sydney Morning Herald, Time, Times on Sunday, Tulsa Studies in Women's Literature, Vanity Fair, Wall Street Journal, Washington Post, Woman's Day.*

# *Index*